☆ ☆ ☆

Francis rushed to Boston to share the news with
Sophia . . .

"I will be the assignment agent for Benson and
Brothers in Oregon. Fifteen thousand dollars' worth
of goods are being gathered to go aboard the *Victoria*.
She departs next week for Honolulu."

"I see," Sophia said slowly. Then she stood up.
"Francis," she asked, "would I be a help to you?"

"Dear Mother of God," he whispered, "you have
not been out of my thoughts or dreams since the
moment I met you. But are you up to it?"

Sophia fought to still the wild beating of her heart.
She was scared stiff; she had never been anything but
a city girl. Still, she knew that Francis Pettygrove was
the only man to father her children. She didn't need to
be told that he had been bitten by the pioneering bug,
and that where he went she would have to follow.

"I shall be packed," she said evenly, "by the time
you return with Parson Jones from the church."

☆ ☆ ☆

Lee Davis Willoughby
is the author of the bestselling series
The Making of America

Other books in the
Americana: The Making of the Cities series:
Cincinnati
Baton Rouge

AMERICANA:

THE MAKING OF THE CITIES

Portland

☆ ☆ ☆

Lee Davis Willoughby

A Bryans & Bryans Book

KNIGHTSBRIDGE PUBLISHING COMPANY

NEW YORK

Published in the United States by
Knightsbridge Publishing Company
255 East 49th Street
New York, New York 10022

ISBN 1-56129-055-6

Designed by Stanley S. Drate/Folio Graphics, Inc.

10 9 8 7 6 5 4 3 2 1
First Edition

Author's Note

History is a fascinating root base for fiction. Unfortunately, the recorders of history in some eras were wont to scribe the names of men of importance and leave faceless and nameless their spouses and children.

To the ghosts of many of the fascinating men who carved Portland and Oregon out of a wilderness, I apologize: I have been forced to invent names for your wives and children.

To those women and children, for whom I have attempted to select names in keeping with the manners and customs of that day and age, I pray that you are pleased with your new christenings.

AMERICANA:
THE MAKING OF THE CITIES

Portland

☆　☆　☆

Prologue

Weymouth, England—1632

He looked at the infant male hands in dismay.

Lorenzo Pettygrove had given up hope of being the father of a son; he had two daughters, Mary and Ann, ten and twelve years of age. And now, just before dawn, his wife had presented him with this unexpected gift. A son! A son to carry on his name was more precious than his dream of someday owning land.

"Francis," Pamela Pettygrove announced weakly, the midwife wiping her fevered brow with a cold cloth. "There has been no Francis in our families for two generations."

Lorenzo's eyes misted with joy. It was a good name and a good name should stay in the family, every generation or so.

"Now be off to work, my husband. This birth has kept you long enough."

His joy turned to despair.

Strong of back, with a keen eye for shaping wood to its natural grain, he had spent a third of his life in shipbuilding. But no new keel had been laid in a year, and yesterday the Master Shipwright had informed him that the Admiralty had no plans for future construction. It was depressing news he did not wish to share with his wife.

It was burden enough being forced to live in a medieval section of twisting alleys and narrow streets. Within walking distance of the docks and shipyard, it was a slum, infested with prostitutes and sailor pubs. The rents were in direct ratio to the number of steps a client had to climb.

Lorenzo's flat was one floor, the sixth, the top, the lowest rent. One hundred twenty-two steps to climb up or walk down. That day they seemed like twice the number. For the first time he thought of Pamela making that climb during her pregnancy. It was a wonder she carried the child to birth.

On the fourth-floor landing he recognized Harry Hill, lingering idly in the shadows. Over the past decade he had made a friend of the rent collector, although everyone else feared or despised the man.

"Cheero, 'Arry. 'Tis a fortnight before me rent's due, right?"

The heavy-set, part-time boxer pushed the battered derby farther back on his head and nervously looked at a list in his hand. "Moving some out," he muttered, "to move better payers in. Best you hurry, Pettygrove. 'Imself is about ready to leave her flat."

Lorenzo grinned, wickedly, and continued down the rickety stairs.

Himself would be Lawrence McFedders, his master shipwright boss and owner of this tenement and others. The *her* would be his sister-in-law, Penelope Randolph.

He liked his sister-in-law. Everyone did. Penelope Randolph was unique. She loved life more than the men who entered her life. Her pride was having produced three healthy and handsome sons. It didn't phase Penelope that there had been a different father for each of her sons, and always without benefit of marriage.

On the second-floor landing the door to his sister-in-law's flat came flying open and Lawrence McFedders came charging out. He caught a glimpse of Lorenzo, blanched, and ran down the stairs.

Out on the narrow street, Lorenzo saw the wispy man jump into a pony cart and pull his shawl over his tall hat, as though the act would make him disappear.

"Blighter should be embarrassed," Lorenzo muttered. "Taking a mistress at his age is a disgrace."

He pulled his scarf higher around his neck. The air was ripe with moisture, suggesting a squall coming down off the North Sea. He took every back alleyway he knew, primarily to reach the shipyards before McFedders, but secondly, because the alleyways were so cramped with overhanging balconies that rain could barely find its way to the ground.

In less than ten minutes he was able to squeeze his bulky figure through a break in the wood fence at the aft section of the keel yards. Normally, the Weymouth Shipyard would have six ships in various degrees of construction. Now, only a single vessel stood ready to be launched. On that murky, gray day the *Falmouth* looked forlorn.

Eighteen months of his life had gone into this consignment ship for Sir Ferdinando Gorges. It was a new design, called an East Indiamen. The shipyard was used to building galleons, with their high sterncastles that housed elaborate living quarters. This vessel had no sterncastle, with the first deck sectioned into barren passenger compartments and crew quarters that seemed cramped. The remaining decks and holds were as plain as a Yorkshire barn. Because there was no inclusion of teakwood, inlaid panels, or expensive captain's quarters, many of his carpenters had resented working on the ship.

In working with Gorges's agents, George Cleeve and Richard Tucker, Lorenzo had come to understand the purpose of the vessel. Sir Ferdinando had a Royal Charter for land in the new world. The *Falmouth* would be a transport for colonists and a mercantile supply ship until their new town was established. He envied those people going to a place where there was new land. He had been born to an illiterate tenant farmer and had escaped at an early age to work in the city and make enough to someday buy his own land, but the cost of rent, food, and the raising of two daughters never left enough for savings.

"Halt! Oh, it's you, Lorenzo. Coming in this way, I guess you haven't heard the news."

"Wot news, Floyd?"

"Master Shipwright is hiring a new crew. I'm here to tell any comin' this way to pick up their personal tools at the shed and be off."

"Why a new crew, Floyd? She was to taste the salt today or tomorrow."

Floyd Smolding giggled. "To put more money into McFedders's greedy pockets. He's having part of her torn apart and rebuilt. What can I do? I am only a guard."

The man got no answer. Lorenzo's heart felt panic, but not his feet. He was running now, his long legs eating up the length of the new ship to the tool shed area. Now he fully understood the conversation with McFedders the afternoon before. The Shipwright had wanted him to stall the launch for a few weeks. It had grated against his moral fiber to lie, and he had refused to go along with any stalling tactics. He had to break through a group of men at the bow section of the keel yard. They were the filthiest, most nondescript specimens of humanity that Lorenzo had ever seen. They were hungry, out-of-work men, not caring if they took a job away from another.

"Wot's this?" Lorenzo thundered as he raced toward McFedders, who was checking each carpenter to make sure they did not take any company tools. He was caught by the arm before he got to McFedders.

"Faulty construction? Faulty construction? Why are you only claiming that now?"

Lorenzo had run up against Richard Tucker before. The tall, red-bearded man reminded Lorenzo of a crane who could not determine whether to fly, awkwardly walk, or strut. The man knew shipbuilding and had made many exceptional alterations to the plans.

"I have made no such claims," Lorenzo mumbled, astounded.

"I thought as much," George Cleeve said, joining them. "All seemed well when we inspected three days ago. Anticipating a launch today or tomorrow, we have already gathered our passengers and cargo here in Weymouth. Do you feel it would be a safe launch?"

"I do, sir," Lorenzo said, without hesitation. In eighteen months he had come to respect and admire George Cleeve very much. Even though rich and powerful, he always treated Lorenzo as an equal.

"I heard that!" McFedders screamed, forcing his way between Cleeve and Tucker. "He lies! He will not take responsibility for his faulty work, so he and his men have been fired."

"That is very good news," Tucker chuckled. The normally

astringent man sounded almost human. "Then, Lorenzo, as of this moment you are on our payroll. Our benefactor has been generous with building funds, but his purse strings are not limitless. Knowing the reputation of this yard, we appeared before a magistrate yesterday and received a paid-in-full document of ownership. The ship is ours. Now, what shall it cost our enterprise to see this vessel taste the salt and be ready for sail?"

Lorenzo almost laughed. They had tied McFedders's hands neatly. "A halfpenny's worth of keel grease and the wages of a dozen sledgehammer men to knock away the supports."

"No, you don't!" McFedders squealed, racing to the men waiting to be hired. "They are going to try and launch her! It will take away the jobs I am offering. A day's wages to any man who stands with me and keeps them from getting the ship!"

"Only a day's wages?" Richard Tucker snickered. "Here, Lorenzo, is a leather pouch of gold coins. Easily a week's wages for each of your crew and yourself."

Lorenzo pushed his stubby, square-fisted hand through his luxuriant dark chestnut beard, his pride and his joy. Pamela Pettygrove would have recognized the gesture at once. Whenever her husband had to ponder a question, he combed his beard with his fingers for a moment to think.

He could have done it with two greasers and four sledgemen, but how could so few get through the knot of men McFedders was now commanding?

"Greasers!" he shouted. "Sledgemen! The real owners want her to taste the salt. I have cash wages for any man willing to help slip her away!"

"No!" McFedders ranted, standing behind a hulk of a man for protection. "Stand them off and your children will eat tonight."

"Listen up!" Lorenzo shouted, his baritone voice carrying far. "Don't listen to his false promise. There is not a shipyard worker here who is not owed back wages by that man." He opened the purse and rifled his fingers through the coins. He knew the musical sound drifted afar. "Who is with me?"

McFedders was not finished. "Any of you men who join me right now will not be fired and will get a raise in daily pay!"

Suddenly, the storm broke with a gust of driving rain. There was a moment of hesitation. Then some of Lorenzo's crew snatched at McFedders's promise like a sodden hope. Lorenzo was not discouraged. McFedders had gained only the laggards, the shirkers, the men who would lie, steal, and cheat with an innocent look on their faces.

Lorenzo still had two dozen strong and trustworthy men. Without comment they grabbed grease buckets and sledgehammers and moved to his side. He moved forward steadily toward McFedders and his motley crew. The wind came crying in from the bay, keening like sailors' wives when they instinctively know a ship has been lost at sea.

They came foot to foot and no one moved. Then, one of McFedders's men threw a lump of pitch. It struck Lorenzo on the head, felling him. Immediately the air was filled with flying pitch.

"Don't be idiots!" Lorenzo roared, rising to his feet, but he was unheard. All that reached his ears was the deep, dull thud of fists meeting jaws, chests, and stomachs. Then came a horrible scream as one man used his sledgehammer to defend himself.

Lorenzo was frantic. He had to put a stop to this bloodshed. "Don't be blind!" he screamed over the melee. "I pay for work, not crushed heads! Here!"

He dumped half of the purse of coins on the quayside and ran for the ship.

Floyd Smolding came running up. "I'm with you, laddie!"

"Then be my paymaster, Floyd. A week of coins for each man who puts his back to the task."

Men were already painting the skids with generous dabs of grease. Others ran to station themselves at restraining poles. Port and starboard, along the entire ship, they had to be knocked away in unison or the ship would turn and hang up in the skid tracks.

Lorenzo turned tyrant. There could be only one master of a launch. Four trusted men he sent up the rope ladder to handle the ship once she was in the bay. He was not surprised to see Richard Tucker scramble up the ladder with them.

The private vessel *Falmouth* was fifty meters long and could carry 370 metric tons of cargo. She was the largest ship to be launched from the Weymouth Shipyard, but with so many greasers and sledgemen, she beautifully slipped into the bay in less than twenty minutes. She bobbed, settled, and waited to be put to anchor. For the moment friend and foe joined, cheering their combined creation. She was proudly afloat.

Lorenzo glared triumphantly at McFedders, who was whispering to the bulky man who had been his makeshift bodyguard. Then, as Lorenzo started to turn away, it began to dawn on him that not only was he a man without a job, but McFedders was also powerful enough to keep him from working in any other British shipyard.

"Look out, Lorenzo!" Cleeve screamed.

Lorenzo turned just in time to see the bodyguard come at him with a knife, as McFedders ran for his pony cart.

"You're a dead man, bloke!" the man yelled and lunged.

Lorenzo fell upon him like an avenging Jove. The knife sliced into his arm and he had to disarm the man before the knife struck him again. The great fists pumped out, delivering hammer blows. The man was caught off guard, thinking Lorenzo would back away after the first wound. He staggered back, unable to get the knife any higher than his chest when Lorenzo caught his arm and twisted him about. The man's feet hit a dropped dab of the grease and they crashed together down on the quayside. The sharp knife ate into the man's chest and he let out a sickening squeal.

Lorenzo rose, his face a pasty gray. "I have done murder," he said flatly.

"Only protecting yourself," Floyd said quietly.

"That will not keep me out of jail until trial time."

George Cleeve leaned close to whisper. "This paymaster man seems to be a friend. I will pay him to row you out to the *Falmouth* and hide you out. One of our people is a doctor and will come right out to see to your wound. Lorenzo, we need a shipwright carpenter for the voyage. If all goes well with the loading, we can make sail with the morning tide."

"I cannot desert me family, sir!"

"Quite correct. Would they be interested in a new life, in a new land?"

"Better than starving with me in prison."

"Give me your address. I shall go see to your family. Now, go before McFedders returns."

Throughout the stormy afternoon and evening, longboat after longboat delivered provisions and colonist families to the ship. Lorenzo had been hidden in the ship's carpenter shop after his wound had been cleaned and bandaged.

George Cleeve brought Lorenzo a pewter plate of food at suppertime.

"I'm glad we never have to do business with McFedders again. By the time I got to your flat, McFedders's agent was kicking your family and sister-in-law out into the street. They are all safely on board."

"Including Penelope and her sons?"

Cleeve looked sheepish. "I say, they are a handsome lot, and you should have forewarned me about your sister-in-law. Knowing that district, I was surprised to find such a charming and beautiful widow residing there."

"Widow?" Lorenzo knew the man had heard wrong.

"A fact that I gained from your good wife. A childless widow—now I find that information quite interesting. Richard is always chiding me for not taking another wife. Now, stay hidden until we set sail."

Lorenzo wondered why his wife would lie about Penelope being a widow, when she'd never been married to any of the men who'd fathered her sons. He decided it would be best not to pursue the subject.

"Sir, how did my family take this sudden move?"

Cleeve frowned. "Your wife said nothing, except to order Jonathan, Philo, and James to load your goods onto the carriage. Then she addressed the baby in her arms. She told him that his father's wish was coming true. Do you understand?"

"Aye, sir," Lorenzo gulped. "The dream of owning land to farm."

George Cleeve smiled to himself. He had other dreams for Lorenzo Pettygrove in the New World.

At dawn Lorenzo heard the anchor pulled free from the oozing bay mud and the high overhead snap of sails hoisted to the main and mizzenmasts. The *Falmouth* moved smoothly toward the ocean waves.

Then Lorenzo began to laugh. George Cleeve would have his hands full trying to get Penelope Randolph to wed him.

CHAPTER

☆ 1 ☆

___

Commonwealth of Maine—1841

The bell-funneled locomotive inched along in the fog-shrouded morning, several hours overdue from New York City. Cautious brakemen walked fifty feet to the front, rhythmically waving whale oil lanterns and muttering an eerie chant.

"Tr-r-r-rain on-n-n-n the tra-a-ack! Tr-r-r-rain on-n-n-n the tra-a-ack!"

Despite the massive fog bank, it was an unusual October morning for Maine. No winds played off the North Atlantic and the calm air seemed almost autumn warm. Throughout the night the few coach passengers had huddled together for warmth. The locomotive, forced to travel at less than thirty miles an hour, had not been able to build up enough steam to supply heat to the passenger cars. Many of the passengers had deserted the train in Boston, content to wait for the blanketing fog to dissipate. Some, who had remained, now hung from the second-class windows for a breath of the warm air and a view of very little.

"Certainly makes you feel all safe inside."

"What does, deary?" asked the older woman, pulling her angular frame out of the window and resettling on the wooden seat.

"That they are lighting the way to keep the train on the

11

tracks. I feared they wouldn't even have trains in a foreign country like America."

Mrs. Adriana Cosbie's horselike face broke into a quizzical smile, which she tried to share with the traveling companion on the opposite bench. The young woman did not respond and kept her face hidden behind a floppy brimmed hat.

"Come back in, D'Arcy," Mrs. Cosbie said, coldly. "Those men are only warning cattle and horses off the track."

Adriana Cosbie was growing to resent the young woman's silence, as much as she had come to resent D'Arcy Broome's constant chatter. Had things run their normal course she would now be sitting in front of her Brookline fireplace with a soothing cup of tea, with a nice tidy profit in her pocket. But nothing had run its normal course since boarding the packet *Lynette* in London. Her hatred centered around Captain John Johns.

"I am master of this vessel," he had barked earnestly. "You may retain your first-class cabin, but if you are chaperone to those dozen sirens, you will keep them under constant check and dine with them in second class."

"Captain," she had growled, "we are both agents for the Tucker Shipping Line. You, as master of this ship, and I as agent to secure domestic help in England for service in America."

"You may look on them as domestic servants," he sneered, "but they are single female vessels and we will face six weeks of hell keeping my sailors from them."

Thus Adriana was deprived of the luxury of first class and sitting at the Captain's table. Still, First Officer Ian Llwellen made sure there was a fresh bottle of sherry in her cabin each evening.

Then the fog had enveloped them like the ending of time. They floated aimlessly for days, without sail. It was impossible to even find the landing for their home port of Portland. Then, having drifted south, they were just able to make landfall at New York.

Adriana still wasn't sure what had turned Captain Johns so

bitter upon docking, but she was advised to get her domestic servants off the *Lynette* and transport them by rail to Portland. She was more than pleased to get her charges off the ship, into hansom cabs and to the railroad depot, only to realize she had thirteen young ladies under tow and not a dozen.

"Me friend from the boat," D'Arcy informed quickly. "She's got her own rail fare and wants to get home to Portland quickly."

Adriana had shrugged it off. She was more concerned over whether the Tucker Shipping Line would repay her for this additional cost. Adriana might have left it at that, had it not been for the stopover in Boston.

The young woman slept on, curled up on the wooden bench and using D'Arcy Broome's shoulder as a pillow. The position had tilted back the floppy hat just enough for Adriana to see a portion of her face. A curious woman by nature, Adriana was now greatly puzzled. Why was this extraordinarily beautiful woman dressed in a simple domestic servant's traveling costume, when her shoes were of a fine patent leather and the hem of the peeking petticoat was Belgium lace? Adriana racked her brain but could not recall seeing this fair lady in the second-class dining salon.

A metallic shriek came from the bell-funnel, along with a soot-laden cloud of smoke.

D'Arcy Broome let out an answering shriek, pulled in from the window, and slammed it down.

Adriana was pulled from her reverie and her sternness convulsed into laughter. "D'Arcy, you are a sight. You have just become blacker than any slave I've seen back in my birth state of Virginia!"

With only a London street education, the girl looked puzzled and then caught sight of her reflection in the train window. "Blimey!" she gasped. "I've done turned black as a chimney sweep. Won't ever get a good domestic position now."

The silent young woman laughed, which caused the floppy, frivolous hat to shake. The laugh was rich, warm, and throaty.

"D'Arcy, don't be a goose! We are now in New England where the people are thrifty, straight-laced, and throw nothing away. They'll just wash you up and plunk you into the pantry or kitchen."

"Oh, Beth," she pouted, "that won't do D'Arcy no good. Like we talked on the voyage, I'm here to find me a husband. That's why I didn't act like them other tarts with the sailors and officers. Oh, my, I've just said too much!"

"Or not enough," Adriana sniffed. "I chaperoned my girls and Captain Johns likewise watched his sailors."

"But who was watching the amorous Captain?" Beth snapped crisply. "You were supplied with your lovely little bottle of sherry to still your night ears, but the decks creaked with silently moving feet. Did you know his wife was on board this voyage?"

Adriana sat back, curious mischief in her eyes. "D'Arcy," she said, in a sweet-mother-knows-all-tone, "we should be just moments from the Portland station. A visit to the wash-closet will remove the soot."

The girl turned toward the back of the passenger car.

Elizabeth Johns felt a strange prickling crawl up her spine. Too much had been said and she did not like the woman's quizzical look. The borrowed hat, shawl, dress, and pinafore apron were not fooling this woman. She was so close to her goal and could not be thwarted now.

"I could resent that comment. I pride myself in bringing only virgins into domestic service for the Tucker Shipping Line."

"For American import, perhaps. Their London offices are not so careful in their selection process. Tucker men select female servants to please Tucker owners and their ship captains and masters."

As though tired of playing this silly game, Elizabeth removed the hat and placed it in her lap. Her naturally curly strawberry-blonde locks had been piled high upon her head, in the manner of the other English girls bound for domestic service. In actual fact, it gave her a more youthful countenance than her twenty years. It exposed the full length of the swanlike neck, upon which was perched an oval face with high cheekbones, a straight nose, dimpled chin, and eyes of such a deep emerald green tint that the time of day could change their true coloration. She now sat erect and her head took on its natural stance of arrogant self-esteem.

Adriana gasped, fully seeing her for the first time. "I've seen you before, my dear."

"Hardly," Beth laughed, crisply. "I took all my meals in my cabin during the voyage."

"Then how did you come to know D'Arcy?"

Elizabeth saw no reason to hide from that truth. "I have lived in London the last two years, Mrs. Cosbie. D'Arcy was my personal maid. She resented the constant advances of my husband, who, to spite me, and D'Arcy, brought her to the Tucker Line offices for your interview."

Adriana sniffed. "Some men are creatures of their own lust. I've met only one true gentleman of late, the first officer on the *Lynette*. Oh, my, what a man! He makes a woman have thoughts she should never have."

Elizabeth felt the color crawling up her neck. For the moment she did not want to think about Ian Llwellen. The Welsh seaman, more than her husband, was cause for her desire to return home to Portland.

"I won't repeat your comment to Mr. Cosbie," she said quickly, to change the subject.

To her surprise the women reared back her head and let loose with a horsey laugh. "Cosbie is but a name I've carried through all twelve of my husbands."

"Twelve?" Beth gasped. It was near impossible to believe that the rather ugly woman, by esthetic standards, had been able to garner even a single husband.

The question did not phase the acid-tongued cynic. "That's a near enough account, as I recall. I'm a woman known for the ability to turn a fair business venture. Hard to do in our rather puritanical society without the attachment of a husband. Most men look for a wife who is a dear and devoted friend, to boss around like a servant and bear offspring. Some men are weak and appreciate a strong woman to give them backbone in their business ventures. Once they begin to feel successful, I take my share of the profits and desert them."

The preposterous truth began to dawn on Elizabeth. "Then, you are not really married?"

Adriana Cosbie smiled vaguely. "Only to Horace Cosbie. He was over sixty and I was only fourteen when my father forced me to marry him. The old goat taught me business finance. When I was sixteen he gave me money to run away from Virginia. Because I learned all he knew about the slave trade business, it was quite easy to convert that knowledge to the domestic service trade."

"Get your parcels, ladies. We are at the Portland depot!"

Adriana's curiosity would not go away. She had a lucrative five-year contract with the Tucker Shipping Line. This woman and her husband were somehow connected with the line. She did not want to get caught in the middle. "Are you to be met, my dear?"

"I am now home and can find my own way, thank you. Have you a placement for D'Arcy yet?"

"The placements are made by Nelson Cleeve."

Elizabeth smiled to herself. Nelson would be easy for her to handle.

A moment later she wondered if she should not have stayed close to Mrs. Cosbie. In New York she had been able to blend in with the many passengers boarding the train. She had been asleep in Boston and was not aware of the vast number of passengers who had detrained. Here, in the sunless October morning of 1841, only their fourteen were stepping down from the second-class car, and only two men and a strikingly beautiful young woman emerged from the first-class coach.

Because of the dense fog, a group of men came around the corner of the depot carrying lanterns to light the way to the awaiting carriages.

Elizabeth felt a pang of dreadful fright. The men were sailors, wearing the uniform of the Tucker Line. And marching in their center was an impossibility.

"Hold it right there, my fair ladies."

The stentorian Welsh voice nearly sent her into a panic. There was no protection in going to huddle with the twelve, and the first-class passengers had already entered the depot. She threw the floppy hat down onto the tracks, pulled the shawl over her head, and moved behind a cart upon which the girls' luggage was being placed.

"I trust you had a pleasant journey," Ian Llwellen said smoothly. "The fog started to lift shortly after you left us, and we made the Portland lighthouse more than an hour ago. And where might I be finding that classical beauty, Mrs. Cosbie?"

Elizabeth felt sick. She knew she was the reason the *Lynette* had pushed to get here first, fog or no fog. And she resented Ian being the agent sent to drag her back to the ship. The man was a devil eating her alive, and she had run away to control her appetite.

"I am here," Adriana said, stepping down from the train. "Just checking to see that the girls left nothing behind."

"Or that none of the young ladies is left behind?"

There was a moment of sudden silence. It was a moment made for Ian Llwellen. Standing between two lantern-bearers, he had purposely dressed in a uniform of white britches, a powder blue cut-away with gold braid and piping. It enhanced his tall, muscular figure. Beneath the cocked hat his stern face had the look of a Roman Centurion inspecting hostages. The flashing hazel eyes searched every face carefully, recalling each one from the voyage. But the one he sought was not in the group.

"I have never lost a charge yet," Adriana snapped. "What do you wish?"

He saluted smartly and bowed. "A formality, Mrs. Cosbie. You forgot to sign the proper papers. The fourteen of you will return to the ship and make proper dock landing here at Portland."

Adriana looked at him coolly. She saw their game now and would not play. No way would they accuse her of smuggling someone into the country. "You can't even count, Mister Llwellen. The manifest will show I brought only twelve girls from England and twelve I have here."

"Thirteen girls left the dock, I have been informed."

"I cannot be responsible for your other passengers. Let's get this petty business over with so I can report to Mr. Cleeve's office."

Adriana marched off and Ian turned a smile on D'Arcy that would have made most other women feel putty weak. "Help me protect her from him," he whispered. "The Captain is in some tirade, D'Arcy. We never should have sailed up in this fog. He even damaged the ship, ramming it into the wharf."

"Ian," D'Arcy cried, "I haven't seen the mistress since just before arriving. I was in the wash-closet."

"Damn!" he muttered. "We will all be under the Captain's thumb if she tells her grandfather of this voyage."

"And why shouldn't she tell the truth?" D'Arcy flared. "In six weeks' time the captain got every one of the girls into his cabin but me, and you know well why he steered clear of me. Makes me sick, him treating the mistress that way!"

Wearily, Ian shook his head. "I could not agree with you more. Now, hurry and catch up with the others."

Ian felt frustrated. It had been a loathsome journey. He hated John Johns for openly cheating on his wife. He hated Elizabeth even more for staying in her cabin and refusing to see him. At least, in London, he had been able to dine at her table once a week, when he was in port.

This trip had stoked his fires like none before. He had escaped the Welsh coal mines at age ten and put himself into naval service. In eight years he had clawed his way up through the ranks, but he could not gain a commission because of his Welsh birth. At the end of that enlistment he had gained a berth with the Tucker mercantile fleet. By age twenty he was a six-foot, four-inch giant, and to his face, beneath a flowing crown of sandy hair, was a certain atavistic handsomeness that gave him the look of a man who would someday become his own captain.

Now he had learned he had a weakness. For twenty-four years he had let women love him, but had never loved them in return. He had tried desperately to keep his feeling for Beth platonic. But the year before, at Christmas, he had

caught her under the mistletoe. That single kiss had made
them both tremble. Thereafter, a single look, a casual touching of fingers were like a torrid affair. Once he dared speak of
love and Beth had fled in terror. He had a consuming love for
a woman he would never be able to possess.

Except, Ian mused with ribald contempt, if only Elizabeth
is fire-brand enough to expose her husband to her family.
Then . . .

A clawed hand came out of the fog and caught D'Arcy's
arm.

"Ouch!"

"You'll be ouching more than that, unless I get the truth
about that woman."

"Wot's in it for me?"

"She asked about your placement."

D'Arcy brightened. "I was her maid, Mrs. Cosbie. She is
Mrs. John Johns, the Captain's wife."

Adriana was disappointed. She thought the young woman
would have been higher placed.

"She is also a member of the Pettygrove family."

"There's a whole parcel of them here in Maine," Adriana
fumed, to hide her fluttering heart. It was important information to possess.

When the baggage man had pulled the cart to the street,
Beth had moved along in its shadow and then hid behind an
oak tree and waited for a hansom cab. A moment later she
heard the rumble of wheels coming out of the fog. Her hope
faded into puzzlement as a resplendent carriage emerged
from the fog and pulled up to the depot entrance.

It was a coach better suited for the streets of London, and
Beth thought it there for the first-class passengers.

Then her heart sang as a familiar figure descended from
the carriage with an aura of gravity and no outward sign of
haste. He whispered softly to the coachman to fetch the
passengers from the depot. Nelson Cleeve was not prepared
for a girl dressed like a servant to step out of the fog, throw
back a shawl, and give him a saucy wink.

"Riding in high style, aren't you, Nels?"

"Hello, Beth," he said, dismally. "It was a present to the Tucker Line from the Hudson Bay Company."

"And here to take me back to the *Lynette* and my ever loving husband."

"Hardly," he laughed dryly. "Francis and I have been betting that you were holed up in some fancy New York hotel, like when you ran away at sixteen. Actually, I am here to pick up guests for Residency House."

"Marvelous, you old love. Then you can get me to Residency House before anyone knows I am really back."

Nelson Cleeve felt the slow sickness spreading through his middle. A thin, frail, and sickly man, his use to the family had been his brain and secretarial acumen. He was not an attractive man to most women, but he was highly attracted to all women—especially Elizabeth. His distant cousin.

When George Cleeve married Penelope Randolph, he gave his name to Jonathan, Philo, and James. Penelope bore George Cleeve four sons, who grew to resent their half-brothers. In two hundred years the split was such that Portland had the have-not-Cleeves and the have-Cleeves. Nelson had sprung from the former.

"Oh, here are your passengers."

Nelson squinted through the fog and broke into a wide grin. "Asa, is it really you?"

The rotund man pushed back his head so he could see out from under the bowler brim. His eyes crinkled and the small mouth opened to expose perfect white teeth. "Good old Nelson! I've not laid eyes on you since our days at Cambridge."

"And you went on to Amherst for a law degree, I understand."

Asa Lawrence Lovejoy laughed. It was a sound that started in his belly and shook the earth when it exploded. "A lawyer," he chortled, "so my father would not have to pay one to handle legal papers for his mercantile business. It has kept me single, but built like a plump kosher pickle, firm of exterior and spicy of interior. But, I am remiss. Allow me to introduce the man I wrote Francis Pettygrove about, Robert

Rowland and his daughter, Sophia. This is Nelson Cleeve, private secretary to Mr. Hiram Pettygrove."

Robert Rowland did not acknowledge the introduction. He was so tall that he did not need the stovepipe hat to make him look taller. Nelson nearly laughed when it got knocked off as the man entered the carriage. Then he turned to help the girl who had been on Rowland's arm.

He saw at once that she was lovely. She was slender rather than thin, high of bosom, soft-curving, and she swept into the carriage in her exquisitely tailored traveling suit like an aristocrat.

"Get in here, Lovejoy!" Rowland snapped. "Bad enough to be met by just a secretary and a servant girl."

Nelson winced as he followed Lovejoy into the carriage. Beth was huddled into the corner, with the shawl back up over her head. There was a twinkle in her eye that Nelson had seen many times before and didn't like.

"How do you do," she cooed, giving her voice a D'Arcy tone. "I'm Beth Johns. Fog put us into New York and we came by rail, too. Of course, being a servant I was in second class, where it was as cold as an outhouse at midwinter. Were you cold, miss?"

"I slept," Sophia rasped, her voice tinged with ice.

"And I slept coming through Boston. I did so want to see that quaint old city."

"Quaint?" Rowland huffed. "My dear girl, many of the finer buildings in that city are my design. Hardly 'quaint' at all."

Asa Lovejoy looked at Nelson, who gave him a knowing wink. He then studied the face under the shawl more carefully. It was a beautiful face. Almost too beautiful. Nelson was up to one of his practical jokes, but he was not sure why. Still, it had exposed Robert Rowland to Nelson at once. The man was an arrogant snob and, although he was a single man, he found Sophia too cold a woman to ever be warmed up by love.

It was not Nelson's joke, but he was delighted to have Beth back. She had always been daring and full of spunk. The only trouble that he and Francis had ever been in was due to Beth.

Margaret Cleeve was so filled with excitement that she nearly bounced. The short, red-faced woman had been the housekeeper at Residency House ever since her husband had been lost at sea, when Nelson was five.

"Lydia, be seeing the lady and gentlemen to the rooms I assigned them. I've got to wrap my arms around my precious Beth."

Sophia Rowland fumed. Proper servants in Boston would not be allowed such a display in front of house guests. Then, as she followed the maid, she heard something that made her very curious.

"Oh, Miss Beth," Margaret bubbled, "a sailor done brought your luggage from the ship. I put it in your grandmother's old room, as usual."

"Don't you think you should go directly to your parents' house in York?"

"No," Beth said simply. She linked her arm through Margaret's and started for the stairs.

Nelson stood there a long moment frowning before he turned and went toward Hiram Pettygrove's study. For twelve years it had also been the bedroom for the old man, who had difficulty navigating the steep stairs. Before he reached it, the uproar burst upon his ears.

"The fool!" Hiram was screeching. "The utter incompetent fool! What idiot would bring a ship through the Casco Bay Islands in such a fog? What's the damage?"

"Nelson will get a full report, as always," he heard Francis Pettygrove answer his grandfather.

Nelson smiled, as he started to open the door. It was a morning of ghostly memories out of the past. As a boy and until he was seventeen, Francis Walter Pettygrove had spent a large part of every summer at his grandfather's house in Portland. As different as dawn and dusk, Nelson and Francis had become close summertime friends. They had shared the love of the incoming cargo vessels from foreign ports and talking with the sailors to learn the news of the world outside of Portland. "Nelson will get the news, as usual" had become almost a trademark.

"And here is Nelson with the news. He took out about half a dock. Even though it appears as only minor damage, I think we will have to send the *Lynette* over to Kittery for repairs."

"Tucker will skin his ass when he hears about this in London. Francis, where is your father?"

Francis grinned. "Nelson and I created a lumber crisis that will keep him in York for a few days. You know his feelings about this scheme."

Hiram Pettygrove nodded and looked at his grandson with affection. He was the one who had insisted they name him Francis. There had not been another Francis in the family since the original had arrived from England as a baby. In his bones he had known it was time for another Francis. In time that Francis had created a family lumber industry in York, moved his father's shipbuilding yards to Kittery, and retained an interest in the Tucker shipping business. But each generation had been conservative in building upon the last.

This grandson was different. There was in his angular frame a driving spirit of questioning, wondering, and adventure. Extremely handsome, at age twenty-nine, he was still single and alert to life. Since the death of his wife, Martha, only three people had been at the center of Hiram's universe: Francis, Elizabeth, and Nelson. And at seventy-five, Hiram didn't care if the rest of the family resented that fact or not.

"Well, which one of you catbirds is going to give me the other news?"

"What news?" Nelson shrugged.

"Elizabeth!" Hiram shrieked. "Margaret says you two were betting that she stayed in New York. Won't take that bet! She tried that when she was a snotty sixteen. Sent you two down to find her and bring her back and what does she do? Talks you into staying with her for three days so you could all see the sights."

"It wasn't all sight-seeing, Grandfather. Remember, that was when I boldly marched into John Jacob Astor's office and got him to tell me about his Astoria fur venture and its failing."

"Don't try to get around me, you puppy-dog. The subject is Elizabeth. Where is she?"

Nelson sighed. "Up in Miss Martha's room. She came up by train. I hardly think that she and her husband are on good terms."

Francis turned toward the casement window to hide his smile. His grandfather was considered the redoubtable one and his secretary the sensitive one. He sometimes wondered, like now, if after twelve years of such a close relationship they did not sometimes reverse roles.

"Didn't approve of the marriage in the first place," Hiram smarted. "Well, I want to rest today, so I am dining with you and the guests. Francis, tell Elizabeth she will take lunch with me. Now, we are fairly up in our facts on Asa Lovejoy. What homework on Rowland, Nelson, and why would the man drag his daughter along?"

"I was also curious. She is most attractive, rather snobbish, and too expensively dressed for their financial condition."

"Oh?" Hiram loved it when Nelson had the full report on someone.

"Frankly, they are near paupery. His company was highly successful prior to the War of 1812, with architect and building offices in London, Boston, and New York. He refused to take sides, so he was considered an American there, and a royalist here. He had married into wealth, but after the death of his wife, he was cut off from the source. His daughter still receives a small stipend from her mother's people. In the past twenty years he has designed and built only seven buildings. Frankly, Asa has probably overwhetted his appetite for the Columbia Project."

"I should hope so," Francis grinned. "I told Asa we could only take along a man we could afford."

"Her dress would suggest they are out to impress and get a good contract. In the carriage she examined the coach and myself quite carefully. Reminded me of Dawson Cleeve weighing coins in his counting house."

"Why would she be trying to impress us?" Hiram mused.

Nelson giggled. It was a strange sound coming from him. "Were not Asa's sisters impressed with our handsome young prince when he was in Boston? We will watch her face when she first views Francis, to see if she has matrimony on her mind."

"Me?" Francis gasped. "I am but twenty-nine and have no plans for marriage until I am at least thirty-five."

Hiram chortled with laughter. "I do believe the boy is blushing. Now, get out of here, both of you."

Outside the study-bedroom Francis held Nelson back.

"Nels, arrange for the two of us to meet privately with Asa this afternoon. And with father gone, we'd best meet with Captain Johns and his First Officer."

"We also have Mrs. Cosbie to deal with."

"I forgot she would be on this ship," Francis groaned. "Warn your mother that we will probably have to invite the old cow for dinner."

He went up the stairs toward his grandmother's old room and knocked on the door. Beth opened it and stood there, looking at him a little fearfully. She still wore the domestic servant's costume. Francis couldn't help but laugh. His laugh was rich and deep. He took Beth in his arms and gave her a heartfelt hug.

"Is this the latest London fashion?"

"No," Beth said, impatiently. "I had to sneak off the ship in New York to get home. I came up by train with Mrs. Cosbie's new domestics." She gulped. "Come in, Francis, so I don't blab to the whole world."

Francis entered the boudoir and crossed to the window

seat. It had once been his favorite spot to have little chats with his grandmother.

Elizabeth watched him carefully. She admired her cousin with an almost religious passion. He had the grace and beauty of a spirited male who had been trained to dance the spars of the mizzen and main masts, with a figure and face she now saw reminded her of a gentleman in a Renaissance painting she had seen in London. To Beth he had always been a friend, who listened with a slightly cocked head and intense gray eyes that constantly changed from interest to amusement to devilish mischief. She trusted him, like she trusted her grandfather.

"Even for you, Beth, this sounds like a rather strange adventure. What's the trouble?"

"I don't know, and yet I do know. I was homesick, lonely, and bored. I thought London would be gay, full of parties and gala evenings at the theater with my husband."

"And that wasn't the case?"

Beth laughed. It was a bitter sound. "I have no real husband, Francis. When he is not at sea, he is at his club, or we are entertaining his friends or officers at dinner. On those nights he is so drunk the butler has to put him to bed. The same butler he pays to spy on me when he is at sea."

"Because of another man?"

"That is almost an ironic question. One of his officers thinks that he is in love with me. But he is always at sea with John, so how could I be having an affair with him?"

Francis was almost sorry he had entered. He was not qualified to be a part of this discussion. He felt embarrassed.

"You could," he suggested timidly, "travel onboard his ship, like some of the other captain's wives."

She began to toss dresses out of the trunk and onto the bed. "Don't make me laugh. I even had a cabin of my own for this crossing, so it wouldn't spoil his fun."

"Fun?"

"I'm sorry, Francis. I used the word *fun* so I wouldn't shock you."

"I see," Francis sighed. "I shipped out with him only once, our first trip for the Hudson Bay Company. He was hardly a gentleman with the native girls in Honolulu. I thought marriage would have—"

"He probably cheats more because he *is* married and can't get caught—" She stopped short.

Francis hardened his heart.

"Elizabeth! You told your mother—"

"I lied!" she wailed. "He was so drunk that night he couldn't remember what he had done. Later, he was the most relieved man in the world, when I told him I had lost the child."

"Why?" Francis moaned. "You are so beautiful. You could have had any man of your choice."

Beth's emerald eyes flashed sudden fire.

"Not of my choice, Francis. The choice of my mother and father. A York man. A lumberjack for the family business. I refuse to end up a hard and bitter woman like my mother, stuck in that dreary town."

"Oh, Beth, my dear, I have no clever words for you. Perhaps Grandfather shall. You are to take lunch with him in his study."

"I shall like that. I've missed him so. Francis, don't ever get married."

He laughed so unexpectedly that she stared.

"Nels thinks that this Miss Rowland might be looking at me with that very thing in mind."

"She'll give up that idea when she finds out that we are cousins. I was simply horrible to her in the carriage. She's probably looking for our outhouse."

"Beth, you didn't?"

"I did. Shall I reintroduce myself and make amends?"

His eyes sparkled to devilish mischief. "You might find out what's on her mind."

He gave her another hug and left. He was unsure what he was to say to Captain John Johns. He knew it would do no good to bring his Uncle Frank over from York. The man had an ax-handle temper and had refused to attend the wedding. He would have to be his own man.

The fog was lifting and he decided to walk down to the office. He could feel a bit of pity for Elizabeth. For the first

seventeen years of his life his winters had been spent in
either York or Kittery. They had been long, dreary winters.
His mother and sister always seemed to have a cold. It was a
cold that had killed his mother when he was fifteen. He could
hardly remember her.

"Good morning, sir. Mr. Cleeve is with Mrs. Cosbie, and
Captain Johns awaits you in Mr. Hiram's office."

Francis smiled. It was still his grandfather's office, even
though he had used it for years.

"Mr. Pettygrove!" Johns greeted him, as he entered. "I
missed seeing you on my last voyage."

Francis looked at the forty-year-old seaman keenly. Johns
was seldom so effusive. He's frightened, Francis thought,
damned frightened. He fingered a gold button on his uniform
and the high brow of his round face showed beads of per-
spiration. He was not an unattractive man, Francis thought,
even though he wore heavy sideburns to cover his growing
jowls, and loose-fitting uniform coats to conceal a rotund
belly.

"Well," Francis drawled, "your explanation for breaking
company policy?"

"London policy is to move cargo fast."

"Portland policy is for the safety of passengers and the
ship."

Johns leaned forward confidently.

"It was an untrustworthy officer on the bridge, sir. Went
against orders to bring her in through that fog. I'll be asking
Mr. Tucker for a new officer on our return to London."

"And how is the man untrustworthy?"

"Philandering at sea," Johns whispered, in a ribald fashion.

"*That* is shocking to you?" Francis asked, his voice heavy
with sarcasm. "You forget perhaps, Captain, that I've sailed
with you."

"I was unmarried then, sir. This time my wife was on
board. She was so upset that she went ashore in New York.
Had the morning train checked, but she wasn't on it."

"Which officer was it, Johns?"

"Llwellen. A Welshman. Covets my post."

Francis frowned thoughtfully. "I've never met the man, though I know of him. I've never been given a bad report on him before."

"A sly one, Mr. Pettygrove. Gets everyone to liking him, including my wife. Yes, he's friendly enough to discourage bad reports."

"I see," Francis said, hiding his amusement. If the man was so untrustworthy, why had the Captain never made his own written or verbal reports? Though he wanted the truth, he knew that to expose Beth's accusations would expose the fact that she was here, so he would not press him now. Francis thought there was nothing in the world he hated so much as a liar. Accused, they would only lie again to cover up the last lie. Liars like Johns had to be caught red-handed.

"Then, Captain Johns, you will deliver a written report to me personally. I will expect it no later than six o'clock this evening at Residency House. Of course, you will stay for dinner. Good morning."

John Johns put on his cocked hat at a jaunty angle and departed. He was most pleased with his performance. Ian Llwellen was a thorn in his side and coddled the crew. It was time to pluck out the thorn. At the next pier, the packet *Rose Ann* was nearly loaded for sailing. Captain Harvey Wouk was an old friend and short an officer. He would go at once and offer the services of Ian. A fat purse would see to it that he never lived to see England again.

As for Elizabeth, he was indifferent. He had used her to secure his position as the chief master of the line, and now found her to be boring window-dressing. He could charge her with refusing him children, desertion, and with Ian dead, adultery.

"Parkinson," Francis called to the clerk after the Captain had gone, "take a message to First Officer Ian Llwellen. He is to report to me as soon as possible. And Parkinson," he added, "get word to the man without Captain Johns gaining knowledge."

The report of Adriana Cosbie on Captain Johns's conduct was quietly accepted. Francis was generous for her aide to his cousin and amused to learn of D'Arcy Broome's former status as maid to Beth. Although it troubled Nelson, Francis wanted the girl placed in Residency House as a serving girl, especially for that evening.

It was Francis's turn to grow troubled with the arrival of Asa Lovejoy. The man seemed nervous and distracted as he laid out his maps on the long table.

"I am glad you did not wish Robert Rowland at this meeting, Francis. Some bothersome news has fallen into my hands. A Captain John Couch has placed a very large order with Cushing & Company of Newburyport for trade in the Sandwich Islands and Oregon."

"Oregon? To deal with what company?"

"Don't jump ahead on my story. Cushing buys from my father, so I had them bring Couch to me. He tried to trade with the Hudson Bay Company and was thwarted."

"Good for John McLoughlin."

Asa frowned. "But not good for us. Couch found a buyer and had Indians canoe his goods to this point on the Willamette."

"Impossible!" Francis fumed, studying the map. "That place is called *The Falls,* just above the Clackamas Rapids. I have been there. It has been an HBC trading post since 1829."

"It would appear, from Captain Couch, that it is now, also, a Methodist mission called Oregon City."

"Then we are doomed," Francis groaned, heartsick. "The Falls was the cornerstone for my Columbia Project, because of the waterpower for sawmills. How many people are there?"

"Only a Reverend Waller and his wife. The mission store is there to service the other Methodist missions above the falls. Here, here, and here. Because they are farmers, HBC is closing its eyes and looking forward to their fresh produce."

"A question," Nelson mused. "Senator Linn's act is stalled in Congress, while Washington fights London on rights to that territory. Are the Methodists becoming British subjects?"

"No, Nelson, they are taking their chances and still laying out their six hundred forty acres. But, let me address how I know that fact." He sighed. "You know how difficult it was for me to convince Lovejoy & Company to open an office in St. Louis. My father was for that, because of the river traffic from New Orleans, and his man, Moshe Shamir, is well familiar with river barges. Three months ago, without my father knowing, I took Moshe's chief clerk, Michael Erin Myers, and set him up in Independence, Missouri. While setting up the store I was approached by a Mr. Elijah White for pricing on supplies for a hundred immigrant party from the depressed farmlands of Illinois and Missouri."

"No!" Francis screamed. "More and more people getting there before us, Asa. It will all be gone!"

"Hardly all," Asa laughed, then he frowned. "But my actions on the Independence store has caused a rift in my family. I have had to use all my savings to pay the company for the supplies there. My father and his associates have washed their hands of me and the Columbia Project."

Francis sat down limply. "Before, I said we were doomed. I did not know that we were fully crushed. How much will you lose, Asa?"

"*We* will lose nothing. Why? Because I depart in three days for Missouri. If Mr. White wants my supplies and my wagons, then I will insist upon going along to protect my investment. Francis, one of us must get there first to establish our claim."

"Beautiful!" Francis gasped, his enthusiasm flowing back. "I will begin pressing my family at once. Now, how about some lunch, so we can discuss what claims we wish to establish?"

Francis's gray eyes danced with amusement when the men gathered in the parlor before dinner. He had been most impressed with his meeting of Ian Llwellen. His grandfather had agreed with his decision on the man and chuckled that Francis had invited him for dinner.

Now it became almost comical. Robert Rowland did his best to impress Hiram; Asa sat grinning with future thoughts; Captain Johns sweated as though caught in the jaws of a trap, and Ian Llwellen remained stoic, his face unreadable.

Francis was waiting to read his face on the entrance of Beth. But even Francis was not prepared for her performance.

She swept into the room in a ravishing London gown that revealed the exquisite female figure she possessed. She was an expert at being the naughty child one moment and sweetness and light the next.

"Hello, John," she cooed, giving each round cheek a kiss. "Mr. Llwellen." She curtsied. "Gentlemen," she said, offering her hand to Asa and then Robert Rowland, "we met in the carriage. I am Elizabeth Johns, the Captain's wife. Grandfather, thank you for a delightful lunch and talk. Oh, and may I present our other houseguest, Miss Sophia Rowland. No one told Sophia that we dressed for dinner in Maine, so we have spent the afternoon together making over one of my dresses."

Francis turned and all thoughts vanished. Sophia Rowland was in a gown of pure white, which enhanced her slim figure and made her black hair and eyebrows almost midnight. At first he thought her decidedly pretty, but when she smiled a greeting at Hiram her dark beauty became magnetic. As though by design, Beth introduced him last.

"Dinner is served, Mr. Pettygrove."

Captain Johns nearly fainted at seeing D'Arcy Broome, and Ian had to hide a smile.

Francis was hardly aware of eating. All he could hear was Sophia's magical voice.

"My plans are a few years down the road," he heard himself answering Robert Rowland. "I think it best for me to come down to Boston a few times to see your buildings and designs."

Elizabeth's green eyes were alight with pleasure over Francis's words. She knew his trips would be more to meet with Sophia than her father. Once she had gotten to know Sophia, she had taken to her. But her real pleasure came in waiting for her grandfather to drop his bombshell during dessert.

"Elizabeth, my dear, how jolly to have you at my table again. You will make this Christmas a pleasure for me."

"Christmas?" Captain Johns gruffed. "We can hardly be back from London by Christmastime, sir."

"Back?" Hiram said gruffly. "One does not cross the Atlantic for a few days' visit. I was speaking of staying. Besides, it is too early for her to leave with you tomorrow on the *Rose Ann*."

"Me, sir?" Johns gulped. "It is Llwellen who has been transferred for that sailing."

"He will need to stay with the *Lynette*. Damage is greater than first thought. She'll be in dry-dock for a good three months. I am sending you back to London, because we have the design ready on a new ship and I want the Tucker approval as soon as possible."

"I am flattered." Johns grinned weakly, feeling Llwellen slip from his grasp. Now the handsome officer would be near to Elizabeth again. "But, sir, that would mean being separated from my wife."

"Grandfather," Beth supplied gently, as Hiram had instructed her, "perhaps I should return with John."

"Nonsense! John, you will stay with your ship and your wife. Llwellen, you will take the draft plans to London. It is settled."

Elizabeth could see the excitement in John's face, but she

did not guess its cause. She had bowed to her grandfather's wishes. For the sake of the family she had to give the man one more chance, under the watchful eye of everyone in Portland and Kittery. If he stepped out of line just once, then the family would decide his fate.

John Johns felt doubly saved. From the reaction of Hiram Pettygrove, it would seem Elizabeth had been smart enough to say nothing about his behavior, and his plans for Ian Llwellen were not altered. The man would soon be dead, and he, Johns, would be captain of the new clipper ship.

Francis was almost smiling as he said good night to the Captain. The man had fallen into the trap without knowing it and was now making the biggest blunder of all. He had protested being away from his wife, but never once questioned if he was also to be a houseguest where his wife was staying. Then, he put Elizabeth and Johns out of his mind. His excitement mounted over the thought of Asa's departure. At last, they were beginning.

CHAPTER

☆ 4 ☆

Boston—March 1842

The two months since Francis had moved from Portland had been the gloomiest he had ever known, even worse than the moments after his grandfather had died in his arms. That was a natural thing, which he was capable of fighting with personal grief. But his father, upon becoming the elder Pettygrove, was unnatural. Mean, self-centered, vindictive, hateful—and little-boyish in finally exposing his resentment at the relationship between Hiram and Francis.

Almost gleefully, Francis had been told that the Pettygrove family would not support the Columbia Project.

His grandfather had left him five thousand dollars, hardly enough to buy his own ship and supplies. Nelson Cleeve had given him a letter of introduction to a New York City merchant house, Benson & Brothers. They hired him as a clerk, but would not listen to his radical scheme. After about a month, though, seeing that he knew buying and selling better than some of their associates, they quietly began to listen and were finally convinced to enter the Oregon trade.

Francis rushed to Boston to share the news with Sophia and her father, but was met by a funeral wreath on the door.

"Last week," Sophia said softly. "I had no address for you in New York."

She was not chiding him, he understood. "I had to establish myself, Sophia, before I could let anyone know where I was, or what I was doing. I'm so sorry about your father."

"Thank you, Francis," she said. After a moment's pause she said, "He knew he could never do your project. How is it progressing, anyway?"

"It seems wrong that I should be excited at a moment like this, but Benson & Brothers are fully behind it. I will be their assignment agent in Oregon. Fifteen thousand dollars' worth of goods are being gathered to go aboard the *Victoria*. She departs next week for Honolulu."

"I see," Sophia said slowly. Then she stood up. "Francis," she said, "would I be a help to you?"

"Dear Mother of God," he whispered, "you have not been out of my thoughts or dreams since the moment I met you. But are you up to it?"

Sophia fought to still the wild beating of her heart. She was scared stiff; she had never been anything but a city girl. Still, she knew that Francis Pettygrove was the only man to father her children. She didn't need to be told that he had been bitten by the pioneer bug and that where he went she would have to follow.

"I shall be packed," she said evenly, "by the time you return with Parson Jones from the church."

September 1842

The Indians let out a scream so terrible that it brought the Reverend Alvin Waller stumbling out of the Mission house in his nightshirt. At first he could see nothing, except the morning catch of salmon left on the riverbank.

Asa Lovejoy rode slowly into view. The sun was barely over the eastern hills and had not yet burned away all the mist that swirled about the rolling banks of the Willamette.

To Reverend Waller this was not a frightening sight. Nearly every day a trapper or mountain man would ride down from the hills. This man looked no more travel-stained than any other. Sitting tall in the saddle, he looked larger than his five feet and seven inches. Six months of constant travel had brought his weight down to a lean one hundred and thirty pounds. This was hardly the same Asa Lovejoy who had left Independence, Missouri, this man who had been forced to turn into a fighting Bantam cock to keep order on the long journey.

Suddenly Alvin Waller's jaw dropped. "Elvira! Children! Come look at this!"

Coming out of the mist behind the lead rider was a string of pack horses, women, children, and cattle herds.

"I take it you are Elijah White," Waller called out to Asa.

"Asa Lawrence Lovejoy," he called back. "Mr. White is on rear guard duty this day."

"Oh, my," Mrs. Waller enthused as she gazed at the approaching pilgrims. "I've not spoken to another white woman in several months. Thank you, Mr. Lovejoy."

For nearly an hour, Asa savored the heady feeling of what it meant to be a part of the first major expedition along the Oregon Trail. When they had left the banks of the Missouri they had been singing; now they were bone tired, weather-beaten, and disbelieving that they had made it.

A sudden realization came to Reverend Waller. "Sir, we were under the impression you were to be a wagon train."

"We were," Asa said. "Our wagonmaster deserted us just before Fort Hall. I told White not to pay him in advance. He said he had to, that it was Methodist mission policy."

"Oh dear," Waller said weakly, not knowing whether or not to take offense. "Still, money would do him little good here. We can only barter and trade."

Asa was fed up with fawning servility. "The man was a thief. He forced us to leave the wagons at Fort Hall. Next time those wagons come through they'll be led by a man like the one who got us here. There he is—Pack McGraw, bringing in the cattle."

"Looks terribly young."

"I think he's terribly handsome," sixteen-year-old Deborah Waller giggled.

Asa laughed. He couldn't remember when the sound had last come from his throat. "He is quite a young man. A trapper's son hired on to herd the cattle. He knew the horse trails, but feared he'd get us lost in making a wagon trail. He was also concerned about the coming of fall and early snow storms in the mountains. A pack train we became."

Asa turned away when he saw the approach of Elijah White. He would let the man tell his own story to the mission man. His worth for the man had frozen into an icy silence after Elijah had forced the slaying of all the dogs on the wagon train. He was glad the man planned on traveling to a mission farther up river.

Asa tethered his horse to the limb of an ash tree and looked around. At first he felt disappointed, but then a slow elation started to creep in. There were only four buildings standing, which was the disappointment. The elation came in realizing there was still plenty of Oregon City land to be claimed.

The Reverend's daughter touched Asa's sleeve. "Can I be of service in showing you around, Mr. Lovejoy?"

He turned and grinned. "I expect you'd like me to introduce you to Pack McGraw, Miss——"

"Deborah Waller," she said demurely. "And though I did say he was handsome, I'm afraid he's too young for me."

"Well, then, Miss Waller, what shall you be showing me?"

"What little there is," she admitted wryly. "Our home, the mission meeting house, and the mission store are all under one roof." She laughed, like a morning lark in an aspen grove, Asa thought. "I certainly made it sound large, didn't I?" she said. "The meeting hall is actually our parlor the rest of the week. The mission store is mainly bare shelves, now that Captain Couch has opened his own store in that log cabin over there."

"I see," Asa said, hiding his surprise as he looked to where Deborah pointed. "It seems to be closed."

"The Captain has returned to New England for more supplies. He left the store in charge of a Mr. Wilson, who sleeps most of the day and only opens in the evenings to sell Blue Ruin to the Indians."

"Blue Ruin?

She laughed again. "It's British slang for an inferior and horrible tasting gin." Then she blushed. "Not that I know of its taste. That is what Papa preaches about from his pulpit. Here Before Christ is furious with Mr. Wilson over it."

Asa was puzzled. "Who is furious over what?"

"Sorry," she laughed. "That middle log cabin is the trading post for the Hudson Bay Company, or HBC. Because of the way they act sometimes, we call them 'Here Before Christ.' They are furious because Wilson has Blue Ruin to sell to the lackadaisical Indians and they do not. Their Tucker Line supply ship crashed and sank off the coast in August."

Asa's heart nearly stopped on that news. Then he realized it was far too soon for the arrival of Francis.

"You know, young lady, you are a walking newspaper of information."

"It's part of my job," she said proudly. "All week I gather information from those coming in to trade from the other missions. Then, Sunday mornings, after Papa's sermon, I get to report the news. It isn't always fun, because a lot of times it's just my family there, and they've already heard it at the dinner table."

Suddenly she stopped chattering and looked at him quite seriously. "Where are you from and what do you do?"

She seemed so mature, though Asa knew she could not yet be eighteen. Her russet hair was long and luxuriant, and she had the palest green eyes he had ever seen. But what really caught his attention was the quirky little smile that now played across her bowed lips.

"I am from Boston, Massachusetts, young lady. I'm a lawyer and merchant, and most recently a shepherd of this flock, which has come across plain, mountain, and too many rivers."

"Home people," she enthused. "We were from Salem— the reason for an up-river mission being named Salem. I wish we had come overland. I never want to see the sea again. I never want to be that sick again! Oh, look! Come and let me show you something you never saw back home!"

It seemed so natural to let her take him by the hand and pull him along toward the falls. Her hand felt good in his. Running together, that close, he could smell the clean scent of her hair and body. He had not smelled anything that clean in six months. She pulled him down on a grassy knoll and pointed.

"His name is Kenwa, one of the best canoe boys on the river. Watch what he does now."

The bronze-skinned young man stood on a rock outcropping, the falling water splashing over his feet.

A streak of scarlet jumped from the river water and seemed to start climbing up through the falling water. The boy froze, and just as the fish passed by the canoe, his hand darted out, caught it behind the head, and threw it onto the bank. Only when it landed did Asa see that it was some two feet in length.

"That's a sockeye salmon, heading upstream to spawn. At first I was sad to think of her as food . . . even before her babies were born. But Kenwa taught me that she dies after laying her eggs and the male salmon then fertilizes and hatches them. Would you like one for supper? They're delicious."

Asa nodded and followed her. He was curious to meet the boy and learn what he charged Fort Vancouver for his fish. To his amazement, Kenwa spoke English with a British accent.

"There was a Fort Vancouver before I was born, sir. My charge is anything I can trade back to my own people."

Asa did not like the way the boy looked at Deborah. He himself might have been too old for her, at thirty-four, but he did not want her with a savage, even one who could speak English. Purposely, he pulled her toward a strange sound that was coming from a smaller fall, around a rock outcropping.

He felt a pang of disappointment. It was two men attempting to build a waterwheel for a sawmill. He was relieved when he realized they were inexperienced and doomed to failure.

"Who are they?"

"When Mr. McLoughlin, from HBC, was here last week he called them claim-jumpers. They own that third log cabin. Just completed it yesterday."

"Any reason they would be called claim-jumpers?"

"Because they want to build a sawmill. HBC has a sawmill and small ship repair yard at the Fort. That's where the lumber came from for our Mission House, although Papa says the mission board will scream at the cost. Will you have lunch with us?"

"I have to sort out the pack animals and supplies."

"Then how about supper?"

"Yes," he grinned, "I think I would like that." He would also like to have an amiable discussion with Reverend Waller, Asa thought, after he saw Mr. White on his way.

It took several hours to sort out over a hundred people, their supplies and goods. Many planned to leave from here to be farmers in the valley. From this point, they would have to use their riding horses as pack animals. His horses were to be taken back to Fort Hall to return the wagons to Independence, weather permitting.

Now that they were here, Asa could take pride in one aspect of these people. They had come prepared, with no space wasted on luxuries. They had food for the winter and seed for the spring, and each man prided himself with a plow and other farm and building tools. The women each possessed a spinning wheel, churn, and Bible.

At mid-afternoon Asa left Pack McGraw to stack his goods and graze the horses. Calmly, as if inspecting the falls, he walked back up to where the two men were still working.

"Bit of trouble, boys?"

"Trouble? Mister, this is enough to make a man tear his hair out. Every time we get one side of the wheel straight, the other goes screwy. Ain't a one of these paddles the same size."

"Let me take a look-see," Asa said, getting down on his knees. Then he stood up and started walking around, scratching his sideburns. "Seems to me, boys, you got enough parts here for two wheels. The big one to turn the blade slow and steady for debarking and the little wheel for the faster speed of ripping and planking. Now, let's see if we can find all the parts."

The sun was dipping low to the west when both wheels were together.

"We can't thank you enough, mister. Tomorrow we'll build the support rigging, drop her into the waterfall and—what was that you said about a blade, mister?"

"Saw blades," Asa said, innocently. "Got to have them to push a log through the cutting table."

"Charley, that damn guy didn't say nothing about saw

blades! Said the whole kit was here for a waterwheel for a sawmill."

"I'm afraid he wasn't lying—but the waterwheel was all you bought. Where did you get it?"

"Downsteam, at the Fort. The guy had just come in by ship and said his wife didn't like the place. Wanted to go back to the Sandwich Islands. Traded him all of last summer's furs for this. Charley, can't you say anything?"

"I'm sick. I didn't want to leave trapping to begin with."

Asa waited patiently while they cussed each other.

"Say, boys, would you be willing to do some trading for those wheels? I've got me a grindstone, and with the wheel I could make flour when the farmers have a crop."

"Whatsha got?"

"Just about anything you need to get back into the fur business."

"Interested in a cabin, newly built?"

"Could be," said Asa. "Let's go take a look."

A half-hour later, Pack McGraw and two of his wranglers were loading up the cabin with Asa's goods. The trappers departed with fresh horses, new rifles, ammunition, traps imported from Russia, blankets, and a winter supply of beans, rice, and hardtack.

Asa whistled as he walked to the Mission House. He had not let the trappers see that he also had a dual waterwheel kit, blades, and the grist mill. Now that he had two sets he could double his desired sawmill plans.

Asa savored the baked chicken, yams, and homemade bread of Elvira Waller. She was an excellent hostess, and he had soon learned where Deborah got her talkative streak. After a prayer and a hymn, Asa and the Wallers adjourned to the front steps to enjoy the beautiful September evening. Deborah sat close to Asa, and he could feel her body heat. It made him uncomfortable with her parents there.

"My daughter tells me you are a lawyer and merchant, Mr. Lovejoy. With Couch coming in, seems like we've got enough in the merchant line."

"I would agree, Reverend, but Mr. Wilson seems to have only native customers over there."

"It's the Blue Ruin," Waller huffed. "Couch established it

with a Yankee tradition, where American settlers would find familiar goods from back home. Wilson ruined it with that gin. I'll eat nothing but salmon before I set foot in that place. It's hard enough to train the Indians for work, without that demon temptation!"

Deborah was pressing too close and Asa had to stand. "How, then, do you get work done around here? The Mission House, for example?"

"We traded goods, when we had goods to trade. A farmer can find a day here and there, if his wife is hankering for some sugar or a tin of this or that."

"Deborah," Asa said, as though changing the subject. "I bought the waterwheel and cabin from those two men. I guess I will be the claim-jumper now. People are going to need lumber to build and I'll need men to work the timber and the mill."

Waller frowned. "You figure some of these folks will stay right here, Mr. Lovejoy?"

"Look at those campfires out there, sir. I know one man who nearly broke the back of a horse bringing an anvil. That says blacksmith to me."

"Workers," Waller mused. "How you going to pay them?"

"Same as you. Trade. Who plotted this land and what lots are still open?"

Waller laughed. It was a sound Asa thought the rather dour man incapable of. "HBC cabin was already here when we just plunked down. Couch and the trappers did much the same. Different for the farmers."

"How different?"

"They got together over this Linn Act thing and made an agreement. They figure out their acres and then go to the nearest mission house and record it in a book of records. That way, when it does become law, we'll have no arguments."

Asa began to laugh and they all looked at him as though he had gone crazy. "Shouldn't we do the same for Oregon City, before someone comes and says they own it as one 640-acre parcel?"

"That's a good idea he's got, Alvin," Elvira said.

"Yes, my dear, it certainly is. I would like a plot for a right proper church."

"And lumber to build it?" Deborah chimed in.

"As long as we're dreaming," Elvira laughed, "I could go back to teaching if we had a schoolhouse."

"Isn't it a dream that got us all here?"

"Not us," seven-year-old Timothy carped. "Church said it was time for Paw to go on mission service and we got stuck here."

"That will be quite enough, young man. Time for you and Annie to go off to bed. Say good night to our guest. No, don't go, Mr. Lovejoy—a worm has been crawling in my brain."

This sent the two younger Wallers off in peals of laughter.

"Would you mind if I called you Asa, sir?"

"Only if I can drop the Reverend. I am not of your faith, you know."

"To be sure. I could tell that when I heard you trying to sing the hymn. But not like a Cantor, either." He paused, thinking out his next words. "This merchandise you have to trade for labor—may I ask what it might be?"

"Surely. General merchandise and dry goods. An associate and I were going into business. He will be coming by ship, but may well be delayed."

"And you might need another associate until he arrives? Someone already established, with a known clientele?"

"I think it is a point worth discussing."

"Good! Then let us both sleep on it and meet tomorrow. Good night, Asa."

"Good night, Alvin. Good night, Deborah. Thank you for the best meal I've had in months, Mrs. Waller."

"It's Elvira, and you're quite welcome. Good night."

Asa did not have to sleep on the idea. It had been his main reason for coming to supper. He did not even have to open a store, yet would still make his investment back and start turning a profit from lumber. It had been a very interesting first day in his new home.

He sighed as he crawled into his bedroll.

"Was she that good?" came a voice from the next bedroll.

"Is that all you ever think about, Pack McGraw?"

"Yep, it's natural when you're only seventeen. By the way, horses are ready to leave in the morning."

"Why the rush?"

"Don't cotton to staying in one place too long. Besides, empty horses and empty wagons move twice as fast. I want out of the mountains before winter sets in."

"As you wish," Asa yawned. "And tell my people that the next time we sell the wagons to them. Hate to think what we're losing hauling them back dead freight."

All he got for an answer was a snore.

Pack McGraw and his crew of twenty wranglers left just after dawn. Asa would miss him. The young man had been a good trail companion and had known the dialect of every Indian they had encountered. He was the type of ramrod Asa would have liked for the saw mill, but he knew Pack was more valuable to him on the trail.

Just after the last horse disappeared, Asa saw Hugh Burns swim his horse across the Willamette and ride up to the mission store. He was inside no more than five minutes when he came out and swam the horse back across. Asa was curious that the man had left the store with nothing in his hands. Burns had been a loud-mouthed troublemaker on the journey, and it didn't seem like him to cross a river for nothing.

The storehouse door opened and Alvin Waller came out. His face was as gray as death. He saw Asa and motioned violently for him to come to the store.

As Asa entered, he saw that the place was neat and tidy, the white-washed shelves nearly bare. Waller was behind the counter, and the trembling in his legs increased so that he had to lean against it.

"We are already too late, my friend," he said weakly.

"Damn! Burns has just claimed this land?"

"No. He has claimed a square mile, just below the claim of Robert Moore. I didn't even think of Moore last night. He was here before the mission and claims to have purchased his land from an old Indian chief in exchange for goods. It is a square mile, encompassing the entire west bank of the river facing the falls. When the farmers began to make their claims he came over and claimed his square mile again, under the free-land bill."

"Then where are we in trouble? Each of their 640 acres are over there."

"Burns wanted to know if I had a copy of the McLoughlin townsite plan. He talked with Moore last night and says that Moore has already marked off lots on his claim, using the same plan as McLoughlin laid out Oregon City. We are HBC and don't even know it."

"I am not going to give up yet!" Asa said suddenly, fiercely. "Get Deborah to find me that Indian boy, Kenwa. I will be right back from my cabin."

"What are you going to do?"

"For one thing, meet the man who was Here Before Christ. But, first, protect us before I go!"

He was back almost before he left. He opened a portfolio on the counter and borrowed Waller's quill and ink well.

"As a lawyer, I came prepared. These are Deeds of Claim. We will make one out for each and every free-land claim in your book and will start a proper Deed of Title book."

"You can hardly do all that for free, Asa."

"I didn't say I would," he laughed. "I will charge twenty-five cents as a filing fee. They can pay in work at the mill or in produce next summer. We must appear very legal when we see Mr. McLoughlin."

"But none of them will be signed, as yet."

"Alvin, I will only take the Deed of Title book with me. As yet, Mr. McLoughlin's name is not in it, but ours shall be. We shall see how good he is at horsetrading."

In the kitchen, Deborah and Elvira could hear them through the wall.

"Isn't he interesting, Mother?"

The round, worried face of Mrs. Waller turned to her daughter. "I watched you at dinner last night, girl. I reckon that man is double your age."

"I didn't mean interesting in that way." Deborah shrugged, and her smile disappeared. "I meant in the way that he is positive and assured. All we've had come through her before this were plow-boys. He's a lawyer. That is interesting."

Elvira touched her daughter's arm. "I wish we were back home, where there would be more young people around."

"You miss your teaching, don't you?"

"I have you three to educate. Isn't that enough?"

"Wouldn't be for Grandfather Henderson. We know he sent you here to education the heathens."

Elvira's sharp nose lifted, and her stare held a hint of dismay. "That is quite enough, young lady. I would not be so well educated if my father had not been a mission head. My choice was to complement your father's talents, not interfere with them. Now, go find Kenwa for Mr. Lovejoy."

Alone, Elvira's cheeks burned. She had an impulse to call her daughter back and warn her never to raise this subject in front of her father. Pride had prompted her to get her husband named to a mission. She had wanted the challenge, but now she felt sinful in thinking only of herself. She was well aware that Alvin was not very effective in the pulpit and that his management skills in the mission store left much to be desired. Even so, he was an excellent husband and father.

"Dear God," she whispered. "Let my husband find Mr. Lovejoy interesting and learn from him."

As Kenwa looked over the offered trade goods, Asa realized that the Indian had a certain candor that revealed itself at once. "Mirrors and beads my people have had for many years," he said with a direct look. "I have ample blankets and woolen shirts. What is in that brightly colored tin?"

"Hard candy."

"I will try."

Asa felt the morning slipping away, but opened the tin. A fragrance hit his nostrils and he was reminded of home.

"My grandmother will like," Kenwa said. "That is the barter."

"But that is only about three cents' worth."

"The value is in how it will please the old woman and her sweet tooth. The tin she can keep her trinkets in forever. Come, we go by bateau today."

"*Bateau?*"

"It is a flat-bottomed boat brought here by the French Canadian trappers. It will be very swift going downstream. We will return by canoe."

The rapids gave them a speedy start on their thirty-mile journey. Because there was so much new to see, Asa lost all track of time and was amazed when they were suddenly at the confluence of the Willamette and Columbia. Kenwa now had to row quickly across the current and up the north shore. Two vessels were anchored in the river: the HBMS *Livermore* and the bark, *Lady Fair*. Asa knew he could gain little knowledge from His Britannic Majesty's Ship, but prayed that the bark was of the Tucker Line.

The interior of the fort was a beehive of activity. Mountains of furs lay stacked ready for shipment. A line of trappers stood with more pelts to be tested, weighed, and accepted. As directed by Kenwa, Asa headed toward the trading post building in the center of the fort.

It was hardly a store in Asa's opinion. Again there were lines, queueing up at six caged windows. Each man had a requisition form that he presented to a clerk, then waited for his goods to be brought back in a wooden box. Amazingly, the lines moved quickly.

"Form?"

"I am here to see Mr. John McLoughlin."

"Around the corner, mate, to the door marked Factor. Next!"

Asa was in for a double surprise. The door opened right into McLoughlin's office, where the man sat talking with Elijah White.

"Excuse me," Asa said. "I'll wait outside."

"No, come on in, Lovejoy," White barked, as though he had the authority. "Mr. McLoughlin, let me introduce Asa Lovejoy, who was in my party."

McLoughlin rose and extended his hand, somewhat reluctantly, Asa sensed. He was a powerfully built man with a round face, a shock of hair that would look uncombed even after combing, and mutton-chop whiskers that seemed nearly as wide as his shoulders. His expression was not friendly.

"Lovejoy," he said, in a voice that was a florid baritone.

"As I was saying," White went on, as though there had been no interruption. "Since I am now the Indian Agent for this area, I'll want a census of what savages may, at times, be on either side of the river. The Methodist missions have been told to provide me with the same."

Asa was shocked. Never once had Elijah White revealed that this was his reason for getting to Oregon.

"Mr. White," McLoughlin boomed, "they are not savages, first of all. Secondly, they travel at will. They consider this their land, not mine or yours."

"I need those figures," White demanded impatiently. "I believe a week will be sufficient time."

With a glare in Asa's direction, he turned and stomped out.

"He was the same way on the wagon train," Asa said. "I didn't know then it was the stench of a bureaucrat."

McLoughlin's big face split into an enormous grin.

"The curse of the world," he chuckled. "I have to live with them, too. What is it I can do for you, Mr. Lovejoy?"

"I am a lawyer and merchant, sir. Until we hear of the passage of the Linn Act, I am keeping a Title Deed Book on the lands being claimed at the Methodist missions. There is a question, however, regarding Oregon City, also known as The Falls."

"There should be no question whatsoever, Mr. Lovejoy. It is British domain and their claims are illegal."

"Are you saying that the missions and their farmers are illegal?"

McLoughlin puffed out his cheeks and let the air escape. "Sir, I spent part of 1838 and '39 in London trying to get our Home Office and our Foreign Office to resolve what would become of this land. Nothing was resolved. They sent me back with a deliberate policy of confusion. As the Factor here, I have long since concluded that the Oregon country south of the Columbia would someday go to the United States and it would remain British territory north of the river. Therefore, I steered the Methodist missionaries south. By their policy I am to discourage settlement by other Americans."

"Mr. McLoughlin!" Asa implored. "How are you to tell them apart?"

The man's big hands came up to his chin whiskers. "In two years' time I shall reach the age of sixty. Half of my life has been spent here. I love this country. I am a doctor by trade, but get to practice very little. Well, that is beside the point."

Asa saw his advantage and jumped on it.

"I think that is the point, sir. You are considering retirement and thus considering a place to retire. Why else would you lay out a townsite plan for The Falls?"

"But, I—" he started to protest. He got no further.

"Robert Moore is laying out your plan on the west bank. How did he get it?"

"That scalawag! He worked for me in this office last winter!"

"Enough said. My point, sir, is that if your plan is not followed, Oregon City will become a hodge-podge of people building where they wish. Do we agree?"

McLoughlin's face cleared, but a nagging doubt clung like a burr in his mind.

"Of course I agree. That's why I laid it out on paper and laid claim under HBC rules. I lose everything if the land goes American."

"Perhaps not," Asa said slowly, for it was time for caution. "The mission and I have also put in claims. Might I see your map to make sure we are not in conflict?"

"We are already in conflict!" he roared, digging in his desk drawer, "but you can see the bloody map all you wish."

Asa studied the map at length, letting the man simmer down, then took out his rough map from the back of the Title Book. He turned them around to face McLoughlin.

"Perhaps not fully in conflict, sir. Here is the square mile you have laid out. Here is the mission house, here Couch's store, the HBC trading post, and the cabin I have just purchased. What I am interested in lies south of you, from The Falls westward. Reverend Waller's desires are for but three lots. The one he is on and one each for a church and school. My desire is for four lots, from the riverfront back to my cabin site. I shall pay for those, if you will deed the mission its desires."

Asa hoped he had been convincing.

The nagging doubt was still in McLoughlin's mind. "That's fine, but how can I claim or sell without being one of your citizens?"

Asa grinned. "As your lawyer, I will draw it up as a grandfather homestead clause, the HBC cabin being the homestead. As your attorney, and an American, I shall do the selling as your agent."

McLoughlin puffed out his cheeks again. "Do it! Now, how do you pay me for the parcels you wish, after subtracting your fees?"

"In lumber."

"I have my own lumber mill."

"I saw it as we rowed across. You don't have enough water power to make it run fast enough. The ripping, I noticed, is still being done by hand. I can give you lumber at half the cost, so you still make HBC's profit and your own. Name your price, for I have brought along all the necessary documents."

"What would you be charging me per document?"

"The same as the others, twenty-five cents a filing fee."

"Then I say twenty dollars a lot."

"Then I say ten dollars per thousand board feet, as you are getting twenty dollars at present from the Tucker Line."

McLoughlin looked at him in amazement.

"How could you possibly be knowing that fact?"

"I have a business associate coming by ship, a friend of yours—Francis Pettygrove, of the Tucker Line."

"Oh, yes, the young man of a million questions. I must be getting old. Once it would have thrilled me for a young buck to take an interest in this land." He paused. "It just came to me, Mister Solicitor, what do we do about Captain Couch's store?"

Asa laughed. "He gets charged fifty dollars for his lot."

"Done! Now, how about a spot of tea!"

The upriver journey was slower, but Asa was content. He wondered if his meeting with McLoughlin would have gone his way had not White riled the man first. He hated to be in debt to the insufferable man but was elated he did not have to fight with "Here Before Christ." McLoughlin had even been helpful in seeing that his message to Francis would go back to Honolulu with the *Fair Lady* for shipment to Maine on a Tucker ship.

"Why are we stopping?"

"Halfway point, Mr. Lovejoy. Arms get tired going against the current."

Asa stepped from the canoe and looked around. For about three acres the brush had been cleared and burned away. The near trees were free of dead branches and fallen trees. A stack of firewood stood beside a fire pit.

"What is this place, Kenwa?"

"Called The Clearing. It is used by the Indians and the trappers as a resting place between Fort Vancouver and The Falls. Here the water runs smooth and deep, so it is easy to land."

Asa tucked that bit of knowledge into the back of his head. He would mention it to Francis. Perhaps the Tucker ships could come this far, rather than unloading at Fort Vancouver and bringing the goods up by canoe or bateau.

"My grandmother is most taken with your hard candy. Will you be getting more?"

"I shall make sure that we do, although I still have a fair supply."

Kenwa looked up at the sky.

"Something the matter?"

"Checking the time. I wish to be back to The Falls before sunset. Not too many days left for the salmon run. Mr. Wilson wants three tonight. I will take him five."

"Why five?"

Kenwa smiled devilishly. It was the first time Asa had seen real animation in his face. "A bottle of Blue Ruin for each. Then he will have only ten left. My canoe boys do not work with Blue Ruin in them."

"What do you do with your bottles?"

"Trade it back to the sailors on the ships. We go now."

Asa nodded. He wished to know a lot more about this young man, but now he wanted to think about getting the sawmill going.

CHAPTER

☆ 5 ☆

The *Victoria* looked so battered and deserted that the outriggers did not row out to greet her with the *lei* girls. With only two main and one mizzen sail left she limped into Honolulu harbor and dropped anchor. A long boat was lowered and rowed ashore a stretchered figure and a gaunt man.

It was October 1842, but dates to Francis Pettygrove were near nothingness. For all the days he had spent at sea, nothing could compare with the last seven months of torture and terror.

There had been too many slate-gray days with no breeze to ruffle the sails; too many days thunderous with storms that buffeted them back six times before they could finally round Cape Horn; too many unusually bright calm days in the Pacific with water and food running low and the temper of the crew beginning to run hot.

Then had come the final terror. The typhoon had come out of a black night sky, crashing down on the bridge of the ship like a cannon's explosion. The helmsman and Captain vanished with the next crashing wave; the First Officer, while unhurt, had been knocked unconscious when slammed to the deck. A frantic sailor had rousted Francis from his berth to take the wheel and bring the ship out of the storm.

Six sailors were lost trying to tie down the sails that had not been ripped and shredded. It was best to do nothing but ride out the storm. Three sailors jumped into the churning ocean, feeling that drowning would be their final fate, any-

way. For forty-eight hours, Francis and the now-conscious
First Officer took turns at the wheel, until they felt their arms
would never rejoin their shoulder sockets.

That they survived should have been a source of relief. But
they could feel no relief with sails barely able to pull their
three hundred tons of cargo and the ship beginning to take
on water from sprung seams. And especially no relief for
Francis. After the storm he had found Sophia on the floor of
the cabin, battered, bruised, and running a high fever. Gently
getting her into the bunk, he had screamed for the ship's
doctor. His fear now was that the six-month-old child was
dead in her womb. He put his hand on her stomach and
prayed, but could feel nothing. The doctor could hear a
heartbeat, but feared what damage might have been done to
the child. Francis cursed their slowness in getting to port.

Francis directed the longboat to take him directly to the
Tucker Line wharf and warehouse. He prayed that Dexter
Farman had not heard about his falling out with his family.

Dexter Farman, like every other ship's agent, had a spyglass on the *Victoria* the moment she had started to enter the
harbor. He had kept the glass on the longboat as it approached and then dropped it.

"That's a Pettygrove being rowed in with a stretcher case,"
he yelled down at the dock. "Get some men to the pulley and
bring the flat wagon out of the warehouse."

He was at the end of the wharf by the time the stretcher
was being lifted and Francis arrived at the top of the ladder.

"At your service, Mr. Pettygrove," he said, not wishing to
admit he could not recall his first name.

"Dexter, this is my wife."

"She—she's not . . .?"

"Not dead, yet. I put a damp sheet over her face to protect
her from the sun."

"Here is a wagon. The mission hospital is the nearest."

Being that he was a Pettygrove, Farman felt obligated to go
along. Francis sat on the floorboards next to Sophia, tightlipped and grim.

Dexter sat on the tailgate and braced the stretcher so it
wouldn't slip out. "May I ask what happened, sir?"

"We were caught in a typhoon. She was badly battered about in the cabin."

"We will insist upon Dr. Charles. They say he is very good with women. Anything else I can do for you, sir?"

For a second Francis was able to put one worry aside and think of another. "That ship is taking water and could sink. Tons of her cargo are mine, under Benson & Bros. label. Kindly shore it and warehouse it. I will pay the fee."

"The company will see to the fee, sir."

"it is my shipment, Dexter, not the family's. I'm off to Oregon to strike out on my own."

The name suddenly popped into Dexter's head. Now he remembered the rash young man from when the trade with the Hudson Bay Company had been set up. He had seen to the refurbishing of the ship with food and water, while the captain had been off getting drunk and playing with the native girls. "I will see to it, Francis, as soon as we have your missus settled."

Dr. Phineas Charles did not believe in mincing words with patient or family member.

"Mr. Pettygrove, the fever comes from an old sea malady, scurvy. Being that far along with child she was not getting enough ample fruits, vegetables, or milk for both of them. But my main concern is with the child. I do not like the heartbeats I am hearing. We will keep her here for a few days. Where shall you be staying?"

Dexter Farman stepped in, having returned from his errand. "We keep extra *lanais* at our house for our captains, Francis."

"Fine," Dr. Charles said. "I know your house. Now, go along, son. I don't want her disturbed for a good twenty-four hours."

Francis didn't protest. He even went willingly. The house was only three blocks away and three of the porches had been converted into private guest quarters. Dexter put Francis in the one facing the sea and opened all the shuttered windows. Within moments of crawling between the cool sheets, Francis was asleep. He slept soundly for forty-eight hours.

When he awoke he found his clothing laundered, their luggage brought from the ship, and a wood tub of water awaiting in an alcove. The tub was too small for him, so he had to bathe a section of himself at a time. Then he smelled something delicious. After quickly dressing, he followed his nose until he found the kitchen door. Beyond it he heard singing and the rattle of a whipping spoon. He entered the kitchen and stopped.

"Hello, there," he said agreeably. "I met you on my last visit here. You're Dexter's sister—I remember that you brought us lunch down at the dock. I am—"

"I'm quite aware," she laughed. "Sit. I'll get you a cup of coffee until lunch is ready. Dex will be here shortly."

"Perhaps I should go see my wife first."

"And fall on your face from starvation? Sit. I popped meself in on her this morning and she was eating a good breakfast. The lass will be fine."

Francis looked at the stout Irishwoman and felt comfortably at home. He remembered that she ministered to her younger brother's needs with scrupulous care, and he recalled that she had worked at the mission school.

"I'm sorry I've been so much bother. You didn't have to do my laundry or put out bath water."

"Not guilty, as charged," she said, putting a steamy mug in front of him. "I have Kanaka girls from the mission school to help me. This month it is Tama. Poor child, she is *tabu*."

"Tabu?"

"Born to a native girl by an unknown sailor. British, American, French, Belgian? Who will ever know. They all fight for this paradise and all they do is ruin it. Oh, here's my brother now."

"Good day, Francis. I see you found your way to Rhoda's kitchen. I stopped at the hospital on my way home for lunch and the little lady is fine. She was glad to hear that you are getting some well-deserved rest. Dr. Charles thinks that by tomorrow bedrest here might be the best thing for her."

Francis felt uneasy. The man's constant chatter suggested that he was avoiding something he did not want to discuss. "Is something the matter?"

Dexter sat down and pulled an oil-skin packet from his pocket. "A ship from Fort Vancouver delivered this today. As it was addressed to you, for forwarding to Portland, it concerned me."

Francis leaned across the table suddenly and caught at the package. Dexter sat back anxious. Rhoda calmly began to ladle fish chowder into an old-fashioned tureen. Francis read the pages with growing elation.

"It is from Asa Lovejoy, my associate. He arrived in Oregon last month and has established a base for us at The Falls. Oh, will he be surprised to learn how close I am! When is the next Tucker ship due, so I can get word to him?"

"They have become most irregular." Dexter sounded so forlorn that Rhoda burst out laughing, putting cutlery and bowls on the table.

"Poor Dex!" she said. "He has so *many* problems with your company and the British. Well, we all have problems with the British. They are fighting like mad to reduce the American influence here and take over the islands from King Kauikeaouli. Tell him, brother."

Dexter contemplated several ways of answering, and chose the only one that he knew would work with Francis, honestly.

"The line has suffered two shipwrecks in the past year, Francis. We are in a trade war, here in the Pacific. San Diego has become a center of the Pacific Coast hide trade. The Mexican cattle ranches draw ship captains into Yerba Buena for shoe hides. And now Oregon. Francis, to survive, I have been forced to deal with more than the Tucker Line."

"And trade with the Hudson Bay Company?"

"When it suited my purpose."

"How many others?" Francis said thoughtfully.

"The Methodist missions, but they are very frugal. Once to a Captain Couch, but when he came back through a few months ago, he headed back to New England. Said that our warehouse charges were too high."

"Are they?"

"You ought to know," Dexter said, a shot in the dark.

"The family needs their capital for these new clipper

ships," Francis said with a grin. "They are pricing themselves right out of the trade routes. But, back to my original question. Do you have a way to get my message to Asa in Oregon?"

"I believe so. This ship, the *Fair Lady,* has quite a shopping list for Dr. John McLoughlin at the fort. As I am in a position of benevolent neutrality, they need not know they are carrying messages for a potential rival."

Francis snorted. "A flowery way to put it, but I like it. And what about a ship for my cargo?"

"Well, Francis," Dexter said, a trace of challenge in his voice, "we need to discuss your need for an agent here in the islands."

"No business talk at my lunch table," Rhoda said indignantly.

An hour later, after three bowls of chowder, Francis was meeting with Dr. Charles, who said Sophia could leave the hospital.

Francis grinned. "This afternoon? That is marvelous. The lanai gets a warm sea breeze and I'm sure she will snap back quickly. How soon will she be able to travel?"

"Not until the birth," Dr. Charles said firmly.

"But that's almost three months."

"You count well," the doctor said tartly and departed.

Francis never knew three months could pass so quickly. Sophia recuperated quickly, what with Rhoda's excellent cooking and the pampering from Tama, the Kanaka girl who had been kept on just for Sophia. Francis and Dexter drew up an agent's agreement and a joyous letter was received back from Asa. Its news kept Francis away from the house during the day, seeking out future customers for Asa's lumber. Because the damp, tropical air seemed to irritate his skin, he began to grow a beard.

On a humid, airless January night, Francis could not sleep. He rose and looked back to see if he had disturbed Sophia. She was in deep sleep, her black hair fanned out on the pillow. He felt so blessed. She had finally taken on that special beauty of pregnancy and his heart swelled with love.

Outside, all the world seemed to have come to a standstill. Not a palm frond swayed, birds were at rest, and the night lanterns on the anchored ships seemed like star reflections. He turned the corner of the house to look up at the mountains and found a strange woman confronting him. She was tall in figure, dressed in a native fabric he had not seen before, and her gray hair stood out as though there was a fierce wind.

"Who are you? What do you want?"

"I am *tutu* to Tama. Tonight is the time."

"For what?" Francis asked, astonished.

"The birth of the child. I wait."

"Nonsense. Dr. Charles sees my wife every other day. He will tell us when it is time to take her to the hospital."

"No time," she said calmly, and began to walk around the house to the lanai.

He ran after her, to bar the way, when he heard Sophia crying.

"Francis, where have you been?" she cried in terror as he ran in. "I woke up soaked. It's time. Get Dr. Charles!"

"Don't you touch her," he warned, as he pushed passed the woman and started running up the street.

After repeated banging on the door, Dr. Charles opened it and grinned at Francis in nothing but his nightshirt.

"Don't panic on me, man. It sometimes takes hours after the water breaks."

"But this is my first baby!"

"Obviously. Did you leave her alone?"

"I'm sure Rhoda Farman is with her by now. But there was a strange woman there, who called herself *tutu*."

Dr. Charles chuckled dryly. "I should have known, with that Kanaka girl Tama in the house. *Tutu* means grandmother, and that *tutu* is the best midwife in the islands. Your wife is in excellent hands. I'll be along as soon as I dress."

"What should I do?" Francis pleaded.

"Get some clothes on for one thing."

Dexter met Francis outside the house with shirt, trousers, and boots. "Use the west lanai. Rhoda is with your wife and the midwife."

"What does a man do at this time, Dexter?"

Dexter patted him on the back. "You are asking the wrong man, Francis. I've been a bachelor my forty-two years. Come to the kitchen when you are dressed. We'll figure something out over coffee."

The coffee tasted bitter, the chair seemed too hard, and the clock seemed to eat up the minutes in gulps. Francis fumed and paced, cursing the tardy doctor. He smelled something frying and nearly ran into a young woman working at the stove.

"Excuse me, Master, if I was in the way."

"Don't mind him, Tama," Dexter chuckled. "My, that smells great."

Francis turned and looked. This couldn't be Tama. Tama wore mission gray smocks, a duster cap, and a downcast face. This was a slim, wiry-hipped girl of fourteen with midnight-black hair that fell to her knees, wearing a brightly flowered one-piece garment. This was a remarkably beautiful girl.

"The baby is here!" she cried suddenly and ran out.

"How does she know?" Francis gasped, as Rhoda came bounding in.

"Saint's alive, it's a boy! Saucy, healthy, and bright-eyed!" On her heels came Dr. Charles.

"When did you get here?" Francis glared.

"In time to hear him cry. Thanks for the offer of coffee, Rhoda. Son, give Tama a few minutes to freshen up your wife and then you may go in. God, you look horrible!"

Francis felt horrible. Everyone had something to do but him. He went outside and paced until he could stand it no more.

Sophia lay there on the double bed in a fresh linen nightgown, placid and calm, although pale. When she saw her husband, she reached out a hand, and he went down on his knees beside her and covered her face with gentle kisses, filled with his tenderness.

"Tama has something for you," she murmured.

He rose and timidly accepted the blanket-wrapped bundle. Eyes of his own shade blinked up at him.

"I would like to call him Lorenzo," Francis said gently.

Sophia smiled her consent. After seven months at sea she knew every Pettygrove story there was to tell. It pleased her that a good name would be continued.

"I take baby to wash now," Tama said.

"Where is your grandmother?"

"Gone. Work done."

"But I haven't paid her."

"Francis," Sophia said, "let Tama take the baby to the kitchen. Dr. Charles wants to examine him. Come and sit beside me."

When he was seated, she took his hand. "I love you, Francis," she said quietly. "I was an only child, and here at age twenty-six I've come to realize the wonderment it is to be a woman and a mother. In a way, I have paid the grand-mother for this birth, and I pray you don't get angry with me. Tama's mother comes from the *ahupuaa,* Hawaiian village people who live off of the mountains and ocean as they have for centuries. They are fiercely proud of their bloodline, and once Tama is not under the protection of the mission school she will be marked for death. Francis, I would like to take her with us as a nursemaid for Lorenzo."

"I think she should have proper clothing."

"Is that an answer?" she giggled.

"Have I ever denied you anything?"

"No, especially love."

A month later another letter arrived from Asa. During the winter of 1842–1843, his sawmill had produced enough lumber for the buildings in Oregon City to increase from four to thirty, and to pay McLoughlin for the four lots. The frame buildings were in need of whitewash and trim paint, which he prayed Francis could bring along. He now had under his employment a very talented Indian boy by the name of Kenwa, who would meet Francis when they knew a window of arrival time. Asa's only woe, with the coming of spring and summer, was a growing lack of lumbermen, now that they were going back to their fields. He implored Francis to send a message to the younger lumbermen of York to become pioneers.

"You haven't told him of your split with your family?" Sophia asked, when he finished reading the letter at the lunch table.

"No," he said softly, "I couldn't. His letters have been so bubbling with excitement, I didn't want to dampen his spirits. Now that Dexter and I have found a vessel, we will be there soon enough to tell him in person."

"Which means it is time to go back to work," Dexter chuckled. "First cargo goes out to the *Fama* this afternoon. You'll be under sail in two days' time."

Rhoda sat frowning after the men had left. Her face was a battleground of emotions. Decision struggled against silence. Decision won.

"Have to leave you with the tidy-up, Sophia, but I've got an errand at the mission school."

She clamped her floppy palm frond hat on her bun top and stalked out the door.

"Whatever got into her?"

"You do not know?" Tama inquired sweetly. "You have become dear to her and she will miss you greatly."

Sophia shivered. She, too, had grown to love the pleasant Rhoda Farman and the lifestyle in the Sandwich Islands. Oregon still sounded primitive.

Rhoda Farman's decision had nothing to do with the thought of missing Sophia, although she would, greatly. Asa Lovejoy's letter had given her an idea. After making an important stop, she went down to the docks where she found Dexter.

"Brother, where is Francis?"

"Rhoda, what brings you to the warehouse, and who is the boy?"

Rhoda gave Dexter a glare that said "Don't get in your big sister's way."

"All right, Rhoda," he sighed. "Francis is in back sorting cargo. Come."

"Francis," Rhoda began, the moment they spotted him, "I have given much thought to a portion of Asa Lovejoy's letter. *Tabu* is for boys, as well as girls. This is Katoro, who will soon be sixteen. His father was Norwegian, this we know. He would make a good lumberjack."

Francis looked at the youth, who was tall and muscular with a handsome thin face and an impetuous smile.

"Perhaps," Francis mused, "but where does he work now?"

Dexter saw his sister's drift and took up the issue.

"There is no work for tabu boys, Francis, except at the mission school. When they turn sixteen they are turned out and become beggars. I hate to say it, but many are turned to prostitution by some of the sailors."

Francis was aghast at such a thought. It was one aspect of the sea life that sickened him to despair. "Are there others?"

Rhoda grinned. "I was hoping for such a reaction. Boys!"

Timidly, five others appeared at the wide warehouse door. They were big boys, ranging from seventeen to nineteen, and they came forward together.

"These we have known for many years," Rhoda said proudly. "They try to stay out of trouble, but there is so little work. Dexter and I try to feed them when we can, but they are getting beyond the age where we can help."

Francis watched them approach, pure joy lighting up his gray eyes. They reminded him of the wiry youths of Maine, just the right age to train for forest and mill work.

Francis grinned at Rhoda. "You will have to get them ready. Each must have two stout pair of boots, heavy trousers, and shirts. Leather work gloves and a cap with a brim to shield their eyes from sawdust."

Dexter did not want to stop the enterprise, but he did have a fear. "Francis, as soon as their clothing is obtained, I would suggest we take them out and berth them on the *Fama*. Even though they are tabu, the Hawaiian government does not like the Kanaka people leaving the island."

Francis saw the anticipation in the eager faces and nodded his agreement. He would now have two surprises for Asa Lovejoy.

The mouth of the Columbia River bombards the Pacific like one giant fighting another for the same footing. Ocean sand and river silt join, are washed apart, and join again in ever-changing and shifting sand bars at the place called Cape Disappointment. Beyond the bar the Columbia narrows, swinging southeastward through the forested rolling coastal range. To the northeast, the dormant volcano, Mount St. Helens, pierces the sky with her snow-topped crown. Without warning, the foothills melt away to fertilize lowlands, just before the confluence with the Willamette and another rise for the Cascade Mountain Range.

Tears sprang to Francis Pettygrove's eyes as the anchor chain was released. He was back to the point of where his dream had begun.

"Fort Vancouver," he enthused. "Come, my love, we will go ashore."

Sophia was not enthused. The logs of the fort and its structures were long since weathered gray. The riverbank was brown earth from constant loading and unloading of cargo. For over a hundred miles, along the riverbanks, she had seen a barrage of color from spring wild flowers. That had given her hope. Fort Vancouver made it fade quickly.

With the gesture of a patriarch, John McLoughlin strode to the boat landing. The HBMS *Barksdale* had come over the bar first and informed him that the bark *Fama,* out of Honolulu, with the Pettygrove family aboard, was close behind.

"My boy," McLoughlin boomed, taking him into a bear hug, "it has been too many years. And with a new beard."

"And a new bride," Francis beamed. "Dr. McLoughlin, this is my Sophia."

"My dear, it may be spring, but you are prettier than any flower I have yet seen."

Sophia knew that marriage had improved her looks; she needed nobody to tell her that. What his flowery words did tell her was that she instantly mistrusted the man. She decided to play shy, hold her tongue, and merely curtsey.

"I'm sorry my wife is not here to greet you. She is in England, where my son is in school. Still, I can offer you the hospitality of my quarters."

"Thank you, no!" Francis answered emphatically. "I must find a bateau boy by the name of Kenwa and get my family upriver."

"Bateau boy?" McLoughlin laughed. "That he was, and he still hires some of the best, but that young Indian is downright cheeky. He took lumber from Lovejoy's mill and made a most respectable river-sized schooner. Oh, nothing fancy, but most acceptable. There he comes now. He brought down a load of lumber for me this morning."

"Not a bad rig at all," Francis said.

"And Francis, if you are a Tucker boat, what might you have for me?"

"I'm not Tucker on this trip, sir. One did sail into Honolulu the day of our departure, however."

"That is good news. Some of my British supplies are totally depleted and my people will touch nothing else, if you know what I mean."

Francis knew exactly. *If you are here to trade, stay away from HBC people.*

"I say," McLoughlin continued, looking out at the *Fama*, "are those all your family?"

Francis turned and saw the rail of the ship lined with his Kanakas and Tama holding Lorenzo. At that distance they looked just like a group of curious boys.

"That is only my son, Lorenzo, held by his nursemaid. The others are from the Methodist mission."

McLoughlin sniffed. "I hope they brought some supplies. Reverend Waller's shelves are bare, from what I am told."

"There are supplies on board," Francis said, without lying. "Ahoy there! Kenwa! I am Francis Lovejoy." He turned back to McLoughlin. "It was good seeing you again, sir."

McLoughlin nodded, bowed to Sophia, and strode off. He had learned what he had suspected from the latest shipboard rumor. He was now sure that Francis Pettygrove had split with his family and was not siphoning off Tucker Line and HBC business to Lovejoy. He now cared little what Francis did, as long as it was south of the Columbia.

But several times that day his curiosity brought him back out of the fort. Not only was the river schooner loaded full, but bateau after bateau came alongside the *Fama* to be loaded. With that much "mission" camp cargo, he wondered why they hadn't sailed the bark halfway up the Willamette for off loading.

Francis wondered the same when they got to "the clearing." It was spring. The Willamette was running deep with a strong current. The bark would have made it to this point in an hour or more. It had taken them until late afternoon and the bateaux straggled in one after the other, their rowers nearly exhausted.

"Mr. Lovejoy is a prophet," Kenwa laughed. He had been granted permission to call him "Asa," but he would only do it when no one else was around. "He said to prepare, that you would come this week. See? I have prepared for this night."

In the center of the clearing were three newly constructed pine bough lean-to shelters with a firepit prepared in front of each. Beside each firepit was a large stack of wood.

"Thank you, Kenwa. It has been nine years since I have been here and it seems hardly changed."

"Here, no, everywhere else, yes."

"What tribe are you, Kenwa?"

"Cayuse," he said, quickly turning to look at the incoming bateaux as though he did not want to pursue the subject.

"Go about your work," Francis said. "Tama, get the boys to bring our blankets and foodstuff."

Standing by the riverside, Sophia was gazing about with wonderous awe. The setting sun was casting an alpine glow of pink upon the snow-capped peaks. She felt a tremor of excitement as Francis came up behind her and encircled her in his arms.

"They are so spectacular," she whispered. "Like rare jewels reaching up to touch the sky. Do you know their names?"

"We saw that one this morning from the bark—but its western side. That's the southern face of Mt. Saint Helens. The big boy is Mount Adams, but my favorite is Mount Hood. She is just somehow special."

"Why *she*?"

He chuckled softly and hugged her close. "The same reason we call ships *she*. We admire them, elevate them, and wish for them to last forever."

"Francis," she said, "we are going to have another baby. Around Christmastime, I think."

"What a marvelous Christmas present that will be for me! What would you like, darling, so I have an equal number of months to work on it?"

She turned and kissed him passionately. She never ceased to amaze him. He thought he had married a straight-laced New England girl. She had proven to be, in their year of marriage, more intoxicating than any wine a man could sip from a glass.

"What was that for?" he asked when the kiss was finally broken off.

"So you won't forget your Christmas promise," she grinned. "Oh, I know it won't be this Christmas, but some year I would love to have a home on this clearing so that I would have this view each moment of every day."

He laughed. "I'd have to get my own canoe to paddle back and forth to work each day!"

"How far is Oregon City?"

"Fifteen miles."

"Francis, you must be joking. That's the same as from Boston to Brookline!"

"With one difference, my darling, they have a horse-drawn trolley."

* * *

That evening, Sophia, Francis, and Tama sat around one fire dining on black bread, cheese, sardines from a tin, and breadfruit. At the center fire, the Kanakas passed back and forth the wooden bowl Tama had prepared for them. It was a cultural shock for the Indian boys to sit and watch the Kanakas dip two fingers into the bowl, twirl them quickly, and raise a glob of pasty *poi* to their mouths and pass the bowl on. Just as curious were Katoro and his friends as they watched Kenwa and the boatmen take a smoked salmon and expertly devour it down to a skeleton.

"They must be from a very faraway tribe," Kenwa told the others in Cayuse.

"I would be afraid of choking on one of the little bones," Katoro said in Hawaiian.

"Did you see the little fish they ate from the tin? Not enough to fill a hole in my tooth!"

"And why did the white lady go behind the lean-to to feed the baby? We have seen that before."

"It is because white ladies have ugly bodies."

"Do you wish another salmon, Kenwa?"

"No, I am ready for sleep and dreaming."

"And what will you dream of, Kenwa?"

He shrugged and started for his river schooner, in which he would sleep, stopping to inform the people at the first fire of the morning departure time. He turned away pleased. He had been able to see the beautiful girl from that other tribe by firelight. She was even more beautiful than he had first thought. He began planning his dream even before he was asleep.

Alvin Waller had thought that he would never have the opportunity to unpack the special little crate he had brought from New England on the *Lausanne* three years earlier. Now, on a small knoll at the north end of town sat his new church, with steeple and uncrated steeple bell in place. He nervously looked downriver and awaited the moment of christening the bell.

The bateaux had been given a three-hour headstart, so they could herald the arrival of the river schooner. Although it was a good four-hour paddle, they made a race of it, and they were at Lovejoy's boat landing by 7:30 A.M. Two hours later, Waller began to strike the clapper against the bell, even though the schooner was still a good mile away.

Asa Lovejoy was in a giddy, jubilant mood. Not even the sight of Robert Moore and Hugh Burns entering canoes on the west bank could dampen his festival spirit.

The owners of Linn City and Multnomah City cursed each other racing for the schooner.

"Ahoy!" Moore shouted. "From the looks of the loaded bateaux you must be bringing quite a party of people. Follow me to Linn City. Choice lots—"

"Hugh Burns here, sir, owner of Multnomah City. Homestead with me and I'll give you the lot for free!"

Francis, who had unboxed his stovepipe hat for this arrival, merely tipped it to the gentlemen and grinned as though he were a foreigner who did not understand their strange babble. His widening eyes were on Oregon City. Even though everything was still raw wood, he saw it as a painter would, in bright colors.

Sophia looked at it through the eyes of a realist, but even so was not fully disappointed. The church and the school, in the center of the colony, were pure New England in design and shape. The homes were small—a quarter of them little more than frame shanties, and the rest single-room log cabins. Two of the larger buildings were belching out great clouds of smoke, and another had stacks of lumber next to it, piled as high as its roof. The two largest structures were two-storied, with peaked roofs. In front of these buildings was a river wharf, to which they headed.

Ten minutes after their arrival at the wharf, they had met so many new people that Sophia was near tears trying to remember names and not cringe at her bruised hand.

"Deborah," Asa whispered, "why don't you and your mother take Sophia up and show her her new home?"

Sophia smiled her thanks, but wondered what the pretty young girl looked so sad about.

Asa could have told her. Although Deborah was constantly on his mind, she was also on the mind of her parents.

Having just turned seventeen, she was to be sent to the Marcus Whitmans near the Walla Walla River for mission work.

Asa's problem was worse, though he was hiding it that day. He had privately asked Alvin Waller for his daughter's hand and been flatly denied.

There was reason enough for everyone else in Oregon City to be in a jubilant mood. When the two-story structure was completed, burlap was put over the first-floor windows and skilled laborers, at three dollars a day, were given Mr. Lovejoy's exacting plans to complete the interior. Shelves and counters meant only one thing to the wives of the laborers— a new store.

"I hope you don't mind my designing it after father's first Boston store."

Francis turned wonderingly to Asa. But Asa simply stood there, his mustache half-hiding a grin.

"The shelves are so smooth," Francis whispered. "Where did you manage to find varnish?"

"I went to the corner paint shop," Asa sputtered in mock wrath, then laughed. "Every ship carries a supply of lacquer to keep sea rust off their metal parts, as well as soda and lime."

"Soda and lime?"

Asa was like a giddy little boy. "Sand we had an ample supply of, and a farmer who had been trained as a glass-blower in his youth. Add soda and lime from the British, a stone furnace, and your store sports glass windows!"

"You overwhelm me."

"The people here say I am enthusiastic, where our friend McLoughlin says I am overzealous in helping a man start a furniture factory. The Reverend Mr. Waller says I am incorruptible, while Wilson, of Couch's store, says I am sanctimonious in fighting the sale of Blue Ruin to the Indian boys. Mrs. Waller thinks I am dedicated in getting a school built for her, but the other Methodist missionaries think of me as ruthlessly ambitious in wanting this to be a real town."

"And now you have the start of your own labor force."

Asa shook his head. "I hope you've done the right thing,

Francis. I've had no luck in training the Indians to do lumber work." Then he brightened. "At least the Kanakas have been taught English. I'll turn my old log cabin into a dormitory for them. Mrs. Tolcott, my housekeeper, won't mind feeding six more. In the meantime, let's put them to work in uncrating and stocking shelves. I want you in business before Couch gets back to replenish his store."

Five days after his arrival on May 19, 1843, Francis opened his Benson & Brothers store. It was a well-stocked store, with items ranging from needles and pins right up to iron skillets and cooking pots. They came in droves, some as far away as Salem. They looked, they admired, but nobody bought.

Francis's mood was as black as midnight.

"How am I to pay you back for the land and building?" he roared. "What little money they have, they keep." He began to pace. "How did you survive? How did the mission store survive? How does Couch survive?"

"My goods went to the mission store in exchange for sawmill labor, so it was tit for tat. Couch's man Wilson gives credit against future production."

"Credit!" Francis growled. "I've never believed in it."

"I was out in the valley a few days before you came. The wheat is already thigh high. By fall I will have the flour mill in place. Next year you won't have to ship flour in and should get a barrel factory going to ship flour out."

"You're saying give credit on future wheat."

"I am. But you left out one company, HBC. They barter their goods for furs."

The black mood lifted, and a happy grin took its place.

"Maybe that would work," Francis chuckled. "How do we spread the word?"

"Announce it from the pulpit."

"Have you gone daft?"

Asa shook his head. "Tomorrow is Sunday. The church may not be your faith, but it's the only one in town. Leave the announcement to me. You just be there at ten o'clock."

* * *

It didn't start as a parade, but nearly ended as one.

As they had to walk from the south end of the village to the knoll at the north end, they had to pass by nearly every shanty, cabin, and house. Women rushed to their windows or doors and then grabbed a bonnet or shawl to take their place in line behind Francis and Sophia, Tama carrying Lorenzo and a straight line of six Kanaka boys. All had heard there would be a special announcement about the new store.

With thirty additional people in his congregation, Reverend Waller was inspired enough to preach rather than lecture. Deborah's "newspaper report" included the advertising in such a clever way that not even Jason Lee, on a mission visit from the Salem headquarters, could take offense.

"A pleasure to meet you, Mr. Pettygrove. I've heard of your good work in bringing these boys from the mission school in Honolulu. Good to see that you are making them retain their church habits."

"Mr. Lee is head of our missions," Waller injected, hoping for a word of praise on his sermon. "He leaves tomorrow morning, with my daughter, for our mission in Walla Walla."

"I'm afraid that will have to be postponed, Alvin. More important for me to get back down the valley with the news of Mr. Pettygrove's kind trade offer."

"But Deborah?" Waller said ominously.

"September is quite soon enough for her to start her mission work."

"But you will stay for lunch, Jason," Elvira insisted. "I've made brown bread and beans, just for you."

This gave Deborah a chance to slip away without having to ask to be excused. Once out of her mother's line of sight, she raced for the falls. In a rock cleft, above the waterwheels, she found Asa.

"How did you find me here?" he asked.

"I've known for some time that this was your secret Sunday spot, when I had to be at Sunday School and church."

"What time do you leave tomorrow?"

"Don't," she said casually. "It's been put off until September."

Asa looked up at her and hid his smile. He had known that Jason Lee would be there that morning and that Jason Lee and his son, David, had cleared and planted some thirty acres in wheat. David Lee, as well, had spent most of the winter in the Cascade Mountains trapping.

"Will you talk with Papa again?"

"I will," he said grimly, "but I don't hold out any hope."

She sank down beside him and was very awkward in giving her first kiss.

Asa scooted back and broke the kiss.

"No, Deborah," he whispered.

Deborah laughed throatily.

"Why can't I kiss you, if we are to be married? Have you kissed many girls before? I've never kissed a boy before."

"Will you stop it!" he growled, taking her by the shoulders. "I am not a boy, either. I am a thirty-five-year-old man and you are a seventeen-year-old girl! You don't know how dangerous a real kiss can become!"

"Show me," she said daringly, pushing herself forward.

Asa felt tempted, and angry at himself for being tempted. He was no saint. Boston was a city and a seaport town, and as a Cambridge student he had known the section of town where young men could learn, for the first time, the feel, the smell, the exotic experience of being with a woman. But that, and the times he'd been with women since, had not been love.

As Asa looked at her, heat rose up the nape of his neck, and his resolve melted. He took her fully into his arms, kissing her with a passion he did not know he possessed. He wanted her like nothing he had ever wanted before. He had daydreamed about placing a hand on her breast and now it was reality. She did not resist, but encouraged him to rub his palm over the cloth until they could both feel her nipple harden.

"I see what you're doing," came a sing-song voice.

They broke apart and Deborah spun around.

"Timothy!" she screamed. "What are you doing here?"

"Papa said for me to follow you and bring you back. He

doesn't want any embarrassment in front of Brother Jason."

He was right at the edge of the rock cleft, within her arms' reach. She felt like slapping him, but held her temper.

"I don't want you telling Papa about this. I only came to tell Mr. Lovejoy that I was not leaving until September."

In a year's time, Timothy's seven-year-old baby fat had turned into eight-year-old gangling growth. He narrowed his eyes.

"You coming with me?"

"Are you going to tell?"

"Depends," he smirked.

"On what?"

"Chores for a month and—"

He got no further. Asa pushed by him, his mouth tightening slowly into a hard line. He ran down the hill to the Mission House so fast that Deborah and Timothy could hardly keep up with him. He burst into the room just as they were sitting down at the table.

"Your son just tried to blackmail your daughter because he saw me kiss her. Show me in *your* Bible where it is sinful to kiss the woman you intend to marry. Yes, *marry*. You said no once, Alvin, but I am going to ask you again—and every day until I wear you down. We love each other and shall be married!"

He realized at once that Waller was not going to give him the satisfaction of a denial, that he would not repeat his ranting scene of the first request. But the deadly silence in the room was infinitely worse.

Then, ever so slowly, Elvira stood up. With deliberate grace she smoothed out her dress and turned into the kitchen.

This was the first rift she had had with her husband. She admired Asa and had grown to see that he would be a very proper, caring, and loving husband. She also knew Deborah. She was as stubborn and bull-headed as her grandfather. What they wished, they usually managed to obtain. But being a woman, and especially the wife of a minister, she knew when to hold her silence.

Asa ran his tongue over dry lips.

"May I have an answer?" he demanded.

"You may," Jason Lee said simply. "Brother Alvin and I have just concluded an agreement. When Deborah finishes her missionary work, she will be married to my son, David."

"I will not marry a plough-boy," Deborah snapped, coming into the room.

"I'm sorry, daughter," Waller said feebly. "I know that women in your family have always married a minister in the church, but—"

Jason Lee's jaw dropped a little.

"There are no *buts* about it! What kind of a father are you, Alvin?"

"A very poor one," he said grimly. "I really have nothing against this man. He has been very good to me and my family."

"Well, I have something against him!" Lee said sternly. "He is not of our faith. Any minister who even thinks of marrying them I will run out of the church and the territory."

"He didn't say he was going to marry us," Asa said calmly. "As to faith, if God had only made Methodists, you would still be a small tribe wandering in the wilderness. What should matter is that I do believe in God and am not an atheist. I don't want to see Deborah hurt by being forced into a marriage she doesn't want. Deborah came to tell me that she does not have to leave until September. We all have a lot of work to do this summer. Why don't we let this subject ride until September?"

Deborah looked at Asa, thinking: He has won mother over, or else she would be sitting here. She had stood outside the door and heard her father start to weaken. But Jason Lee ran the missions as though he were God.

Jason Lee was caught between his Methodist doctrine and his desire to be successful. He had once called Asa Lovejoy "ruthlessly ambitious" because he envied him. He also resented Oregon City having a proper church, while in Salem they met in a log cabin. Oregon City had a school; Salem didn't even have a woman educated enough to teach. But the bottom line was business. His wheat would be useless to him without Lovejoy's mill and wherewithal to export it.

"September is a long way off," he said, without making a commitment, one way or the other. "I will make my excuses to Sister Elvira."

As he stepped into the kitchen, he looked into Elvira's triumphant face.

"You are for this union?" he asked.

Elvira looked at him, the triumphant smile widening on her lips.

"My husband was right, Jason. My grandmother, mother, and I were all forced to marry ministers. They grew to love their husbands, as I have mine, because we shared a common interest in the church. They, too, seem to have many of the same interests. We will see what September brings."

Later that night, Elvira went and sat down gently on her daughter's bed.

"Promise me, Deborah," she whispered, so as not to wake Annie, in the next bed, "that you won't do anything foolish?"

"Mama, I must confess that I started it by kissing him first."

"I had to kiss your father at the altar, he was so shy and timid. I was only seventeen, just like you."

"Mama!" she gasped. "You are younger than Asa."

"That's right," she said, and left the rest of her thought unspoken.

"How long were you betrothed?"

"Our bans were read a year before the wedding date."

Deborah was silent for a long moment. "September seems very close, all of a sudden. There is so much to do. Why, it took Carrie Watson forever to get her hope chest together back home in Salem."

"Let's make a list up tomorrow," Elvira said, leaning down and kissing Deborah's forehead. "Good night, my darling."

Outside the bedroom, she leaned up against the wall. Her mission had been successful. She was not against the marriage, she just wanted a breathing space so everyone would be sure.

The summer of 1843 did not give breathing space to many. Because of the deep, rich soil in the valley and the mild climate, garden vegetables expected in June were ready for harvest in late May. Francis had to build a small warehouse to store his traded furs and waited on word from Dexter Farman on a ship to transport them to New York. Captain John Couch returned in mid-June. He had sold half his cargo in Honolulu, reloaded with fresh fruits for Fort Vancouver, feeling his half cargo was an ample year's supply for his small store in Oregon City. Not only was his cabin nearly lost in the jumble of new buildings, but most of his supplies not only duplicated the items at Benson & Bros., but were of an inferior quality. Nor would he pay a "bloody Englishman" or "Yankee lawyer" fifty dollars for the puny lot. He changed his tune when he learned he had to buy lumber from the Yankee lawyer to build a larger store. The blacksmith shop bellowed out darker smoke and the anvil rang from sun up to sundown. Elijah Perry recalled the beached skeletons of several ships around Cape Disappointment. On Kenwa's still unnamed river schooner, Perry made a scavenger run and brought back enough scrap metal to make wagon rungs for the new wagon shop at Linn City. The Kanaka boys fell in love with the forests, harvesting and hauling enough trees to keep the sawmill buzzing all fall and winter. Asa, when not bogged down with paperwork, finished the new waterwheels and flour mill. He got to see Deborah only about once a week, Sunday dinner at the Waller's, which was becoming a ritual.

In New England, a hint of Jack Frost in the air announced a change from summer to fall. In Oregon City it was the arrival of the Indians with their thin spears, for the spawning of the salmon. And that year a new sound wafted through the air, which would ever after mean fall—the grindstones turning wheat into flour.

In mid-October Francis got a shipment of goods from Dexter and news that he would have a ship for the furs by early December.

Standing at the curtained windows of her second-story bedroom, Sophia was still upset that Asa had built the house facing the river, because she had to go out on her back porch if she wanted a view of Mount Hood. The second floor also bothered her because ten-month-old Lorenzo was a crawling terror and Francis could never remember to close the inside stairwell door.

She was only half listening to Marsha Talcott. The woman basically had three stories: how she had lost her husband on the wagon train; how Mr. Lovejoy should marry a widow woman and not that young girl; how she would never be able to learn to cook to please the Kanaka boys.

Still, Marsha had become a friend and a help at expanding her less-than-expert cooking talents. Looking at the changing fall colors across the river, she had to count her blessings. The past six months had gone well for her; the number of women who came to her home was a demonstration that she had been "accepted." She had come to know every woman in town by name and to like the easy camaraderie, the informality of a small town. It wasn't a Congregational Church, but she was comfortable with Reverend Waller and dearly loved Elvira. She shied away from any discussion about Deborah and Asa, for she had her own thoughts on the subject.

As for her husband. . . . She frowned and then pulled the curtains apart. A bateau usually had four paddlers. This one had eight and was flying toward their wharf as though it had the devil on its tail. Then she gasped. God himself could not have looked more wrathful than the arriving John McLoughlin.

"Marsha, mind Lorenzo a second. Tama is watching the store and Francis is . . . Lord, where did Francis say he was going?"

"To check Mrs. Ferris's produce," Francis answered himself, coming from the back entrance, gnawing on a raw turnip. "What's the problem, my love?"

"Mr. McLoughlin! He's probably in the store by now."

Francis laughed. "Well, I can't say that I haven't been expecting him."

Without another word he went down the inside stairwell. Tama came up a second later.

But John McLoughlin was not in the store. He still stood on the wharf, gazing at Oregon City. The last time he had been there it had consisted only of his HBC trading cabin and the half-finished Mission House. He was greatly impressed with the whiteness and growth of *his* city. Then he recalled his mission and stormed in on Francis.

"Well, Mr. Pettygrove." He grinned. It was the grin of the wolf about to devour the rabbit. "A very handsome establishment you have here."

"Thank you, sir. Glad you finally decided to visit us."

"Visit, hell!" he bellowed, like a steer being branded. "I'm here to put you on the damn rack. Best you get that lawyer of mine over here, so he can hear what HBC has to say."

"Asa? Why, he is down at the fort with a William Overton. The man brought in a shipment for the mission and the captain is trying to pull a pirate job on his charges."

"Will you stop babbling!" McLoughlin started trembling all over as though he had the ague. "Six months! It has taken six bloody months for that corpse who runs my trading post here to let me know what a cheeky-assed thief you are!"

"I've never stolen a thing in my life, sir."

"Furs! I'm talking about furs. HBC furs you have illegally taken in trade!"

"I think I'm entitled to barter at a fair rate for the merchandise they received in exchange, Mr. McLoughlin."

"The Hudson Bay Company has a monopoly on all the fur trade in this region."

Slowly Francis shook his head, a grim smile lighting his eyes.

"My grandfather tutored me well, sir, on the history of the Hudson Bay Company. The reason I was sent to London to negotiate the trade route agreement with the Tucker Lines. HBC, in itself, has always had full right of all trade on all watersheds into Hudson Bay. The North West Company had the watersheds right of the Columbia River. Don't stop me! I know you know this well, and about the fighting and bloodshed between the companies, until the British government had to step in and merge you in 1821. While the world wasn't watching, you and George Simpson built thirteen forts in the region, with Fort Vancouver as the main base. When I came here, almost ten years ago, you had an empire. I recall eight hundred people working and living in that fort. What are you now? Less than four hundred? What has happened?"

Although he was normally a temperate man, McLoughlin's voice rose to a frenzied shriek.

"The furs!" he cried. "Give me back my furs!"

"They are not your furs. Under the joint occupancy treaty of 1818, I am within my rights as an American citizen to trade in this region. I believe that 1818 precedes your merger by three years."

The wind went out of McLoughlin's sails.

"What shall you do with them?" he asked quietly.

"I have made arrangements to ship them to New York."

"Do you mind if I see them?"

"Not at all. Tama," he called up the stairway, "come watch the store. I will be in the warehouse."

"You have them in a warehouse?"

"We also used to trap in Maine, sir. Hides trapped in the winter and spring still contain vermin and woodticks. If you rack the pelts, keep the warehouse slightly steamy with a boiling kettle, the vermin soon realize there is no more blood to suck and they drop to the ground. It also keeps the furs in a better condition before being shipped. They are then better when they arrive and bring a better price."

McLoughlin didn't comment. He followed Francis into the warehouse where he examined rack after rack of beaver, otter, silver fox, and an assortment of other animal pelts.

"I would like to keep the monopoly for HBC," he finally said. "I don't deny your right to trade, but why not retrade with me? These will bring a better price in Britain and Europe than in New York. This is a handsome gathering. Your discard pile tells me you were selective before trading. I judge you have in British crown sterling the equivalent of fifteen thousand dollars American. Is it a done deal?"

"I can see that we both judge fur by the same standard. It is done."

"I'll arrange transportation. How would you like the delivery of the payment?"

"A receipt to me and payment in *gold,* delivered to Benson & Bros., New York City."

Francis walked him back to his waiting bateau and then reentered his store. Only then did his legs begin to tremble, and he had to go behind the counter and sit down. He was dazed. His books showed only a little over $8,000 exchanged in goods for those furs and had saved him the cost of shipping them to New York. Now he saw why HBC was so rich and powerful. They cheated the poor trappers blind. Still, he knew that HBC would make triple that amount in the fur markets of London.

Even though he had just paid Benson & Bros. in full for the initial shipment, he had to consider their profit and . . .

"Lord have mercy! What am I going to send back to Dexter on that ship?"

"It really is some country," William Overton said, warming his hands at the clearing fire. "Would you look at those trees. So tall and straight as an arrow."

Asa chuckled. "Those are fir trees, called 'Douglas' by the British. In some of the timber stands they rise to seven and eight stories high."

"That's city talk, Mr. Lovejoy. I'm a backwoods Tennessee country boy, myself."

"What brought you to Oregon anyway?" Asa asked, handing Overton a tin plate of lunch that Kenwa had prepared.

"Came with the Methodist mission group and got assigned at The Dalles. Good spot for hunting and fishing, but boring mission work. I was so bored that Brother Lee sent me to Honolulu to secure these supplies for the mission stores. Ain't much good at it, it would seem."

Asa did not want to comment by answering. The tall, well-built young man was better suited for the outdoors than as a trading agent. It had taken every bit of mission gold and Overton's small hoard to quiet the captain and get the goods off-loaded onto the river schooner and three bateaux. The captain had demanded more, but Asa had shown him his empty pockets.

"I really think I'd like to settle down," Overton said, handing Kenwa the empty plate.

"Then you should be like the rest of the settlers and file your claim for 640 acres of free land."

"Do you mean like this place? I could claim it? It sure is right pretty."

Neither saw the fierce scowl that crossed Kenwa's face.

"That's right," Asa said. "No one has filed on it, I know because I do all the recording. I can do the paperwork when we get to Oregon City and you can pay me the twenty-five cents filing fee."

Overton's face dropped with disappointment. "You saw that pirate take the last of my money. I hate to lose this spot. Say, Mr. Lovejoy, I don't need no 640 acres. I'll give you one-half the claim if you would do all that fancy paperwork and pay you the two-bits when I get my commission from the mission."

"Sounds very fair to me. Ah, Kenwa is ready."

After Overton was aboard, Kenwa pulled Asa aside.

"Asa, *the clearing* has always been the clearing. What will he do with it?"

"Nothing! That's why I agreed to part of the claim. When the mission finds out what a miserable job he has done, he won't stay in these parts long. But it will still have my name on it, so no one else can file. We need it as our halfway point, Kenwa, always."

Kenwa was relieved.

Asa forgot to file the claim when he got to Oregon City. The streets were as though a carnival had hit town. Asa's thirty-family wagon train had arrived and were circled just west of town. After six months of trail life, the wagon people were like little children upon seeing civilization again. They roamed in and out of the four stores, "ooohing" and "aaaw-ing" and chatting with every town person they could corner. Asa found Pack McGraw waiting for him in his law office.

"My boy, how very good to see you."

"Yep," Pack drawled, as laconic as ever. "Here I am. Won't do it again with this wagonmaster."

"But you were to be wagonmaster."

Pack only shrugged.

Asa knew better than to press the boy. Boy? He had to correct himself. In that year away Pack seemed to have grown a few inches and put some meat on his sinewy bones. The scraggly, trail-grown beard and mustache gave him age that was not his at eighteen.

"So," Asa began slowly, "how many wagons?"

Pack sat and stretched out his long, buckskin-clad legs. "Left with forty. McCarty the wagonmaster said some were a troublesome lot, so he kicked them out before we hit Whitman's place. Think they headed northwest. Idiots turned half their cattle free, because I couldn't send any wranglers with them. I rounded up thirty of them. McCarty says they belong to the train. I say they are mine. You say."

Asa could stand it no longer. "Who is McCarty and who hired him?"

"That Moshe Shamir. Says you're out of it, according to your old man. Has that clerk in Independence scared out of his drawers. I kept my peace, because of you."

"Damn! That means no supplies on this train."

"Plus they sold your wagons to these people and kept the money."

Elvira Waller rushed in the door and stopped. "Sorry, I didn't know you were busy."

"What is it, Elvira?"

"Alvin is in a real stew with that Overton. Could you come?"

"I'll be right along."

Pack smiled. "She's the one with that pretty daughter, isn't she?"

"Who is to become my bride after Christmas."

Pack whistled. "You sure got good taste. Sure a parcel of ugly ones on this train and no fun. Prayer meetings every night. Must be five ministers in this lot."

"At least they grow good crops," Asa chuckled. "Look, go over to the Benson & Bros. store. Tell Francis Pettygrove that I sent you. If he is interested in the cattle, I'll go in with him."

"Good. I'd like to get rid of them and hit the trail tonight."

"No more wagon trains?"

Pack shrugged. "We'll see when I get back, but not with this wart-hog."

A pretty young girl told Pack that Mr. Pettygrove was busy. Pack could see that he was talking in the corner with a young Indian man. Cayuse, Pack thought, by his face and body. They always had powerful arms and chests from paddling and spearing fish. But his interest was in the girl. He knew every tribe west of the Mississippi and she wasn't from one of them. She was so graceful with her hands and body as she waited on the customers, and polite. Definitely no squaw from any tribe he knew. When he glanced again in the direction of tall, bearded Pettygrove, he noted that the Indian kept diverting his eyes. Pack smiled. He wasn't the only male taking note of the girl.

"Then you feel it is too late for any more salmon, Kenwa?"

"For chinook, yes. Only a few schools of silver still coming in from the ocean."

"I have lumber, flour, and whole kernel wheat I can ship. I had hoped I could round out the cargo with salmon packed in salt brine."

"Wouldn't work, Mr. Pettygrove. HBC tried that and people would not eat them because they ended up too salty. Smoked is only way."

"But we don't even have enough fish to smoke," Francis sighed.

"My people have," Kenwa shrugged, as though everyone should realize it. "We cannot eat everything fresh that we catch on the Columbia. The women spend the fall smoking many fish and putting them on layers of cedar chips. This was very good year for chinook. Most three feet and longer. We will sell soon to HBC and sailors."

"Will you sell to me?" Francis said with a direct look. "Ten cents a fish."

"Fifteen cents and all trade goods from this store. No HBC. Your things better."

"How many can you supply?"

"One or two thousand," Kenwa said indifferently.

"Whew! I'll order the barrels."

Kenwa frowned. "I mean no disrespect, but that would ruin the fish. For one cent more per fish I will supply the packing crates and cedar chips."

Francis calculated quickly. It would take no more than twenty crates and he could get them at a dollar a crate. A barrel would cost him $1.50.

"Done. You are going to end up a very rich man."

Kenwa grinned and headed for the counter.

Pack started toward Pettygrove just as Asa came through the front door.

"My grandmother thanks you for the hard candy," Kenwa said, smiling.

Tama dropped her eyes and flushed. "We should not be seen together."

"I am here as customer," he insisted. "I will take five of those candy sticks. The penny can go on my account."

Their fingers barely touched as he took the candy. "Will you walk out with Katoro this evening?"

"Yes," she whispered, her heart fluttering.

"Perhaps we will meet?"

"Perhaps."

He moved his index finger onto hers and then turned and walked out proudly.

"It's a horrible mess," Asa said, after introducing Pack. "Every barrel of flour is full of weevils, the seeds are moldy, and half the tins look as though they are pregnant. And there is an officious young minister over there who has been assigned as Alvin's assistant."

Pack's shaggy eyebrows lifted up with disdain and his laugh was ribald. "That would be the newly ordained Reverent Mister Percy Thorpe. The wranglers took bets on whether he wore lace on his drawers. We tried to leave him behind at Fort Bridger, but McCarty pulled a gun on me and made me go back for the psalm singer."

Asa didn't want to hear anything more about Brother Percy Thorpe. He had already been informed that the thin-voiced man would be at the Waller's Sunday table the next day. "Let's walk out and look at your cattle, Pack."

"Cattle?" Francis said. "What cattle?"

"The ones that we are going to buy, so that you can have a butcher shop and I can have a proper New England pot roast."

"Wild cattle can be very stringy," Francis laughed, taking his hat from the hook, "even at ten dollars a head."

"These are Michigan valley cows, Mr. Pettygrove, with a bull and calves, so some heifers are milking."

Francis licked his lips over the thought of a glass of fresh milk. The milk that came in from the mission farms always had a hint of the tin container it was carried in.

"How many head?" he asked.

"Thirty, not counting calves."

Francis stopped short. American cows were going for sixty dollars to seventy-five dollars a head. Beef at the HBC was seven cents a pound. The investment was too great.

"Asa, do we have a price?"

"Nope," Pack answered first. "I'm not much into cattle, except herding the bastards these two trips. You said wild cattle were fetching ten dollars. I'll take twenty dollars and throw in the calves."

"No! No! I say twenty-five dollars a head and that's my final offer." Catching the astonishment in Asa's face, Francis explained, "We just made a shipping deal with Kenwa for salmon, which will net a profit of seven hundred eighty dollars. Seven hundred fifty dollars for the cows leaves a net profit of thirty dollars for the day. We will send the majority out to Joseph Gale in Tualatin Valley. His wheat didn't bring in what he expected and is still on the books. Book is clean if he feeds and cares for them. We'll keep some milkers here, and a calf. Will veal chops satisfy you till Joe figures out one for slaughter?"

Pack McGraw was stunned. He'd never had more than fifty dollars put together at one time in his life. He was also impressed with Francis Pettygrove and his store. He wouldn't mind doing business with him again.

At nightfall, a canoe was in a small cove around the bend from the church knoll. The paddle was in place and beside it were five sticks of peppermint candy.

Sophia had been pleased when Katoro had taken an interest in Tama; he was so polite and gentlemanly and could now be left in charge of the sawmill without Asa being in attendance. Their walks, two or three times a week, were sweet and innocent, in her eyes.

"An hour and no more," Tama warned.

"Thank you, my little sister of spirit," Katoro grinned, kissing her cheek. He began to paddle across to a wooded area below Linn City. Although he had never been an outrig-

ger boy in Hawaii, he paddled with a sure excellence, thanks
to the teaching of Kenwa.

During the summer, Robert Moore had been able to snag a
chair manufacturer off a boat at Fort Vancouver. The man
had brought with him from Honolulu a Kanaka family who
were caners. Moore had promised the man the moon and had
done little more than build him a twenty-by-twenty frame
building for a factory. His wood supplies had to come from
Asa's sawmill. It was while delivering lumber, with Kenwa,
that Katoro had met Pelani.

Tama waited until she saw Katoro safely across the river,
then her heart began to beat happily.

She turned and walked slowly, demurely, toward a grove of
hemlock.

She found him waiting before a small hut he had made of
fir boughs and bent and tied branches. Her mission training
told her that what she was about to do was bad. But her
mother had told her that among the people of the *ahupuaa*, it
was accepted to taste of young men until one was found to
your sweetness. She knew her mother had tasted outside of
her own people, and now she was tasting even farther away
from her people, but she had found a sweetness she could
not give up.

"He is across?" Kenwa said simply.

"We have but an hour."

"You are so very beautiful. My heart flew into you on
meeting. You are *saki,* little flower petal."

Tama laughed, delighted at the comparison, and did not
resist as he swept her up into his powerful arms and carried
her into the hut. Filled with happiness, she pressed her lips
to his, and when he placed her on the fir bower she pulled
him down on her.

But as the hour waned, as he lay exhausted beside her, he
swore against their having to be secret lovers. He had to
make money to get away from his people and to marry this
girl. He knew he would be banished, but he no longer cared.

A whistle came from the river. It sounded like a nightlark.
It was time to go, again.

Asa reached for Deborah's hand under the table. It was rudely snatched away.

Everyone at the Sunday dinner table, except Elvira, Will Overton, and Asa, seemed intent on any jewel that might drop from the mouth of the twenty-two-year-old Percy Thorpe.

"Although Dr. Whitman's mission is an ecumenical endeavor, I do share his fear of the colored."

"Colored?" Asa mused. "We have no black African slaves in Oregon."

Percy looked down his thin, pious nose as though Asa was unworthy of an answer. "I saw several 'colored' at church this day, and the river is filled with 'colored' paddle boys."

"Tommy-rot!" Asa cursed. "The boys you saw in church are Kanaka, Hawaiian. The rest are Indian."

"Their skin is darker than ours," Percy simpered, "so they are colored, as the mission's provisional government laws state."

"Government? Organic laws? Alvin, what is he blathering about?"

Alvin Waller blinked, a little confused. "Asa, he's talking about the meetings at the Champoeg mission. I told you about them. You said you were too busy to be political. Don't you recall that they made you the official Title Book recorder?"

"I was doing it anyway," Asa gruffed, "but I recall nothing about colored laws."

"Well, Brother Percy is a little mislead on that topic. The

89

law mainly prohibits slavery and forbids the residence of free black persons. Our Indian friends are not mentioned."

"And what of our Hawaiian friends?"

Alvin blushed. "Those already here will be charged a three-dollar resident tax, those who come later a five-dollar nonresident tax. There is only one problem. They made no provision for the collection of the tax."

Asa roared with mirth. "I smell the fruitful hand of Jason Lee. A rafter-shaking preacher, a tenacious wheat farmer, but ill equipped to deal with the law."

"Sir," Percy quavered, "you are speaking of the man who leads our faith. You will apologize at once."

"Like hell! The Methodists don't own Oregon any more than the HBC. Until everyone has a say in the government, I recognize none. Excuse me, Elvira, I've suddenly lost my appetite."

Percy Thorpe did not let a sliver of silence fall between Asa's departure and his continuation. "Brother Alvin, I now insist that we hold separate services for the colored and our loyal congregation. Is that not the way it is done in Hawaii, Brother William?"

William Overton nodded, without knowing what had been asked. He was miserable. Asa Lovejoy had not only saved his hide but had also helped him secure land. He hadn't attended any mission services in Hawaii. He was sick of the type of hypocrisy that Thorpe preached.

"That's a very practical suggestion, Papa," Deborah cooed, to win favor with the young minister. "We are nearly full every Sunday, and the Kanaka boys do take up a full front row."

And are the only ones who seem to listen to me, Alvin thought dourly. Nor did he like the rumblings coming out of Jason Lee and the other mission ministers. All new arrivals were to be examined to make sure they had "gained Christ." If they were "unsaved," the ministers had an obligation to reform them or make them feel unwelcome. But the hardest part was that he had been unable to find voice enough to face Asa. At the July 5th meeting it had been determined that each Methodist male could claim a square mile and that each mission site was to claim a six-square-mile townsite. In the eyes of Jason Lee, Oregon City was all owned by the Methodist mission.

Percy helped clear away and wipe the dishes. It was not to Elvira's liking. It was her kitchen and she did not take kindly to being told the way Percy's mother had taught him. She had already begun to resent him as an intruder. She was proud of the growth and strength in her husband, and could not abide the constant superior attitude of Percy Thorpe.

"Sister Elvira, may I ask the pleasure of Mistress Deborah's company in helping on my Sunday afternoon parish calls? I would hate to make a fool of myself calling someone by the wrong name."

Elvira nodded, then frowned. Deborah usually took a Sunday stroll with Asa. She thought of going and chatting with Asa, but the thought was quickly taken away. Timothy and Annie were fighting again and she rushed to find out what the disagreement was over this time.

Sophia lay in the four-poster bed and felt of her stomach. "Tama says it will be a girl."

"How does she know that?" Francis laughed, getting into his nightshirt.

"Because I am quite small going into my ninth month, and I am carrying the baby very high."

"Tama is not her *tutu,*" he said, crawling into bed and pulling the down comforter up to his chin.

"Don't worry, my love. Tama will do fine and she will have the help of Elvira and Grandma Perkins."

"That wasn't my worry, if I looked worried. That was some lecture dished out this afternoon by our new young minister. Do you suppose that was his message all over town?"

"No doubt," Sophia sighed. "What do you intend to do about it?"

"With your approval, I will not force the boys and Tama to attend a segregated service. Likewise, I shall boycott the regular service and keep the store open next Sunday."

Sophia giggled. "That should raise a few Methodist shackles."

That he would not mind doing. Percy Thorpe had also scolded him for selling to some of their people when they had a moral obligation to use the mission store. Never, since he had been a young man at sea, had his fingers itched so to strike a man.

On the second week of December, unexpected visitors arrived. Dexter Farman had decided to come along with the supply ship and to bring some surprises.

"Rhoda!" Sophia cried as she was engulfed in the big woman's arms. "What a marvelous pre-Christmas present!"

"I just had to be seeing you," Rhoda said, wiping the tears from her eyes and cheeks, "and my Lorenzo, and Tama and the boys, God love them."

"And Francis?"

Rhoda pursed her mouth in mock guilt. "Himself I've already seen at the wharf. I think he's of a mind to throw me in the river and make me swim back. I done brought eight more Kanaka boys and four girls."

"Oh, my!" Sophia gasped, knowing how Francis must have felt. "Where shall we house them, and what work can we put them to?"

"Himself said he would jaw that over with Mr. Lovejoy. Tama, come and help me with our luggage."

Sophia nodded approval, then had her own moment of disquieting alarm. She ran to the back porch and hollered up the hill to the boys' cabin.

"Katoro, run over to the furniture man and see if he still has those two beds and mattresses he took in exchange for Mrs. Carter's dining room set. Send up the rest of the boys to help me move things around. Dexter and Rhoda Farman are here."

"Oh, my dear girl," Rhoda said behind her, putting down a wicker suitcase. "I never gave a thought that you might not have extra living quarters. No bother! Dex and I will just go along to a hotel."

"You might have to go a long way," Sophia laughed. "We have no hotel yet. Anyway, Tama can go into Lorenzo's nursery and I have a bed coming that we can put into Francis's study for Dexter. Oh, Rhoda, it's so good to see you!"

* * *

"Sorry to disturb you, Asa," Francis said, coming into his law office next to the store.

"Give me a moment, Francis. I just want to finish filling in this Title Book entry on The Clearing."

Francis was stunned. "The Clearing? Damn me for being a busy fool. Asa, for Lord's sake, don't let Sophia know it's in someone else's hands."

"And why is that?" Asa asked.

Francis sank down in a chair. "I made her a rash promise on arrival, I'm afraid—a Christmas-future promise that she would someday have a home on that site."

Asa laughed. It was the first time he had laughed in the three weeks of the church boycott. As if he were responsible for half the town staying away, Deborah had been spiteful and nasty each time they met. The only Waller family member who was civil to him was Elvira, who had stopped by several times with wedding preparation questions. Now he was sorry the wedding had been put off from September to late December.

"And what is so funny?"

"Sophia is still protected, Francis. William Overton gave me half the claim for the paperwork and filing fee, which he still has not paid me."

"And may never," Francis said. "All I get are complaints from ladies who go to the mission store first and then have to come to me. Sorry, Asa, finish your work."

"Already done," Asa said, closing the book. He looked up. "I saw the bateaux arriving. Looks like quite a supply from Hawaii."

Francis sighed. "And more than we expected. Dexter and Rhoda Farman came on the ship and brought another dozen Kanaka—eight boys and four girls. I don't know what we're going to do with all of them."

Asa rubbed the dome of his forehead, which was starting to go bald. "The second floor of this building is partitioned into a dozen rooms. We can move Katoro's crew here and some of them will have to double up."

"Girls are a different matter."

"As I have been finding out the past few weeks."

Francis ignored the comment. He had never really approved of Asa marrying Deborah, but had managed so far to keep his silence on the subject. "Say!" he said, on an instant thought. "Mrs. McGuire is always complaining about not having enough to trade for goods. She has vacant rooms on her second floor. I'll trade her goods for rent. How do you think Marsha would take to feeding such an army?"

Asa relished the thought. "For two days it'd be as thunderous as the Second Coming, but then she'd dearly fall in love with each and every one of them."

"How did you know there was to be a Second Coming?" Francis grinned.

"Been around the Methodists, that's how. Now, as for work, best we find out if they have any skills."

A piercing male scream came from the wharf, and a second later Percy Thorpe ran by the office window, blood spurting from his nose.

Francis and Asa ran to the dock, as the sash windows opened and Rhoda and Sophia leaned out. The bateaux boys had formed a protective ring around a stack of unloaded supplies and Kenwa.

"Kenwa!" Francis demanded. "What happened?"

"Trouble coming," he said, shaking his fingers, which still stung. "That minister guy started counting the crates and bundles, putting figures on a slate. Asked him what he was doing and he said counting. Sorry, but I told him I wasn't stupid. I wanted to know what he was counting. He ignored me and tried to start opening that crate. I pushed him away and he said he was there for Jason Lee, who is over at the Mission House. Said I had to open every crate so they would know what import tax to levy. When he started going through the crate again, I swung him around and caught him on the nose. Trouble coming!"

"I say," Dexter said, coming out of the store with an oilskin packet in his hand, "I don't think I've ever heard a native talk with a British accent."

He realized at once that it was a rather inane statement,

but he was kept from further embarrassment by the arrival of Jason Lee, Percy Thorpe, and a stranger.

"All right," Lee barked, "I've had all I am going to take from the likes of you two. This is George Abernethy, the new business manager of the missions. Brother George, might as well•tell them now as later."

"Hold on a minute," Asa cut in sharply. "If you're going to talk taxation, I've done some checking as a lawyer. Your provisional government made no provision for taxation, so this matter is moot."

"Perhaps," Abernethy said smoothly, "and I regret that Minister Thorpe overstepped his authority, of which he had none." He smiled at Percy, who seemed to shrivel. Then he paused, as though thinking over his next words.

At any other time George Abernethy seemed as though he would be a most congenial fellow. The slight burr of Scotland was on his tongue, he wore homespun trousers and shirt, but the woolen winter coat had the woven pattern of the Abernethy plaid.

"I would have seen ye gentlemen later, had this not occurred. Having received my training in New York City, I prefer an office discussion to a street brawl. But, as we are here, I see no point in hesitating to tell you that your various enterprises are located on the six-square-mile townsite of the Oregon City Mission. You will cease all operations and be moved along by the New Year. I'll be at the Mission House for a few days to answer any questions. Come Brother Jason, Brother Percy."

"Wait!" Dexter called. "Are you Jason Lee?"

"I am, sir," Lee said coolly.

"Then this is for you. It is from the mission office in Honolulu. It was received from your New York headquarters for delivery by the first ship out of Honolulu."

Lee snatched the packet away and left without a thank you.

"What will we do?" Francis moaned.

"Nothing," Asa grinned. "I have the Title Book and know what is what. If they continue to scream, I will scream back 'squatter's rights.' Kenwa, get the boys back to work. Mr. Pettygrove has need of some of those supplies on his shelves. Then, Kenwa, we must sit down and discuss what we will need in manpower to get Mr. Farman's supplies downriver and loaded." He turned to Dexter. "What is your sailing desire, Mr. Farman?"

"Oh, no rush, sir. Francis owns the vessel with me."

"What?" Francis started.

"Dear boy, that was the only way that we were going to get furs out of this region without having the British navy down our throats."

Francis and Asa looked at each other and broke into peals of laughter. Dexter looked baffled and hurt. They each took him by an arm and pulled him back inside the store.

Dexter was still stunned later as they sat eating lunch.

"Ten thousand board feet of Douglas fir," he mumbled. "Two thousand board feet of cedar. One hundred barrels of flour, two hundred barrels of wheat, twenty crates of salmon. I certainly hope that old bark can hold it all."

The bell sounded down in the store.

"I'll get it, Tama. You finish feeding Lorenzo."

Standing at the counter was an ashen-faced William Overton. "They are closing," he mumbled.

"I beg your pardon?"

"The missions, Mr. Pettygrove. The Methodist Board in New York has ordered the immediate closing of all the Oregon missions. Financial failures, they called them. Mr. Abernethy is to take over the store and sell off the inventory. I'm ruined!"

"Not knowing your situation," Francis said sympathetically, "I hardly know how to answer."

Overton clutched the edge of the counter in desperation. "They will not be able to pay me. I'm penniless. And I'll be stuck here unless I can get at least fifty dollars for clothes, equipment, and food."

Francis crossed his hands over his stomach. "I am not a charitable organization, my friend, and that is a handsome amount of money you're talking, when you've nothing to trade."

"But I do have something of trading value." Overton gushed. "I have half of a six-hundred-forty-acre claim downriver."

An alarm bell went off in Francis's head, recalling the Title Book entry Asa had made that morning. "My dear Mr. Overton, there is nothing downriver but wilderness. It is hard enough to get twenty dollars a developed lot here in town. I'm afraid—"

"Please," Overton begged, "will you at least take a look at it and then tell me what clothes and equipment it is worth?"

Francis had trapped himself by not claiming to know the piece of land and setting a price.

"Very well," he said. "How far downriver?"

"Just fifteen miles."

"Tama," he called, "come mind the store. I will be gone downriver for a few hours."

Outside, bundled up against a growing chill in the air, he motioned to Kenwa.

"I will need four strong canoe men. I want to look at some property Mr. Overton owns downriver and be back by early evening."

Kenwa remembered the man and the land he was going to claim. He had trusted Asa's word, but it was not working out.

"I will go along on the journey, or else they will not speed to your liking."

Kenwa selected a small canoe, because it would be lighter and faster with four paddle men. Overton sat in the stern, brooding over his dismal luck. As Kenwa barked his orders in Cayuse, Francis gathered he had picked men who did not understand English. The reason became obvious when Kenwa chose to sit next to Francis.

"Is it true, as Asa tells me, that you also wish Kenwa to call you by your given name?"

"I do. When you say Mister Pettygrove, it sounds as though you're giving me a British title."

Kenwa nodded and fell into a long silence. "Francis," he finally said, trying the name out on his tongue. "Do you know Overton's property?"

"I didn't know it was his until this morning, when Asa told me."

"The Clearing is very important to my people and the trappers. What shall you be doing with it?"

It was Francis's turn to lapse into silence. Normally a very methodical man, a rash idea had come to him while bundling up to take the trip. He had put into his woolen coat pocket a roll of twine and a lead weight from the scale.

"Kenwa," he finally said, avoiding giving an answer, "you know the river better than most. How deep is she around The Clearing?"

"Deep this time of year. Very, very deep in spring and summer."

"Deep enough for a sea ship to sail up that far?"

"Captain Couch did it," Kenwa grinned. "He brought his brig *Maryland* as far as the rapids on his first trip. Kenwa has wondered why no one has tried since."

The news stirred Francis's imagination. "I would like to try. Think of how much easier it would be to get our supplies to and from the ship."

"Think how that would put me out of business," Kenwa said, as the realist.

Francis shook his head. "I don't see it that way. I see it as an advantage for your river schooner and more like her. Some of my people are ship builders. Back home we have a small working boat called a scow. I will draw out some plans and show you the advantages of a scow over the bateau."

"Once you asked about my people," Kenwa said. "Cayuse were once hunters and fishers, always on the move. What with trappers, HBC, and missions, some villages now stay put. Ours was one of those, and my grandfather ordered me to work at the fort to learn the tongue of the white man. He wished to learn if their words rang true. It has not always been the case. The young men are bitter and resentful over losing more and more hunting and fishing grounds. Someday that bitterness will boil over into bloodshed. These four paddle men are a generation that has not tasted war . . . they pant for the opportunity to get *coup* feathers in battle."

Francis knew he had been accepted by Kenwa as a confidante, and that he had to step carefully. "And what of your desires?"

"Kenwa will never go hungry again. He is learning the way of the white man to make money. Money will give him power to take a wife and have children."

"Do you have a girl in mind?"

"I have," he said proudly, but he did not mention Tama's name. "We are there."

Francis looked at the clearing with new eyes, while Kenwa did sounding depths with the twine and weight. But the three-to-four acre clearing was not his prime object. A quarter of a mile farther west he found a clear running stream. He headed south. The land was flat and the timber was good. Hills rose in the near distance. He turned east and came out again at the river, a half mile above The Clearing. His excitement grew as he walked back along the bank.

"Kenwa, have no fear, The Clearing will remain as a stopping place."

Kenwa grinned broadly, then his face instantly changed into a deep frown. A bateau was speeding downriver toward them. He began to shout at the paddle boys in Cayuse, but they ignored him. As the bateau shot by them, the two passengers turned their heads to the east bank to keep from being recognized.

"I feared something like this," Overton moaned, running to them.

"Who are they?" Francis demanded. "And what are they up to?"

"They would be the Reverend Mister Percy Thorpe and Mistress Deborah Waller, or my name ain't William Overton. Thick as fleas they've been of late. When Brother Jason announced that the Board was going to reassign the ministers to missions in China, Brother Percy became quite irate. He announced his intention of offering his services to Dr.

Whitman at the *Waiilatpu* mission near Walla Walla. When I saw Percy and Deborah with their heads together, I knew they were up to no good."

Francis and Kenwa looked at each other, stunned. Each, without knowing the thought of the other, felt relief that Deborah was out of Asa's life, and then realized what a horrible blow this would be to him.

Francis's heart was heavy when he saw Asa waiting for them on the wharf. The temperature had dropped by twenty degrees and a fierce storm was about to break.

"Overton, go into the store and begin gathering your fifty dollars' worth of goods," Francis said as they docked.

"Where have you been?" Asa demanded, anger edging his voice. "I have been out here every five minutes looking for you. Well, come along to my office where it's warm."

Francis sighed and reluctantly followed. Kenwa silently stole away before he was invited to join them.

The office was toasty warm, but Francis refrained from taking off his outer clothing. He knew he would be no good at consoling his friend and wanted to make a hasty retreat as soon as the news was broken.

"We are going to win, Francis, my boy!" Asa chuckled, warming himself at the potbellied stove. "Abernethy has been around three times looking for you. The store he finds a disgrace and wants a conference on how to keep it in operation and still not be in competition. He senses a rebellion, starting with Jason Lee. Lee does not wish to give up his wheat farm for a rice paddy."

"I see," Francis said, with relief, but questioned how the Wallers had kept the news quiet. "And where I have been concerns you. I have just purchased Overton's half of the claim." He reached into his pocket. "And here is my quarter for the filing fee. All that leaves me is the copper penny my grandfather gave me at age twelve!"

"Poor man," Asa chided. "You do make yourself out a pauper. Well, what shall we do with The Clearing?"

Francis's eyes glinted with excitement. "Asa, Kenwa did some depth soundings for me. I am convinced that a ship drawing twelve or even fourteen feet can ascend to the clearing. I propose a townsite to accept ocean ships."

Asa laughed. "With what advantages, other than the deep water?"

"Being on the west bank it gives us direct access to the Tualatin Valley, which most of these new people are homesteading. Moore and Burns will get their trade or charge a ferry fee to get them across to Oregon City unless we act first. And, Asa, coming back this evening, I even thought of a name—Portland."

Asa broke into a roar of laughter. "All the way from Independence I thought of naming this place Boston. McLoughlin beat me to the punch with Oregon City. No, it is half mine and it shall be called Boston."

"That is idiotic!" Francis flared. "Everyone in America knows Boston as Boston. You can't have two!"

"Every seafaring man," Asa retorted, "knows Portland as Portland. *You* can't have two of them!"

"I am firm on this, Asa! I will have no other name but Portland!"

"No firmer than I, Francis. Boston and no other name!"

Francis looked at him, his face flushed and angry. "Are you willing to take a chance on the flip of this penny?"

"All right," Asa said. "I will take the denomination side."

Francis flipped the large penny so high that it bounced off the low ceiling before it hit the wood-planked floor.

Asa stood very still and looked down at the coin, then he laughed. "From Portland to Portland, they will be able to sail. Well, when do we start?"

"I thought about that, too. After Katoro has the new boys trained to timber work, we can transfer them down there to start clearing the land."

"Except for one," Asa insisted.

"Which one?"

"The stocky one that they call Matoa. He worked in the hospital kitchen in Honolulu as a butcher."

"And Asa Lovejoy can smell his pot roast cooking." Francis saw Elvira hesitantly peek through the window and pull back. "Well, I'd best see to Overton's supplies."

"Fine," Asa said. "I shall see you shortly. Sophia has asked me to dinner this evening." He picked up a form. "Have Overton sign this and we will fill in the details later."

To the amazement of the weeping woman, he had let her tell her full story without interruption. He stood there, staring at her, then a wicked grin lit up his face.

"Now Jason Lee doesn't have to worry about my faith. What little I was gaining has been dealt quite a blow. I think I could have stood her marrying David Lee before this thieving blackguard."

"Will you be all right?"

"I shall be fine," he said, without a grimace, although his heart was broken. "What really hurts is the manner in which she has treated you, her mother. A note! That is cruel, heartless, and cowardly on the part of the *man* she is to marry. I shall never forgive either of them for that. Would you mind if I were now left alone?"

But once alone he could barely stand it. For thirty-four years, being alone had not necessarily meant loneliness. He sat down, knowing he could not face another thirty-four years of being alone. The tears of self-pity came without warning and he buried his face in his hands and let them flow.

When Asa had not arrived in time for dinner, Francis broke the news of the reason for his tardiness. When he looked up, meeting Sophia's eyes, he was amazed at her anger.

"Francis Pettygrove, what manner of man are you? Even if we silently disapproved, that is no reason for us to leave him alone now. Tama, get me a shawl. I'll go fetch him back for supper."

Francis did not protest. The friendship that Asa and Sophia had shared in Boston had grown even stronger in Oregon City. They were like brother and sister, who could communicate without speaking.

Once off the back porch and down the stairs, she had to pull the shawl up over her head. The wind came down through the branches of the fir trees in fierce gusts. She stood holding the railing for a moment, debating whether to go on or return upstairs. She recalled Rhoda's excitement in announcing that it was starting to snow. That was excitement for a woman who had not seen snow in eight years, but it had meant little to Sophia. Now the wind tugged at her body, swirling the snow about her face. She hunched down and fought her way forward against the wind.

Her intention had been to enter through Marsha's kitchen door, but the kitchen windows were dark and she recalled that Marsha was going to feed the boys early so she could attend a quilting bee. At the dining room window she saw that all the Kanaka boys were huddled in front of the fireplace, shivering. As cold as she was becoming, her logic was not numbed. *I will have to talk to Asa about getting them heat for the second floor,* she told herself.

Rounding the corner, a northerly gust caught her off guard and knocked her to her knees. She got up slowly, holding on to the side of the building until she reached the office door. The warmth of the office was unexpected and took her breath away. She stood there shivering and totally ignored.

Asa had been unable to control his weeping. Tears flowed down his cheeks as he stuffed legal books and portfolio files into a carpetbag.

"Going somewhere?" she said, her teeth still chattering as she moved to the stove.

"You said you'd leave me alone for a while," he sniffed.

"Asa, it's Sophia. I've just arrived."

"You know?" His usually deep, rich voice was paper thin.

"Yes, Francis just told me. I've come to take you to supper."

"How does Francis know?" he wept.

"They saw Deborah leaving on the river."

Asa's eyes were swollen from crying and he could hardly focus. "My fears are starting tonight, instead of tomorrow." He gulped. "Tomorrow I will be the laughingstock, when everyone starts to gossip. Foolish old man trying to take a child bride."

"Asa, stop it! She is the one who will be blamed! She is the one who ran out on your wedding!"

His face puckered into an ugly mask. "Pity? Those are the words of pity and I dread that more than their laughter." His voice began to climb, octave by octave. "I can't stay. She has ruined my life here. It is finished. I can't look them in the face."

Slowly, Sophia had come up beside him. She had faced this scene before, with her father, during his last few months of life. Self-pity, hatefulness, and blame. Unless stopped, it would be like a cancer that devoured him.

The slap was quick, leaving the red imprint of her fingers on his cheek. He stepped back, stunned and glaring.

Sophia's hand began to tremble in midair. Her face twisted into anguished pain, as a lightning bolt shot from the pit of her stomach to her heart. "Asa," she gasped, "it's the baby!"

"It is too soon . . ." he started to say, but her eyes rolled to white and she crumpled to the floor. He threw open the inner door to the living quarters and dining room. "Katoro," he shouted, "go quickly for Mr. Pettygrove and the women. Something is wrong with Sophia!"

Sophia came out of her faint as strong arms were lifting her, and she looked up to see Francis's bearded face, sick with fear, and the concerned face of Rhoda.

"What a foolish thing for me to do," she said.

"Hush," Rhoda whispered. "Asa and Tama are preparing Mrs. Talcott's room. We'll keep you here tonight, rather than taking you back out in the storm."

"Is Asa all right?"

"He is," Francis said, taking her toward the bedroom off the kitchen. "Said you knocked some sense into him, just before you scared him right out of his wits."

He no sooner had laid her down on the bed, in the care of Rhoda and Tama, when the dining room erupted with wailing, weeping, and chest pounding. Asa, Francis, and Dexter ran in to see what this latest outburst was all about.

"Baby no born here!" Katoro was wailing. "We got sickness, no give child!"

Asa and Dexter looked at the Kanaka boys aghast. They had all begun to turn a sickly blue, with Katoro's shade the darkest. Only Francis began to laugh.

"You are not sick," he chortled, "and have no illness to pass on to the baby. I saw this when I was here that other wintertime. Some trappers had brought some Kanaka up to work their trap lines. There is something about this North-western winter climate that gives a blue tint to Hawaiian skin. They called them the *Blue Men*. But, Asa, it is beastly cold in here. Where did you get your potbellied stove?"

"At the fort. With their cold-blooded English staff cut in half, they have a surplus of used stoves."

"Then tomorrow we shall send down for some. We want these lads warm and healthy. They have a city to help build."

CHAPTER

☆ **9** ☆

_____

Cartagena, Colombia—April 1844

Elizabeth Johns stretched out on the oversized bunk in the captain's quarters and luxuriated over the warm breeze wafting in through the portholes. She giggled wickedly and stretched again. The night before had been magical.

She closed her eyes and combed her fingers through her strawberry-blonde hair to bring back the memory.

The full moon had lighted the quiet sea with a silver radiance. Cartagena, scattered on islands and shoals in the curve of the great bay, shone with a myriad of golden lights. She had been so enchanted by the city in the moonlight that she could hardly wait to see it by daylight. But preparing for bed, her husband began to make amorous suggestions. It was his first approach in over six months. Had they been in London she might have denied him and retired alone.

But Elizabeth now took Captain John Johns at face value. With George Pettygrove in charge of the family, she accepted the fact that she was married forever. Her return to London had been fortuitous in that Harold Tucker, eldest son of David Tucker, became her mentor, friend, and open door to society. The shipping magnate had approved of the relationship, because Harold squiring about a married woman was less of a scandal than his son associating with the "teddy boy" clique.

Under the hand of Harold, Beth had matured, gain valuable knowledge, and learned to handle her husband with quiet words and avoid screaming bouts.

One piece of Harold Tucker advice, given to her before sailing home for the launching of the clipper ship, she had not been able to employ until the night before.

"Bethy, my sweetness and light, don't go pompous on me. That romantic new vessel, *The Elizabeth,* is being named for the Virgin Queen and not you, ducks. However, you might learn something from that old girl and her secrets of lovemaking. Court circles still chuckle over the rumor that she brought to the palace a well-used Harcourt 'ore to give her verbal instructions on how to be better than a man's wife or his mistress. Thus, when a paramour was finally granted access to her bedchamber, naively thinking he was gaining a virgin, he wound up shocked with the best night of his life."

Beth giggled again and rose, the silk and lace of the nightgown clinging to her exquisite body. She blew a kiss to the faraway Harold Tucker.

"It worked, dear friend," she whispered, going to the porthole. "John was so shocked at my wanton willingness that he didn't sneak away during the night to taste the girls of Cartagena. Oh, no!" she cried, viewing the small town by daylight. "I should have known it would be like an old lady, flattered by the soft lights of evening. I would need half the crew to protect me, shopping in those narrow, filthy streets. Good thing we start for England today. I don't think I want to see it by moonlight again."

"Ahoy, *Elizabeth!*" came a call from astern of the vessel. "Prepare for the *Rose Ann* to come alongside and board!"

Beth gasped and felt her heart skip a beat. She raced to her wardrobe to find a suitable dress for this arrival. Then she stopped short. She had not seen or heard from Ian Llwellen since his departure from Portland in October of 1841. Only at the launching, two months before, had she learned from Nelson Cleeve that Ian had gained the captaincy of the *Rose Ann,* with his main duties being in the Caribbean. When she had pressed Nels for details, he had shrugged and acted as if he knew nothing. It had peaked Beth's curiosity, but the maiden voyage of *The Elizabeth* had taken it out of her mind.

On purpose she chose a very matronly dress, with a high collar, long sleeves, and a very small bustle. She felt the two ships bump and heard an order to lash them together. She took her time pulling her hair back and twirling it in a bun at the nape of her neck. She waited until she heard the piping aboard of an officer and then went up on the deck.

Beth was astonished at the sight of Ian. At twenty-three his sandy hair showed silver at the temples and an ugly scar crawled from his right ear lobe to the cleft of his chin. He was clean shaven, as though he wished the scar to be seen and not hidden behind a beard. As always, his uniform was immaculate and made Beth feel she had overdone the matronly bit.

With a sweeping gesture, he took her hand.

"Mrs. Johns, a pleasure to see you on this voyage."

"Isn't she a beauty?" Johns gushed.

"As much so as in the original drawings," Ian carefully sidestepped, not wishing to indulge in a conversation about Beth. "Thirty-five sails, they tell me."

John Johns could be friendly, now that Ian Llwellen was no longer his First Officer and a threat. In his singsong voice he filled Ian in on the marvels of the clipper ship: from Portland to Jamaica she had cut through the water at twenty knots, with a full cargo of fifteen hundred short tons. Sailing empty, through the Caribbean Sea, they had no need for all the sail power and she had floated like a cork.

"Then she is seaworthy," Ian said, bringing the conversation back to his purpose." I have just come up the main from Barranquilla with coffee for you. I also have to offload, sugar, molasses, and rum. Only a thousand short tons, but I can make up the difference with cargo in Honolulu."

Johns's sunburned face paled. "Honolulu? You? Sir, we are on a maiden voyage that takes us back to London. My present navigator is untrained to take us down around South America and into the Pacific."

"That thought must have struck Mr. Tucker in London, Captain. Last time I was in Portland I was ordered to take on board company passengers to deliver here. Murton Boddick, a navigator, late of the Royal Navy, has been around the

Horn to the Northwest many times. As we are mercantile, he will require quarters for his wife, Eliza."

John Johns stood stunned. Automatically Beth answered for him. "This is all out of the question, Captain Llwellen. We are on our way back to London, for I have no intention or desire of going to the Sandwich Islands."

"They didn't think you would," Ian said, without expression. "You may return to Portland on the *Rose Ann* and take the next packet for England."

Captain Johns came back to life, his old jealousy renewed. "With you?" he flared. "Not on your life, sir!"

"She won't be with me, sir, for I shall be a part of this ship's company."

"I have a full complement and wish no changes."

"I don't make the orders, Captain Johns, I just carry them out. I'm assigned as your cargo master for this trip to Fort Vancouver."

Beth smiled. It was just like Ian to give a direct, honest answer that was irrefutable.

John Johns smiled to himself. It was true he did not have a cargo master on this maiden voyage, for he had only had the shipment to Jamaica. Finally he murmured: "Cargo master on this ship is only a second-rank officer." The flat words carried their own meaning.

Ian Llwellen only shrugged, and Beth felt a bristling anger. Anger at her husband for being snide and renewing the feud and equal anger at Ian for accepting such orders.

"Then I suggest, Captain, I be granted permission to start moving the cargo."

"Agreed. And send the navigator to me so I can reacquaint myself with the route. I've made the trip only once, and that was a decade ago."

Then, only Beth saw the change in Ian Llwellen's face. His eyes took on a fresh fire, as though he had just won something important, and Beth's interest livened.

She caught up with her husband and put her hand through his arm. She felt him shiver from memories of the night before.

"How long is the journey to the Northwest?" she asked

innocently, as though she had not heard Francis Pettygrove talk about it for years.

"Normally, my dear, about one hundred and eighty days. With our ship we should be able to cut some sixty to seventy days off that schedule."

"That doesn't sound half-bad. I think I shall just stay with you."

John Johns looked at her with a small smile. "As you wish, my dear." Turning her back, so she could see Ian issuing orders, he grew bitter. "But that does not mean I will allow you to renew your past with *him*!"

At his first words her heart had pounded happily; now, with a sick sensation, she let her hand fall from his arm.

"There was never anything between us! Nothing!" Her voice shook in a way that she could not control.

"And, there won't be . . ." The care with which he chose his words made her suddenly furious. Never once had he questioned her running all around London with Harold Tucker. Nor had she ever been allowed to question his numerous affairs.

Suddenly, she realized that her husband had left her side. She was still turned toward Ian and for the first time since he had come onboard their eyes met. And suddenly, she knew why he had taken this lesser assignment. His eyes were still as hungry for her as they had ever been.

Independence, Missouri—April 1844

Pack McGraw stood at the second-floor window and looked out across the Missouri River. For two months he had savored the heady experience of sleeping in the same bed with the same woman. But spring was taking away the winter brown of the plains and he felt restless. Each day it was getting harder to tell Kitty that he belonged back in the mountains. Even the limited civilization of Independence was too much civilization for him.

He heard the cursing coming down the hall and he smiled. Kitty Flynn was like no other woman born to man.

"Get me a wee dram," she demanded, pushing through

the door and soundly slamming it shut. " 'Tis the last time I'll be singin' 'n dancin' for two old drunks, even if Flynn's is me own joint. Me talents too precious to waste on yokels. Thanks, love." She took the jigger of fiery Irish whiskey and downed it in a gulp. "That's betta! John, help the girl out of her workin' togs."

John Packwood McGraw started to correct her, but knew it would do no good. On his first visit to Flynn's Irish Pub he had been polite and given Kitty his full name when asked. John came off her tongue like liquid music and Pack stuck in her throat like a raw piece of baked potato. Still, he grew embarrassed each time he had to help with the hook eyes, buttons, and bows.

Kitty was a small woman, only five foot even, without her high-heeled dancing shoes. She wore her hair, with strands of braided-in wigs' hair, high on her head to make her more statuesque. It helped, because she was built like an hourglass, with ten hours of sand still on the top, dainty hips, and two hours of sand equally divided from the wide hips to muscular thighs and nimble legs. Legs that kicked high enough to make any stout man tremble at what he thought he viewed under the costume covering. Ireland lay thick on her singing tongue and thicker in her fierce determination that she picked her men, they did not pick her. Few ever guessed that she was only seventeen years old, because she wore her makeup thick and possessed a business sense that had made her independent by the time she was fifteen.

"You're getting good at that," she laughed, reduced to just a short chemise. "Too bad you'll be leaving."

"Am I going someplace?"

Kitty's lovely brow knitted with frowning, as she started to take off the makeup. "John, my Daddy-do introduced me to men at age twelve. By thirteen he had me in America and dancing in the Bowery. When 'imself kicked off, I worked my way out here, gaining enough money and experience to open this joint. Don't tell me about men. I can smell it when they want to leave."

Pack's big face split into an enormous grin. "I have been growing restless, that's for sure."

"Pour me another wee dram, John."

Her interest had started with his shock of unruly black hair and eyes too dark for her to swim in without drowning. She had wanted him like she had wanted the other men in her life, for an evening of pleasure and good-bye.

But five minutes after she had brought him up to her room, she had felt male arms around her like no other male arms. They were massive in size, but sensual in their embrace. She had trembled at his brawny hands, fearing other brawny extremities, but, surprisingly, his hands had had a butterfly touch in exploring her every curve under the costume and then removing it as though trained to the task. His gentleness told her she was not his first, but his most wanted at that moment. But she knew those moments were over now.

Pack was pouring the jigger of whiskey when the door came flying open.

"The barkeep said I would find—oh, sorry, Kitty!"

Pack spun, his hand on the neck of the bottle as though it were a weapon. "What in the hell do you want?"

The slightly built young man cringed. He was not used to addressing a woman in her chemise and a man in nothing but buckskin trousers. "We have met, sir. I'm Michael Myers, from the Lovejoy Company."

"Which means nothing to me," Pack barked.

"Please," the young man begged, twisting his bowler hat around and around in his hands. "A dispatch rider came in this afternoon from Fort Williams. There is some trouble with the wagon train."

"Then I suggest you hop down to St. Loo and take it up with the great Moshe Shamir."

Kitty frowned. This was not going as she had anticipated.

"Hello, Mick," she said, putting on a dressing robe.

"Sorry, Mrs. Flynn. I was under the impression this was Mr. McGraw's room."

"Mrs.?" Pack queried, pulling a buckskin shirt over his head.

"A title only," Kitty laughed musically. "Needed when doing business with men like Mick. I don't like to make their wives feel uncomfortable. Thank you, Mick, for those last cases of whiskey. A very fair price."

She winked at Mick as she went by and out the door. She had done her part, now it was up to Mick. When he had delivered the whiskey she had learned of his desire to talk with Pack McGraw. She had arranged it, for it was time to cut him loose. His West was not ready for her. She needed people and towns to make money. Once there were people and towns she would look Pack McGraw up again. There was a lot of man there to like.

"Would you mind coming to the store to talk?" Mick said.

Pack considered the question and nodded. Nothing lost in listening.

He sat on the bed to pull his boots on. "From what Kitty says, you're married."

"In a way, yes," Mick mumbled.

"In a way?" Pack McGraw smiled, the slow rare smile that brought the crinkles into the corners of his eyes. "Ain't ever heard of just being married 'in a way.'"

Michael Erin Myers blushed furiously while his eyes twinkled. "Nor have I had to explain it before. I was fifteen when I came on immigrant passage. The crew spread a rumor that only married men and women could land at Boston. An Irishman got me drunk to drown my woes and the next morning I learned that the ship's captain had married me to the man's daughter."

Pack grunted and went out the door. Either the man was stupid or just plain foolish. He went out the back entrance and down the steps. Mick had to nearly run to keep up with him.

"How'd you find me?"

"It's a small town," Mick panted.

The Lovejoy building was just a block away. Mick took him to the side of the building and pointed at the outside stairs.

"My living quarters, if you don't mind. The other clerk is not aware we have trouble."

The living quarters were small, simply furnished, but spotlessly clean.

"Coffee, please," he called into the kitchen, and indicated they should sit at the dining room table. "I could not comment on your suggestion to go to St. Louis, because I did not want Mrs. Flynn to know that Moshe Shamir is not there, but with the wagon train at Fort Williams."

"And has himself in trouble, I hope."

"He has the whole train in trouble, and McCarty has vanished. The army commander at Fort Williams refuses to let them go on and Moshe refuses to bring them back."

"What's the army's beef?"

"The garrison commander here has no idea. He has sent a telegraphic message to Washington."

A young woman came from the kitchen and presented them each with a steaming mug of coffee. Pack McGraw couldn't help but take note of her and admire Mick Myers's good luck. She was petite, with her dark brown hair pulled tightly back into a bun, which made her pretty oval face more pronounced. Her little bow mouth was puckered with trouble, but her brown eyes glowed with a gentleness when she looked at Mick. He thanked her with a loving smile and she returned to the kitchen.

Pack drew close and whispered. "For one who woke up married, that's not a bad hangover."

"Anita?" He was about to explain and then caught himself. Knowing McGraw's feelings about Moshe Shamir, he might ruin everything by explaining that Anita was Moshe's wife. Nor did he want to admit that his own wife had taken one look at Missouri, left on the next train east, and had not answered any of his letters in three years.

"Myers, what was it Kitty called you?"

"Mick. My father is also a Michael, so I was always Mick."

"Fine, Mick, so why drag me into the trouble?"

Mick looked him square in the eye. "Asa Lovejoy trained me and gave me this job. I've never agreed with the way his father treated him and the manner in which Moshe became so superior. There are nearly two hundred wagons in the train and over six hundred people. Five of the wagons are mine. They carry crates that belonged to Asa, that Moshe knew nothing about. It's the least I could do for Asa, after what he did for me."

"I can buy that, but I've been with my last group of psalm-singing pioneers."

"Haven't you heard? The Methodists have pulled their missions out of Oregon. It was in the paper. These are all farmers and merchants looking for a new beginning."

Pack didn't want to admit that he had never learned to read and came back to an unobvious question.

"Why is Shamir there?"

Mick grinned in such a way that Pack saw he had a certain Gaelic handsomeness.

"I could say that it is his ego wanting to be called 'captain' on his own train. But he is incapable of that task without McCarty or you."

Pack sat back, his eyes unreadable. "And now boil it down to the truth."

Mick sighed. "Moshe is personally taking two wagons through with a shipment for Elijah White, the Indian Affairs Commissioner. Crated rifles and ammunition."

"Dammit! White is the man we kicked out as 'captain' because he shot all the dogs for bothering the cattle. I wonder what he's up to? Last thing we need is a hothead like that setting up his own private little army. Army! No wonder they've been stopped. Who's the commander holding them up?"

"A Colonel Nelson Wende, according to the dispatch rider."

"I met the man once," Pack said, indifferently. "Perhaps I can be of help to you."

"Thank you," Mick sighed. "When I get word from Washington City, I'll send that word along with a dispatch rider."

After Pack left, Anita came to clear the table.

"Moshe will never accept him," she said miserably.

"I disagree. Your husband sounded worried in his dispatch. He will really start to worry when he finds out Pack McGraw knows about the guns."

"Oh, what a fool I've been! I never should have told you about the guns! I never should have stayed here after he left!"

"Hush," he soothed, taking her hand and putting it on his cheek. "He treats you no better, being in the same room, as Liddy does me, being far, far away. It comforts me so, that we can be such good friends. And don't worry. Even the clerk knows that I have a bed down in the store."

She took her hand away. Years before they had promised not to touch, not to look at each other, not to give Moshe the slightest reason for suspicion. They could only be friends and live with the misery of their individual marriages.

Two days later a fire swept miles of prairie land, threatening the Bear Creek Station. At first it was only a cloud on the horizon, like a thunderstorm invading from Canada. But this time the cloud came from the east. It thickened. The mushroom fringes darkened, tinged with black. It floated across the plains toward the mountains as if to connect with a real bank of storm clouds. That night the air hung heavy with ashy clouds.

A lone rider rode the northern fringe of the fire.

Pack McGraw sat his plain saddle, his tall, broad-shouldered, lean-as-a-broad-ax body leaning slightly forward, his brawny hands resting lightly on the pommel. With the exception of two brief interruptions he had remained in that position for hours, but there was still, in the lines of his immobile figure, that which suggested expectancy, incessant alertness.

He had known since leaving Fort Kearney that a grim, hard giant of a soldier had been cutting his trail. At the confluence of Bear and Horse creeks he let the Pinto pony drink deeply and then gave the horse its head. They were both back in an area where they had hunted buffalo, antelope, rabbit, and grouse. It was a place he had vowed never to visit again. He slept in the saddle.

Whether a quirk of fate or because of the blessed breeze that always played around a bend in Bear Creek, the fire had gone south at that point. The trading station, built by his father in 1830, stood intact.

On one side of the creek the cornfield was newly plowed. Opposite, the cottonwood grove was just taking on the hues of spring green and the vegetable garden already had month-old rows. A woman was bent over a hoe. In homespun brown and a sunbonnet, she was unrecognizable to him, but he rode forward.

"Hello, John," she said, without looking up. "Thought you might be in the territory."

She let the sun bonnet fall back on her shoulders and leaned on the hoe.

Molly Spragge had been sixteen when her father had come to Bear Creek Station to work as a blacksmith. Dainty and serene, she had excited his fourteen-year-old mind enormously. She had been surrounded by a sensuous glow, but it had taken him a full year to get brazen enough to learn the meaning of the glow.

"What's behind me?"

"Soldier on the bluff," she said. "Not unusual. One or two scout from there most every day, ever since that last wagon train went through. Hear tell you been on a couple of those trains."

"With the cattle," he said, as a lame excuse. "Kept them moving northwest."

Molly could accept it. All Pack McGraw had at Bear Creek Station was the unmarked graves of his parents and two sisters. Not much to come home for.

"Wende's back," she said, turning toward the long mud-and-log hut that was trading post and living quarters.

"I've heard. Not setting too well with Major Sheffield at Kearney. He was one of the officers on the Board of Inquiry."

"Board of Whitewash!" she scoffed. "Twenty-seven dead in the massacre and all Wende and his men got was a polite slap on the wrist and reassignment back East. Now, he's back at Fort Williams as a light colonel—and asking all manner of questions about you, I hear."

"Why in the hell did you stay, Molly?"

She snorted. "Paw refused to leave this Godforsaken country. He's got a wife and two sons buried here, remember? When he's gone I can run away from death, like you did."

"Murder!" Pack exploded. "I've lived around the Cheyenne long enough to know that was an innocent hunting party Wende's patrol gunned down. The war party was attacking the station to get Wende, but he had left us alone, stealing away in the black of night."

Molly looked at him steadily, almost insultingly, then laughed.

"Doesn't matter anymore. It won't bring back our dead, or the Indians we killed that day. Now, they try to burn us out."

"That's not the work of the Cheyenne. I've a hunch those thousands of burned acres of grassland were to keep wagon-train cattle from grazing between Kearney and Williams. Don't blame the Indians."

She colored angrily, blood coursing across her face.

"How can you abide them," she snarled, "after they massacred our families? Get the hell away from here! I don't give a crap what Wende might want you for, but I pray to God it's a good enough reason to hang you!"

He slowly turned and with a single, fluid motion rose to the saddle. The horse did not wait for a command but slowly started walking away from the station.

He, at least, had learned from Molly that Nelson Wende was looking for him. It was time to get rid of his tail, but still let them think he was heading toward the fort.

It was midnight when he got to Fort Williams. It was dark, as were the circles of Cheyenne tepees, a little way to the east. In strange contrast, the four circles of fifty wagons each were illuminated by bonfires. Pack circled wide until he determined the reason for the all-night fires.

"Wende's scouts are back," he muttered, seeing the sentries patrol around the wagon train, as though it were a prison. But, in this case, it was to keep him out and not keep the prisoners in. He dropped into a dry creek bed and dismounted. "Stay here, Thunder, old boy." He took off his boots and put on mocassins. Then he began walking backward up the creek bed to the nearest wagons. That way, if a sentry happened to spot the tracks, he would think it was an Indian returning after having traded with the people in the wagon train.

Once within the circle, he had little difficulty in locating the man he sought. The "captain's" wagon always had an honored spot right behind the chuckwagon for the cattle herders. Moshe Shamir was huddled over a bonfire with Joe Bellam, a cattle herder Pack knew from one of his earlier trail trips.

Pack sat on the ground and put his boots back on. Moshe stared with his large brown eyes, then weakly smiled.

"They have run us to the ground looking for you. Are you so desperate a criminal they would stall the whole train?"

"Depends upon the crime. Somehow, I don't think I am the only thing holding you up. Might have something to do with your cargo."

Moshe was surprised at the subtlety, after the harsh way he had treated the man in Independence. Something tight relaxed in him. He had never dreamed that Mick Myers would send him Pack McGraw, but it might have been a fortuitous choice. If the army was so interested in McGraw, he might be able to turn over the man for their release to proceed. He squatted down by the fire and laughed. The laugh was more than a trifle unsteady. "The army fears our going into hostile Indian country."

"Have we ever seen any hostile Indians, Joe? No! This fort has been here since 1834, Mr. Shamir. This is the first time I've seen a Cheyenne village camped this close."

"According to Colonel Wende—"

"I accept nothing according to Colonel Wende," Pack interrupted rudely. "He served here once before, with a very warped sense of reasoning. He sees the West as a marvelous training ground. Live targets, in the form of savage warriors, to make his soldiers supreme shots. But the one time he had to put his theory to practice he ran away and left people to be massacred. Shown force, he will crumble."

"What are you suggesting?" Moshe asked coldly.

"Go ahead and move out!"

Moshe scrutinized him. He could read nothing in the stoic face. Moshe's hard eyes found eyes that were harder. Here was no hesitation. Curious as to Pack's plan, he rose and leaned across the fire.

"You do not fear the might of the military to stop us?" he asked.

"Might?" Pack asked, vexed. "In your six hundred you must have a good three hundred men with guns. What does Wende have? Seventy, eighty troops at most. Move out in the morning and regroup after a mile. It will startle Wende, but give you a show of force until Myers gets a dispatch man here with word from Washington City."

Moshe started to disagree, then gasped and grasped his chest. Pack and Joe Bellam were instantly up and by his side. The long-bladed knife in his chest had caused instant death. Pack saw the handle design was Cheyenne.

"Attack!" a sentry shouted. "Cheyenne attack!"

"Bullshit!" Pack growled. "Cheyenne don't attack at night!" He removed Moshe's hat and shawl. "Dump him in his wagon, Joe. We've got to keep him alive or Wende will turn this into an Indian war."

"No attack!" he called, walking to the center of the circle, as heads popped out from the wagons. "False alarm! False alarm!" In that dim light all they could see was the familiar round crowned hat with the broad brim and the flap of the shawl as he waved them back to sleep. Now, he prayed that the advancing sentry had never been too close to Moshe Shamir.

"It would seem there is no attack," he said sternly, before the guard could speak.

"But—I saw the savage knife enter your chest!" The man's voice was hoarse and unnatural, for he had been selected to throw with his deadly aim.

"The night plays games with the eyes," he mocked, keeping his face hidden in the shadow of the brim. "The Cheyenne village seems quite asleep, to me."

Inside the fort, Nelson Wende cursed. Silence from the wagon train meant the man had missed and there would be no panic and general alarm. But quiet from Moshe Shamir also meant that Pack McGraw had not reached him. Only two men remained who had evidence of his cowardly act at Bear Creek Station—Captain Bryon Sheffield and John Packwood McGraw. Sheffield he could handle in an army manner, because he had only sat on the Board of Inquiry. McGraw had to be eliminated, because he had been a witness.

The incident had nearly ruined the career of Nelson Wende. At first he had resented a desk job in Washington City. But when he found that his department handled all files on Indian Affairs, he relaxed. It had taken him four years, but he had expunged the record of the Bear Creek Massacre and filed a greatly altered version. Every Indian report from the West came to his desk first and left with his slanted views having been added. He created the fear in army circles that the wagon trains would bring about great attacks by the Indians, convincing them that he was the most experienced officer to command the last civilized fort before the trains went into the western wilderness. He had been given the promotion and the command to also be a peace maker. That he was doing at the present with the chief of this Cheyenne tribe. He had already shown the chief his power to stop this train and not let it move on into Cheyenne and Arapaho country. But, once he had Pack McGraw, he would let the wagon train go, as though they had broken his orders. One way or another he would talk the Cheyenne into pursuing them. He had lost four years in his quest to become a general. He would gain that back with an Indian war, real or imaginary.

The wagon train did not move out the next morning, or for four mornings. The word spread that Moshe Shamir was very ill in his wagon. Joe Bellam became Pack's ears. Neither liked what they were hearing. Factions were growing. Factions could split a wagon train faster than a street brawl. On the third night after his arrival, Pack disappeared. Two hours before dawn he was back.

"Damn your hide!" Joe got out. "I thought the army had nabbed you and I couldn't say nothin' to nobody. Where you been?"

"Talking a little Cheyenne. That knife was a present to Colonel Wende during their peace talks. Peace, hell! He's really fed them a forked-tongued line of crap. I have convinced them that these people are going far beyond the mountains of snow to the great lake that one cannot see across. As they have no interest in that land, they wish us the speed of the eagle."

By dawn the Cheyenne village had vanished. An hour later a dust-laden stagecoach pulled into the fort and a short time later came out to the train.

"His authority does not extend beyond this fort," Mick Myers sighed in triumph. "He can only restrain a train if he feels it is ill-equipped, ill-supplied, or too small to travel safely. Captain Tanner, in Independence, thought I should deliver the word in person, as it was a political decision."

"Political?"

"It's an election year, Pack. There is talk we'll go to war with Mexico over Texas territory, which means a war would give us California, as well. They want more people going into Oregon, so we can get it away from Great Britain without a fight. Hell, I even had to buy this stagecoach to get here."

"Why not ride a horse?"

"We don't talk the same language and . . . and . . ."

Pack turned to the stagecoach and lost his temper. "Just so you could bring your wife?" he snapped.

"She is really Moshe Shamir's wife!" Mick snapped back, not needing one more word on the subject. The clerk had not been discreet and Anita had been caught in the middle of Independence gossip, which she could not handle. "Her husband is on this train and she has elected to go forward to Oregon with him."

Pack lifted Mick by one arm and half carried him out of hearing range. "Her husband is dead! Don't interrupt or change the look on your face. That fact is known only to Joe Bellam and myself. He took an Indian knife to the chest the first night that I got here. It was supposed to have caused trouble, but keeping him alive in everyone's mind helped stop that. He is secretly buried under where his wagon sits. Tell her now or tell her later, but Colonel Wende is about ready to land on you."

Pack sat down with his back to the wagon wheel and pulled his hat low.

Anita was near to panic. Not being immediately greeted by her husband led her to believe that she had erred in making the trip. She now dreaded the scene she knew was to follow. Her husband had definite opinions on women: mindless creatures who had no right to make decisions.

Pack held his breath as Mick approached the pretty woman to whisper in her ear. Her reaction in front of Wende could ruin everything. But there was nothing. Pack had expected some show of emotion: a gasp, a sob, a face pinched into grief, but she made no response at all. She was like a wooden statue, unmoving, staying by Mick's side as Colonel Wende alighted from his horse and walked stiffly over to them.

"Where is Moshe Shamir?" he asked with constraint.

"At his wagon site," Anita whispered, putting a restraining hand on Mick's arm. "My husband is quite ill, Colonel. I am Anita Shamir. I came as soon as I received the word by the dispatch rider. There is a doctor with him at the moment, so I don't think we had best disturb them."

What a cool little liar, Pack thought.

The colonel smiled, but weakly. "Then, you will not be moving on."

"We will be moving on," Mick said evenly.

Wende became belligerently excited. "I have carefully read the dispatch you presented me, Mr. Myers. Your political friends may think they have thwarted my military command, but they have not totally stamped it out. I was about to forge a peace treaty with the Cheyenne, but they have departed. I can only read into that the fact that they do not wish peace and have gone off to prepare an attack, and possibly upon this very wagon train. One of the most important pieces of equipment for a wagon train is a wagonmaster. With an ill wagonmaster, I cannot let you proceed."

"But we do have a wagonmaster," Mick said without hesitation.

Pack gasped and cursed himself for not telling Mick about his problems with Wende.

Wende nearly foamed at the mouth with excitement. "If

you have Pack McGraw hidden down trail, it will do you no good. He is wanted for cattle rustling. I have the sworn testimony of your own man, McCarty."

"McCarty?" Mick said snidely. "If he were my man, Colonel, he would still be with this train. And I do not have Pack McGraw hidden down the trail. He was not employed by Mr. Shamir for this trip."

Pack couldn't call Mick a cool liar, but smiled over the beautiful way he had evaded the real truth.

"But who shall be in charge?" Wende demanded, a hard suspicion in his voice.

Mick's decision had been made the moment he heard of Moshe's death. "The safe arrival of these people lies with the Lovejoy Company, sir. Hence my quick arrival from Independence after learning of Moshe's illness. I have full authority from Mr. Asa Lovejoy to get this group to Oregon. Now, good day, sir."

Colonel Nelson Wende hesitated a moment, then slowly returned to his horse. It had all been for naught and he had been made to look the fool in the bargain. He could not help but feel that Pack McGraw was somehow involved. He would not rest until he saw that man in his grave.

That night Pack met with Mick, Joe Bellam, and four key men. Without hesitation or interruption he outlined his rules, a moral code, a daily schedule, and who would have final say on all matters.

"For a moment I thought I was back on a Methodist train," Joe chuckled.

"I learned from them, Joe, but they all got through. These folk have been rotting here for near a month. Enough time to take away that first rush of adventure. Ain't going to be easy, with this lot."

"Handle them like you do the cattle, boy. Take no guff, prod 'em in the ass once in a while, but let 'em graze peacefully each night."

CHAPTER

☆ 10 ☆

Oregon City—1844

Sophia had looked forward to the picnic all week long. It would be the first time she and Francis had been alone since on the ship to Honolulu. It would be a relief to get out of the house and away from the children. Ellen, the baby, was driving the household wild with her crying at every little thing.

But now she was growing impatient. The hamper had been ready for a half-hour, but each time she went to the window she could see that Francis was still in deep conversation with Robert Moore, down in front of the store. Then, to her amazement, she saw Moore spit, very deliberately, upon the ground.

"Politics," she growled. "I'm sorry Francis ever went to that provisional legislature meeting. Asa and George Abernethy should have gone alone."

She continued to talk to herself as she put on a bonnet and cape and took the hamper downstairs. Moore was walking toward his canoe as she came out of the store.

"I thought he would never leave," her previous thoughts went right on. "I thought you were all quite happy that you had removed the Methodists right to the townsite and all those other little things. What was he so angry at you about?"

Francis frowned, looking down into her lovely face. He opened his mouth and then closed it again grimly.

"I was about to lie and say it was politics, but it wasn't. It's a matter I will not let spoil our picnic."

"Good!" She slipped her hand through Francis's arm and they went down the river path.

"Where are we going?"

"Only this far, for the moment."

"Francis," she laughed, looking down at Kenwa's canoes on the riverbank, "I thought we were to be alone."

His gray eyes were filled with mischief. "That we shall, my love. Kenwa has been giving me lessons on our many trips downriver. He still doesn't trust me coming upriver, so we may have to walk back."

"What a delightful thought to start out on. I hope it is not too far."

"No, just to a lovely little spot I found. Let me help you in."

Francis paddled along silently, while an April breeze caught at his heavy hair and lifted it back from his forehead. Sophia sat facing him and saw the wrinkled brow.

"You said you were going to put Robert Moore out of your mind."

"I know," he sighed, "but it's a hard matter to put aside. Moore has a Kanaka family living over there. The man is a caner in the furniture factory. He has a daughter, Pelani, who is with child. The father beat the girl until she admitted that the father was Katoro."

"I've been fearing such a thing, Francis. It wasn't a problem when it was just Tama and the original boys. But with these new girls and boys, we can't constantly play mother and father. Tama was trying to tell me some of their customs the other day and I had to close my ears. I am not a missionary, but I still have moral standards. Will you talk with Katoro or have Asa talk with him?"

"Asa?" he laughed. "He is a turtle that hides in his hard shell of business and politics. Let a woman even try to get close to him and he snaps in his head. Hey! I'm getting pretty good," he said, steering toward the west bank. "We've made it in less than an hour."

"And how fast is the spring current running, to bring us fifteen miles?"

"You are a kill-joy," he said, banking the canoe and helping her out. "You knew where we were coming all along."

"I had a hunch, but . . . Francis! Someone has built a log cabin! And where are all the trees?"

"My dear Mrs. Pettygrove, may I be the first to escort you around Portland, Oregon, and wish you a belated Merry Christmas!"

"Oh, no! You don't get to say that until my house is built. But, guide on."

Francis was giddy. "Actually, it belongs to Asa and me, and I promised Kenwa I wouldn't disturb the original clearing site and the boys have done wonders clearing the trees, and the Kanaka boys built the cabin to stay in and here is the penny we tossed so it would be Portland and not Boston, and I'm glad it wasn't a vote or it would have been two to one for Boston. What do you think?"

"That you are about ready to run out of breath. Let's spread the blanket here and you can point out everything while we eat. I'm famished."

"Are you trying to tell me something?"

"Definitely not! Ellen and Lorenzo are enough to handle for the moment. Tama has her—" She stopped short. "Oh, Francis, Tama! How could Katoro do this to her, when they go about walking all the time!"

"Our picnic, remember? What's to eat?"

Francis wanted to evade the issue. His respect and admiration for Kenwa had steadily grown, except in one area. He had slowly come to realize that the girl in Kenwa's plans was their Tama. It was not the time or place to unearth that thought with Sophia.

"This timber," he said, slowly eating, "has been taken by bateau back to Asa's saw mill. As soon as it is cured, that spot, just south of the old clearing, will become a wharf, in the durable New England style. I have already drawn up the plans for a warehouse, to be built at the same time."

"There are stumps everywhere."

"Surveyors and women must see the same thing. That was Tom Brown's first comment when I brought him down last week. For the moment I told him not to be concerned and start thinking about laying out a grid of sixteen blocks. Those that buy lots can remove their own stumps."

Sophia was the practical daughter of an architect father. "But what if the stumps are in a street way?"

Francis laughed. "My love, a worry over that matter is still a good year away. Ah, here are Tom and Katoro now."

"What are they doing at our picnic?" Sophia sniffed indignantly.

"Kenwa showed me an Indian trail into the Tualatin Valley. For the past week they have been surveying it as a possible roadway and taking a good look at the whole valley. Please, Sophia, no words with Katoro at this time. Hello, you two."

Sophia was not enamored with the bumbling, unkempt Thomas Brown. When the ladies of Oregon City would meet, it was always Nancy Brown who complained about people not wishing to pay a proper fee for a survey and the odd jobs her husband was forced to accept to put food on their table. Still, at that moment she had to be gracious.

"Of course, join us. You can see that I have fixed enough for a small army and I know Francis is probably anxious for your report."

Tom Brown ate like he looked, in great gulps to keep the lumps of his body filled. Katoro ate sparingly, as though this were an intrusion on his time and he had plans to be elsewhere for the remainder of the day.

"Not a great route," Tom said between mouthfuls, "and not a bad route. Some swampy areas, but that could be due to spring runoff. In the canyon of that creek we might find ourselves with a few sharp curves and steep grades. But the valley is not what I expected, having done most of my work down in the Willamette. Joseph Gale should stick with raising cows and not wheat. He placed his claim all wrong, because a mile below him the soil is crying to be planted in good midwestern wheat. Useable land can easily handle some seven hundred family farms."

"Why, that's over forty-five thousand acres," Francis gasped. "Think of the wheat we can export then!"

"Well, thanks for lunch, Mrs. Pettygrove," Brown said, picking up his pack. "I'll keep my eyes open on my hike home, Francis, though I still think it's a foolish notion for a road between here and Oregon City, what with the river being so handy. Come on, Kanaka!"

"Wait, Katoro," Sophia blurted.

"Not now," Francis warned.

Sophia would not be put off, but expressed her desire for him to stay in a different light. "Mr. Pettygrove may need your help in paddling back the canoe, Katoro."

"Well . . . I . . ." Katoro stammered.

"And don't even think of lying," Sophia snapped. "You must have some knowledge of the canoe to get back and forth to Linn City, to see Pelani!"

Thomas Brown silently departed. All he had heard about for a week was the Kanaka boy's desire to get back with his girl. He didn't like Katoro. He didn't like the Kanaka workers being there. He had been one of the strongest backers of the organic law to keep out blacks. He had treated Katoro as though he were in that class and was delighted that he had been found out and might be sent away. His real fear was that the boy was too damn intelligent and had corrected too many of his mistakes that week.

Instead of denial, Katoro stood tall and proud. He was hardly a boy any longer. He was now taller and more muscular than when he had left Honolulu a year before. The thin face was taking on a mature handsomeness and the impetuous smile had a grave curve.

"It is good that you finally know. I am soon to be eighteen and would be with wife a year now, if back home. Here, I have done no wrong, except keep a secret."

"*No wrong*?" Sophia scathed, before Francis could open his mouth. "The girl is bearing your child out of wedlock!"

Katoro looked at her as he might a mission Sunday School teacher, who knew only their rules and were deaf to the rules of Hawaiian custom.

"Pelani good girl," he said softly. "Before she would give

herself to me, we participated in the most ancient and sacred ritual of Havaiki. As we had no coconut to plant, we planted the cone from a fir tree. Pelani is thus my wife. As the seed of the tree grows, so shall our seed."

"You are still not married in the eyes of God!" Sophia insisted.

"Which God?" Katoro came right back. "We had many gods before the missions came. Nor did we have *kapu* children. That is the problem, isn't it? Pelani is afraid of her father, because I am tabu. We are in a new land. Mr. Lovejoy says each man should be judged by the worth of what he gives to this new land and not what failures he may have left behind. May I be judged the same? If it means I should be married in your way, I shall do so."

"Sophia," Francis asked hesitantly, "would that solve it in your mind?"

Sophia began to repack the hamper. "Francis, you will speak to Reverend Waller on our return."

"We are not exactly on speaking terms."

"Francis, I know good and well that you secretly contribute to the fund to pay his salary and keep him in Oregon City. If you do not feel comfortable in speaking with him, find someone who will." Then her thought changed. "And, as for you, Katoro, I am ashamed of what I shall have to tell Tama. It was cruel of you to walk her out and have no interest in her."

"It was the only way I could be with Pelani and she could be with Kenwa."

He realized his mistake at once. Sophia's face moved in segments from shock, to outrage, to quiet fury. She challenged Francis with her eyes on the point, but he only helped her into the canoe and held his silence.

It was a very silent return to Oregon City. To avoid a clash with her, he went directly to see George Abernethy.

The arrangement he had made with Abernethy had been most agreeable for each of them. Abernethy had taken on consignment the majority of Francis's hardware and manufactured items, giving Francis the room he needed for the butcher shop and more sundry goods. Plus Francis's approval of the man had grown watching his natural leadership abilities. There was even talk of George Abernethy for governor, when the provisional executive government was established. As Francis thought he might, he found Asa with George.

"And so, George," he said, coming to the end of his request, "will you speak to Alvin for me?"

"Seems to me," Asa said dryly, "you've left out an important step. From what you said about Moore, that Kanaka father ain't too keen about his daughter marrying Katoro. I know what the lad is up against. Of course, on the other hand, the man is a damn idiot. Katoro is not only a fine worker but also smart enough to run the whole saw mill on his own."

"And what is he paid for those services?" Abernethy asked pointedly.

Francis looked at Asa, and Asa gave him back a long, slow look. Then they both looked guilty.

"Well," Francis said, clearing his throat, "we feed and clothe our Kanaka workers and give them liberty of the store for any other things they may desire or need, within reason, of course."

"Of course," Abernethy laughed, rudely. "Odd how that has the ring to it of a plantation owner justifying the care he gives to his black slaves. Both of you voiced your opinions on not wishing slavery for this territory and in a form you are practicing just that. Now you ask for one of your *slaves* to marry. Does the coming baby become 'chattel' to you or the parents?"

They considered the question in silence, then Asa laughed.

"We have been soundly put in our place, Francis. And I see your point, George. How can a man marry unless he is earning a living wage to support a home, wife, and child? I'll start paying the other boys a dollar-and-a-half a day, common labor, but will feel justified in holding back twenty-five cents a day for room and board. Katoro is skilled and worth three dollars a day, but can set up his own household. I've some lumber business to discuss with the furniture man in Linn City. In the old days my family used nothing but matchmakers. I'm some poor excuse for a matchmaker, but I'll give it my best shot with the Kanaka caner."

"You might also ask him to find a minister," Alvin Waller said, tartly. No one had seen them come through from their living quarters, where they had heard all, but the look on Elvira Waller's face showed that she was in deep disagreement with her husband again.

"We had hoped—" Francis started.

"You took them away from my flock," Waller cut him short.

"Your *son-in-law* forced that issue," Asa said, meanly. "Nor have I seen you asking them back, since the good people of this town saw to keeping your church open. George, you originally came out here as a missionary. Do you still have the power to marry a young couple?"

"Well, I do, but—"

"And the schoolhouse, with its steeple, looks like a church. Any objections if I rent it back for a wedding, Elvira?"

"Well, it is—"

"Good! I'm finding that it is easier being the matchmaker for a bridegroom than being an actual bridegroom."

"And then Alvin Waller caved in," Francis chortled. "I think it really rattled him to see Asa come out of his shell and not sound hurt when the subject of marriage came up. We must also think of a wage to pay Tama and Matoa in his butcher duties. If he keeps selling meat at this rate, I shall have to see to more livestock . . ."

Francis noticed that Sophia was still peeling the same potato as when she started the story.

"Are you all right, my love?"

"I am fine," she said, through thin, emotionless lips. "And I shall consider no wage for Tama after her deceit."

"Except that it makes her a form of a slave."

Sophia Pettygrove's face darkened. "My father brought indentured servant girls from England and Ireland all the time. They were very happy with the same arrangement we have with Tama."

"And you quickly lost them to the first single delivery man or policeman that came along," Francis laughed. His laughter was cut short when he saw the look on her face.

"They were men of the same race as those girls," she said, cold as ice.

"I see," he sighed. "You will tolerate Katoro and Pelani because they are both Kanaka. But suddenly Kenwa has turned into a devil with horns. I think you are being—"

"Francis," she snapped. "You run your store, with or without that Indian. I will run my home very nicely without him seeing Tama ever again. I have made myself quite plain to Tama. One step out of line on this subject and back she goes to Honolulu."

"Don't worry," he said gruffly. "I will not interfere with your running of the household, but I will not tolerate that attitude toward Kenwa. Where is that draft coming from?"

Sophia did not answer. Her back had stiffened over his words.

Francis opened the door to the children's nursery and closed it. When he knocked and opened the door to Tama's room, his heart sank. He walked slowly to the open window and peered down. Old packing crates had been stacked up so she could easily drop down to them and climb the rest of the way down. There was no one on the street and Kenwa's personal canoe was gone. He slowly closed the window and turned. Sophia stood in the open doorway, trembling with real fury.

"Her name is not to be mentioned in my home ever again!"

Kenwa was gone for a week.

"We . . . I have been concerned about Tama," Francis said, when he and the young man were alone.

Kenwa gave a grimace of disgust. "She has told me of the words of your woman. She is safe in the care of my grandmother. Tama calls her *tutu*."

"Grandmother, it means. What are your intentions, Kenwa?"

Kenwa glared at him, suspicion written all over his bronze face.

"How does my answer affect our business arrangements?"

"In no way whatsoever. I have no authority to tell you who to marry or who not to marry."

Kenwa stood looking at him with his eyes suddenly brimming with happiness, but the smile upon his thin lips was pure gratitude.

"My intentions will take time, Francis. It has taken a week to convince my people. That is why she is in the care of my grandmother. I am not to see her for the period of a full moon, while she learns the ways of my people and how a Cayuse woman treats her Cayuse husband. Then there will be a week of ceremony for our traditional Cayuse wedding."

"And a wedding in our custom?"

Kenwa's black eyes widened; then his cleft chin came up and he loosed his strong baritone laughter. "I have heard of what you and Asa are doing for Katoro and Pelani. A church wedding next month. I think this is good, for them." Then he grew serious. "Kenwa's thoughts on the subject are far ahead of yours, Francis. Part of my training came from the Catholic priests at the fort. I have already made my wishes known to Father Bernardo. He will attend our Indian ceremony and then recite the mass to unite us in the eyes of his church. My only sadness is that you and Asa will not be there."

"You might invite us," Francis said incisively. "Despite what my wife said, I would be honored to give away the bride."

Francis knew he would fly in the face of Sophia's fury. He really didn't care. He had loathed, since a child, the class structure in which he had been raised. Just because two centuries had passed, the present generation should not feel themselves any better than their ancestors who had arrived to a wilderness on the *Falmouth*.

Francis would have reason to recall his thoughts with the arrival of the wagon train of October 1844.

Where other wagon trains had started their journey with song, ending with silence, this group came to their new home with their voices singing with joy. They were the voices of America. Not a group brought together by a religious mission, but over three hundred families and individuals who had been strangers at Independence. Obediently, they had allowed a nineteen-year-old giant to mold them into a single unit, with a common goal. The train of '44, after leaving Fort Williams, lost not a soul, animal, or yapping dog.

Oregon City gained a doctor, a dentist, a Congregational minister, and various tradesmen. The Tualatin Plains did gain a good share of wheat farmers. The Willamette gained six family groups with patience. Two of their wagons carried nothing but carefully wrapped cuttings for future orchards of pear, apple, cherry, peach, and plum fruits. While they waited, they had seed bags to plant acres of snap beans, green peas, onions, potatoes, and the finest sweet corn to come out of the Ohio River Valley. In 1833, Nicolas Zarundy escaped the serfdom of Russia with a small, carefully hidden bag of seeds. At several small farms, from Massachusetts to Missouri, he had planted a few rows of the seeds and let the plants mature to seed to increase his seed stock. On the journey he had laughed about being a beet farmer, because the Russians loved their beets. He never mentioned that his beets would be white and not red. Now he could feel free. For two generations his family had been serfs on a carefully guarded farm where they raised and extracted sugar from the beets for the exclusive use of the Tsar and his large royal family. Nicolas had brought his seeds and secrets to the Tualatin Valley.

Some were not pleased with the news they received with the arrival of the train.

"Shamir is dead?"

Seeing the expression of horror on Elijah White's face, Anita stepped in.

"I am his widow, sir. May I be of service?"

"I certainly hope that you can. I'm the Commissioner of Indian Affairs and he was bringing me a rather large shipment of great importance."

Anita looked blank. "I'm sorry, sir, but my husband's wagons only carry furs for trade."

White had been cheated, but how could he scream against a dead man or accuse a widow of fraud?

"Like I said before," Pack grinned, "that little lady is one cool liar."

"What did you do with the guns and ammunition Mick told me about?" Asa whispered.

"Jim Bridger will make a small fortune at his trading fort selling them to the mountain men and trappers. Mrs. Shamir should get a good start out here trading those fine-grade Rocky Mountain furs."

"She's staying?" Asa frowned.

"I think your Mick Myers wants to stay too, but not in the stagecoach business."

Asa didn't have time to ponder that problem. George Abernethy and Sophia Pettygrove were bearing down on him at the same time. George won.

"Reapers? Horse-drawn reapers? Six of them? I am that excited, Asa, but who will ever be able to afford such expensive equipment?"

"They won't be able to for a couple of years, George, so in the meantime you and I are going to rent them out for a share of each acre of wheat. Oh, Sophia, allow me to present the wife of my late chief clerk, Anita Shamir. Anita, this is Sophia Prettygrove."

"Why would she come here as a widow?" Sophia asked, practically ignoring Anita.

"Her husband died on the trail."

"Too bad," she said without interest. "Asa, I must speak with you. The Reverend Mr. Richard Fulton and his wife Annie are most charming and are Congregationalists. I just must have your schoolhouse to convert into a church for them. The teacher hardly uses it anyway."

"It's been summer and harvest time, Sophia. Elvira will be using it again soon. You might ask her about its use on Sundays."

Sophia flounced away in a huff.

"Who put a burr under her bustle?" Pack said.

"Dear boy, it's a tale longer than you want to hear right now. Come along, you three. Francis wants to see you, Pack, and we can drop Anita and Mick off at my house. My housekeeper, Marsha Tolcott, will love snooping around to find you each lodging space."

"Any stray cows this trip?" Francis kidded, vigorously shaking Pack's hand.

" 'Fraid not, sir. All together though we increased the herd by a couple dozen calves and the human herd by three boys and two girls."

"And now it's back to gather another group?"

Pack shook his head. "Didn't aim on bringing this lot. At one time I got mad as hell that I wasn't given the wagon-master job. I found out that once is quite enough to play full wet nurse."

"Have you ever been to Spanish California, Pack?"

"Can't say I have."

"I was impressed by their cattle," Francis said. "I even tried to bring a few up by ship. They grew so seasick that I lost half of them on the trip. While you can see that I now have a butcher shop, as well as fresh milk and butter, Asa and I have need of a larger herd. Would you be interested in a cattle drive from California?"

Pack's eyes sparkled. He and Joe Bellam had discussed giving up the long trail and looking into a cattle ranch. Problem was, he had blown the money from his windfall sale to Francis on a fancy set of pistols, a buffalo rifle, and Kitty Flynn. He had thought of talking to Asa, but never Francis Pettygrove.

"Guess I could take a look at California," he said. "I'll need a couple of men. Especially the cow boss from this trip. He speaks some of that Mexican lingo."

Francis was about to open his mouth to settle the deal when Sophia came marching through the front door of the store.

"Francis, I will see you at once, upstairs."

"Sorry, my dear, but I am in the middle of a business discussion. You had better go look after Ellen. Not even this Kanaka girl can calm her down."

Sophia's face purpled at being put off, but after a moment she recovered.

"All right," she quavered. "I shall handle this family crisis by myself, as you seem incapable of handling little more than business these days."

Francis had no idea that he would be faced with a real family crisis within a few days.

The bark *Enda* stood off Cape Disappointment and waited. It was an hour before sunset and Captain McIntyre did not like the look of the sky on the horizon or the turbulence of the waves in the sandbar area. Dexter Farman had picked him off the garbage-heap of beached sailors and officers in Honolulu. Although it was his first command in five years, he had determined in the last few days that it would have to be his last. On the beach he could lavish himself with rum. On board ship his body was racked with craving.

"Ship ahoy!" the man in the crow's nest called. "Three master ten degrees to the stern."

She was still just a white dot on the swell of blue-green-gray, but moving with tremendous speed.

"Break out the signal flags that we are standing off," the Captain ordered, then put a hand to his temple. The sudden throb he put down to not having had even a nip of rum since daylight. In an hour he would be relieved by Mister Fallow, and would have twelve hours to ease away the pain.

For an hour he kept himself moving here and there on the bridge, putting his eye-glass on the advancing ship from time to time. The pain was fierce, but he tried to remain calm. Twice he stumbled, but the helmsman, whose eyes and mind were busy keeping the ship in its steady circling course, had not noticed.

"Another visitor," Henry Fallow commented, coming on the bridge. McIntyre turned and walked right into him as though he were stone-blind.

"Sorry," he mumbled. "That cheapskate has got to learn we have to be more than a two-officer ship and left to do our own navigating. Who's with us?"

"British sloop, sir. She has seen our signal and will stand off as well."

"And the other?" McIntyre asked, not wishing to admit that he could no longer focus his eye through the eye-glass.

"It's that clipper ship which was so long in Honolulu harbor," he answered with envy. Then, like a pang of pain, he recalled his visit to *The Elizabeth* a few weeks before to seek a berth. Brutally he had been told by its captain that his experience was laughable. He had come back to the *Enda* gloomy and prepared for his second visit to the Columbia for Dexter Farman.

"Sir, she's ignoring our signal. She has not slacked a single of her thirty-five sails. Do you think it possible, with such a deep hull, for her to get over the sand bars?"

When the Captain didn't answer, Farman turned to find himself alone, except for a new helmsman. He mumbled to himself, "How do you get experience, if you get to talk to your captain only a minute a day?"

McIntyre was not thinking of Fallow or the ship. He was lucky he had made it to his cabin and his chair. He felt extremely cold and weary. Then the final pain ate from temple to temple and to the top of his skull.

The ocean waves had been steadily rising. *The Elizabeth* rose to the crest and then plunged downward to a bone-jarring momentary stop before starting another climb.

Murton Boddick had come onto the bridge an hour before sunset. He had not liked the darkening of the northwestern horizon. He had watched the cloud rise like an opaque wall, until it had devoured a third of the sky.

"Beg your pardon, Captain, but I don't like the look of the weather, what with Cape Disappointment dead ahead."

John Johns turned on him a piteous stare. "The waves may be a might high, Mr. Boddick, but there is no wind, no rain, or smell of storm. It is night coming on and little more."

Boddick bit his tongue. Since departing Cartagena he had

found himself under a captain who was hopelessly wrong-headed and crazy. They would have made Fort Vancouver in August, but the captain had cavorted away six weeks in the Sandwich Islands. Now he dared not protest too noisily that nightfall came from the east. But, as navigator, he would protest one point.

"Beg pardon again, sir, but you do have to consider the sand bars at the mouth of the Columbia. Those other two vessels must have tested them, for they are standing off for the night."

Captain Johns caught at Boddick's lapels and drew him close.

"I can read signals," he said scathingly. "I also see that they are a bark and a sloop. With our speed we will slice right through the sand and be in calm river waters before your mythical storm is upon us."

Boddick wrung his hands and then saw the cargomaster on the fantail. In his opinion Ian Llwellen was the only officer of merit on the ship.

"What do you make of it, Mister Llwellen?"

Ian frowned. "Never have seen anything like it. But then, this is my first trip into the Pacific."

"I've seen it off the China coast. It's a Pacific squall if I have ever seen one. They make an Atlantic squall look like a summer shower. He plans on taking her over the bar and not standing off."

"How bad is the bar?"

Boddick turned and darted a desperate look at the nearing coastline and the cliffs and rocky shoals of Cape Disappointment. "My fifth trip to this country, but that sand bar is never, and never will be the same, for any two ships. She can shift and change in a matter of moments, just like the wind and sand on the Sahara. My judgment is that the bark and sloop have been here before and are giving that spot respect until the morrow."

Ian sighed. "And you wish for me to alter the course of the captain's mind?" He laughed disdainfully. "I am not too much in his favor, after tossing those native girls off the ship."

Boddick grinned. "I've never thanked you for that. My wife has been with me at sea for three years, but she is still a woman and—" He stopped to look up as the cloud swept over them, bringing a shadowy darkness.

There was no warning, not even a bolt of lightning, but in the next second they were drenched from the downpour of the rain and had to grasp the rail to keep the fierce wind from taking them overboard.

"Now he *must* stand off!" Boddick screamed above the wind.

A blast came that took Ian's breath away. When he turned to answer the navigator, the man was gone. In his mind's eye he could see the man going over the rail without even the time to scream out. It would do him no good to warn that a man was overboard: the ocean was a boiling cauldron. He had to grab the safety rope on the railing to inch his way forward to the bridge.

Elizabeth Johns sat up abruptly in her bunk and felt herself pulled to its edge and crashed to the floor. She sat stunned, looking up to see the peculiar dance of D'Arcy Broome as she tried to come through the cabin door with Beth's dinner tray. Back and forth and up and down, D'Arcy tried to counterbalance the tray to keep the food from toppling. Then the ship plunged into a wave well, and that third motion was too much for the maid. The tray flew from her hands, hit the deck, and slid into a corner.

"Nothing toppled over," D'Arcy laughed hysterically.

"Did we hit something?"

"No, m'um. It's a storm that has the sea hissing like a whole stove of kettles gettin' ready for tea."

"Well," Beth said, picking herself up and sitting on the edge of the bunk. "Little we can do about a storm but ride it out. Seen *himself* today?"

D'Arcy groped her way upward, using the cabin door-frame. "Did. He asked how many more days you planned to stay in this cabin, in your bunk. I told him as long as he kept buggering around with whatever would spread their legs for him. Hit a red-hot coal there, m'um. He's been pushing the crew and ship hard all day to get to this Fort Vancouver. Do they got women there?"

"If not, he'll be lunatic to try you again."

"My legs are locked," the maid said indignantly. "Only one man I'd unlock 'em for. Gore, m'um, I swear that Ian Llwellen is a better-lookin' bloke now than we first sailed with him from England. Even Liza Boddick talks about him in that way, when her old man ain't a bad piece to feast your eyes on, either."

"D'Arcy, will you get out of here," Beth said in a scolding voice. "I want to be alone, so don't disturb me until breakfast. And close that cabin door tight!"

Beth sat and wrapped her arms about her breasts. Her teeth began to chatter, but it had nothing to do with the gossamer-thin negligee she was wearing. It was cold fury and hurt. It had been maddening having Ian so close again and not being able to even talk with him. In six months she had been close to him only once, riding in the same longboat as they were rowed into the Honolulu dock. But her husband had seen it and it had started him on a binge of debauchery that would have Honolulu talking for years. All at once she began to cry. She wept and blubbered like a child, catching her breath and sobbing, "Oh, if only I had done something wrong! I almost wish Ian would have taken me off to one of those lagoons. I bet he would be fascinating to be with!" She was quiet for awhile and started on another thought. "I know that Francis is somewhere in this part of the country. I must find someone at this Fort Vancouver who can take me to him. Francis will know what to do. Francis will help me get away from this beast. I can't go on living this way. It's fine in London, where there are things to do and people to divert my mind. Right now I am in a living hell."

A convulsive jerk nearly toppled her from the bunk again. She crawled under the covers and put a pillow over her head.

Eliza Boddick opened her cabin door to find a startled pair of eyes and a face white about the nostrils.

"D'Arcy, luv, come in."

"Awfully sorry," the girl mumbled, "but I couldn't stay alone a moment longer."

"No one likes to listen to a storm alone. The sounds bring about too many vivid thoughts, which really aren't true. I was sitting here sewing on my hats and thought sure I had heard Murton calling my name. Gore, he's probably trying to work out a course to get us out of this mess."

"You sure do make fine hats, Liza."

"Get on with you. I make 'em just for meself and to get a laugh out of me Murton. Ain't sayin' I'm ashamed of being a big girl, luv, but it does take some captains back a bit to see me waltz up their gangplank wearing a hat that is nearly as wide as my Murton is tall."

D'Arcy giggled. It had also amazed her when she saw the couple come onboard in Cartagena. At twenty-three, Eliza was a formidably built woman, with a commanding bust and a built-in bustle to match. At six-foot-two inches, with hats that towered several inches higher, she seemed to dwarf the five-foot-five, barrel-chested Murton Boddick, who was ten years her senior.

Liza's beauty lay in her sharp wit, sparkling smile, and eyes that were always dancing. Without them she would have been rather man-handsome plain. Her courage lay in having survived an upbringing in a London orphanage and street life without turning to prostitution. At sixteen she became an apprentice in a millinery shop and learned that her talent was in hats. Murton Boddick was a naval navigator who came to the shop to pick up a hat ordered by his mother. They were married a week later and she had waited until she could go to sea with him. She felt she had learned as much about the sea in three years as she already knew about hats.

At that moment she did not like what she was hearing, but kept her face calm. In such a storm they should have been slacking off on the sails. Murton had told her that they would see landfall before sundown, but she had felt no course change. And now, above, she heard the squeal of a winch starting to lower a long boat. She knew that her husband would not come for her, that was their pact. If trouble came, he would be busy with the ship and couldn't look out after her. But he had taught her what to listen for and what to do.

Over the keening wind she heard the foghorn warning from two other ships. Calmly, she opened a sea chest and took out a couple of winter coats.

"D'Arcy," she said quietly, "put this on. I fear the ship might be in trouble and it will be a might chilly in the longboat. Come."

D'Arcy was used to taking instructions, but stopped in the passageway.

"Oh, I must go for Beth."

"Her cabin is too far aft, girl. We are right here at the ladderwell. If she isn't on deck, we'll send a sailor for her."

Sailors were very hard to find. They were either below deck, to keep out of the storm, hiding in corners on deck, or cowering away from the near mutiny taking place on the bridge.

John Johns had refused to listen to Ian. He kept the helmsman steering for the mouth of the Columbia, although each slow plunge would take her off course and he would have to fight the wheel to get her back. The rain swept over her like she was a part of the sea. It was like being sucked through a tunnel by a flood.

"Johns," Ian screamed, his hat long since blown away. "If you crash this ship, I'll get those captains to testify at your trial. Turn back man! Turn back! Or—"

"Give up my command to someone who will?" Johns shouted. Even though the storm had taken away some of their speed, they were still at ten to twelve knots. "Too late! Here we go in and over!"

The ghostly images of land passing on each side gave the illusion that they were flying along. But below, Ian heard a sound that made him sick. The bow was beginning to eat through water growing heavy with silt. Then she hit the sand bar as though slamming into a brick wall. The hull timbers began to scream and pop their wooden rivets from the pressure. The full sails fought to drive her even farther forward. The current of the river fought to move the object out of its way. Unable to be of use, the sails began to rip and tatter, and then flapped and caught on the forward spars. This added force cracked the main mast, and like a felled timber it cut through the spars of the forward mast and crashed down with such weight that it ripped through the deck and opened a gaping hole in the starboard side of the bow.

The water came rushing into the forward hold, soaking the thousand bags of coffee beans and making them heavier. The water forged on to the next hold and the ship began to list to starboard.

The sailors began to panic and fight over the longboats. From belowdecks came the screams of those caught by the onrushing water.

Liza Boddick pulled a benumbed D'Arcy along to where she had heard the winch lowering the boat. Whichever sailor had thought of making his escape had put down a rope ladder and then gone back for his gear. She was not going to wait for him. D'Arcy was too frozen with fear to think. Liza pushed her down the ladder and followed. Then she pushed off from the listing side of the ship. If it rolled over or sank, she did not want to be pulled down with it.

The sails of the aft mast, as though angry at being left out of the tragedy, caught the changing wind and tried to twist the ship to port. The bow was stuck so deep in the sand bar it would not give. The gaping hole where the main mast had stood weakened the midships. With a rumbling like a growing thunderstorm the ship began to split in two, the stern listing farther and farther to its side, while the aft sails took that section and began to spin it around back toward the sea.

Ian was hoarse from shouting down orders from the bridge, orders that were only half obeyed. Captain John Johns stood with a sickly grin on his face. In his mind there had been a hope to save the vessel and crew, right up until the actual moment she had been split asunder. Now he walked down the stairs from the bridge to the main deck and out to the jagged edge, as if to inspect the damage. But he did not stop; he stepped right off into nothingness and disappeared down into the tumbling cargo in the water.

Ian's breath was driven back into his throat. There was no longer any need for orders for this half of the ship and the other half was beginning to slowly sink. The four longboats, which had been winched down, held less than a dozen survivors. He crawled up to the railing. His only hope for survival was to dive into the river and pray that he could fight back up out of the current.

It was an excellent dive, but it took him too deep. Although a strong swimmer, he had to work with every ounce of his energy to break the surface. Exhausted, his lungs near bursting, he relaxed and let the current carry him along.

"There's one!" he heard a female voice call. He lifted his head and saw an offered oar. He grabbed ahold and let them pull him to the side of the longboat.

"Luv-a-mercy," Liza gasped. "It's Mr. Llwellen."

She looked down and read his eyes. She didn't flinch, but knew she was never to see her Murton again.

Ian hung on the edge of the boat and looked in. Liza had already pulled four other sailors out of the water, and D'Arcy sat at the tiller about ready to break into a fit of hysteria.

"Mrs. Johns?" he wheezed. "Is she in one of the other boats?"

"Don't know," D'Arcy suddenly wailed. "I think she's still in her cabin!"

They were less than a hundred yards from the aft section. It was fighting hard to stay afloat but slowly losing ground. He looked beyond the wreckage. The yellow gleam of a masthead light was bobbing closer and closer.

"Row toward that light, Mrs. Boddick. Their sailors will be fresh and can come back for me. If the aft goes down, don't even bother, she'll crack like an egg from the water pressure inside."

He swam away. From some deep reserve came a new strength. His strokes became powerful, and despite his boots, he was able to kick with ease. In five minutes he was hanging onto a jagged hull beam and determining his best way to enter and climb up to the first deck. He could see into the aft hold and saw what was giving her a fighting chance.

The sugar was dissolving and floating out, and the rum barrels were floating under the third-deck flooring as though they were empty and not two hundred pounds each.

Then he became conscious of silence. It was bizarre. The squall had vanished as quickly as it had arrived. It had done its vengeful worst. He fought down the impulse to think of how many of the crew of eighty-two were part of the silent sea. Nor did he have any assurance he would find Beth alive, but look he must.

He used the jagged hull beams as a ladder to gain access to the third deck. Going aft he was appalled by the destruction caused by the storm. He took the ladder to the second deck, which brought him out near the door to the captain's cabin.

His heart sank, seeing the cabin door swinging back and forth with the sway of the half-ship. With trepidation he approached and entered, fearing that Beth had departed and was now lost forever.

The pungent odor of spilt oil from the wall lamps enveloped the chamber. A candle stub, on the night table, gave a faint glimmer to show that not even the sacred chamber of John Johns had escaped destruction. It was as though a naughty child's hand had entered the room of a doll house and stirred everything about.

Then, his worst fears were realized. Crumpled in a corner was the twisted body of Elizabeth Johns. His heart beating a hollow tattoo, he knelt and reached out for a pale hand and wrist.

Tears sprang to his eyes as he felt a weak but steady pulse. Gingerly, he straightened out her limbs, feeling and looking for broken bones. Looking about, he saw that the mattress had been tossed from the bunk but he was not going to take time to lift it back up. He picked Elizabeth up from the deck and transferred her to the mattress. On the back of the skull he felt a knot, where her head had crashed into the bulkhead. He knew it would be near impossible to get her topside in this state. He began to rub her cold hands with his own, to circulate the blood and bring her around.

He sat on the edge of the mattress and stared at her beautiful body in the gossamer fabric, a sight he had dreamed about for years. Now that the initial violence of the past two hours was over, he felt little of anything except a paralyzing numbness. He was incapable of thought, oblivious to any emotion.

From far off he heard a name whispered. He pulled himself back to reality and looked down. Beth's face was white and her green eyes frantic. But the fact that she was awake and alive gave him acute pleasure. Yet for the moment he could not speak.

She saw at once that he was soaking wet. She said, unsteadily, "Are we leaving the ship?"

He stood up without saying anything. Coming out of his stupor he had felt something, even through the mattress. Water lapping against the second-deck flooring. They were sinking at a much faster pace.

Beth blinked. For the first time, in the dim candle glow, she realized it was not her husband who had come to rescue her. She bit her lip and tried to keep her voice level. "Why you, Ian? Where is my husband?"

"He's dead!" he said brutally. "He wrecked the ship trying to take her over the bar and then played the coward's game by taking his own life."

Grief would come later. All Beth could feel at the moment was anger at his brutal way of telling her. She used every bit of her strength to rise. She wanted to beat on him with her fists and force him to say it was a lie. When she raised a hand to slap him, Ian grabbed both of her wrists and pulled her close. His brutality had paid off. He had her on her feet and fighting mad. Now she could help with her own survival.

"You can hate me later," he snarled. "Now we only have minutes to get off this ship before it sinks."

"Then get your filthy hands off me," she hissed. "I've got to get dressed."

Despite the desperate situation, Ian laughed. "You're not going to Mayfair, Beth. We've got to go—"

He never got to finish. The super structure of the aft mast and spars was too great a weight for even the water-filled lower decks to keep straight. In a matter of seconds it fell to the starboard, shearing off as it scraped the rocky sandbar ridge, leaving only the hull exposed above the water line. Then, the hull, too, began to sink.

Beth clung to Ian, in those desperate seconds, as they were tumbled from bulkhead to the ceiling. The dim candle spluttered in its uncommon upside-down position, because like most things on the ship, the candlestick was bolted to the nightstand and the nightstand bolted to the bulkhead. Bunk, desk, sea-chest, and washstand were suspended above them. Everything that had been loose was scattered about them on the flat surface of the ceiling.

Ian let the breath out of his lungs slowly, then reached out to retrieve a loose, fresh candle and light it on one of the final sputters of the wick being drowned in its own dripping wax. He stuck it into the small loaf of bread from Beth's uneaten dinner.

A look of surprise replaced the bewilderment on Beth's face. She crawled back onto the mattress and let out an inane giggle. "I think we are already dead and this is our hell. I am left to stare at a bunk I shared with a man I never really knew or loved. What are you doing? Where are you going?"

Ian had crawled over to the outside bulkhead, peered out the porthole, and then closed the metal covering. Sitting with his back against the bulkhead he had then taken off his Wellington boots.

"All I can see out the porthole is black water. Still, we have no water seeping in about us. We must be in an open air pocket. It's not hell, yet, but soon could be."

He stood and removed his uniform coat, shirt, and peeled down the skintight trousers until he was in just his under-britches.

Beth had started to look away, but had been fascinated to find that he was even more muscular than he had ever appeared in full clothing.

"The slant of the ceiling suggests that we may be near the water surface. With luck I should be able to swim down to the main deck and out to the surface to bring rescue."

Her desire to get even for his brutality was gone. Her fear remained. "I don't want to be left alone," she quavered.

"I didn't go to the trouble to come for you only to let you perish now."

Before she could protest further, he fought to get the upside-down cabin door open and stepped out onto the ceiling of the passageway. It was like entering a black hole. He inched along, keeping a guiding hand on the bulkhead and then stopped short. The bottoms of his feet had come in contact with icy water. He waited until it had covered his toes and then he returned to the cabin and firmly closed the watertight door.

Beth knew without being told that he had found no escape. She burrowed into his arms and held him tightly.

"Sorry, Beth."

She looked up and her green eyes turned soft. "After all these years you've finally gotten up the courage to call me Beth."

She was so beautiful that Ian felt ashamed at how he had treated her. He bent and kissed her gently on the cheek and she didn't move a muscle. Shaking all over, he tasted of her lips and felt her arms encircle his neck and return the kiss.

"Let's go back to the mattress," Beth whispered with meaning emphasis.

He obeyed like a lovesick boy. Love? It was a word that did not set well with him. But for five years he had known that he loved her with a force so strong that everything else in life paled by comparison. The barrier of a husband had done little to daunt his thoughts of her. The fact that she was the wife of John Johns had kept him from killing the man upon learning he was responsible for the attack on the *Rose Ann* which had left him with a scarred face. He knew that his revenge would have brought her contempt and he would have lost her forever. Now that Johns was dead, he could win her for his own, even if it might be for only a few minutes.

Beth gave off a throaty, suggestive laugh. "Your under-britches are still wet. I don't want a soggy mattress!"

He peeled them off and stretched out on the mattress.

"I hope his spirit is watching," she said bitterly. "He never believed that we had not had an affair."

In a single motion she let the gossamer fall from her body and knelt on the mattress. Her voluptuous breasts were at Ian's eye level.

She shivered as his fingers traced the rim of each ivory treasure. He leaned forward before the dream might fade. His lips touched the taught nipple with a kiss and then his tongue circled it again and again as his hands kneaded the pliant breasts.

"I knew you'd teach me new feelings," she whispered, writhing and moaning. She let herself fall backward as his mouth moved from nipple to nipple until they were stone hard.

Her words encouraged him to continue her newfound sensation. He kissed and tongued the cleavage, made patterns on her belly, and was drawn to the musty aroma of the strawberry-blonde forest. It tickled her, but he probed until his tongue found the nether lips.

"I don't know the words," she panted, "but—"

She thrust her legs apart and he understood. Never having known foreplay, he had overly excited her. He crawled between her lithe legs. He looked down and saw a Beth he had never seen before. Her face was aglow with the fascination that she was about to experience the first meaningful female-male communion of her life. He could feel her heat of desire as he settled on her, and slipped gently into a euphoric cavern as her pelvic muscles tightened and relaxed and tightened again.

He wanted to plunge, as he had done with countless, nameless women, but Beth was reliving a dream. Only to herself had she admitted that during her wanton, lusty night in the harbor of Cartagena, she had thought of Ian Llwellen, while accepting John Johns. Now she wanted to feel the real man enter inch by swollen inch to produce real ardor and not a dream.

"I'm ready!" she panted, clasping his butt cheeks and pulling him to her so tightly that he could feel his sac touch her buttocks. Mentally, they locked into an equal rhythm that stoked her sexual inferno.

Her eyes flared, but she did not cry out as she rose to a

shuddering climax. Her silence was from habit, never wishing to give John Johns the knowledge that he might have pleased her. Nor had she ever been the first to climax. She began to kiss Ian passionately to bring him to an equal point of exhilaration. Her hands kneaded his shoulders and back until his muscular form quivered, his every sinew as tight as steel, his breathing heavy with five years of waiting for this intoxicating moment of pure satisfaction.

He started to roll away when their airtight world was intruded upon.

They had not heard the heavy axes cut a hole through the hull into the ballast hold. Now the axes were chopping away a section of a beam, and crowbars were prying off the planks of the flooring to the captain's cabin.

It meant rescue, but also a few moments of desperate embarrassment. Ian's clothing was too wet to put on without much difficulty. Beth searched the ceiling for suitable garments that had fallen out of the seachest.

While Ian was directing the sailors as to which planks to remove, Beth reached up and opened a bottom drawer to her husband's desk. She had learned, by secretly watching, how to press the back panel to spring open the door to his money vault. In Cartagena, Johns had been dead broke and borrowing heavily from the ship's account for his personal use. In a drunken stupor he'd admitted to her that the only way he had been able to support his expensive cavorting life in Honolulu had been to sell the rum, cask by cask, and fill the cargo space with empty barrels. The evidence was gone, the theft would never be discovered, but she was not about to start off her widowhood as a pauper. She put four heavy bags of gold coins into her pantaloons and felt justified.

Ian chided himself as he climbed up through the hold to the hole in the hull. He had forgotten about the small ballast hold under the captain's cabin, half filled with roped-together circles of cork. He was grateful it had saved his life.

Onboard the *Enda* Beth was spirited away by Liza Boddick and D'Arcy Broome. Being of a near size, Ian was taken by Henry Fallow to his quarters for a change of clothes.

"The Captain is dead," Fallow said.

"I know," Ian said, "I saw him go over the side."

"No, sir, I mean our captain. Captain McIntyre. Died sitting in his chair, after his watch. So, I was wondering, sir, as a senior officer, will you be taking command to see us in?"

"When did you take your watch, Mr. Fallow?"

"Eighteen bells, sir."

"Well, if you are capable to have properly stood this ship off, to have saved it in the storm and directed our rescue operation, then you are capable of taking her in. Your navigator will give you help."

Fallow scoffed and his gloomy face returned. "Cap and I were our own navigators and everything else. It's only a crew of twenty and four, sir."

"Who's the owner?"

"It's registered as Farman, Pettygrove, and Lovejoy."

Ian smiled to himself. He had totally forgotten about Francis Pettygrove and Asa Lovejoy and their dinner talk of coming to Oregon. He recalled a sailor's rumor that Francis had been all but kicked out of the family, but as he was not one of George Pettygrove's favorite captains, he had never pursued the rumor.

It would be interesting to see how they had fared.

CHAPTER

☆ **12** ☆

"Katoro, these lines look as though they were laid out by a drunken man."

Katoro bowed his head, and nodded miserably.

"I may be Kanaka," he whispered, "but still a man with feelings. Mr. Brown does not like me or my corrections. When I told him he had started too far north, he sent me away."

"How far north?"

"He's got The Clearing right in the middle of your grid plans. Said you were a fool, and that the land there was too valuable to be left to 'injuns' and the like."

Francis was beyond anger. He had been spending most of the last few days at the site to escape the growing pettiness in Oregon City. Once he had been content to think of his Portland being a year or two into the future. Now, he was determined it would be established in the new year. With that in mind he had secured the services of the HBC wharf-master, John Waymire, to begin selecting the proper trees for pilings. Kenwa, needing money for another scow, had begun to move the lumber for the warehouse to the site. To stave off the tart tongue of his wife, Francis had bought a lot from John McLoughlin for the site of a new church and quietly commissioned John Morrison to begin designing a house for Sophia in Portland. On one thing Francis could count his blessings. The day after the arrival of the wagon train he had Mick Myers firmly in place as the clerk of the Oregon City store. It gave him breathing space to spend time at the townsite.

"Are you," Francis asked Katoro earnestly, "capable of correcting such a gross error?"

"Yes, but what will Mr. Brown say?"

"I don't give a damn! I'm just plain filled up with his carping, through his wife, that I am cheating him out of a fair fee. If I learn he has done this shoddy work out of spite, I'll pay the fare for a proper surveyor to come out from New England."

He uttered the threat so emphatically that Katoro knew he was serious. He also knew there would be trouble later in the day when Tom Brown came back from laying out farms in the Tualatin Valley for some of the new arrivals. Then a sight startled him. Coming past Swan Island was a bark in full sail.

"It's the *Enda*," Francis cried merrily. "I'll row out to greet her. Tell Kenwa to join me when he gets here with the scow."

Katoro nodded and prayed that the ship from Havaiki was not bringing any more Kanaka. His first boys were quite content with their lives, but this last group had been too long on the streets of Honolulu. They were, in Francis's words, "more shirkers than workers," and Katoro would be happy being rid of them.

Francis's merry spirit turned dismal five minutes after climbing onto the deck of the *Enda*.

"What a needless loss," he said sadly. "Still, I am grateful for the lives saved. It is very good to see you again, Ian."

"And what about me?" a voice said behind him.

"Oh, Bethy!" he cried, taking her into his arms for a hug and then twirling her around and around as he laughed. Then he put her down and held her at arm's length.

"Beth, though you look like an angel, why, every time we meet, are you wearing some silly costume?"

She twirled around. "This, dear cousin, is called 'ensemble for a shipwrecked widow.'"

The casual manner in which she had connected her new status shocked Francis. She saw the look and put her hands on his bearded jaws.

"I always said you were a good-looking young man, Francis, but the beard makes you devilishly handsome." Then she looked deep into his gray eyes. "I have no tears to shed for him, Francis. I can't playact and be the hypocrite."

Ian Llwellen held his silence. Either she was playacting now, for the benefit of Francis Pettygrove, or D'Arcy had been lying to him when he had tried to see Beth and had been told that she was too griefstricken to see anyone.

It wasn't grief that kept Beth chattering away. It was guilt, and fear, that Francis would see right through her and know that she had gone to bed with another man with her husband less than two hours dead. She had been afraid to see Ian, terrified of her emotions if left alone with him. During the night it had slowly started to sink in that John Johns was dead and Ian was within calling range of her voice. By dawn she had come to a startling discovery. To steal a casual glance at him, or dream about him, had been a dangerous and fascinating game. Last night the game had become a reality, but with it had come a truth. Ian Llwellen was in love with her, but her feelings were still stuck on fascination. She dared not look at him, or be alone with him, until she had her emotions under control.

"But where do you live? I see only one cabin."

"Oregon City is still fifteen miles upriver. I'm afraid I have no Residency House to offer you, but Sidney Moss has converted his home into a proper hotel. Here is Kenwa. He will take you, Ian, and the ladies along, while I see to the cargo with Henry Fallow."

"Oh, Francis," she teased, "what a divine man. I think I'm in love."

"Get on with you," he laughed. "This is a happily married man, so put your fangs back in."

Then he frowned thoughtfully. It had been so natural to kid her right back. He now feared she was still in shock and realization would dawn when she was on solid ground.

"D'Arcy, my store is right at the wharf where you will land. Be a good girl and tell my wife Sophia that we will be five extra for dinner."

Then he turned to Eliza Boddick. "We will get word to the

Tucker Line as soon as possible, Mrs. Boddick, to arrange transportation back to England for you."

"Very kind of you, sor."

"Francis," Ian said, pulling him to the side. "Might I wait and return with you?"

Francis hesitated, suddenly recalling Ian's former interest in Elizabeth. If the naval officer wished a conversation on that topic, Francis felt ill-prepared to handle it. "If you wish, but why?"

Ian grinned. "You may have noticed how quiet Fallow was when I gave you the report on the wreck. He's scared to death, both of you and his inexperience. I stood on the bridge with him while he brought the *Enda* over the bar and up the river. Damn fine officer. Made the decision on his own to come up the Willamette."

Francis laughed. "I've never considered myself a frightening figure. Please then, Ian, stay."

Francis tried not to intimidate Fallow, but certain aspects of the cargo Francis strongly questioned and Henry took it personally.

"Dimity? Calico? Crepe? Dexter has lost his mind! It will take me a lifetime to sell that many bolts of cloth. Raffia? What in the hell am I supposed to do with two dozen bales of raffia? And what in the hell *is* raffia?"

Henry Fallow gulped and his gloomy face grew longer. "It's a fiber from the palm leaves, sir. It was ordered by a man in Linn City, according to Captain McIntyre's manifest."

"Manifest?" Francis scoffed. "I'm hardly able to read half of this hen scratching. This is the last time this ship sails without a proper cargomaster. Look at this! What does 'P.Press' mean?"

Surprisingly, Fallow answered without hesitation. "That is my entry, Mr. Pettygrove. Mr. Farman brought the printing press out just before we sailed. It was a hell of a job getting it and everything that went with it into the hold."

Francis was aghast. "Printing press? What does Dexter expect me to do with a printing press?"

"Thought you could sell it for a profit, Mr. Pettygrove. It was returned from Yerba Buena, for shipment back to New

York, because the fonts were in English and not Spanish. Mr. Farman said to tell you that he only had to trade fifty dollars' worth of your wheat for it."

"Ian," Francis smirked, "I think it is time to head for home, before I uncover any more surprises from my Honolulu connection. Mr. Fallow, you have been to Oregon City before, but by bateau. Allow a little over an hour for six of your rowers to get your longboat there by dinner at six o'clock."

"Me, sir?"

"You, sir. You will need to start calculating the lumber, wheat, and salmon for your return trip."

Ian was impressed with Francis's ability with a paddle and canoe. He soon picked up the knack, so they could paddle in unison.

"I like what you said about a cargomaster for that ship, but are you aware that Farman sent them out with just two officers and a very short crew?"

"I was picking that up from things Fallow did not say. Dexter is not naval-minded, Ian. We know that the cargo means nothing, unless you have the proper ship, men, and officers to deliver it. I didn't even know this McIntyre or that the other captain was gone. Is Fallow worthy of the captaincy?"

"Worthy? Twelve hours on and twelve hours off makes a man worthy. Capable, I have already said. But he needs a few tours under a seasoned captain to bolster his knowledge and give him confidence."

Francis laughed. "Applying for a berth, Mr. Llwellen?"

"Yes," Ian said simply.

Francis thought he was kidding and laughed.

"I'm most serious," Ian said, after a long pause. "When we came over the bar this morning, the night and the tide had floated what was left of *The Elizabeth* away. As if she had never been. David Tucker wanted me on this voyage so I could see how a clipper ship would take to such a long voyage. She was beautiful, her master was not. I lowered myself to be cargomaster, so I would stand in his favor to skipper the next clipper to taste the salt. Francis, you know the company and your father. I will never get another command from them, because I will be suspect for not wresting the command from him and saving the ship. Damn, I tried, but everyone who could back up my version is dead. If I'm going to be on the beach, it might as well be here."

"You will never be on the beach as long as I am around, Captain Llwellen."

As Francis washed up at the kitchen washstand, Sophia babbled on about her very disconcerting day. Because she was not carping and her tongue was not tart, he gave her the benefit of his ear.

"My lands, what a shock," she said, basting the roast in the wood stove oven. "Imagine that maid and your cousin all the way here from London. Poor dears losing everything in the shipwreck!"

At least I am spared her thoughts on Captain John Johns, Francis thought.

"Five extra for dinner did give me a moment of concern," she went right on, "because I took your advice, Francis, and asked Anita Shamir over to make my apology. It seemed only proper to include her, Mick, and Asa with the Fultons for this evening."

"Sorry," he said, with deep-rooted irony. "I'd forgotten all about the minister and his wife."

Sophia had started to roll out the biscuit dough for cutting. "No need to feel sorry, Francis Pettygrove. Annie Fulton came waltzing in here while I was having my chat with Anita, and blithely announced that they had erred and had a previous dinner engagement in Linn City with Mr. Moore. Previous, my grandmother's petticoat! Good thing I saved the news about the lot until this evening. We'll still be ten. I certainly hope no one will mind eating off their laps."

"Don't fret, my love. Is that quiet I hear? Where are the children?"

Sophia sighed, putting the biscuits in the warming oven to rise. "Marsha was a dear and took them down to her kitchen. Francis, the girl you hired off the wagon train got to the point where she was crying more than Ellen. I let her go back to her people. I will not have another Kanaka girl in the house—" She stopped, gasped, and then laughed. "Francis, Beth once kidded me about outhouses. What will she think when that is all we have to offer here?"

Francis smiled to himself. It had finally dawned on him that Sophia was nervous, and yet excited, over the sudden appearance of Elizabeth, someone of the "back home social standing" she could communicate with.

"Mick, I am not going upstairs for dinner when you close the store. I've already told Mr. Moss that I will take supper at the hotel."

"Anita, I think you are being overly sensitive."

Her brown eyes flashed and a pout had replaced her usual smile. "*That* woman had no regard for my feelings, sensitive or not. I regard what she said as even ruder than our first day here. I am no nursemaid, Mick Myers, and she all but inferred that was all I would be capable of doing in this town. She even acted like Lady Bountiful in offering me fifty cents a day, room and board. Proper work for a widow, she called it. *A dank, nit!*"

Mick knew she was upset when she spoke in Yiddish.

"Hello, children," Asa bubbled, coming into the store. "I could smell that roast all the way next door. Anita, I talked with Elvira Waller, as you asked. If she gets five more students from the in-close farmers, she'll be happy to have you as an extra teacher."

"Thank you, Asa," she grinned, giving him a hug. "Now I can go to dinner and not feel like I am being pressured into something I do not want."

Mick was hurt that Anita had not consulted him on the matter. In St. Louis and Independence he had been her only friend. On the wagon train, and the few days in Oregon City, the warm charm of her youth in New York was returning and no one was a stranger.

"I hear you down there, Asa Lovejoy," Francis called. "Bring them up! Mick will close the store after everyone has arrived."

Mick held Asa back, as Anita started up the stairs. "Asa, does anyone but you know of my marital status?"

"No, except Anita."

"Good. Please keep it that way."

Asa shrugged, but did not agree. He liked each of them, and had not been fond of either Liddy Myers or Moshe Shamir. But Mick was still married and Asa couldn't forget it.

Henry Fallow waited at the wharf until he saw the approach of Ian Llwellen and then reluctantly joined him to enter for dinner.

Three women stood for a few minutes outside the store in deep conversation. Mick recognized D'Arcy Broome, who had brought the message to Sophia. Having overheard that conversation, he knew at once that the beautiful woman was Francis Pettygrove's cousin, and that the extremely tall woman was the navigator's widow who had saved the life of D'Arcy and Ian Llwellen.

"D'Arcy," Beth snapped, "stop being a little prig!"

"Know why I was invited, m'um, and I'll not be bartered over like I was one of Adriana Cosbie's domestics again!"

"Hush!" Liza Boddick warned. "This berg is so small and quiet they'll hear you upstairs. Even though the women offered you a nursemaid job is no reason she is going to steal you away from Mrs. Johns. Besides, D'Arcy, you and me ain't citizens. We belong to Queen Vicky. I'm takin' meself in now."

"M'um," D'Arcy cried. "I'll stay with you, even though you can't pay me anymore."

"Dry your foolish eyes," Beth sighed. "I haven't figured out what to do with myself, let alone you."

"Mrs. Johns," Liza cried, as they came in the door, "we have stumbled into civilization. Just look at this selection of bolt goods, buttons, and hooks. Tomorrow, Eliza Boddick will put her sewing fingers back to work for a proper outfit for you."

As Beth feared, Sophia turned their reunion into a tearful event, although the tears were all on the part of Sophia and seemed somewhat false.

"Oh, my dear cousin, what a horrible loss."

Beth accepted the hug, but not the false pity. "Hardly a full loss, dear Sophia. I've learned that Liza is a milliner and your store has bolts of goods."

Sophia was startled and then recalled that Francis said she was still in a state of shock.

Francis, seeing the look on his wife's face, jumped in before a dead silence could develop.

"You haven't seen anything yet. The *Enda* has bolts and bolts of dimity, calico, and crepe."

"Crepe!" Liza enthused. "Exactly what I need!"

"No crepe for me, Liza. Elizabeth Pettygrove Johns refuses to go into widow's weeds at age twenty-three!"

"Not for you, luvy. Need it fer me children." Liza giggled. From such a large woman it was more like a bad case of hiccups. "Me hats are me children and I lost them all."

She fell silent, but before she could dwell on the loss of her husband, Francis dove in again.

"Crepe wasn't the only unusual thing on the shipment. Sophia, can you believe this—Dexter has sent me a printing press! Fonts, tins of ink, and reams of newsprint. Whatever shall I do with it?"

"Raise more daughters," Anita laughed, and they all looked at her strangely. "I'm sorry, but it is an old joke in our family. My father was not only a rabbi but also editor of the *Hebrew News*. My sisters and I were all trained to handset the type. Each time a matchmaker would marry off one of my older sisters, Papa would say it was time to start raising another daughter."

Sophia did not laugh at the story. Right now she was fuming at Asa Lovejoy, whom she felt had snatched a potential nursemaid right out from under her. But the biggest insult was that Elvira Waller would gain her as a schoolteacher.

"Dinner is ready," she announced. "I am sorry that you will have to help yourselves, but I am temporarily without help."

D'Arcy felt the sting of the message, but Liza pinched her to silence, quietly urging her to get in line.

There was a loud banging at the back porch door. Francis went, so that Sophia could see to the guests.

The moment Francis opened the door, Tom Brown stuck in a booted foot so it could not be closed in his face. He was drunk, belligerently drunk.

"Want every cent you owe me, Pettygrove," he sneered.

"I am entertaining, Tom," Francis said, keeping his temper. "I will discuss this with you in the morning."

"Like hell! I ain't one of your Kanaka boys you can order around. No man has a right to change my work and cheat me!"

Francis lowered his voice until it was thin and brittle. "And no man has a right to force himself on my privacy, give me shoddy work, or change my plans without my authority. As for pay, Mr. Brown, you are already overdrawn on the trade books. You have done your last day's work for me, so get your foot out of my door before I'm tempted to chop it off with my wood axe!"

Brown stepped back, blinked, and then glared. "You and your 'stumptown' ain't heard the last of me!"

Francis closed the door, composed himself, and turned to get a plate of food. He hated the fact that he had been shaking, as he had shook in fighting with his father. He loathed bullheaded men who could never see when they were in the wrong.

"That was most interesting," Henry Fallow said shyly, timidly taking a seat on the parlor floor next to Anita Shamir. "It certainly brought back a memory, even though my father had all boys to help run his print shop in Concord."

"Then how did you become a sailor?"

"Too many brothers. Too small a print shop. Sea life seemed glamorous . . . then."

"There's room here," Anita called to Francis as he came from the dining room.

"My next house will seat twelve at the table," he chuckled, putting Brown out of his mind. The parlor was crowded, but he noted that no one seemed to mind. Even Sophia seemed to be animated, talking with Ian and Beth. Asa, surprisingly, was keeping Liza and D'Arcy well entertained. Only Mick seemed glum that Anita had let Henry Fallow sit down with them and now his boss.

"Have you plans for the press and materials, Mr. Pettygrove?" Anita asked, after she had let him eat for a spell.

"Not really."

"Would you consider a trade for furs?"

"Anita," Mick scoffed. "What would you do with a press?"

Her eyes sparkled and a devilish grin came to her lips. "Start a newspaper, what else? If you can handset Hebrew characters, you can handset English."

"That you could do," Henry agreed, "like my mother. But it takes muscle to put those heavy flats into the press and strength to lever down the wooden platen."

Anita looked at him with warm encouragement. "It sounds like it is time for you to come home from the sea, Henry Fallow."

Henry blushed and looked at Francis. "She might be right, sir. I was going to talk to you before we sailed, to express my thanks, but offer my resignation. I'm twenty-five, been at sea for five of those years, and know little more than when I started. Of course, I'll want to help get the *Enda* back to Honolulu."

Ian had heard part of the conversation, going to get himself a second plate. He winked at Francis.

"Better to grab him for what he is good at, rather than put in time training him and losing him."

"It is utterly ridiculous!" Mick flared. "A woman running a newspaper!"

"Better than being a school marm," Sophia gloated.

"And I shall be your first paid advertisement," Liza announced.

"For what?" Beth queried.

"Mr. Lovejoy and I have been talking," Liza beamed. "I've got nothing to return to England for, so why not open a hat and dress shop?"

The clanging of the church bell broke off the conversation.

"That's also our fire bell," Francis exclaimed, rushing to a window. "Lord, Asa! It's the new house Katoro just completed. Mick, get every bucket in the store! It's close enough to the river to form a brigade!"

Ian and Henry didn't need to be asked for their help, and raced down the stairs after Mick. Asa and Francis sped out the back door to round up the Kanaka boys.

It was futile, from the first, to try and save Katoro's house. Even before the first bucket of water was dipped from the river, the four outside walls were an inferno.

"Wet down the buildings on either side!" Asa directed. "George, take a group of men and work on the houses to the left. Francis, Kenwa's house is too close. The paint is warping! More water! Matoa! Keep the Kanaka boys putting water on the burning building. We've got to cool her down! You boys! If you see a shingle fly, run after it and stomp it out. Tama! Take Pelani to my house. Does no good for her to stand and watch this! Kenwa! To be on the safe side, remove your valuables!"

It took an hour before the structure was reduced to hissing embers. Francis was disgusted that Tom Brown had come for a few moments, grinned at the blazing flames, and departed without helping. The *Enda* sailors were more help than some locals, when they saw it was Katoro's house. The women started arriving with kettles of coffee and tin cups. The water brigade continued. They were surrounded by forests and it had been a dry fall. Every last spark would be drowned to ensure they wouldn't wake up to a forest fire.

"It was so sudden," Katoro told Francis and Asa. "Pelani has been real sick lately with the baby. I fed her some soup and we went to bed at sundown. I woke to smoke and fire everywhere. I tried to get out the door, but I guess a burning log had already fallen across it. I had to break out a window to get Pelani out."

"Can I see you three over here," George Abernethy called, his brow deeply furrowed. He had been digging in the ashes to uncover any glowing embers. "Katoro, what fuel do you use to light your lamps and to cook with?"

Katoro looked at him strangely. "Kenwa taught me how to make candle bowls from beeswax. Only wood in the fireplace, made by the stone mason, Mr. Moss. But the fire was almost out when I went to bed."

"Made any enemies lately?" Abernethy asked pointedly.

"No, not that I—" he stopped and turned to Francis. "I haven't had a chance to tell you, but when Mr. Brown came back to the townsite he got real angry seeing me redoing the stacking. Said he would get even with both of us."

"He came to see me, too," Francis said. "He was drunk and I let him know what I thought of his shoddy work."

Abernethy puffed out his cheeks and exhaled. "Got ourselves a real problem, gentlemen. A strong smell of kerosene is all about the base, and both doors had a fireplace log jammed against it. Only you, Couch, and I carry kerosene, Francis. Get your new man, I've already sent my son for Wilson. Katoro, ask Kenwa to excuse himself from your wives and we'll all meet in Asa's office. Least said, for the moment, the better."

The small law office was crowded. Even though Abernethy had raised the issue, he whispered to Asa and let him take charge.

He found out quickly that Mick had sold only a pint of kerosene to Mrs. Crumley for lamp fuel.

"Thanks, Mick. Now why don't you tell the others to go on with dessert without me and Francis."

"And Mick," Francis said, "you'd best find quarters for Mr. Fallow and his men. Getting too late for them to go back to the ship tonight."

Mick nodded, but wasn't happy over that order. The first person to whom Anita had offered coffee was Henry Fallow and not himself.

A. E. Wilson had never been sociable or a good merchant for Captain Couch. He resented having to close his store, being the only one who stayed open into the evening.

"Wilson," Asa said, beckoning the man inside, "I'll only keep you a minute, so you can get back to your store. Have you sold any quantities of kerosene lately?"

"Yep! Three gallon tins late this afternoon."

"Regular customer?" Asa asked evenly.

"Nope, except for Blue Ruin. Surveyor man gets most of his stuff from Pettygrove in trade for his work. Said he had some stump burning to do on a project."

"Thanks, Wilson, we'll let you go now."

Asa drummed his fingers on his desk. "Katoro. Kenwa. Mr. Abernethy whispered to me why he wanted you here. Some of us have been talking about needing a local government, as we're forming for the territory. Many are asking me to run for mayor. George knows I won't do it, if in any way there is prejudice against the Indian and the Kanaka. We both feel, as do many others, that you are damn fine businessmen and an asset to our growth. What has happened tonight makes me sick, because we don't have a government in place and no law to go after this disorder. We've got evidence enough to know who did it, but how do we really prove it?"

"Do we have to?" Kenwa said, without hesitation.

"Are you going to let the bastard get away with it?" Katoro shouted.

"No, but we all know the man to be a liar. I am suggesting Indian justice. Francis, you and Asa saw it practiced at my wedding ceremony. Because the festivities could not be put under a dark spell, what happened to the young brave who was known to have stolen, but lied?"

"He was totally ignored, not allowed to participate, denied food and drink, and disappeared."

"A renegade, outside the family circle, even though his father was white and he uses the name Lewis."

Abernethy frowned. "Do you think that would work with Brown?"

"It would with his wife," Asa chuckled. "Let the women of this town stop talking with Nancy and she'll die for lack of gossip."

"But how do you let the women know?"

"Tell Marsha Tolcott," Katoro laughed.

"One more thing," Asa said. "This was George's idea and I'll give him credit. We are a community and as a community we will start tomorrow to clean away the ashes and have a house raising. Katoro, you will be in your own home again before the baby is born."

Francis could not help feeling a little sad returning to his guests and his home. He knew that he had lost Asa to Oregon City, and Portland would have to be his dream alone.

C H A P T E R

☆ **13** ☆

Sophia saw Francis only on weekends for an entire year. But he was so enthused with the progress of Portland and with her new home nearing completion that she refrained from speaking of her own lonesome state.

To a certain extent she was pleased that Beth had decided to stay for a spell. Never one to have suffered with her previous pregnancies, she was becoming more and more dependent on her afternoon naps. Not as a servant, but as a friendly gesture on the part of Beth, D'Arcy would spend each afternoon seeing to the children and a bit of tidy up around the house. For D'Arcy it was a break from boredom. The two-bedroom house that Beth had rented hardly kept her occupied. Sunday afternoons she had come to love. After dinner, with Sophia napping, Francis would use Beth as his sounding board and D'Arcy could help out down in the store.

"It's ridiculous," Francis complained. "Every time I seem to make headway, another enemy pops up to give me fits. Imagine, my own father putting the blame of the wreck on my shoulders."

"What did you expect, Francis? It's not the wreck, as much as your stealing Ian away from them."

"It's so unfair," Francis said, "what they have done to Dexter. He's had a hard time getting us supplies and a new warehouse. He's also afraid we might lose Ian, although I can't blame him for being unhappy over the age and condition of the *Enda*."

169

Beth sat silent for a moment, recalling the fierce argument she had had with Ian on his last voyage.

"Then buy him another vessel," she said at last. "The Tucker Line has not been able to ruin your connection with Benson & Bros. Their bark *Toulon* should arrive soon, but you will still need a ship for the Honolulu run."

"On the surface that would seem a good idea, dear cousin, but in Honolulu they would want gold or coin for a ship. Here, we have 'Hudson's Bay Money,' 'Abernethy Money,' and 'Pettygrove Money.' Orders on paper for goods at the face value of the order. The last gold I received from McLoughlin for furs went for the cattle Pack brought back from California. Your idea will have to wait."

"Why?" she insisted. "I found out from Ian what a privately owned bark is going for in Honolulu. Francis, I have ample resources to buy such a bark and should be thinking of a way to support my widowhood."

Francis looked at her lovingly. "You can't buy the man, if that is your intent."

With each passing day, her year of self-imposed "widowhood" was drawing to a close. She could share Ian's companionship in this parlor, and there alone. Ian's frustration was great. He had warned her to make a decision by his next trip, or else he would get out of her life forever.

"Maybe I am buying time," she grinned, "but you will be the one who gains."

Francis frowned. "You are really serious about staying, aren't you?"

"Oh, Francis!" she chided. "I did not buy a lot from you and Asa as a lark! My money is not that great that I would throw it away having Mr. Morrison build me a house."

"Or order furniture through Benson & Bros. in New York," he joked.

"How did you learn that?" She giggled.

"Even though Anita has been thwarted in getting her newspaper started, the news is called gossip. D'Arcy told Liza Boddick, who told Mrs. Morrison, who told her husband, who told me." He frowned. "If only all of it was such simple gossip. That is the one thing that disturbs me about this place. Everyone argues over the least little thing."

"Perhaps that is because they never had a say in anything where they came from. But how will it be any different in Portland?"

"Because it will be mine, and *I* will decide who to approach about settling there and buying lots. I have already convinced John Couch that Portland will be the head of navigation and he has taken a claim north of mine at the mouth of the creek."

"When you say it's yours, aren't you forgetting Asa?"

"Not really," Francis said grimly. "As the Mayor of Oregon City he is being whiplashed over having a double allegiance. Rather than ruin our friendship, we decided we would look around for a buyer for his half of the claim."

"And what about me?"

"Your lot purchase is quite enough," Francis said thinly. "Besides, being a claim owner would do you little good, Bethy. Only men gain a vote by having a claim."

Beth held her temper. For the moment she pitied Francis for still being New England "narrow" in his regard of women.

Mick Myers was having a different problem in regard to women.

Every Sunday afternoon, for six months, D'Arcy had spent her time dusting merchandise and shelves, rerolling cloth bolts, and restocking items from the back storeroom. She was witty and a joy to be around, as Anita had once been.

He could not fully blame Anita for their strained relationship. She had been totally crushed when Henry Fallow had decided not to return from Honolulu. She sat with a crated printing press and no prospects of anyone capable of helping her start and edit a newspaper. She had sold the rest of her Rocky Mountain furs to Francis for a credit balance and, to spite Mick, had taken a position with George Abernethy to keep his account books. Even though she was a widow, it was a shock to the women of Oregon City. An educated wife might keep books for her husband, but not an "unattached" woman. Perhaps it was Abernethy's pending governorship that kept the gossip from getting blown too far out of proportion.

"Mick! Micky! Ducks, what's keeping you so long with the corn starch?"

D'Arcy roared with mirth upon entering the back room. In getting a bulk bag down from a top shelf it had split on him. Sweeping up the mess, he looked like he had been covered from head to foot with fine snow.

"Gore, you're a ghostly sight. Let D'Arcy help dust you off."

"No," he said quickly. "I can do it myself, when I'm finished sweeping."

"Fraidycat!" She giggled. "Scared the touch of me hands might make you do something foolish. You look like the type that likes to steal kisses."

"I think," Mick said coldly, "that you'd best go back and watch the store."

"Oh, don't be shy. We ain't had a customer all afternoon."

Her blue eyes suddenly devilish, she walked very slowly to where he stood and took away the broom.

"I don't mind if you kiss me, luv."

Six months of temptation was all he could take. D'Arcy's face was blush pink after the kiss. Wordlessly, she backed away from him, a wild notion racing through her brain. Gossip had him linked with the Jewish woman, even though they fought and argued all the time. Cheerio, Anita! she exulted. She had come to America for a husband and this was the closest she had come to starting something.

Mick stood stark still, his eyes staring and his face turning whiter than the covering of corn starch.

"Anita!" he gulped.

D'Arcy spun and looked into the cold, hard face of Anita Shamir.

D'Arcy shrugged. "Were only a kiss, ducks."

"*Ducks!*" Anita said mockingly. "Only a whore would kiss a married man!"

"Go on! He ain't married."

Anita smiled—a slow enigmatic smile. "Ask Asa Lovejoy, if you don't believe me." She turned and fled before they could see the coming tears.

"Gore, you're married?"

"Yes—" he whispered, looking at Anita depart through the store.

"And you're sweet on her?"

"Yes," he repeated, his voice hoarse and unnatural.

"And where might your wife be?"

"Damned if I really know," he snapped, a slow flush of anger stealing over his handsome face. "D'Arcy, I was married at seventeen, with a train coach honeymoon ride to St. Louis. She took one look and fled back to the protection of her mother, leaving me without the honeymoon benefit of . . . well . . . I—"

"Gore!"

"Oh, stop saying 'Gore!' and looking so shocked. Mind the store! I've got to talk with her!"

D'Arcy nodded. *Damn him to hell for being married*, she thought.

He caught up with Anita at the top of the stairs, going to her room in the hotel.

"I don't spy on you in the back room of Abernethy's store!" he spluttered and knew it was the wrong beginning.

"Nor was I spying on you," she said coldly. "I was coming with some good news for us . . . for me. Mr. Abernethy has found me a man who could be a potential editor."

"Go on," he said calmly, because they were momentarily not shouting at each other.

Anita shrugged. "All I know is that he was on one of the wagons that came northwest with one of the first wagon trains. This fall he lost his wife and two children to the measles. He is on his way down from the Whitman's at Waiilatpu. End of report."

"The kiss was innocent!" he said quickly, before she could leave.

"That, Mr. Myers," she said tartly, "is none of my business!"

"It is your business! After you left, I told D'Arcy something that only made sense to me after I started chasing after you. I was in bed with Liddy once, and she started to cry so hard that I slept on the floor. Anita, I've been married seven years and never had a wife. In my heart I am not married. I don't give a damn what others may think. You are going to marry me, or live with me, or we will move to where no one knows us so that we can get some happiness out of this life. Now, I'm going to show you what a real kiss is like!"

As Mick bent down to her, her arms came happily about his neck. He was aware, tasting her lips for the first time, of feeling a sharp pain. It was Anita, so frantic over the thought of losing him that her nails dug into the nape of his neck, possessively.

He bent down and picked her up, starting to step toward the door to his room.

"My door is nearer," she said clearly. "I am not"—she paused, lending bitter emphasis to the word—"a virgin."

Mick stood still. Her meaning was clear, but the tone cut him like a knife.

Carefully, he put her down again.

"I love you! I've loved you for six years! I can wait until we are married."

"We have no rabbi," she scoffed, "and the nearest Catholic priest is at the fort. I doubt that either one would marry us anyway. You've heard the near blackmail they had to go through to get a Methodist to marry two Kanakas. I love you! If you had taken me into my bedroom I would have been the happiest woman alive, but you keep me so confused. Well, I'm not confused now. I talked with Ian the last time he was here. We are not yet a territorial part of the United States. We can be wed by just saying that we are wed, and he can do a ceremony on his ship when he comes back. When I get ready for bed tonight, I shall leave my door unlocked. If you wish to be wed, come to me."

Mick stood still, watching her turn away. The close of her

door, like the purr of a cat, slowly brought him out of his reverie.

"I must get back," he muttered. "It's near dusk and time . . . No! D'Arcy knows how to close the store."

He went back down the stairs to see if Eleanor Moss had hot water on the back of the stove for the tub room.

The bark *Toulon*, with colors flying, arrived at the completed northern end of the wharf in October 1845.

Deboarding at the wharf, Nathaniel Crosby, Jr., was jubilant. As master of his own vessel, he had been instructed in Honolulu by Ian Llwellen and Dexter Farman, on the proper approach to the bar and travel up the Columbia and Willamette. Even though it was October, he had been assured the river would be deep enough for his craft.

Francis Pettygrove was also jubilant. He would no longer be looked upon as a mere dreamer trying to make something out of his "stumptown." His warehouse was a cavernous monster, with a retail section four times larger than his Oregon City store. He had hired George Bell away from HBC to be his chief clerk, and, to the chagrin of Sophia, Annette Bell became the first white woman to live in Portland. On Washington Street, behind the warehouse, Bell had constructed a neat and cozy three-room frame house.

"I am rather stunned," Crosby wryly admitted. "Llwellen said I would find anchorage at The Clearing. The Clearing seems to have sprouted some fifteen buildings, in various degrees of completion."

"They say I am a man who never sits down," Francis laughed, but felt pride at the man's words.

"The wharf is a grand size to moor against. No longboats and shoremen to row the cargo in. Right off the ship to the wharf and into the warehouse."

"Tomorrow you will see how Kenwa's men will bateau part of these supplies to Oregon City. Some of the heavier cargo will go by way of his river schooner or scow."

The heaviest pieces, Kenwa was to discover, were staying right in Portland. Still, he had to borrow a few wheelbarrows

from the Morrison carpenters to get the crated furniture to
Second Street and Jefferson. It was only eight blocks, but
there had not been a fall freeze to harden the muddy ground
and they had to keep dodging around stumps in the streets.
Still, at the wages Kenwa was paying, it was easier than
paddling it all the way to Oregon City.

"That is my cousin's house, receiving the furniture. My
house is the one by the river, at Front Street and Jefferson. If
my wife doesn't keep making changes, we may be moved in
before it becomes a town all the way to Fifth Street. As I go
home only on weekends, may my wife and I accept you for
dinner on Sunday?"

"My honor. And as you are here in Portland without
family, will you honor my table on the ship this evening?"

"Very gracious and I accept. It will give us a chance to
discuss your return cargo."

"Then I shall ask my cargomaster, Benjamin Stark, to join
us."

Beth had excused herself from dinner that Sunday, but left
D'Arcy behind to help. She was just too excited and wanted
to dig into her treasures.

"All right," she warned the Kanaka boys she had brought
along to help. "I'm paying you the same wage as Asa, so
don't try to bluff me. I've brought plenty of food, so no one
will starve and you have that log cabin to stay in tonight. Oh,
my, one other thing. Only Henderson & Mott would crate
their furniture in such good wood stock. Be careful uncrating
everything. Our local furniture maker will give me a good
price for those slats of oak."

Saturday evening Beth was exhausted after having fed the
five Kanakas, but still she had to roam from room to room
and hug herself. In twenty-four years this was the first house
that was hers, alone. She loved the colonial front, with the
shuttered windows and three gabled windows to light the
third-floor attic. Piece by piece she felt of the furniture and
drapery material. She wanted it special, to pop Ian's eyes.

On Sunday, she worked alone unpacking the china and
glassware, placing them in the Queen Anne breakfront. She

was so absorbed in her work that she didn't hear the man enter.

"Hello, there! Are you finding everything in order?"

"Oh!" she gasped, turning. "You took me by—Benjie! Benjamin Stark, is that really you?"

"Beth!" he cried. "Holy Hannah! The Tucker people have everyone believing that you went down with Captain Johns."

"Just like them, so they wouldn't have to pay a widow's mite."

"I saw Ian in Honolulu and he never let on that you were here."

"And just like him. Sit! Oh, it is so good to see you, Benjie, and as dashingly handsome as ever. But what brings you here?"

"Cargomaster on the *Toulon*. Had to get away from Tucker and Pettygrove, Beth. All of their money goes into clippers and captains. They've even downgraded cargomaster to a second officer, so they don't have to pay him as much, yet they still get the same amount of work. Honeychile, I told them which end they could whistle out of and put myself on the beach in New York City. That's where Nate Crosby picked me up and a finer man I've never worked for."

They chatted and laughed and wiled away a good share of the morning. Beth didn't mind. It was the first time she had laughed so naturally in a long, long time.

"Benjie, please, don't breathe a word of what I have received. I want it to be a surprise for a party I have been planning in my head. Oh, how long will the ship be here?"

"A good two to three months. The HBMS *Modeste* is at Fort Vancouver because of the international boundary negotiations. The U.S. Navy put cannons in our hold, in case the British get any funny ideas."

"Good," she sighed. "Then you will be here. I really wanted the party to be just before Christmas."

Benjamin Stark was standing at the rail, looking toward the light in Beth's house, when the long boat returned Nate Crosby.

"Nathaniel, my good man, you know me to be a true

Southern gentleman from New Orleans and thus not one to prevaricate on the facts about women. In that lighted house is this century's version of Helen of Troy."

Nate laughed. "Have you been nipping at the rum? That's the house of Pettygrove's cousin."

"To be sure," Stark smirked. "Elizabeth Pettygrove Johns, widow of the infamous Captain John Johns who wrecked the Tucker Line's first clipper ship. A widow who was not wearing weeds this day."

Nate pursed his lips. "And all along I automatically assumed that Pettygrove's cousin was male and married. When do we get to meet your 'Helen'?"

"She needs time to get her home in order, then she is going to give a party."

"I can hardly wait."

"Beth, you are being spiteful and hateful," Sophia wailed. "Why can't you wait and move when I move?"

"Sophia, your house may not be ready until the new year. My house is ready, my things have arrived, and I've got to have time to get it in order."

"Then, please," she pleaded, "at least leave D'Arcy with me."

"I can't, Sophia. There are a million things she has to do for me."

"You're selfish, that's what you are, Elizabeth! Some days my ankles are so swollen I have to use a chamber pot instead of getting down to the outhouse. Little you care that I am seven months along and can't do for myself and my children."

"Sophia," Beth said thinly, "this has got to be said. I've seen you trot up and down those stairs in the morning to have coffee with Marsha Tolcott. It's only in the afternoon, when you have D'Arcy here to coo and pamper, that you pull your little act. You had it made, from what I hear, when Tama was here. The only woman in town with a maid. Was that what turned you bitter against her? You lost your status symbol?"

"Get out!" Sophia hissed. "And don't you dare come here

for dinner next Sunday. Nathaniel Crosby will be here and I don't want a fine man like that meeting a slut who couldn't keep her husband happy and runs after other men!"

Beth remained quiet and aloof as she put on her bonnet and cape. She knew that once Marsha Tolcott got ahold of this tale she would be branded as more than just a slut.

Beth stood in the street for a long moment, unsure if she should back down and allow D'Arcy to stay for a few more days. She turned, just in time to see Sophia race between the two buildings to Marsha's kitchen door.

With her skirts flying, Beth raced the two blocks to her little rented house.

"Now, D'Arcy!" she ordered. "We are leaving now, and not tomorrow! I want my home and Portland! I don't give a damn if I ever see this place again!"

Beth planned her party for Saturday, December 20th. It was the closest date to Christmas to give the *Enda* time to arrive.

A few times she saw Nathaniel Crosby from a distance and wondered what impression he had gained of her from Sophia. She found him to be a pleasing-looking man, with his bushy muttonchop sideburns and connecting mustache. Benjie Stark, who had become her male helpmate and confidante on the party surprises, was gentleman enough not to repeat any comments made by his boss.

Francis was so irate with both women that he refused to be the punching bag between them.

In late November, John Morrison completed Liza Boddick's home and dress shop on Front Street and turned his meticulous attention to the Pettygrove house. Although she had not asked for a reply to her invitations, she was rather hurt by the small response. From Liza she learned she could count on four ladies who had ordered dresses: Mrs. McLoughlin, Mrs. Abernethy, Anita Shamir, and, amazingly, Elvira Waller.

She also knew she could count on Katoro and Pelani, because they were helping with the party. She feared it would not be a glowing social event in the eyes of Nathaniel Crosby.

By Friday morning Beth was near tears. She had received a polite note from Mrs. Couch that her Alice was "sick a bed," but that Captain Couch would attend to represent the family. The dour Philip Foster, upon delivering her produce, curtly announced he would attend.

"Some party," she scoffed, helping D'Arcy clean the vegetables. "Philip Foster is not my idea of a lively party man."

"M'um! Would you look at that. While we've had our heads down in the wash tub, the *Enda* has docked."

"Oh Lord, no! I look a fright!"

Racing up the curving stairs, she paused at the round window to check on the *Enda*'s activity. Her heart sank.

Because there were no buildings on Front Street, from Madison to Salmon, she could see the ship clearly, and the man and woman who were picking their way through the stumps.

Even had it been a mile distance, she would have recognized the towering, dashing figure of Ian Llwellen. The woman barely came to his chest, in a prim and proper black bonnet and a neck-high dress with brooch and flowing cape. The manner in which he had her by the arm, gently guiding her along, infuriated Beth.

"The bastard did it! He went off and got himself married and now thinks he can waltz his new bride into my home!"

To spite him, she turned and went back downstairs, without changing or brushing her hair.

"D'Arcy," she called, "you'll have to get the door. I've decided to change a few things around on the tree."

To D'Arcy's delight, Ian picked her up and swung her around, then his eyes rolled in disbelief.

"This is one hell of a fine place! Beth, are you going to stay up on that stepladder all day? I've got a surprise for you."

"Ian, I am in no mood for surprises," she said sharply, without looking.

"This one came all the way from the other Portland, via Tucker Lines. Handed over to me by Nelson Cleeve in Honolulu, for safe transport to Francis."

Beth turned, and nearly fell coming off the steps. "Mary Charlotte Pettygrove! Saint's alive!"

"Skinned alive, Cousin Bethy," the thirty-year-old woman laughed, "when Papa really finds out what Nels and I have done."

Beth went to her with open arms. She had never paid much attention to Francis's younger sister, but saw that maturity had made her a pure Pettygrove, with the high forehead, curly hair, slightly cocked head, and gray eyes filled with amusement and mischief.

"Nels is with you?"

"No, in Honolulu, to find a new agent. In a word, with Nels's help, I've pulled an Elizabeth Pettygrove. I grew tired, Beth, of taking care of Papa and Residency House. Papa will die when he learns I've run off to visit Francis. At his store they told us that he was in Oregon City. We're waiting for some Indian craft to take me there."

"No!" Beth laughed, her spirits soaring again. "I've a much better idea, and I'm delighted you got home in time for it, Ian. Tomorrow I am having a Christmas party. You will stay here tonight and surprise Francis tomorrow. D'Arcy, we'll put Mary Charlotte in the blue bedroom. Oh, I'm so excited, I forgot. Ian hasn't seen his room yet."

"I have a room?" he grinned. "I certainly hope that the floor and ceiling are in their proper place."

Beth flushed. "I think you will find everything to your liking."

"I like the homecoming already, although I feared we might never make it. That old tub has almost had it, Beth. I've got to talk with Francis, because all Dexter will do is shrug."

Beth also shrugged. This was not the time to spring her Christmas present on him.

The weather was on Beth's side, even though she still fretted over who might not attend. Saturday dawned bright and mellow. Because for some it would be a long trip, she had planned an all-day affair. An hour after the house was astir Pack McGraw brought a string of pack animals in from the valley, with the cream and eggs she would need for the egg nog, and a quarter of aged beef.

"Thank you, Pack, for getting it here so early."

"My pleasure, Beth, but it's going to cost D'Arcy, because she's my kind of woman."

D'Arcy giggled, working at the stove, frying slabs of bacon and ham. She loved the attention, but no single woman had been able to figure out what type of woman suited the cattle and dairy rancher.

"Joe Bellam ain't much of a cook and the Kanaka girls can only milk and churn. I came for some of D'Arcy's cooking, but don't think I can stay for the whole party."

"Pack," Beth said, getting him a mug of coffee, "how close are you and Joe to having your own cattle?"

"Soon, but I don't mind running these for Asa and Francis. It pays enough for us to pick up a few of our own each trip south."

Beth was ready for her first ploy of the day. "Would you run cattle for me or anyone else?"

"What's the offer?"

"You're interested in breeding. Run my stock as breeders and we'll split the calves fifty-fifty."

"Fair enough. When do you want to get a herd?"

"Maybe today, Pack. But it can't be in my name. Certain people don't like women being in business."

Pack shrugged indifferently. Women in business didn't bother him.

Bateau after bateau began to arrive by mid-morning. Katoro and Pelani brought the four Kanaka boys in their new dark pants and matching shirts, made by Liza. By the time for the noon buffet, Beth knew the party would be a success, except for the absent Francis and Sophia.

"Don't worry," Asa whispered, breaking away from a conversation with Benjamin Stark. "Francis said they would arrive with Mick and Anita."

Benjie was beaming as he steered Beth toward the punch bowl.

"It is done for you, my little manipulator. Tomorrow, Benjamin Stark will become the owner of Asa Lovejoy's half-interest in this town and his cattle. Plus, dear girl, I saved you money on your hidden investment. We gained it for twelve hundred fifteen dollars and not fifteen hundred. As a speculative investment, partner, I think we are off to a roaring start!"

Beth's second ploy came quicker than she had expected.

The sound of wheels on the streets of Portland was so unusual that everyone rushed to the front windows.

"Would you look at that! Never thought we'd see that stagecoach roll again!"

Mick Myers had spent a month burnishing and polishing the vehicle to a high luster. The horses had red and green ribbons tied in their manes, and brightly decorated boxes were tied on the top as though presents. The arrival got an ovation that made Mick blush. But the alighting passengers looked more like the gloom of Christmas.

"We couldn't get Sophia to come without Marsha," Anita told Beth, with more casualness than she felt. "I've been glared at for twelve miles like a scarlet woman."

"Who is that?"

"That's Dennis Landry, my new editor."

Beth had never seen such a sad-looking man. Still, she greeted him warmly.

"Ah, Anita and Dennis, just the two I have been waiting for," John Couch boomed, with his gentlemanly deportment. "May I show you the way to the excellent punch bowl?"

Francis kissed Beth on the cheek and went to join the waving John McLoughlin. She would save her surprise for a few minutes.

Sophia Pettygrove and Marsha Tolcott sailed in the door, tightlipped and unsmiling. They only nodded at Beth and she smiled in return. She would not let them ruin her party.

"What a lovely tree," Marsha gasped. "Ain't seen one like that since I was a girl. And look at the people!"

"All the wrong ones," Sophia replied icily. "Mainly came to gawk at her new house, I would assume."

Tama timidly approached them and Sophia went stiff as a board.

"All fall," she said softly, taking the flower lei from around her neck. "Pelani and I have kept plants in the sun, to keep blooming. You remember the lei, Sophia. I sewed the petals together all night long. I wish it as your Christmas present."

Sophia's hand darted out and knocked it to the floor before Tama could put it over her head.

Beth scooped it up before anyone else saw and held Sophia in a hard glare.

"This is my home, Sophia," Beth said. "That was a beautiful gesture of friendship by Tama. It's a shame it was wasted on such a cold heart." Before Sophia could react, she put the lei over her head, her eyes defying her to take it off.

"Tama," Beth cried, grabbing her hand, "what is that sound?"

Glad for an excuse to get away from the two women, they ran to the door and threw it wide.

Coming up Jefferson Street were John Morrison and Hugh Donaldson O'Bryant, his chief carpenter, dressed in their kilts and playing the bagpipes. It was the second ovation of the day.

"What a grand reception," the tall and sparse Morrison grinned. "In the wee bachelor house on Ash Street, Hughie and I thought it might be a grand sound wafting over our town."

"So fine," Francis called, "that I'm going to give you a Christmas present early. As of this moment, Ash Street is now Morrison Street."

"You might have waited until he got *our* house finished," Sophia said.

Unlike Tama, John Morrison did not need Beth to come to his aide.

"Lassie," he cooed, "even God rested to view the wonders of his work, and this *mon* is here to view his wonder with laughin' people in it. Now, Hughie and me need a wee dram for our whistles."

Beth clapped her hands. "And now for a Christmas surprise for Francis and Sophia. Ladies and gentlemen, I would like to introduce Miss Mary Charlotte Pettygrove from Portland, Maine."

Francis gasped and ran forward as Mary Charlotte came

skipping down the stairs. Sophia frowned and then a sly smile crossed her lips.

"Poor girl," D'Arcy whispered, passing Beth with an empty tray. "Someone just got wind of a live-in nursemaid."

"Don't count on it. While I was still playing with dolls, Mary Charlotte was racing around the countryside in a pony cart. Oh, Ian, are you having a good time?"

"Delightful. Anita and Mick were just telling me a strange thing. John Couch told Anita that some businessmen have put together a printing association and want to buy the *Spectator*—even though it hasn't yet issued its first edition. They plan to keep this Landry on as part-time editor. Anita doesn't know whether she should be glad to get rid of it or if it's a slap in the face."

"Coming from John Couch I would say it's honest in presentation, but Pelani says that even Mrs. Moss is upset over renting two hotel rooms and having to make only one bed."

"Speaking of beds," he said wickedly. "I'm glad I have mine and Nate Crosby does not. He may be talking to everyone in the house, but he keeps looking at you like he knows what you look like nude on a ceiling mattress."

She put a finger to her lips and then pressed them against his lips. "We have a roomful of eager gossips."

"Ah, Mrs. Johns," John McLoughlin enthused as he and two young men approached, "a most charming party. This is my son, David. You were busy when he arrived. I'd also like to present a newcomer. Daniel Lownsdale. He's taken a claim just to the west and had the courtesy to ask Francis if he objected to his business being on the creek."

"Mr. McLoughlin, Mr. Lownsdale," Beth said graciously. "May I ask, Mr. Lownsdale, what is your business?"

"A tanner," he said, fixing Beth with a pair of crystal-clear blue eyes. He had such an honest, open gaze that she liked him at once. "I have been in Europe for three years studying some of the old tanning methods. Their secret was hemlock, and that creek is bountiful in it. Now that I have found it, I shall send for my family in Kentucky."

"This is good news. We can certainly use a leather tanner

on the creek. And what are your plans, David, now that you are home from school in England? A post with HBC?"

The eighteen-year-old looked a little startled, but then his Eton training saved him.

"Sorry, but I gather you did not hear father's statement to Mr. Pettygrove. We have resigned from Hudson's Bay. On the new year we shall take up our residency in Oregon City and begin to build a home. Father has secured a clerk's position for me with Mr. Pettygrove. Please excuse me, I see that your girl is bringing more of that excellent eggnog. Father?"

McLoughlin looked down his hawkish nose and nodded his permission for the boy to be excused. "My dear," he said to Beth, "having lived in England, you will appreciate the reflections of a sixty-two-year-old man who had forgotten the pomposity of British youth."

"If you don't mind me asking, Dr. McLoughlin, why are you leaving the fort?"

He laughed, and his white mane seemed to float like a cloud around his head. "One might say the fort left me, my dear. Booted to Chester, so to speak. For eight years we have had a young queen and empress on the throne at home. India is her concern, not America. Any month now we shall hear that your country not only has this land, but even farther north. Here they say I am too Tory, while in Whitehall they accuse me of being too lenient a Factor in letting the Americans come in to dominate. But let's not talk of such things! Politics can always ruin a good party. Do you think we can talk John Morrison into piping us up some good dance tunes?"

"We surely can, as long as you save the *Flora MacDonald* for me."

"Bethy, Bethy, Bethy," Francis sighed as he joined them. "I can't think of a grander time, and to see my sister is such a treat. Even though the day did start with hurricane warning signs."

"Who did you leave the children with?"

"Mrs. Couch, because Alice was feeling poorly. First time I can recall Ellen not crying. I must say my idea of bringing Sophia on the stagecoach was not well thought-out. My only excuse is that on a horse one is not aware that our grand new road is not exactly a Boston Street!" He gestured toward Morrison and O'Bryant. "I see you've arranged for dance music. Are you trying to run the Methodists off early?"

"Hardly," she laughed. "Look at Marsha tapping her foot and gazing at Asa. Oh, oh, too late—Liza Boddick got to him first. Francis, have you ever seen Philip Foster smile before?"

"Never! The man was born with a pursed mouth."

"Better look again. He started grinning broadly the moment he got Mary Charlotte up to dance. Boys, come and help! Move the furniture back to the walls. More want to dance than I realized."

Dr. McLoughlin was organizing a reel when D'Arcy tapped Beth on the shoulder.

"M'um, is it proper for me to accept a dance?"

Beth looked at the suddenly beaming face of David McLoughlin and turned to his father.

"My dear," the elder McLoughlin said, "the lad is eighteen. He's soon to become an American citizen, wishes to be called "Dave," and wouldn't give a hoot if I did disapprove."

"Harriet McLoughlin," Marsha sniffed on the other side of the room. "Do you see who your son is dancing with?"

"A very attractive young girl."

"A *maid*!"

"I understand," Mrs. McLoughlin said evenly, "that you are now a cook and housekeeper for Asa Lovejoy and his Kanaka boys."

"Well! I never!"

Sophia smiled. "That's our problem, Marsha. We can dish it out, but we can't take it when it's dished back." She struggled to get to her feet. It was painful but she made it to the kitchen.

"Katoro," she said, "please call Beth in from the dining room."

She gripped the table, blinked her eyes, and waited.

"Sophia? What is it?" Beth said with concern as she came through the door.

"Too much bumpy stagecoach, I fear. Can the boys help

me down the street to my house? I know the new bedroom suites have been delivered."

"Is it . . . time?"

"I'm afraid so."

"Then we'll get you right upstairs."

"Please," Sophia said weakly, "allow me this, Beth. If this is to be the first child born in Portland, I would like to be in my own home and not ruining your lovely party. They will just think that I left for the outhouse."

She started to crumple and Katoro and Pelani caught her.

"What now?" Katoro said, his eyes wide.

Beth was calm. "Have the boys get a blanket. They can carry her in it as though it were a stretcher. She wanted her house and that is where we shall take her. Pelani, please ask Tama, Elvira, and Dr. McLoughlin to come here. No use turning Francis into a nervous wreck at the moment."

The party went on, unaware. The trio gathered together what they would need and soon smoke curled up from the chimney of the new fireplace.

By the time D'Arcy had started to ladle out the steaming bowls of oyster stew, John McLoughlin had returned to announce that Portland had a new male citizen.

As though she had been deprived of her duty, Marsha bustled down the street to take charge.

"What's that poor woman going to do when Asa gets married?" Liza Boddick asked. Everyone looked at her like she knew something that they did not.

Reluctantly, people began leaving after the supper of soup, ham, and fresh bread.

Francis came back to borrow pillows and blankets for the night.

"We're going to leave the stagecoach," Mick said, "and go back by bateau. We didn't want to infringe on your party, but Anita has something to tell you."

Anita kissed Beth on the cheek and held her hands. "This is my first Christmas party, and it was lovely. But not as lovely as this morning. Reverend Waller married us, so we can move up over the store without Marsha fainting away next door."

"And, Asa, you can stop frowning," Mick said. "One of

the pieces of mail that Crosby brought from New York was from my parents. I wasn't even aware there was a potato famine in Ireland, but they have arrived safely in America. They were able to find your father to locate me. Asa, Liddy has been remarried for five years and has three children. That was enough to convince Reverend Waller that I was a free man."

Kenwa came to Beth. She felt guilty about having ignored him all day.

"May I also have the honor to kiss the cheek and hold the hand?"

"The honor would be mine."

His lips were soft as he brushed each cheek, his hands warm and strong.

"The woman who gave my mother life was of Yam-il tribe and captured by Cayuse as young squaw. Yam-il women, like my grandmother, are great women. Francis has named a street for my grandmother, although he spelled it Yamhill. Today, because of what you did for my Tama, I have met another Yam-il woman."

Beth was suddenly blinded by tears. She had never been so honored.

She was glad they were the last to go. She had heard enough "thank yous" and heard enough praise.

"Ian, why don't you stir up the fire and snuff the candles and lamps? D'Arcy, go to bed, dear. The boys are staying in the cabin and will clean up the mess in the morning."

Then Beth stood for a moment and looked around her kitchen, relishing the fact that it had been one of the most popular party rooms in the house. When a light tapping came at the back door, she was tempted not to open it.

"Mr. Zarundy! What a surprise!"

He removed his cap and nodded his head in a little bow. "I am sorry to be so late for party, Mrs. Johns, but the climate of this country takes longer for my process than in Russia. Still, by sundown I have dried enough to make you Christmas present."

"Process? Present? I hope you did not feel you had to bring a present to the party, Mr. Zarundy!"

"It is my thanks for you helping me in the store."

Beth had almost forgotten the incident, it was so minor. Mick had been busy and the man's wife was totally confused on the differences in yard goods. With Zarundy as interpretor, Beth had determined that the woman wanted a fabric to make small sacks.

Now, one of those sacks was being thrust at her, tied with a red ribbon.

To be polite, she opened it and was stunned.

"Mr. Zarundy, this is sugar. I can't accept such an expensive item for such a small favor!"

"It is sugar from my beets," he protested, "not expensive like from cane. This year only half the crop will be sugar, other half to mature for more seeds. But, a favor, again. I do not know how to speak with Mr. Pettygrove about the purchase. Will you help? My food supplies I think will not get me through winter."

"Yes, I will help. Come by Monday and we'll talk."

"Thank you. Now I have process, can dry maybe a hundred pounds a day. Well, goodnight."

Ian had pulled two chairs to the front of the fireplace. He was warming a bottle of brandy between his hands.

"My Christmas present from the crew. They got it off a French ship."

"That sounds delightful and soothing. Before you pour it, though, taste this."

"It's sugar," he said, licking his lips and then his finger again. "Very good sugar."

"Beet sugar, Ian, grown and processed by that quiet Russian family in the valley. Nicolas Zarundy has asked me to talk to Francis about purchasing it. He says he can process about a hundred pounds a day. I gulp when I have to pay two dollars and thirty-five cents for a pound."

Ian whistled. "I've heard of the sugar beet in Europe, but not in America. Louisiana is very protective of their cane sugar. They won't even let it be grown in the Sandwich Islands. But it is, illegally."

"Then there is a market for beet sugar?"

"One hell of a market."

Beth rose and went back to the tree in the hall. "I think it is time for your Christmas present."

"I hope it includes you."

"In a way, it does."

"It's heavy," he laughed, putting the package down on the floor and squatting down beside it. He frowned, puzzled. "What's it for, Beth?"

"There's 4,000 Pounds/Sterling in that wooden box, Ian. Francis can't afford a new ship or to fix the *Enda*. There is your new ship."

Ian sat silent for several moments. "With you as a partner?"

"Yes."

"In how many ways?"

"In as many ways as you desire. I can't run away from you any longer."

He put his head on her knee. She could tell that he was crying. She stroked his hair and looked deep into the dying fire.

It had been a good day and her final ploy had made her content. Never again would she be afraid to love this man.

CHAPTER

☆ 14 ☆

"How quickly the years do evaporate," Beth wrote Harold Tucker on Sunday, November 28, 1847.

> To think that I have been in my home for two years is startling. As to your inquiry, now that you are the "pompous" head of Tucker Lines, the news of the boundary settlement did not evoke pitched battles between the Americans and British, as you say was reported in the *London Times*. We learned of the settlement in rather a remarkable way. Captain Nathaniel Crosby departed Portland in late September for his third trip back to Honolulu. He was back, with the news, in a startling thirty-five days. Not even a clipper ship has made such a round trip record!
>
> But poor Nate! I think he was trying to break another record, the race for my hand in marriage. He lost and seemed rather a sad-faced little boy as Ian and I were wed during my Second Annual Christmas Party. Elizabeth Llwellen! How does that sound?
>
> Yes, Harold, I am most happy and it is not the "wild, wild West," as you imply. Portland grows daily, though not fast enough for Francis. Even though we are some thirty buildings and one hundred souls, we are still sneered at as "The Little Stumptown." It did not discourage Nate Crosby, even though he had lost out on me, from building a most unusual home for himself.

Harold, it was assembled in Boston and brought by ship in sections. John Morrison delighted in erecting it, as the whole structure was put together with wooden pegs and not nails.

A couple of personal notes that will be of interest to you. Mary Charlotte, after a stormy month of trying to live with Francis and Sophia, married Philip Foster, in February of 1846. Their wedding was overshadowed by Asa Lovejoy's announcement that he had sold his sawmill to George Abernethy and that he was engaged to Eliza Boddick. To the chagrin of Francis, Sophia hired Marsha Tolcott and moved her to Portland. We have our fingers crossed that the new blacksmith has a real interest in Marsha.

Now hold onto your hat, Harold dear, for our little D'Arcy has created the greatest gossip story of 1847. Although we had seen signs of David McLoughlin's interest in her, it was not until April that we knew that the "bun was well in the oven." The McLoughlin's being Catholic brought about the first official visit of a priest to Portland. After the wedding, Father Bernardo was so impressed with the neatness, thrift, and industry of Portland that he secured a free lot from Francis for a Catholic church. McGraw, who "runs my cattle," feels that while we may be a three-church town (Methodist, Congregationalist, and Catholic), we lack the real necessity of life—a tavern.

Now, let me tell you of my plans for my Third Annual Christmas . . .

Beth's pen stopped in mid-sentence. In the distance she thought she heard thunder, but they never had thunder storms at the end of November. She rose from her writing desk and went to the window. The full moon made sparkles in the Willamette current. Not a single breeze stirred the branches of the Douglas Fir. The night was peaceful. Then the sound came again.

"Gunfire," Nuua said, waddling from the kitchen.

"Impossible! No idiot hunts at night."

"Too many guns for just hunters," Nuua quavered. "I go home, please."

"Of course," Beth said, her attention now on watching Francis come out on his sideporch and look up river. "And tell Matoa that the roast was excellent."

She turned, intending to give Nuua instructions for the next day, but the girl had already vanished.

Beth smiled to herself. She would never admit it to D'Arcy McLoughlin, but she was very pleased with the clean, efficient, and cheerful girl.

Nuua had been brought from Oahu in 1846 as a bride for Matoa. From his butcher salary Matoa had saved three hundred dollars in "Pettygrove Money" to purchase a bride who was a Havaiki girl with no *haole* blood. Dexter and Rhoda Farman had been able to convert the script to local trade goods. It was a handsome price to pay for a bride, and Ian Llwellen fretted all the way from Honolulu that the Farmans had been cheated in getting full value for Matoa.

As Nuua had come off the *Yam-il*, Matoa had nearly swooned with rapture and Pack McGraw had to catch him. Nuua was as wide and short as Matoa was wide and short. A native girl who had always lived in a hut, she was awed that her husband-to-be had a butcher shop on Front Street, even though the lot, building, and business were owned by Pack McGraw. The second-floor living quarters were superior to any *haole* dwelling she had ever seen at home, but when she saw Beth's house, she told Matoa that not even King Kauikeaouli could have such a fine palace.

The front door banged open and startled Beth out of her reverie.

Marsha Tolcott came marching in, as if it was her due, dragging Lorenzo, Ellen, and Robert in their nightclothes.

"What is it, Marsha?"

"Himself can't tell for sure, but a mile or so upriver he can see a whole armada of torchlit canoes chasing and shooting at something. Heathen Indians, if you ask me."

"Marsha, we don't have any hostile Indians around here."

"That's all you know," Marsha replied icily. "I keep me

ears open at our dinner table and don't waste me time planning fancy parties."

"Where is Sophia?" Beth snapped, to cut off the prattle.

"Gone to the store to have George Bell break out guns and ammunition. We've known for two weeks that Indian trouble was coming."

Wordlessly, Beth brushed by the woman and went into the study. She took a Sharps rifle and ammunition from Ian's weapon rack.

"What do you think you are going to do?" Marsha sneered, as Beth came back to the foyer and grabbed a cape from the coat rack.

"Not stay here and help you baby-sit," she said curtly and ran from the house.

She found Francis standing on the riverbank, in front of his house, with James Terwilliger, the blacksmith.

"What is it, Francis?"

"Beth, this is no place for you. Go back to your house!"

"Francis," she snapped, "I have always been a better shot than you, so don't tell me what to do!"

Francis Pettygrove was not used to being snapped at; it shocked him into what he thought was the truth. "That half-breed, Joseph Lewis, has been stirring up the Cayuse for nearly a month. Two weeks ago all of the men started disappearing from the villages down around the fort. Last week, Kenwa's bateau boys disappeared."

They heard the muffled gunfire begin again. The torches looked like a ship burning at sea.

Within a minute they could see the form of a man floating downriver. As the body drifted by them, they could see that the man's back was an open wound from a high-caliber weapon.

"Cayuse," Terwilliger said and began to load his ancient rifle.

Beth felt a slow sickness spreading through her middle as they saw Indian after dead Indian float by, each with a cavernous hole in their back that suggested they had been shot from the front—possibly by someone they knew. Not a single Indian was in battle attire.

"I don't understand," Francis mumbled.

"Don't play the idiot," Terwilliger hissed crisply. "Them's the first ones that must have attacked Oregon City. Too much firepower there, so their comin' down to where they know we are weak on manpower."

Beth's green eyes snapped fire. "Then who are they firing at and since when did the Cayuse have guns? Look! There's Kenwa's scow. Oh, Lord! It's been half burned away!"

From under the canvas of the broken mast, Kenwa crawled out and started to paddle in toward the wharf. Terwilliger started to raise his rifle.

"Shoot him and you'll never make another horseshoe, blacksmith!"

Pack McGraw stepped out of the darkness, a pistol holster tied to each leg. He called to Kenwa in Cayuse and the scow veered to come into the bank where they stood.

Just as they were ready to touch shore, Sophia arrived with George Bell, John Morrison, and Hugh O'Bryant.

Francis grabbed the sharp prow of the vessel as Kenwa crawled to throw back another half-burned piece of canvas sail. He looked fierce and frightened. Half of his hair had been burned away and he had no eyebrows. It made his black eyes larger, the whites glowing in the moonlight.

"My child," he said hoarsely, holding up the three-year-old chubby boy. "And Tama is much burned on hands and arms. They burned our home and she tried to save it."

"Give me the child," Sophia supplied gently. "John, help Kenwa get Tama off the boat and then bring her into the house. George, go back to the store and get me two five-gallon tins of honey."

She walked away with the child. Hugh had to help John Morrison, because Tama had fainted from the pain.

Kenwa looked at them take her away and frowned. "They wished us dead, too. They burned my river schooner and took my bateaux."

The cold, cynical Beth came out. "They? Whoever they are, they'll be here in a couple of minutes. What has been going on?"

For the first time Kenwa realized Beth was in the group.

He was still in a state of shock. He looked at her with eyes burning with fury.

"Friday night six of my men returned. They did not like what the madman Lewis had talked the tribe into doing, nor would they tell me. Late this afternoon that Tom Brown came riding in hard from Waiilatpu. His horse was so lathered and foamy that the beast fell over dead. He was screaming like a crazy man. Because of what he did before, Katoro grew frightened and took Pelani to Mick and Anita at the store. He was shouting so that he drew a crowd of men. They all went into Couch's Store and it grew quiet. Just before sundown they started the shooting and burning."

"Where were Asa and Abernethy?" Francis demanded.

"They, and all the business owners and their wives, are at that territorial meeting at Champoeg."

A shot rang out from the lead bateau and twanged into the side of the scow. Instinctively, Beth raised the Sharps and fired. Pack fumed and turned to storm at her, but all he could see was excitement in her face. When he looked back at the bateau, he saw a torch flying through the air.

"All right!" he cried out. "Put down your weapons!"

"Not till we kill that murdering Indian!" Tom Brown bellowed.

"Unless that was a lucky shot," Pack grinned, "that buffalo rifle will give you six more reasons to change your plans."

With time to aim, Beth had her sights on the broad section of the pitch-dipped torches, just below the flame. What had looked like a fleet were only seven bateaux. Like shooting a flight of Canadian geese in the Maine marshlands, she came from the back bateau forward, knocking all six torches into the river.

"The next shots will be for real," Pack shouted. "Get into the shore!"

"Only if you turn over the Indian," Brown insisted. "They killed my wife and many others yesterday at Waiilatpu!"

"Kenwa's men came back Friday," Francis said scornfully.

"He's a liar, just like you, Pettygrove. Men, an Indian lover ain't no better than an Indian. Open fire!"

He was met with silence. The other eighteen men cowered down in the bateaux. In the darkness they thought the rifle shots had come from Pack McGraw. Every one of them had been on a wagon train with the man and knew of his expertise with the rifle and pistols. No one wanted to test his aim now.

Once they were lined up at the riverbank, and faces were recognizable, Francis's disgust at them was bottomless. His eyes centered on Amos Crumley. "What gives you the right to take the law into your own hands?"

Crumley stumbled onto the bank, his face ashen with fear.

"As Brown said," he rasped, "the Cayuse did a massacre at the Whitman mission. Ain't just Brown's wife that boiled our blood. Our own Deborah Waller was taken prisoner and her preacher husband is dead."

"What were you doing up there, Brown?"

Tom Brown stepped out of his bateau, his body hunched over as if he were ready to spring.

"Marcus Whitman was a Christian man and took us in after you cheated me, lied about me, and chased me from my home and livelihood."

"I ain't interested in ancient history," Pack snapped. "What happened there yesterday?"

Brown blinked, unaware that he was still in a state of shock. "Wagon train came in Friday," he mumbled. "Among them the half-Indian daughter of Jim Bridger, sent for schooling at the Lapwai mission. Breakfast cooking at dawn. No warning. They came from all sides of the mission, racing in on their *Cayuse* ponies, nearly naked, all painted up, clashing their shields, burning, looting, killing. I found a horse and made tracks. They had no reason to do that."

"No reason?" Kenwa sputtered. "I don't go along with Joe Lewis's argument that all the missionaries should be killed, for they and HBC have never been the problem with the Cayuse or the Nez Perce. We could trade with them in harmony, like with Francis Pettygrove. But you men, and hundreds of others like you, killed our game, fished out our streams, grazed your cattle and horses on our pasture lands, stole our land and horses, and brought your sickness. Joe

Lewis's only problem is that he massacred the wrong people. I am sick at what I saw this evening. My men were unarmed. They didn't fear you as you approached. Then, at the goading of Brown you shot them and started to burn me out. Who are you to call others savages?"

"It's an 'eye for an eye,'" Brown wailed, "and I ain't yet got my revenge for my wife! Everyone get away from the killer!"

He started for the gun in his waistband to back up his demand. Pack had been reading the wildness in his eyes as Kenwa had talked. The man had so garbled things in his mind that he had convinced himself that Kenwa had been at the mission and killed his wife. Pack knew that no amount of talking would bring him to reason. The moment the hand started to remove the pistol from behind the belt, Pack sprang into action. The bullet caught Brown in the chest and threw him hard into the river. No one else went for a gun.

"Get back to your homes," Pack ordered sharply. "He's not the first man I've been forced to kill and he may not be my last!"

It was a long night.

Marsha, fearing that Tama might worm her way back into her domain, bustled the Pettygrove children back home to their beds, but refused to look after little Peter Kenwa.

Her arms coated in honey to draw out the sting and keep air from getting to the wound, Sophia awoke, smiled lovingly at the boy, and fell into a deep sleep.

Some time later, Beth and Pack took Kenwa and his son to her house. After the boy was asleep in bed, they sat at the kitchen table. No one talked, as any discussion of the future seemed futile.

Francis paced from Jefferson Street to Washington Street and back again. His disgust now was with his own people. Why, he wondered, hadn't Mick and David tried to stop the slaughter? His answer came a little after 2 A.M., when the stagecoach came wheeling into town.

"Brown set fire to the fur warehouse," Mick explained. "We were all working to put it out when we heard the gunfire. Not until we heard the church bell did we know that they had torched Kenwa and Katoro's houses. The town is hostile. The hotheads are blaming you and Asa for bringing the Indians there in the first place."

Despite the situation, Francis couldn't help but laugh. "Who was where first? And who in the hell do those damn idiots think have been paddling in their supplies? Those are the people I left Oregon City to get away from." He paused and frowned. "How are the Wallers taking the news?"

"They are in Champoeg, like everyone else. Being a four-day meeting, all the wives went along. After David and I locked and boarded up the store, he left for Champoeg to tell his father and the others. I brought Anita, D'Arcy, Pelani, and Katoro here."

"That was wise of you."

It was shorter and quicker for Governor Abernethy, Asa, and Dr. McLoughlin to get to Portland via what was becoming known as the Twality Road because the farmers couldn't get Tualatin twisted around their tongues correctly.

Abernethy called a meeting to be held in the Pettygrove store.

"Pack, I've sent my son to Salem to start signing up recruits for a militia. Stephen Coffin has military experience and will be in command, but he will need you as a scout and because you speak the language. Dr. McLoughlin will go immediately to the Factor at Fort Vancouver, to get the Hudson Bay people to make contact and see if we can't ransom the women and children. Francis, for the moment I don't think it is wise for you to reopen your store."

"It is better protected open, than closed and unguarded."

"Haven't you done enough to rile the people?" George Abernethy suddenly flared. "You could have prevented bloodshed here, but you took the law into your own hands."

"You've got that all wrong—" Pack tried to explain, but Abernethy cut him short.

"It's his town and he should have had better sense."

Francis was so instilled with rage that he was unable to defend himself.

"Abernethy," Pack said icily. "I'm not some Methodist

layman you can codfish over. You may have just been re-elected governor, but that doesn't give you the right to be judge and jury. Before you start accusing us in Portland, you'd best get your fat ass back to Oregon City to determine the bloodshed there."

"It's not the same," Abernethy hissed piously. "Those were Indians!"

"Is that how you feel too, Asa? Your silence has me puzzled."

Asa was uncomfortable, as was Dr. McLoughlin. Abernethy had been like a fierce tiger since hearing the news.

"There is reason for silence," he said sourly. "At first we only had the report from David McLoughlin, who was not an eyewitness. Twenty minutes later Amos Crumley rode in and related how Brown had tracked Kenwa's men back from Waiilatpu and that Kenwa was attempting to take them downriver for hiding in their village."

"Idiot!" Francis screeched. "You know damn full well my feelings about liars and yet you can stand there and repeat the words of one without ever once, since entering that door, asking for the truth of last night. Out! If this is my town, then I have the authority to order you out!"

"Go to hell!" Asa snarled and he and Abernethy stormed away.

John McLoughlin stood for a long moment, unsure of what he really should do next. He was more upset over the territorial meeting than the incident at Waiilatpu. Abernethy had sprung an insidious surprise at the meeting. Before Asa could protect his client, the legislature stripped any British subject of all their land claims and gave them thirty days to redeem them at the present market value. Ironically, Abernethy could then put on a different face and ask the British people at Hudson Bay to assist with the Cayuse. Now, he had seen another face of Asa Lovejoy. It left a strong suspicion in his mind that Asa knew of Abernethy's proposal long before they went to Champoeg.

"Francis," McLoughlin said, at last. "I, for one, have need for the truth. Will you paddle with me to the fort?"

"Yes. It might help my mood." Then his voice took on a

note of concern. "John, all night long I have been pondering another concern. Kenwa's family are good people and devout Catholics. Last night I saw there were no innocent bystanders when it comes to hateful prejudice. Do you mind if Kenwa goes with us, to check on his family?"

"But, of course not!" Then he let out an audible sigh. "I wish I had a parcel of land to give Kenwa's family. Some at the meeting were already starting to covet the land north of the Columbia."

Beth's Christmas party was not the only fiasco to finish off 1847.

Not wishing to admit that they had listened to a liar, Abernethy and Lovejoy concentrated their efforts on the Cayuse War, while perpetrating a war that would last longer.

On December 6, the packet *Liberty* sailed right by Portland. On the bridge, with Captain Irving Paine, was Nathan Abernethy, a cousin who had brought a shipload of manufactured goods from the East Coast. Having been assured by Nathan that Oregon City was the "head of navigation," Paine was not even ordering sounding depths. Within the hour they were being buffeted back by the rush of the Clackamas Rapids. Barely able to get the 137-foot vessel turned around, Paine made his fiasco move. With no charts of the river, he mistook the east channel around Ross Island to be the main channel and was no sooner committed to that course when he went aground on the sand bar of the shallow-watered channel.

Without bateau boys, but feeling it was within his right to commandeer Kenwa's bateaux, Abernethy ordered the Kanaka boys out of the timber and to paddle up his supplies. To drift with the current, using the paddles to steer and brake was not difficult. To paddle against the current, with eight hundred pounds of cargo, spelled fiasco time. One after another the bateaux were forced sideways by the current, capsized, with the cargo sinking or floating away with the upside-down bateau. The water was December icy and the Kanaka boys turned a deep blue. It was twelve miles of swimming against the current back to Oregon City and three miles with the current to Portland. As though they were in the ocean surf they swam hard for Portland and presented Katoro with an ultimatum: find them other work or send them back to Hawaii. Abernethy was stalemated in getting his cargo, and thus his lumber business came to a standstill.

Mick and Dave had been making daily roundtrips since the 1st of December to keep the store open in the daytime, but tightly closed at night. They were doing very little business, but on the 8th, a disgruntled customer came back to Portland.

"No one tells Eliza Boddick where she can shop and not shop for dress material. I'm reopening my shop here, Beth, and Asa Lawrence Lovejoy can swim in the River Styx before I will marry him!"

Liza wasn't Asa's only fiasco. When John McLoughlin came with "Pettygrove Money" to secure back his unsold lots, Asa refused to accept it, except at a greatly reduced value. Asa knew that John had put all of his money into building McLoughlin House and was anticipating lot sales to live upon. Asa also knew that Abernethy wanted some of the McLoughlin property, because part of the cargo stranded at Ross Island was a supply of bricks for a new store.

"As I don't see us doing much trading in 'Pettygrove Money,'" Asa said, "I think you'd best go back to Francis and get a cash loan."

The word *loan* was enough to boil John's Scots blood. Nor was he about to tell Asa that he had sold Francis his claimed land upon which the Fort Vancouver sawmill sat. North of the Columbia the "Abernethy rule" was not valid.

John Couch did not pull a fiasco, but made a wise business move. He gave McLoughlin par value for the script and made a quiet trip to Portland.

"Francis, when I sailed the *Maryland* to The Falls, it was spring and the backwash from the flooded Columbia made the Willamette twice as deep as normal. Can't make money waiting for a flood to get a ship in. The stranded *Liberty* convinces me that Portland is the head of navigation. My claim is still a little distant from your downtown and I seek permission to buy a lot and move my store from Oregon City."

Francis was jubilant. He was gaining in the war, without having yet fought a battle.

His fiasco, and Ian Llwellen's, came as one as the *Yam-il* docked the next day. Rhoda had sent along another twelve male Kanaka workers, and Francis's folly had followed Ian up the Willamette like a parade.

"I opened my mouth, spoke, and then forgot I had made such a rash promise," Francis moaned. "To keep them from any retaliation, I told Kenwa he could move his family here. Ian, there must be fifty canoes on the river. They'll never fit on the old clearing."

"What about that meadowland which is half on your land and half on mine?" Daniel Lownsdale asked. "It's much larger than their spot above the fort, the creek runs right through it, and I can use the labor of some of the men to get the bark off the hemlock without killing the whole tree."

"That's fine with me," Francis said. "I'll tell Kenwa."

"Oh, Ian," Daniel said, remembering why he had come down to the ship. "I was wondering if you had some of my kin aboard. Mrs. Elizabeth Caruthers-Thomas and her son, Finice Caruthers?"

"Didn't know they were your kin, Daniel. They have been a pain in the . . . hold! Had to build stables down there for her eight horses. She treats them like spoiled children. Don't know how they ever survived such a trip from Kentucky."

Daniel smiled. Eccentric people and the things they loved always seemed to survive. When he had filed his claim, he had also filed a claim for the six-hundred-forty acres just south of the townsite in the name of Finice, because Asa wouldn't record a claim in a woman's name.

Kenwa's fiasco was in allowing his grandmother to decide who was "family." His grandfather had had three wives, his father two. His grandmother, called "Old Wife," didn't wait for her husband to come back from the war party to make a decision. In the matriarchal custom of her Yam-il tribe, she

gathered up the one hundred eighty-seven whom she wished
to call relatives, and moved them. They ranged from a month
old up to her sixty-eight years.

To Francis, whom she remembered from the wedding, she
shouted a joyous greeting.

"My grandmother," Kenwa interpreted, "say she is happy
to be near the source of the hard candy."

Pack's fiasco was getting involved in the Cayuse War to
begin with. Stephen Coffin resented the manner in which he
was given the command. He had only arrived the spring
before, with his wife and children. He had had only one
summer of militia training in Maine. As a builder, he had
asked to bid on Abernethy's new brick store. Curtly, he was
told he could have the contract if he commanded this mission. In business he was decisive, but his military leadership
was marked by indecisiveness. He had left Fort Vancouver
with a force of one hundred fifty, a pack supply train of fifty
horses, a self-appointed staff of five officers, and Pack
McGraw. The "officers" were of the original Methodist stock
and ceaselessly denigrated HBC for even attempting to negotiate for the hostages.

Pack figured the Cayuse would have gone north to the
Horse Heaven Hills, using the Toppenish Ridge to get back
unseen to the Cascade Mountains. The officers determined
that they needed to go all the way to the mission and track
the Indians from there. That night they lost 20 percent of the
force to desertion. After a hard sixty-mile ride, they were
opposite the HBC trading post at The Dalles. Fording the
river, the officers were hostile to the Indians camped there,
to the embarrassment of Pack and Coffin.

They were Nez Perce and were distressed over the destruction of the mission.

"Why your interest, one who speaks our tongue?"

"They have women and children. I want them back safe."

"Three little squaws dead already from the sickness."

"We have not heard there was sickness, wise one."

"Reason for the tragedy, my son. Our chief bears the
Christian name Timothy. When the salmon ran late, the
Great Spirit in the fish told him the white man's sickness

would strike the Cayuse, because they do not cross themselves when they pray, as we have been taught. Priest say
sickness called 'measles.' Many, many sick at mission and at
villages down the river. Medicine man say put hot rock in
hut, pour over with water to sweat, and then go jump in cold
river. Dr. Whitman say medicine man wrong and the Cayuse
die so fast no time for proper burial. Bad medicine man from
Eastern tribe tell Cayuse that doctor was poisoning sick
Cayuse so he can take land. He says whites get well from
sickness because no poisoned. Cayuse stupid, not smart like
Nez Perce. White squaws no like be Indian wives, yet three
ceremonies already.''

"You have much knowledge, wise one. Can you tell me
how many were captured?''

"Fifty-one in all.'' He looked at Pack with hard, piercing
eyes. "From one of the pillars that holds up this corner of the
sky flows a mountain river. The home of many little vales
and caves. But a land of terrible winter storms. Not fifty-one
by spring.''

Nodding with due seriousness over the statement, he dug
into his pack. Although Pack was not a smoking man, he
made sure he always had several lengths of braided burleigh
for moments like this.

Stephen Coffin thought Pack had gained valuable knowledge.

"Utter nonsense,'' Moses Ruby scoffed. "A deliberate
attempt to lead us off on a wild goose chase. We press on for
the mission.''

"Moses, that's another hundred and twenty-five miles.
We'll never get home by Christmas. If we go down The
Dalles trail, we are only forty miles from Oregon City.''

Too many had overheard the comment about that shortcut
home. During the night they lost another sixty men.

"It is obvious you can't command their respect to keep
them,'' Moses preached at Coffin. "The five of us have met
and determined that you should relinquish the command.''

"With great pleasure. Men, Moses Ruby and the others
are in command. Those who wish to stay can. As for me, I
am going home. What about you, Pack?''

"Think I'll snoop my way back down the Columbia."

Moses lost all but twenty of the men, including three of his officers and his son.

By noon all three parties were caught in the same driving snowstorm. Coffin, having been raised through bitter winters in Maine, got his men deep into the trees and hunched down to wait out the storm. Pack had been trained to smell out a trapper's cabin from a distance of a mile. He stumbled in on a French-Canadian who spoke Umatilla. No one ever learned if the Moses party perished in the storm or ran into a hothead band of Cayuse.

Because of the trapper's daughter, it took Pack until December 15 to reach Fort Vancouver. The Factor, Peter Skene Ogden, took Pack's report with great seriousness.

"They consider Adams and Hood as pillars. They wouldn't go south into American territory, so we can forget the Hood River. That leaves the Kicktat runoff from Mount Adams. Good on you, old boy. We've been floundering. Can't talk to the blokes, unless you can find them. Wouldn't get your folks' hopes up, though. The old man was right about winter. The Cayuse are used to this elevation and river valley winters. That area is a good mile higher than here. I've held the sloop *Larksdale* from sailing with a great score of my senior staff and their families. Might do her marines a bit of good to stretch their sea legs before the long voyage home. Home . . . what a strange-sounding word. I left England exactly twenty years ago this month, at the age of twenty. Don't relish having to pack up, is my problem."

Pack never thought about age, but Ogden's mention of it reminded him that he had turned twenty-two while sitting in the trapper's cabin.

"Fitting place," he said sourly.

"Does that horse walk on water, cowboy?"

"Kenwa, what in the hell are you doing here?"

"Been repairing the scow at the shipyard. She's ready to go home. You ready?"

"Sounds good to me. Come on, Thunder, this will be a new experience for you."

George Abernethy was not only in the humiliating position

of having to explain the failure of the militia, but in having to accept that Ogden had the hostages back to Portland by December 20.

"Why Portland?" he flared. "Oregon City is the capital of the Oregon Territory!"

McLoughlin loved his moment of retribution. "The *Larksdale* and Kenwa's scow delivered them to the head of navigation. Besides, Peter gives great credit to Pack McGraw. The information he obtained at The Dalles allowed them to accomplish the rescue without loss of life."

"Then let Pack McGraw and the rest of the Portland pack pay for the ransom!"

"George," the former Factor said sternly, "although history does not always paint us in that light, we English are a compassionate people. There has been no mention of charging you for the ransom HBC paid to retrieve those poor women and children, nor will there be."

"Well," George sputtered, "at least I have a right to learn of the Waller girl."

"Her parents have been informed. Deborah died of measles a week before the massacre. Mrs. Brown also died of measles, George. Tom Brown knew both of those facts and the survivors have reported on his cowardly desertion, without knowing a thing about the incident here. If restitution is in order, it should go to Kenwa and Katoro."

"That is ridiculous and unthinkable. It is not Oregon City's responsibility if Brown set fire to their homes and destroyed Kenwa's boats. We are the ones who are being made to suffer without his bateau service!"

"Sophia," Beth said, over coffee, "I should have known that it was wrong to hold my party so early in December. Now we have these women and children with us, until they can be relocated. They deserve some holiday cheer. Do you think anyone would mind if I redid the party on Christmas Day?"

"Oh, Beth, what a marvelous idea! Why couldn't we all share, so you don't have all the burden. One thing I miss about Boston at Christmastime are the progressive dinners."

Beth clapped her hands. "That's it, Sophia! We have your house and ours. Liza would love it, and if it's a nice day, it's not too far of a walk to the Lownsdales'."

"I wonder," Sophia mused, "if Tama might want to talk with Old Wife. The woman is wonderfully amusing. What do you think, Ian?"

He looked up from the last issue of the *Spectator*. "Might let those orphan waifs know that not all Cayuse are killers."

"Speaking of amusing women, I think Elizabeth Caruthers-Thomas would participate. I've rented them the Crosby house until Nate's return."

"You've rented?" Ian asked, on a raised eyebrow. "How do you have that authority?"

"Very simple," Beth said in a low and very sexy voice. "He slipped me the keys in bed while we were making wild, passionate love. My ecstasy was such that Nuua could hear me panting all the way down here in the kitchen."

Nuua broke into a fit of giggles and covered her moon face with her hands.

"That proves what a liar you are, Elizabeth Llwellen! Had Nuua turned silent and frowned, I would have feared it was true. Now, when are you three going to break the news to me?"

"Ian," Sophia scolded. "it's supposed to be a Christmas present."

"Your act of being inscrutable didn't work. Lord, I've been sleeping with the woman each night since my return and am not blind to change. When?"

Beth sighed. "In July, Ian. About the same time that Nuua and Matoa are expecting."

"Nuua? I thought I noticed you getting bigger, girl."

Nuua giggled again and ran from the room. Her husband was her husband, but Ian was her god. He had brought her to her land of happiness, but it was *kapu* for her to let any man but her husband sing her praises. Still, she loved Ian's kidding.

"Well, I've got to get back. Marsha is not happy with our newest patient, and Marsha wears her unhappiness like a martyr's cross."

"What's her complaint with . . . Molly Spragge, isn't it?"

Sophia nodded. "Seems she and Pack were raised at the same trading post, but Marsha can't get any more than that out of her or Pack. After all of these years of his masculine charms troubling Marsha's dreams, she's furious at his tight lips. Her romantic nature has turned it into something dark and mysterious."

"How badly was she hurt?" Ian asked.

"Physically, only bruises. It's the humiliation and embarrassment of having been forced to become the bride of a brave. Pack started to tell me of a previous Indian experience she had been through, but stopped when Marsha came into the room."

"He's saving it for the *Spectator*," Ian laughed. "All they print are second-hand stories."

Sophia grinned at him. "Because first-hand news might be too embarrassing to the government."

CHAPTER
☆ 15 ☆

The quixotic rivalry between Oregon City and the struggling communities of Multnomah City and Linn City was a battle of words.

By the spring of 1848 the other rivalry had turned vehement and bitter.

"Kenwa," Abernethy chuckled, with a sickeningly sweet grin, "you've been most busy this winter. Three scows! Most impressive. I need the rest of the cargo off that ship before the spring runoff floats it free."

Kenwa looked at him without smiling. "Fee seven dollars."

"That seems very high."

"That is per scow, per day."

Abernethy blew out his lips. "That is outrageous! I used to pay $1.00 per bateau, per unloaded ship and in trade."

Kenwa didn't flinch. "Bateau boys who worked for dollar trade all dead. Bateaux destroyed or stolen. Scows cost Kenwa much money to build. New boys want same pay as timber men. Kenwa not in business for pure fun."

Abernethy listened to Kenwa's report with a deep scowl on his face.

"What do you charge Pettygrove to keep this store supplied?"

"Yearly contract," Kenwa answered dryly.

"All right," he said slowly, "but I want it done today."

Kenwa shook his head. "Next week, maybe. Must finish with *Toulon* cargo, float timber to the fort, deliver lumber to

Mr. Coffin, rocks to Mr. Moss, and supplies to Milwaukie. Next week, maybe, maybe no."

Abernethy turned away in disgust.

Katoro, who had been helping train the new Kanaka boys to the sail and tiller, sidled up. "Why didn't you tell him we pulled the *Liberty* free this morning?"

Kenwa grinned. "Not our place to tell a white man his business."

George Abernethy was fuming by the time he found Asa, Stephen Coffin, and Sidney Moss together in the tap room of the Main Street House Hotel. It was the first time he had set foot in the place since Moss had obtained a license to be a retailer of "spiritous liquors."

"Lumber?" he stormed. "I don't recall you putting in an order for lumber, Coffin!"

"Didn't," he answered evenly. "You couldn't deliver, so I had to order it from Pettygrove. Work is in Portland, anyway. No work here."

Abernethy sputtered. He dared not bring up the growing stack of bricks for his building, as he had taken the contract away from Coffin.

"And what do you need rocks for?"

Sidney Moss liked to think of himself as a man of diverse parts. As the organizer of "The Falls Debating Society" he loved to take any stand that was opposite the views of Governor George Abernethy.

"The lady wants a rock foundation for her stables. Can't make a rock foundation without rocks. No more than Steve can finish her house or build the stables without lumber." He got a warning glance from Coffin to stop right there. He didn't want Lovejoy or Abernethy to know that they were also building a two-story hotel on Portland's Front Street. "Any other questions, Gov?"

"Yes! What in the hell is this place called Milwaukie?"

Asa shrugged. "Nothing more than a name Lot Whitcomb put on his claim when he arrived last November. He's only started to erect a sawmill at the mouth of Johnson Creek."

"Only?" Abernethy scathed. "I can't even get my lumber

downriver and now a new competitor! Why am I always the last to learn anything?"

For the second time that day, he stormed off. If an Indian could build scows, then he could build ferries to handle his ship cargo and lumber.

"You can come out now, Dennis," Asa said. "Your chief critic has departed."

The part-time editor of the *Spectator* came out from behind the taproom bar like a jack-in-the-box. Of Nordic blood, Dennis was tall, big-boned, and ashy blond. A sad-faced man, he moved as though he were dragging along the bodies of his dead wife and children.

"Thank you," he said softly. "I didn't want another hour-long lecture on why I was wrong to have written against his taxation plan. But, to answer your question, Asa, in the Michigan Territory we really didn't have any provision for the adoption of orphans."

"Nor do we here."

"Then you can just write it up to please your client and so it conforms with their will."

Asa pursed his lips. "I've always been more of a business lawyer and not personal. Can you write it up for me?"

"Can," Dennis Landry said laconically. "But why?"

"It was Philip Foster who approached me. He and his wife have taken in the six Johnson kids from the massacre. Mrs. Foster was Mary Charlotte Pettygrove. See my problem?"

"Yep. Two stubborn lead mules who won't go into a double harness. Best tell you all right now. That was my last *Spectator*. May starve, but I'm going back to my law practice. I've rented a second-floor office and living space in Portland. I'll still write it for you, though."

"Better yet," Asa said, "I'll have Philip come and see you. Your first client. Why the second floor?"

"The owner, Finice Caruthers, has his own use for the first floor."

"I can attest to that," Coffin broke in. "Shelves, shelves, and more shelves. He's got more books in crates than we had possessions for a whole family on the wagon train. While his

mother raises her pure breed horses, he's going to open a
library. How do you like that? Portland ain't even got a
school, like you have here, but they're going to have a library."

Asa smiled to himself. Coffin wasn't up to date on all the
Portland news. Foster was not afraid of adopting the Johnson
children, because a schoolteacher had arrived in Portland
aboard the *Toulon*.

"Sophia, what a chatterbox he has become. And don't
anyone correct him! I can be 'Auntie Rhodie' if Lorenzo
desires. Beth, are you sure you should have walked down
here?"

"Rhoda Farman, I am fine," Beth said. "I may be big as a
horse, but I'm getting tired of people pampering me."

"A married lady should be pampered," Sophia insisted. At
the mention of the word *married*, Rhoda's mouth started to
pucker. Sophia saw it and jumped right in.

"Rhoda, don't you even think of sniffling. We can't even
hold a normal conversation without some word setting you
off. It's not as if Dexter were—"

"He might as well be dead!" Rhoda overrode. "The old
fool! Almost a sin to marry at his age. I hope he starves
because of her cooking and that she puts too much starch in
his collars!"

"Green-eyed monster jealousy talk again?" Marsha sing-
songed, bringing in the tea service.

Wordlessly, Sophia glared her out of the room. Out the
south window she saw the approach of a horse and breathed
a sigh of relief.

"Elizabeth is coming now."

The rider was coming hell-bent-for-leather, over a newly
cleared pasture. Rhoda, looking out, thought Sophia was
mistaken. This rider wore pants, a flat-brimmed hat, and
cleared the split-rail fence by a good four feet.

"That's a man."

"Hardly," came a wheezing laugh behind them. "That's
my maw-ther."

They had forgotten that Finice Caruthers had already arrived and sat in a straight-backed chair next to the fireplace.

Rhoda had nearly giggled when she had met the twenty-seven-year-old man. As thin as a bamboo-shoot, he wore straight-line suits that exaggerated this appearance. Finice was precise in everything; each word was spoken as though he had to breathe life into it. The angular face was not unhandsome, but had a jutting appearance from his habit of tilting back his head to peer out of his pince-nez glasses. The impression he gave was not in any way feminine—he was just too much a part of his only vocation and avocation: books.

"You should know, Miss Farman, that she was regarded as the finest horsewoman in Kentucky, sidesaddle or astraddle. There are some southern gentlemen who will not ride except on a Caruthers-bred horse, you know."

"I've never ridden myself," Rhoda admitted.

"Nor I," Finice laughed. It was a deep rich sound, like the bass notes on a pipe organ. "I was given a pony when I was six years old. The beast took a bite out of me and so I bit him back. He never wanted to see me again and the feeling was entirely mutual."

Elizabeth Caruthers-Thomas breezed in laughing, as though she knew no other sound.

"Sorry to be late, but I had to show the mules who was boss—and how to pull out stumps!"

Rhoda was puzzled. "Why are the stumps coming out of that pasture, Mrs. Caruthers-Thomas, and not from the streets in town? Why, I nearly broke a toe coming here from the ship!"

Elizabeth's bell-like laugh came again as she took off the hat and let her carrot-orange hair fall to her shoulders. Without the hat she shrunk to the mite of a woman that she was. For a woman of fifty she still had the body and complexion of a girl.

"One of my horses, Miss Farman, costs more than this whole town put together. Horse breaks a leg and all I can do is shoot him. So the stumps go. Once these mules are trained, I might start working on the streets just for the exercise. Now, let's you and I get one thing clear from the start: You can drop the 'Caruthers-Thomas' crap. It's either 'Elizabeth' or 'Mrs. Caruthers.' Joe Thomas was a worthless no-account who drank his way to New Orleans and vanished. I never should have married again. Meriwether Caruthers was one hell of a man, before he broke his neck trying to take too high a fence. But, like my horses, a filly gets an itch and there's a stud in the next pasture. Hell, Joe Thomas wasn't even good as a stud!"

Rhoda blushed scarlet. Even though she was five years younger than this woman, she was still a virgin and intended to keep it that way.

Just then Marsha brought in a tray of dainty sandwiches, sniffed, and departed.

Sophia and Beth looked at each other and nearly broke out laughing. Marsha was greatly upset that Elizabeth Caruthers had not invited her to this little tea-party meeting.

"Well," Elizabeth launched right in, taking a sandwich and devouring it in a single bite, "I told Francis that I hate meetings of any nature, but I love a hot cup of tea and something to nibble on. The bottom line—go ahead and pour, Sophia—is that I will donate the timber, if Francis gets it cut to lumber. Morrison, O'Bryant, and Coffin will build it, after they get my house finished. Captain Crosby seemed overjoyed that he was going to be staying at Beth's house, until he saw her state of pregnancy. He has looked like a gelding ever since. What else do we need for a school?"

"I've taken care of the books, Elizabeth," Finice reported. He had stopped calling her "Mother" when he turned twenty-five and she'd married Joe Thomas.

"Good. Rhoda, these are books we used to educate our slaves. Look them over and let Finice know if they are proper or not. If not, he knows every publisher who has ever printed in New York or Philadelphia."

Rhoda frowned. "I haven't even said I would stay. It was only for a visit to get over my—"

"We have all summer to think about it," Sophia said quickly, before Rhoda could start pouting over Dexter's marriage again. "And you won't have the full responsibility. Finice will also be teaching certain subjects."

"We can make a shopping list and return it with Ian when he gets here next month for the birth of the baby. If there are no objections, I say meeting adjourned."

Marsha brought a fresh pot of tea in; she still wasn't asked to stay.

"Elizabeth," Beth said, "I've never figured out your desire to settle and raise horses here. Was it because of your kin, Daniel Lownsdale?"

"He's not really blood kin, Beth. In Kentucky all your county neighbors are kin. When Daniel sent for his wife, I told her to tell him to get me a claim, because it sounded like fine horse country. When Meriwether died I grew most unpopular by freeing our slaves. Men we had sold horses to for years stopped buying. Knew right then they were not the type of men I wanted owning one of my little darlings. It was time for Finice and I to move on to newer pastures."

"Sophia," Marsha hissed, but so everyone could hear. "Molly ain't back with the milk yet, and Finice just used the last we had."

"I've had ample tea, thank you, Mrs. Tolcott."

"Humph! All we're running around here is a boarding-house. Six months and she's not asked to lift a finger. If you ask me—"

"I didn't, Marsha. Thank you."

Beth saw the hurricane warning signals go up as Marsha made her exit. She was happy that Sophia was in charge of her own house again, but Molly Spragge was a worry. She was so quiet, so uncommunicative, and glared at Pack as though she hated him fiercely. And because she was there, they had seen very little of him in the past several months. She knew part of his absence was for her benefit. When they received word that American troops were about to capture California, Pack had left Joe Bellam on the ranch and made several trips to trade with the frantic Spanish ranchers. At five dollars a head, he had built the herd to over 2,000 head of cattle.

* * *

Pack stretched out on the grassy knoll and sniffed the air. Joe Gale had three hundred acres plowed and planted in hay. The old farmer and his wife had given up on wheat and cattle. They could make more raising hay for the winter use of Pack and Joe Bellam, who owned the next two claims to the west. It was all undeveloped grazing land, except for the ranch house, milking barns, and chicken coops. Mrs. Gale had become friendlier when one of the Kanaka girls had become Mrs. Joe Bellam. That arrangement pleased Pack, as well. Lilano was Nuua's older sister and had cost Joe only one hundred dollars. A strong, forceful woman, she had been able to take charge of the other Kanaka milkmaid girls and bring peace and harmony.

Pack was content. They had 1,280 acres and miles of grazing land to the west, because no one had set claims on it, as yet.

"You look quite relaxed."

Surprised out of his reverie, Pack took the hat off his face and looked up.

"Jehsophat, Molly!" he exploded. "What in the hell are you doing out here?"

"Prune-faced Marsha needed milk," she laughed. "The store was out and I convinced Bell I could handle a team and wagon better than a man. That Indian woman told me where to find you."

"She is not Indian!" he snapped. "She is Hawaiian!"

Molly shrugged indifferently and looked around. "You've come quite a way, John Packwood McGraw! Quite a way!"

He remained prone and didn't invite her to sit down on the grass. "Why did you come out here to Oregon, Molly?"

"I told you that someday I would be able to run away from the dead."

"And right into another massacre and Indian marriage."

She laughed, and it had a wicked sound. "They understood enough of my Cheyenne to know that I was not a threat to them. The other two ninnies fought and screamed over becoming brides. It wasn't my first Indian, as you well know. It was just one more chance at survival."

"Then why the big act for the past six months?"

"I deserved it!" she glared. "To live in a real house, eat good food, and be treated like a lady and not a squaw. Yes, squaw! That's how your mountainman father treated your mother and how my Paw came to treat me. Female slaves. No more of that for Molly Spragge! I've played my quiet game so I could listen and learn. Prune-face is a wealth of information. Look at me, Pack McGraw!"

He rolled on his side, looked up, and gasped.

While she had been talking she had removed the simple cotton dress. She was an embarrassment to Marsha because she refused to wear a breast support or pantaloons. She stood before him, full-breasted, slender-trunked, snowy-limbed, brunette-downed. He had known her as a sixteen-year-old girl, had thought of her as a haggard old woman at Bear Creek Station, and now saw that she was an exquisite woman.

"You see," she snarled, "it hasn't been fully used up or abused. Twice, you had an opportunity to take me away with you, for it to be yours alone. You owe me for those times."

The sight of her had stirred his desire, but her words were like a splash of cold water.

"I owe you nothing," he said, rising.

Molly's eyes narrowed. "You owe me for a murder, which convinced Colonel Wende that you were also dead."

"What?" he gasped.

She came close, so he could smell of her clean scent and get the full impact of her words.

"They kept scouting the station, in case you didn't leave on that train. I 'befriended' a scout, made it look like he had a shootout with you, and dug you a grave next to your parents."

He grabbed her by the wrists and held her so firmly that she blanched.

"One time, when I was fourteen, did not make us lovers, Molly! You and your sister were also wanton playmates with the Indian boys who came to trade. Owe? I owe you nothing! Put your clothes on! I leave for California in the morning. I'll leave passage money with Francis Pettygrove for you to get out of here. Don't you ever try to blackmail me again, or I swear I'll kill you!"

Molly Spragge dressed slowly and deliberately. Her lustful desire for John Packwood McGraw had shriveled and died years before. She had scared him, as a boy, into his first sexual experience. Now, as a man, she'd scared him into the only thing she desired from him—money for a new beginning. She had no intention of using the money for passage. The ranch and the cattle had confirmed Marsha Tolcott's words: Pack McGraw was becoming a wealthy and respected man. She would bleed him until he was dry.

Two weeks down the trail, Pack crossed the path of an army patrol, riding hard cross country.

"War going against us?"

"The war is over in California, but the murders and claim-jumping is such that martial law may have to be declared. We're under orders to have General Nelson Wende move his entire Western Army to the American River."

Pack grinned. "He's more suited to Indian wars than claim-jumping squabbles."

"Where you from?"

"Oregon Territory."

"Then you ain't heard. Yerba Buena, which we now call San Francisco, is near a ghost town and the greedy are pouring into California like ants to a sugar crumb. This sugar being yellow gold that they found back in January at Sutter's Mill above Sacramento. People have gone crazy. Over half the army's deserted to become gold-diggers!"

Pack sat debating after they rode away. He feared what this would do to the price of California cows and wondered if he shouldn't go back with the news. Then he determined it might be interesting to see that they might wish to pay to get some of their cattle back. He headed directly south for Sacramento.

The baby refused to come, but Beth was having no difficulty or pain.

"We counted wrong," Tama said. "Nuua didn't know how

to count and look at her baby boy. Baby here soon, you see."

Ian debated daily whether to leave or stay. The *Yam-il* had been loaded for two weeks with timber and wheat, although it might be the last lumber Francis was able to obtain from Lot Whitcomb's new mill on Johnson Creek. Abernethy, in a political move, named Whitcomb Commissary-General for the Provisional Government, responsible for organizing the supplies for the new militia who were to spend the summer chasing the still-wandering Cayuse braves. As Commissary-General, however, he could only order supplies from Abernethy's store, could only use Abernethy "barges" to transport the supplies, and was quietly discouraged from doing any business with Portland.

Francis retaliated with a "wharf tax." Any ships offloading goods for any upriver destination were charged a fifty-dollar fee, unless they used the services of "Yamhill River Transport—John Kenwa, proprietor." The "John" had been Beth's suggestion, so that some ships' masters didn't get the idea they were dealing with an Indian they could hoodwink. Besides the *Toulon* and *Yam-il*, the Willamette was receiving about a ship a month for trading. It was Tama's suggestion to keep the company name consistent with the street, and mainly because the scows moored at the foot of Yamhill Street.

"That's odd," Ian said, as a ship whistled for permission to dock behind the *Yam-il*. "That's the *Honolulu*. Newell normally only runs her between Hawaii and San Francisco." He climbed down to the wharf and walked back to greet the arrival. "Ahoy, Brice! Did you lose your navigator?"

"Hello, Ian," the sixty-year-old captain called crisply, disgusted there was someone in port he knew. "Ran short of provisions."

That didn't strike Ian as logical. The water line of the ship told him the ship was on a dead-head without cargo. The ship had not been in Honolulu when he departed, so he knew its last port had to have been San Francisco.

"Got any California newspapers for us, Brice?"

Newell looked nervous in his moment of hesitation. "Sorry, mate, but we're just up from the islands." He didn't want Llwellen knowing that it was a seller's market in San Francisco and Sacramento. Nor did he want to admit that there were no San Francisco newspapers because all of the printers were off to the gold fields.

Casually, Ian wandered back to his ship. The man had outright lied. Even though it was near lunchtime, he loafed about until he saw Francis leave for home. He didn't hurry to catch up with Francis, for he didn't want Newell to know they were closely acquainted. He caught up with him at the foot of Yamhill Street, as he was giving quick instructions to Kenwa.

"Hello, Ian. Do you know this Captain Newell?"

"Yes, and he's got my curiosity up. What provisions does he seek?"

"Picks, shovels, washstand basins, and all manner of men's heavy clothing. I've sent Kenwa to get what we have at the Oregon City store and whatever he can from Abernethy."

Ian whistled. "How do you know the Governor will even talk to Kenwa or accept 'Pettygrove Money'?"

"Because"—Francis laughed, sarcastically—"neither of those are in the picture. Dave McLoughlin has been running John Couch's store for him while the good 'Captain' has been back in Massachusetts. Couch always gets such manufactured goods for both stores through Abernethy. As for money, I can't see Abernethy turning down gold dust for payment."

"Francis," Ian said, after a long pause. "Newell barely has money to pay for each cargo load and his crew. If he is buying with gold dust, he knows something we want to find out about. And if we can't learn it, I want to set sail after him and tag him to his port."

"What about the baby?"

"Francis, my gut tells me that I'll be around for other babies, but this is too important not to follow up on."

At midnight, Francis was aroused by the strangest sound. He laid for several seconds before he realized someone was throwing pebbles at his bedroom window.

"Ian!" he hissed. "Are you drunk? Is it the baby?"

"No baby, and only a little tipsy. Get dressed, Francis, and meet me at the store. I'm going up to say good-bye to Beth."

Francis fumed as he pulled his clothes on over his night-shirt.

Approaching his store, he was sure this was all a dream and he would wake up momentarily. There was a non-speaking line of sailors stretching from the warehouse door to the ship and down into the hold. Without a sound they were passing along the heavy sacks of potatoes, dried beans, sugar, and flour barrels that had been accumulated for the next *Toulon* run to Honolulu. Inside the warehouse he found George Bell meticulously putting the items on manifest sheets and Ian calculating his cargo load.

"When do I wake up from this strange dream, Ian?"

"Just be thankful we do not have a tavern," Ian said, still a little flushed, "and that Newell doesn't allow grog on his vessel."

"I beg your pardon?"

"By turning my quarters into a friendly bar for the officers and navigators of the *Honolulu*, I was able to loosen a tongue here and there. Francis, an exceedingly rich gold mine was discovered in the Sacramento Valley. It's not ore, Francis, but pure virgin gold! When the *Honolulu* left San Francisco it was bringing fifteen dollars per ounce. I want to sail at dawn but make Newell think it was my normal departure for Hawaii. You'll have time to restock for the *Toulon* and *Henry*."

"The *Henry*? Kilborn is one of Abernethy's main suppliers."

Ian grinned. "Think like your grandfather. Any man can be bought if the price is right. And don't worry about Beth. Tama is with her, and Beth is so excited about this news that I wouldn't be surprised if the baby came tonight."

Ian was off by two days and a baby. No one had even thought about twins. Dana came kicking into the world at 6:01 A.M., August 3. Donald waited until 6:12 A.M. with yawning indifference to everyone and everything about him.

During those days Francis was nervous and agitated, trying to keep the news away from Marsha Tolcott's ears. Because she had not been included in on the school discussion "tea," she had renewed some of her acquaintances in Oregon City, walking the twelve miles a couple of times a week.

Then Francis did begin to fret. On the day that the *Honolulu* was to depart, a longboat came upriver from the HBMS *Constance*, stopping at Fort Vancouver to take more HBC employees home. Captain Courtenay was sending copies of the *Polynesian* to the *Spectator*. By Thursday, waiting for Kenwa to bring him a copy of the local paper, Francis was not fit to live with.

"Hello, Mr. Pettygrove."

"Molly," he barked, "I am a very busy man today."

"Don't mean to bother," she said, sniffling just enough to win his ear and sympathy. "But are you sure that's all the money that Pack left for me?"

"I was not even aware it was money. He just left the packet in my care for you to pick up."

She turned her face into a pout, although she was elated. He did not know it was supposed to be passage money. "Weren't much. Not enough for me to live on until he's back to marry me."

Francis answered without having really listened. "Then you never should have moved out of our house, Molly. Sophia warned you that it was a waste of money for you to go out and rent."

"Couldn't take it no more," she cried. "Ain't one to make trouble, but Marsha was downright hateful and spiteful."

"Excuse me a moment, Molly. Thank you, Kenwa."

Molly was left to hold her playacting while Francis put on his reading glasses and scanned the front page of the *Spectator*. He began to smile. There was an article on the gold strike, but the new part-time editor, a part-time lawyer like Dennis Landry, judiciously cautioned his readers not to run after "fool's gold."

"Now, what was it, Molly?"

She had seen the smile and knew something had pleased him. "Can't see how I can survive till Pack comes back for the wedding. Suppose I should *walk* out and see if he left me money with Joe Bellam."

"No need for that, my dear. Pack has an account with us, get what you need, whenever you need it, and George will put it in the book."

"Thank you, Mr. Pettygrove," she simpered, taking his hand and touching it to her cheek. "I'll let Pack know of your kindness when he returns. Oh, one favor. Except for a few friends, we're keeping the wedding plans secret. I'd just die, before I'd let Marsha Tolcott know."

"I fully understand," Francis agreed and excused himself as he saw Nicolas Zarundy pulling up with a wagonload of sacked sugar. Beet sugar was costing him $.25 a pound; illegally grown cane sugar from Hawaii was $1.50 a pound and when he could get it from New Orleans and the Caribbean it was $2.10 a pound. He couldn't help but wonder what Ian was getting for it in California.

Molly was quiet and demure in making her selections, accepting George Bell's offer to deliver everything except the yard goods, which she would carry along herself.

The moment she walked into Eliza Boddick's dress shop, a thrill of ecstasy made her shiver. All of her dresses had been homemade from flour sacks or homespun woven cloth.

"Hello there . . . Oh, it's . . . Molly Spragge, ain't it. I've seen you of late going up to the quarters over the butcher shop."

"Yes, ma'am," Molly said shyly. "Pack . . . Pack McGraw, that is, said as long as he owned the building, and Matoa had built a new house, I should be using it until we got married."

"Saint's alive! That's a parcel of news to drop so gently. Sit. Sit! I'm all ears to hear how you landed that gorgeous male."

Molly was delighted with herself. Liza had fallen for the story as easily as the Kanaka butcher. She could thank Marsha for every tidbit she had learned about Pack McGraw.

She would let some think she had rented and was starving, but she still had every cent of the passage money hidden away.

"It ain't real romantic, Mrs. Boddick. Known each other since we were kids. When he started making good he sent for me to come out on the wagon train. He ain't ever been one to tell others his plans."

"That's for sure."

Molly hesitated, fingering the string of the wrapped parcel, as though timid to raise a subject.

"Before he left for California, Mrs. Boddick, he went and picked out some dress fabrics. Said he wanted me looking pretty again and not like I was still part of the massacre survivors. Said to come to you . . . but I've hesitated. He didn't leave no money for me to pay you with."

"Now that is just like the man, but, luv, don't you be worrying your little head. He's good for the money, even if I have to take it out in trade for beef and eggs. Let's take a look-see. Oh, my, for a man who lives in buckskins, he's got excellent taste in what he wants his princess to wear! Come over to the table and let's start looking at patterns."

Molly cooked an excellent meal from what she had obtained from the store and butcher shop, where Matoa had also been more than willing to charge things for the future wife of his boss. She set the table fancy, like at the Pettygrove house, and opened the bottle of liquor that her dinner guest had brought back from the "spirits" sale shelf at the Main Street House in Oregon City.

This dinner had not been spur of the moment. The second floor of the butcher shop looked right into the second floor of the library. For several nights, sitting in the dark, she had watched Dennis Landry, drink himself into a stupor so he could sleep.

This had been the longest Molly had been without a man since she was fifteen. The more she looked at Dennis Landry, the more appealing he became. One night she left a bedside candle glowing as she totally undressed and lay on the bed nude. She knew she had captured his attention when his lamps went out. She rubbed her hands over her body, as though they should have been his hands. Then she blew out the candle and left him to wonder what she had done next.

The next day in his office he was shocked to see her and then acted like a little boy about to be scolded for being a peeping-tom.

But Molly's visit was only to obtain legal advice.

"That is a strange business matter, Miss Spragge. I'll take it up with Asa Lovejoy in Oregon City. He might have an answer as to whether Pack is entitled to any profit from the sale, after having deserted the property twice."

Molly pressed her fingers to her mouth in a sudden gesture. "Oregon City. Might a lady ask a great favor, that must be kept a secret?"

Landry laughed. A sound that would have startled everyone who knew him. "Lawyers are supposed to keep their clients' secrets."

Molly turned shy and timid. "This is out of the realm of lawyer and client. Since my . . . ah . . . experience with that . . . Indian, I've been taking a little tonic to relax my nerves. Sometimes I can feel his hands all over me . . . and . . . and—"

"Don't go on, I think I understand. Is the tonic whiskey?"

She nodded as though confessing a great sin.

"Don't worry, I'll get it for you."

He had been quick to accept the dinner invitation, when he delivered the liquor.

The dinner was served warmed over and late.

Five minutes after they had started their second drink, she had him in bed.

Two days after the brig *Henry* arrived with confirmation of the gold discovery, Ian brought the *Yam-il* in riding high in the water.

"It was faster to dead-head back and besides—"

"Good to see you," Francis overrode in a strong voice. "You must be anxious to see the twins!" Then he whispered, "Everyone thinks you've been in Hawaii. Go home! Sophia and I will join you for dinner."

Ian started away puzzled, then stopped dead in his tracks.

Twins? He started running blindly and amazingly missed every stump in the street.

"I'm sorry I was brusque," Francis said, pushing his plate away. "We are awash in enough gold mania."

They had kept the dinner conversation to news of the twins' birth and trivial matters. Once Nuua had finished serving, she was excused to go home.

"Kilborn is a total ass, Ian. To remain respected, in the eyes of George Abernethy, he's anchored below the rapids and will take back only lumber and passengers."

"I can't blame him on the lumber. You paid thirty dollars per thousand board feet and I sold it for one hundred twenty dollars in San Francisco. All told, Francis, we've made a net profit of ten thousand dollars on this run."

"That's fine for now, but my concern is this fall and winter."

"Concern?"

"Ian," Sophia said, playing with the rim of her water glass, "I know we have all laughed in the past about Marsha and her gossip. But to show you the scope of this mania, Marsha is on Captain Kilborn's passenger waiting list. She has already paid him two hundred dollars for a one-way passage. If Marsha thinks she can go dig for gold, what's to stop the farmers, the carpenters, the lumbermen, even your sailors?"

Ian frowned. "I wasn't thinking from that point of view, although I've already seen it down there. The *Toulon* will be running late. Crosby lost half of his crew to gold fever and has gone back to Honolulu to pick up whatever beached sailors he can hire. I sensed that feeling in my own crew when we left here. When we got beyond Cape Disappointment, they knew we were California bound. Immediately, I raised the crew to six dollars a day and the officers to two hundred fifty dollars a month."

"What does that do to our profit margin?" Beth asked, a little concerned over such a huge salary increase.

"Beth, my beautiful mother of two handsome sons, I told Francis *net*, remember. Our percentage of the sugar profit alone more than paid for the crew. But Francis is right, even though California has a desperate demand for food and lumber, supplies are stacking up on the wharf because the importers lack labor to build warehouses and to ship the supplies up the river to Sacramento. Lord only knows what the miners are paying for it by the time it reaches them. Oh, I saw Benjie Stark. He's back from his trip to Connecticut. Came from New York in forty-six days on one of the new steam and sail ships. He sends his best to all. Francis, how soon can you get me loaded for a return trip? Francis?"

"Oh . . . ah . . . sorry, my mind had strayed. Immediately, if not sooner. Sophia, we don't want to outstay our welcome. Thank you, Bethy."

Later, as Beth snuggled against Ian's chest, she sensed he was far away in another world.

"Dreaming of steam ships?"

"No," he sighed. "A little impractical for us, unless someone strikes coal instead of gold. But I was thinking about ships, my darling. It would tear your heart out to see the San Francisco waterfront. It's one big forest of masts of deserted vessels. Their masters are selling them for a tenth of their original cost, so they can get to the gold fields, too."

"And you're pondering how many we should buy."

He turned his head and kissed her forehead. "Did I say as much?"

Beth giggled and grabbed a handful of chest hair. "You forgot my bloodline. I've sensed this conversation coming since you took your first look at your sons." She tried to give her voice a deep Welsh tone. "Aye, Dana's a grand name for a sea captain and Donnie looks inscrutable enough already to be a cargomaster." She paused as he lightly laughed. "But they are still a wee bit young. Ian, where will you find officers and crews for our new vessels?"

"Don't laugh, but I have thought of a source that many would not think of, and I won't take full credit. When the American fleet blockaded San Francisco Bay, they caught several Mexican vessels by surprise. Santa Ana had been using Spanish officers and crews. With California all but lost, the Spaniards did not want their country pulled into a losing war. They burned and scuttled their vessels, only to receive a chilly reception. After the surrender Mexico would not claim them, and certainly not Spain. The men are stranded and homeless. Crosby put me onto them for day laborers to unload the ship. I was pleased with the number of officers who spoke enough English to foreman their crews for me."

"How many have you hired?" she yawned.

"Beth, if we had five more ships not a fortnight would go by without our having a ship here for loading."

"Uh huh. What about the *Toulon?*"

"Stark let something slip from the bag, but I thought it best for Nate to tell Francis, himself. Nate put in a claim for land down opposite the tip of Sauvie Island. He's got a man onboard, by the name of Thomas Smith, who is going to build him a sawmill."

"Everyone wants to build a sawmill," Beth murmured and drifted off to sleep.

The lamp burned late in Francis Pettygrove's study. He poured over the charts he had obtained from Nate Crosby on the California coast, its bays and riverways. He would study, look off into space, and then study again. An aroma made him turn.

"What's this? Sophia, my dear, no need for you to be up."

"The bed is empty without you," she smiled, putting down a tray. "I've mulled some cider to ease your mulling mind."

"And how did you know it was mulling?" he asked, sipping at the spicy hot brew.

Sophia crawled into a wing-backed chair and tucked her feet up under her legs. "The only time your mind usually wanders at the dinner table is when Marsha is talking, for one thing. The other tip was our quick departure. What did Ian say that stirred your interest so?"

His fingers began to beat a tattoo on the chart. "The inability to get the merchandise from the waterfront to the buying public. Nate Crosby once said that Sacramento could never become a Portland, but could become like a St. Louis for New Orleans. Six years ago you asked if you would be a help to me. You have been my helpmate, my lover, and have given me three beautiful children." He paused and listened to the drumming of his own fingers.

Sophia unfolded from the chair regally, walked over, and put a hand on his shoulder. Then she laid something on the chart by his hand.

"The penny is not for your thoughts, Francis. It's the penny you used to name Portland. Do you need to use it on this decision?"

Francis's deep lines of concentration softened. "Perhaps the decision has been coming for a long time, Sophia, and today turned the tide. I went to Milwaukie to see Lot Whitcomb about lumber. I must say I like the man and his industry, but I'm damned if I will pay one hundred dollars per thousand for rough, unplaned three-inch thick planks. Katoro does better than that with the ancient equipment down at the fort." She patted his shoulder, as though to tell him he was wandering from his point. "Then, after giving such a price, he informed me it might be December before I could buy. Marsha and the *Spectator* have missed out on the fact that he and Joe Kellogg have built a shipyard and have laid the keel for a twenty-two-ton vessel. Lot intends to make Milwaukie the head of navigation and will build his own ships to prove it. His dreams, Sophia, sound like mine of a decade ago, but he is bringing them to fruition. I refuse to go through a battle with him like I am going through with Oregon City."

Sophia slowly walked to the window and looked out at the Willamette. Over his shoulder she had looked down at the chart he had been studying. If he were just a dreamer, rushing off for elusive gold, she would put in her heels and rebel. But in six years' time he had built this dream into a reality. Perhaps it was time for him to move on to another dream and turn this one over to others.

"Sacramento," she sighed, turning. "I like the sound of its name, Francis. Can we afford a new venture?"

He pulled a length of foolscap from under the cart, with columns of figures.

"For two poor New Englanders, my dear, who arrived here with no more than a promise of a share of the Benson &

Bros. profit, we have done well. We've built up personal assets of seventy-five thousand dollars. I have put our liquidation at a very fair market value."

"How soon?" she asked, the realization dawning on her that this was all more fact than conjecture.

"Before I put it in stone, I would like to make an inspection trip to weigh the advantages and disadvantages. If things appear to be in our favor, I would like a California operation going by the end of September. Once I have a suitable home established, Ian can move you, the children, and the household goods."

Even though his decision was this far along, she knew he was waiting for her final comment. But at the moment only one thought lodged in her brain.

"Francis, the children and I will go wherever you wish us to go, but don't tell Marsha we are going to California, too."

"Woman, I love you so."

Francis boarded the *Yam-il* with everyone assuming that he was just going as far as the fort, to see to the lumber for this shipment and to prepare a shipment for the *Toulon*. No one thought to question the ruse, for few had reason to visit the old "family quarters" outside the fort.

Katoro had learned much from Asa and Francis in his five years in Oregon. When Francis acquired the old sawmill, Katoro had no problems running it with just his Kanaka boys, though they loathed the daily trip between Portland and Fort Vancouver. Katoro approached Peter Ogden to learn the price for the one- and two-bedroom frame houses that had been for the use of the married HBC personnel. Because the price was reasonable, the young Hawaiian, taking a page from Asa's book, approached Pack McGraw to borrow the money. Pack, who had expansion plans of his own, agreed to the loan and Katoro was able to purchase the houses for his crews. Then, in a fast-moving business deal that left Katoro stunned, Pack bought the sawmill from Francis on credit, and leased it to Katoro. His sly comment to Katoro was, "Those houses are better suited for married folk."

The message was not lost on Katoro. He began to move out the Kanaka boys, replacing them with married Kanaka couples who spoke only Hawaiian. Katoro convinced Francis there was a profit to be made in importing Hawaiian foodstuffs, and one of the Kanakas used his savings to set up a commissary near the new community.

Man and nature had left Katoro with a problem that was difficult to solve. The British had been harvesting the timberlands in this area for eighteen years, and the Kanaka crews were having to work farther and farther inland and upriver, hauling the logs out by draught horses and floating them down the Columbia to the mill. Katoro saw only one solution. He doubled the number of crews, keeping his expenses the same by paying each crew on a board-foot production basis.

On the Monday before Francis returned, a new vessel came into the Willamette, the *Molly B.* out of Boston. She was a run-down old brig with a crew to match. They had dropped their manufactured goods in San Francisco and had heard that cheap produce was to be found in Portland.

George Bell was a stoic merchant and not one to haggle.

"Those are our prices, Captain Stacey. Four dollars a barrel wheat and six dollars a barrel-milled flour."

Stacey spat out a stream of tobacco juice on the floor. "Two and four is all I'm payin', boy. Sweet corn only one dollar a thousand ears."

"I'm afraid we can't do business."

"Look, you little runt, I know what other ships have been paying here 'cause I talked to them. Do I get the same price as they, or no?"

George was flustered. He had a store full of ladies, and the man was a rude bully and twice his size.

"I believe you are quite mistaken, Captain," came a woman's voice.

Stacey spun around and glared. "Lady, where I come from skirts don't mess into the business of men, so butt out!"

Beth's back stiffened. "My husband and I own the only vessel that has taken cargo out of Portland in the last month, and my cousin owns this establishment. The prices are as quoted to you, sir. Make your manifest order, or weigh your gangplank."

"I see," he mused. "And who's to stop me boys if they do a bit of midnight pirate work on that mountain of wheat barrels out front?"

"You might ask the people upriver how good I am with a Sharps buffalo rifle, Captain."

Beth caught a sudden, smoldering look in his eyes. She had seen the look in enough sailors' eyes to know he had more on his mind than the purchase of provisions.

"Well, me little beauty, as you seem to talk a better trading game than this poor excuse for a man, why don't we mosey onto the *Molly B.* and have a little business talk over a dram of something tasty?"

"But, Captain," she smiled sweetly, "you just said women shouldn't mess into the business of men. I was just pointing out that our prices are our prices. George, I will leave him in your capable hands. Kenwa will be right in to pick up my order. Come, Sophia."

"Beth," Sophia whispered, when they were outside, "why did you say Kenwa would get your order, when you didn't order anything?"

"Because," she giggled, "the bully looked out the window when I nodded my head. He can bully George, but I don't think he wants to tangle with Kenwa. Lord, I'd forgotten how rough waterfront life could be. If we keep losing men, we women will soon have to start toting guns to protect the town from the riffraff."

Sophia grew silent. She had not been able to bring herself to tell Beth of Francis's plans.

"*Molly B.,*" Molly Spragge enthused, looking at dress fabrics with Liza. "I think that's just the most exciting thing I've ever heard of, a ship named after me."

"Is that really your name, little darling?" Captain Stacey called, ignoring George and wanting to make him nervous.

"Hush!" Liza hissed. "Ain't proper for an engaged woman to talk to strangers."

"Oh, Liza, don't be a sourpuss. Won't do no harm to

answer him." She sidled to the end of the counter, where the bolt goods were stacked. "Molly Beatrice is my name. I ain't ever been on a ship before."

Liza hissed again. "You were brought upriver on one, girl!"

"Oh, Liza, that was only the Indian scow." She batted her eyelashes at Captain Stacey. "I mean a big ship like yours."

Stacey came close enough so that his hand could casually brush over her butt, without Liza being able to see. "Be more than happy to show you the *Molly B*, little darling."

"Molly!" Liza warned.

Molly turned so she was facing the man. "I'm sorry, but I don't think that would be proper." Then she let the back of her hand brush his crotch.

Stacey didn't need to say anything more. She would find her way to the ship, one way or another.

"Storekeep, I'll check with you in the morning to see if your prices are the same."

The store was very quiet until Molly made her purchase and left with Liza.

Marsha Tolcott had been standing in the pots and pans section with Alice Gale. The Gales had decided that hay for the McGraw-Bellam Ranch was a fair living, but gold might put them on easy street. And Marsha had decided that a wagon trip with them, even though she might lose her two-hundred-dollar deposit with the captain of the *Henry*, would put her at the gold site faster.

"Matoa," she said, going up to the butcher, who was waiting for George to grind his knives, "isn't Molly still living over the butcher shop?"

"Yes, Mrs. Tolcott, she still lives there. Waiting for Mr. Pack to come back to marry her."

"I *thought* I heard Liza say something about her being an engaged woman," Louise O'Bryant said.

"First I've heard of it," Alice Gale sniffed. "Seem's he would have told his old neighbor friends. Sure is taking him a long time to bring these cattle back."

"Well, dear ladies," Finice Caruthers chuckled, "this is

one time when 'absence doesn't make the heart grow fonder,' if you know what I mean."

"No, we don't!" was the almost universal chorus.

"Oh, my, I thought it was common knowledge, but I guess we are kind of alone at this end of town at night. I mean the library, my lawyer tenant and the butcher shop. I assumed that everyone knew that Dennis Landry was Molly's regular dinner guest."

"Thought she ate a lot for a single gal," George Bell said dryly.

"That settles it, Marsha Tolcott," Alice Gale simpered. "They need to know the embarrassing thing we saw happen in this very store."

For once Marsha was flabbergasted that she had to be the gossip. She turned crimson and clamped her lips shut.

"Well, I'm not afraid," Alice growled. "Boils me even more knowing that sweet Pack is engaged to that . . . that *whore!* Why, she put her hand right up to the Captain's—"

"I don't think you have to be explicit," Finice said. "I, too, saw his ungentlemanly approach to her. I don't think we have the right to say anything. Pack will have to deal with her, in his own way, when he returns."

He began to feel differently about it as the evening wore on. The sailors were miffed that the town didn't have a tavern, so they brought their tankards of rum ashore. They roamed the streets, kicking and cursing the stumps and shouting ribald desires for the "one good woman" in town to come out and play.

Working in the library, he heard Molly go up the outside stairs to Dennis's quarters. The voices were muffled, but the angry tones were obvious. Later, he couldn't recall if he heard her come back down. Everything was quiet, including the street. He went back to sorting his books into alphabetical sections on the shelf. The room grew stuffy and he opened the front door and stepped out for a breath of air. It was only 8:00 P.M. and still September daylight. He could see right across the clearing to the moored ship. The sailors were sitting on the deck drinking, but quiet. Then he saw a hatch fly open and heard the captain's voice boom out.

"Have a go at her, mates! She's a little darling!"

A very drunk and nude Molly came prancing out onto the deck. She threw back her head and laughed wickedly. Dennis had become a bore, talking marriage and giving up the bottle. The ship had been a God-send. The captain had not been able to get it up, so now she was ready to take on all comers.

The cry over Finice's head was pitiful, then he heard Dennis pounding down the back stairs. He was so drunk he fell in the middle of Washington Street, rounding the corner. Finice started to go to help him, but Dennis struggled up and started to run for the wharf. Finice then saw that he had a bottle in one hand and a gun in the other.

"Dennis, you damn fool!" he shouted. "Come back!"

About this time, Aaron Wait and George Abernethy were being paddled on one of his barges back to Oregon City. They were silent, because the trip had been a disaster. As the Provisional Governor, he had wished to overthrow HBC's sale of some thirty buildings and land to the alien Hawaiians. First, he was informed by Peter Ogden that he had no jurisdiction in that area. Second, according to the treaty, the British Empire was given "reasonable" time to dispose of their "developed" land in a "businesslike fashion." And, last, said lands and buildings had been sold to an American, whose name Ogden would not disclose.

Now they were silent, watching a very nude young woman covert in a very lascivious manner before a bunch of leering and cheering drunken sailors. Suddenly, a drunken madman came running toward the ship, firing a gun into the air.

Finice raced back into the library and took a rectangular box down from a top shelf. Quickly, he took out the matching dueling pistols from their velvet pockets, loaded them, and ran toward the ship.

Dennis had done no harm, for the five bullets were expended before he got to the edge of the wharf. But four of the sailors had jumped down and were jabbing at him, trying to grab the bottle away and urging the other sailors to start with

Molly, so that her boyfriend could have a ringside seat.

"Get away from him!" Finice hissed, as cold as death. Then he shouted. "Captain Stacey, get your drunken ass out on deck!"

The sailors hooted and howled. "Cap, there's a scarecrow out here with a couple of cap pistols."

Finice aimed and took a bosun's cap off at thirty paces.

"All right, asshole," Stacey belched, staggering out of the hatch in his knee-length undershorts. "You've had your fun. You've only got one friggin' shot left with the other dueler."

"And it's for you, Captain," Finice said without a trace of emotion. "Get your men on board, release the girl, and aweigh your mooring lines. This is our town and we don't cotton to you or your behavior."

Stacey laughed until he was almost choking. "Shoot me, you thin-shit and two minutes later me boys will have you dangling by the neck from the yardarm. If you're all this town has to protect it, then it ain't got a future."

"He is not quite alone."

Finice did not have to turn to recognize the distinctive voice of John Kenwa. As the four sailors around Dennis backed up and climbed on board, he turned his head.

From behind the towering stack of wheat barrels, around the corner of the warehouse, and starting to stand up where they had been lying in the clearing, were some fifty Indians.

"Beth was afraid they might try to steal some of the unguarded provisions," Kenwa whispered. Then he spoke quietly in Cayuse.

Two of the men came and took Dennis by the arms and led him back toward his quarters.

It was like the seconds of waiting before the tintype photographer's flash powder went off. The only movement was from Molly, who darted into the hatch and a second later came out pulling her dress down over her head.

She marched through the Indians with her head held high, a disdainful smile on her lips.

Stacey disappeared, but obviously had given a silent order, for the sailors began to unlash the mooring ropes from the wharf cleats. They were just pushing the ship away, to catch the current for a turning, when Molly began to scream.

"Wait! Hold that boat! Wait!"

She came tearing down Washington Street, one arm filled with dresses and the other struggling with two hat boxes, and a pillow case filled with shoes and her toilet articles. She stopped for only a second beside Kenwa.

"Tell that son-of-a-bitch Pack McGraw that he still owes me!"

The incident was not mentioned the next day, except behind closed doors and then with guarded snickers.

By Wednesday morning, when Dennis had still not made an appearance, Finice went up to check on him. Embarrassment had made him leave in the dead of night. He was the latest male to depart for California, but his quest wasn't really for gold. He promised Finice, in his note, that if he outlived his embarrassment, he would return.

Aaron Wait made sure that the Thursday *Spectator* was off the press and on barges at dawn for delivery to Milwaukie, Portland, and Fort Vancouver.

WATERFRONT FROLIC

While the terrible fever of gold is depopulating our riverfront towns and farms, our neighbors downstream were visited by a different form of fever. The fever of lustful, wanton sailors wishing to turn our God-fearing towns into the hell ports they are accustomed to anchor at. The actions of the sailors and the willingness of the women to oblige them, on the open deck, are too unspeakable to mention here. When founded by Francis W. Pettygrove, he boasted that Portland would be the head of navigation on the Willamette. Is this the image we want for our "major" port? And what protection do our citizens have from such drunken lawlessness? We note that Mr. Pettygrove did not deem it worth his bother to come forth to put down the lustful acts and order the wrongdoers off of his privately owned wharf. We note that Mr. Pettygrove also owns the wharf at Oregon City. Are we to suppose that he will allow such ships as these to visit our town? Mr. Pettygrove is silent!

The work of turning that evil brig back into the
Willamette was left to an unlikely individual, Finice
Caruthers, Esq. Perhaps to keep our honor pure we
should advise other ships that Milwaukie can load from
the shore or rafts. Our enterprising friend, Lot Whitcomb, Esq., is building an ocean-going vessel. We
should all wish him God's speed in building an entire
fleet of vessels, so that the manner of ships and captains
coming to Portland could be turned away at Cape Disappointment.

There was also a smaller article that was of interest to
some in Portland.

SESSION SOUGHT

Governor George Abernethy, after reviewing a case
with Hudson Bay Factor, Peter Ogden, is considering
calling a special session of the Legislature to determine
if the sale of former HBC property to alien Hawaiian
parties is contrary to the Organic Law.

CHAPTER

☆ 16 ☆

The bosun's whistle sounded a little shaky as he piped for docking privilege.

A small group had gathered at the store, mainly to chew over the *Spectator* articles, but to also gawk at the caravan of ships sailing behind the *Yam-il.*

Several had suggested to George Bell that he send Kenwa down to the sawmill to fetch Pettygrove. He had only shrugged.

When Francis was the first figure to step off the *Yam-il,* clutching a copy of the paper in a tight fist, they knew the news had reached Fort Vancouver. When their greeting went unanswered, they sensed the depth of his wrath. With his gray eyes fixed firmly ahead, he marched out Washington Street toward Tanner's Creek.

"Where do you think he's going?"

"To jaw it around with Dan Lownsdale, I'd venture. Never seen men respect each other more than those two."

"Would be better if he was taking a horsewhip to that editor," Liza fumed. "Made it sound as if every woman in town were part of the bawdy scene."

"At least your 'unlikely' person was not mentioned by name," Finice chuckled. "I'm aware of why they would exclude mention of Kenwa and his brethren, but why omit Dennis Landry?"

"A very careful oversight to protect the fact that he was the former editor of the paper."

"He's sure building Whitcomb up to something that he's

241

not, at least as yet. It'll be a good year before Kellogg and Whitcomb's son-in-law finish that' vessel, and it's hardly more than a yacht."

They fell into a nervous, embarrassed silence. Pack McGraw had ridden up and was entering the store.

"Hello, everybody," he said, a quizzical grin on his face. "Quite a greeting I got on arriving from California last night. Joe Bellam tells me I've got a few debts to settle."

"As it was authorized by Mr. Pettygrove," Bell sputtered, "perhaps you'd best discuss it with him."

Pack shook his head, but the smile remained. "Francis may have done the authorizing, but Molly did the asking in my name. Hear you're also out, Liza."

"Forget it, Pack. I was taken in like everyone else."

"No need for you to suffer at the hands of such a convincing liar. I should have known she'd be trouble the moment she stepped off of Kenwa's scow. Add up my charges. I'll take care of them and then we can drop the subject. Right now, I have to see Beth and Ian. I've finally found a wedding present for them."

No one said a word. They had all expected Pack McGraw to take the news like a raging bull. He was too calm, too collected, too *un*-Pack McGraw.

Externally, Pack was no different than before, but internally he was vastly changed. In two months, his American River claim had netted him as much profit as it had taken Francis six years to acquire. Content with his gain, he had sold his claim for three times what he had taken from the ground. By Sutter's Mill standards, he had "quit" as still a poor man. By Oregon standards, he was exceedingly wealthy and would have to keep it very quiet.

"Hey, Mick!" he called, as he saw him paddle into Kenwa's scow landing. "I was going to come up and see you in a day or two. You'll never guess who I saw in California."

Mick Myers stepped onto Front Street, but his face showed that he was not too interested in Pack's news.

"What's the matter, buddy? My good news can wait."

"You said the magic word, Pack. California. Dave McLoughlin and I are probably the youngest men left in

Oregon City. Even Asa Lovejoy went down on the *Henry*. I've come to find Francis and tell him I've got to go try my luck, too."

Pack shrugged. He had seen every manner of man and woman trying their luck and he sensed this was only the beginning of the rush of people to that area. "Then walk along with me. When I came out of the store I saw Francis cutting across the pasture toward Jefferson Street. He's either on his way home or to Beth's. And if you do go to California, you won't be among strangers. One of the biggest tent saloons is owned by Kitty Flynn. She's as beautiful and brassy as ever. No mining for Kitty. She's getting rich mining the miners. Mick! You haven't heard a word I've said."

"Sure I have, but I can't help wondering how Francis will take my news."

"We'll soon know. Hello, Francis!"

Francis halted. He was about ready to knock on Beth's kitchen door. He felt a second of displeasure that he would not have a few minutes alone with Beth and Ian, but he calmed himself and waited for them. They were friends, after all, and the secret could not be kept a secret much longer.

They entered together, learning from Nuua that Beth and Ian were in the parlor. Mick decided to hold his news for the moment.

Beth was pacing. Ian had only been able to give her a brief outline of what Francis had accomplished in San Francisco and Sacramento.

"You'd best sit down, Beth," Francis said.

"I'll sit, Francis," she said narrowly, "but I don't think I'm going to like what I hear."

Francis smiled blithely. "It's not all bad. Ian, Dan Lownsdale will be bringing down to the wharf five thousand dollars in leather for that boot man in San Francisco." He paused and sighed. "You all might as well know that I have sold my half-interest in Portland for that leather."

Beth pursed her lips. "You might have discussed it with others, before you sold it to Daniel."

"What could you have done? You've got all of your capital invested in ships."

"Exactly," she flared. "Because I thought you would still be here, the enterprising merchant who'd keep them filled with export cargo."

Francis would not be pulled into that argument. He answered in a rumbling, authoritative tone. "The cargo at the other end is far more important, and you stand only to gain. Ian and I have been able to put together a fleet of rivercraft and two of the older vessels as warehousing space in San Francisco Bay. And after reading this paper, I'm damn glad to be saying good-bye!"

"And leaving us to the vultures," Beth moaned. "What is to become of your stores and other interests?"

Francis began to smile. "I could start a very interesting bidding war between Couch and Abernethy. John Couch would love to expand his mercantile business to include Portland, and George Abernethy would love to close Francis Pettygrove down and force people back to Oregon City to trade with him. They're the only two capable of capitalizing on my departure."

"Damn you, Francis Pettygrove!" Beth hissed, starting to pace again. "That was your father I just heard speaking and not your grandfather! Hiram Pettygrove must be spinning in his grave. You're not giving one minute's worth of thought to the people who helped you get where you are!"

"Elizabeth," he said sternly, "don't you dare lecture me. I have certainly thought of them. My first instinct on reading that damn newspaper was to scuttle everything I had done here, but that would have played right into Couch and Abernethy's hands. I was only jesting when I suggested a bidding war. I'll wait for Couch to return. I'm sure Mick and George Bell can keep things running normally until then. Listen, I must go to Sophia. She doesn't know of the sale yet."

Pack pinched Mick to silence. "Just a moment, Francis. Am I to understand that the cattle were included in the purchase to Lownsdale, like they were with Stark?"

"No. I was going to wait until Stark came in on the *Toulon* and then talk with both of you."

"Get your price fixed and Joe and I will buy you both out."

Beth started to open her mouth and then closed it. Francis did not know the deal she had made with Benjamin Stark and so neither did Daniel Lownsdale.

Pack had earlier bought the sawmill from him on credit. He hated to disappoint him.

"I can name the price at twenty dollars a head right now, Pack, but would really like to liquidate everything for cash."

Pack didn't bat an eye. "We'll have a full head count of your share in two days. I did enough business down in California to pay you in gold."

"Thank you. Mick, I wish I could extend you a line of credit to buy out the stores and merchandise, but I have already learned that business in California is cut-throat and cash on the barrel head."

"Fine with me, Mr. Pettygrove," Mick laughed, "maybe I'll go to California and make my own nest egg."

The four sat silent for several moments after Francis left. Ian was extra silent because he had been so engrossed in getting his ships, getting them manned, and helping Francis get operations set up at that end that he had not given a moment's thought to the supplies at this end without Francis being here.

"Perhaps there is something I can do," Pack finally said.

"You will have trouble enough if Abernethy digs deep into your helping Katoro."

"That may be some little time," Mick advised. "No way he can call a special session with the Speaker of the House, Asa Lovejoy, and three-quarters of the legislature down in California."

"Still doesn't worry me," Pack mused. "Ian, did you leave off a shipment for me at Fort Vancouver?"

"The *Spanish Lady* did. Those crates were so damn heavy they had to be winched over the side."

Pack grinned. "It will make Katoro happy. Some joker had just started a sawmill on the Sacramento and rushed off to the gold fields. He wasn't doing too well, so he sold all the equipment to me for a grub-stake." He smiled. No one had yet thought enough to ask what he had been doing in California. "Mick, I know your desires, but look at the other side of the coin. You can still get a good meal at the Main Street House for twenty-four cents. Down there a loaf of bread is a dollar, and eggs are fifty cents apiece, when you can find one. I had a steak that cost me five dollars and I swear it was horse. Remember, I told you Kitty was mining the miners."

"I know what you're getting at, Pack, but you heard Francis. The only thing that Anita and I have is some credit coming from those furs."

"That's a start, and what about you two?"

"You heard Francis," Beth repeated. "We're up to our waterline, so to speak, in ships and crews."

"Except for the fact that Stark's cattle profit from me will go to you. I'm also willing to buy out the other cattle I've been running for you. As long as we are among friends, let's go a step farther. Your half-interest, under Stark's name, is about forty-eight acres from Washington Street to where it joins Couch's claim. It hasn't been surveyed for lots, so let's just talk per acre."

"I'll talk," Beth shrugged. "But why would you be interested in it?"

"More wharf and warehouse space," Pack answered calmly. "I'll go one thousand dollars per acre and twenty dollars a head on the cattle. Mick, I know that Anita has to have at least a thousand left out of the furs. That's almost ten thousand dollars. I'll make up the difference of what Francis is asking. I'm proposing that we buy up his whole kit and kaboodle and form our own import-export business."

"Jesus Jennie!" Ian cried triumphantly. "We'll completely cut out the middleman costs! What did you do, strike the mother lode down there?"

"No," Pack said, cautiously, "just enough to help pull off a deal like this."

Pack was reverting to his childhood. At each meal he would squirrel away half his portion, just in case there was nothing for the next meal.

Abernethy and Wait were triumphant, as if they were responsible for forcing Pettygrove out. But Wait was unable to print the news, because he had lost his printers to gold fever. Alone he was able to get out a handbill before Christmas, apologizing to the advertisers and claiming that over three thousand of the previous five thousand people in the area had departed and that "Little Stumptown" had been reduced to three males: Daniel Lownsdale, Colonel William King, and Keith Warren.

"I am not counted," Mick laughed. "I assume for the same reason they haven't counted the male Indians and Kanakas."

"I am not counted," Finice chuckled, "because I am an 'unlikely' person and the 'Colonel' should have been on the society page because of his visit to mother. Why are you listed, Keith, and not Joe Terwilliger?"

"'Cause Joe says ain't no need for a blacksmith to advertise and I'm only the assistant blacksmith."

Deep into 1849 it stopped being a laughing matter. Ninety-five percent of the Willamette and Tualatin farms were being run by women and children under fourteen years of age. It was a bumper year for crops and even Old Wife and the squaws were pressed into harvest duties. Normally, the river had seen about nine vessels a year. In 1849 it was an average of five a month. At harvest time, twenty vessels clogged the Willamette and waited for loading.

Desperate for warehouses and wharfs, Pack commissioned Stephen Coffin to move from Oregon City and take on the project. There had been little work in Oregon City and Coffin had no interest in gold. In the two years since his arrival in Oregon City he had accumulated enough capital to now acquire one-quarter interest in Portland, from Lownsdale, for six thousand dollars. Beth could see Pack's subtle hand behind that move. Pack and Steve Coffin were cut from the same cloth.

When Dave McLoughlin developed gold fever, Mick was relieved and brought D'Arcy and her children to live with him and Anita in the old Pettygrove house. For the time being he would use the old store and warehouse to store flour barrels from the grist mill, because Abernethy was still businessman enough to supply the Portland Provisions Company milled flour at ten dollars a barrel and still have a four dollar net. Lumber he refused to sell them, because he couldn't keep labor long enough to produce five hundred board feet of lumber a week. In Milwaukie, Whitcomb's mill was producing six thousand board feet a day, in two twelve-hour shifts. It was still rough lumber, while Katoro was producing three thousand board feet a day of planed lumber. Henderson Luelling, while waiting for his nursery stock to reach retail size, had also built a sawmill on Johnson Creek in 1849.

Even though Lot Whitcomb was his neighbor and had traded his "yacht" for a 239-ton bark, Luelling would still not ship with him, because Lot tried to tell him what to produce out of his mill. Luelling had once worked in a shingle mill and that's all he knew how to produce. The Portland Provisions Company was willing to pay him two dollars a bundle, for which they got twelve dollars a bundle in California. He and his family were able to produce one hundred bundles a day.

By late November, Mount Hood looked like a mound of white icing and the rain seemed to fall daily. Beth didn't mind. She was terribly tired and the rainy days let her stay at home. With this child she was just as large as with the twins and she did not want to repeat that act. It seemed of late, as though they were all constantly at the store or the ware-houses. Even with she, Mick, Anita, and D'Arcy all working, they never seemed to get ahead of the next ship ready for cargo. And it didn't help matters any that she, Anita, Tama, and Nuua were all pregnant at the same time. They laughed about it, saying it proved they did occasionally have a few moments alone with their husbands.

They got a small reprieve when Dave came home in early December, luckless. It was still foolish to reopen the Oregon City store, so he was given the position of manager of the warehouses.

Beth decided not to have her Christmas party that year. Still, Daniel Lownsdale asked if she would mind hosting a "business discussion" dinner. It turned out to be one of her worst days for leg and thigh cramps, but she dressed and had

Nuua seat her at the table before the men came in from the parlor.

She had been told that Lownsdale and Coffin were bringing a man by the name of William W. Chapman, but she could see by the look on the faces of Pack and Mick that they'd had quite enough of the man during the social hour.

"Very nice to meet you," Chapman said when introduced to Beth. She detected a lack of sincerity. "Nice that you could be here representing your husband."

"And myself, Mr. Chapman. There are four of us with interest in the company."

"How nice. I've never done business with women before."

"You'll find that we don't bite."

By the time the soup was finished he had repeated everything he had said in the parlor. All about his Virginia birth. His extensive legislative experience in Iowa. His law practice in Salem since 1847. His gained wealth in the gold fields and his exploration of every townsite to determine which required his wealth and talents.

"Steve and I have sold him one-third of each of our interests, Beth."

Chapman chuckled. It was the first time his voice had risen above a monotone. "As our leader of business, let me assure you that I will not, as a new owner, try to dictate to your enterprise. However, one thing does bother me about *my* new town, and that is the Indian village. I propose talking to the Indian Affairs Commissioner about it."

"William," Daniel said, "it is not on townsite property."

"My understanding, based on the map you drew up, puts half of it within the square mile."

"On that point you are correct, but ten acres of this meadowland and ten acres of my meadowland were originally set up by Francis and me as the village. Since that time it has been purchased."

"Good. If purchased, then the owner will be moving them soon."

Daniel started to correct the man's misinterpretation and caught Beth's smile. He smiled back and changed the subject. "Beth, I know you've been acting as Stark's agent, but we three agree that once this gold fever has settled down, we will start expanding. I'm going to San Francisco next month to set up a leather line for a shoe manufacturer. Would you put me in contact with Stark, so we can discuss buying him out?"

"But, of course, I will. It might be less cumbersome getting Benjie out of the picture."

Nuua came in and whispered.

"Thank you, Nuua," she said softly and looked up with a frown. "Kenwa was just here. There have been severe flash floods above The Falls and on Johnson Creek. Both sawmills at Oregon City have been washed away and Luelling's has been damaged. Whitcomb is all right, Kenwa is racing the rising water down to the fort, because they are on much lower ground."

"Then please excuse me," Chapman said. "I had best ride back to Oregon City at once and check on my wife."

It was said with such a lack of emotion that Beth blanched. He was not going to be a jolly addition to Portland.

The rain, flooding, and mudslides continued through most of January. It slowed the ship traffic down, but it did allow Ian to be home for the birth of his daughter.

"Lord, what a little beauty, Beth. What have you decided to name her?"

Beth looked down at the bundle Tama had put in her arms. The child already had strawberry ringlets and the shape of Beth's face, but her body was long and slender like her father's. She recalled a portrait in the Cleeve house of another tall, beautiful woman.

"I have always been fascinated by the stories of one of my ancestors—Penelope Randolph Cleeve. I've always loved that name, Penelope. Rather fitting, when you think that a penny was tossed to name this town."

"Well, then, hello little Penny. I hope you are a lucky piece for your parents."

"Speaking of luck, how did things go with Benjie?"

"It was almost comical. When Lownsdale learned that most of Stark's property had been sold, Daniel was going to get the others to pay Stark back until he learned that Benjie had been compensated, so to speak. He's most pleased with the profit he made on the deal. He plans to visit you this summer. He's sick of the sea and the bachelor life."

"Will you ever grow sick of the sea, Ian?"

"If I was still on those six-month treks, I would say yes. This is not a bad run, but every moment that I'm away I miss you, the boys, this house, and now it will be Penny. We are now bringing as many back from California as went down in the first place. The big gold finds are near ended, but the business will not stop booming. San Francisco and Sacramento are changing month by month."

"I don't want to move, if that is what you are driving at."

Ian laughed and played with one of Penny's little hands. "Not us, but I think we need a shipping office there. We've got to get our triangle going again between here, Honolulu, and San Francisco."

"And where else?" she laughed.

"The East Coast," he said and waited. When there was no response he took a flyer from his pocket. "These are all over San Francisco. It announces that Empire State Shipping is now exclusive agent for Abernethy & Co. of the Oregon Territory, with shipments on the Milwaukie Line on a scheduled basis. They're going to have the jump on us and undercut us in pricing."

"Or make it appear that way. It's ridiculous that if we want to advertise we have to do it in the *Spectator*. What we need is our own newspaper."

"I'll put a bug in Steve Coffin's ear. He's going down on this trip with me. His interest in steam is really fired up. He's meeting with a ship builder from New York and with another company about a steam engine for a sawmill."

"Does Pack know about that?"

"He's the one who encouraged Steve to look into it."

"And we're still not interested in steam ships?"

"No, not yet, my love."

The sound of hammers nearly clashed together between Portland and Milwaukie, while Oregon City was still fairly quiet.

In June, Joe Morrison and Steve Coffin counted one-hundred-fifty houses and thirty business and commercial structures being built. The "Oregon Forty-niners" were returning with gold to pay off debts, improve their farms, or advance to commercial ventures. Their stories of Oregon, in the mine fields, brought a new wave of people looking for commerce and industry.

"Elizabeth," Finice told his mother, "Rhoda and I have been counting noses. We are over five hundred people. The schoolhouse was built to accommodate fifty pupils. By fall we could have four times that many."

William Chapman, who had imposed himself into Sophia Pettygrove's vacant seat on the "unofficial" school board, was not sympathetic. "The owners of the town cannot afford to take carpenters off needed construction to add more rooms to that building."

"The carpenters," Beth reminded him, "as well as the lumber, were all donated."

"As was the land," he said sourly. "I thought to make a profit here, but every time I turn around I find nothing but donated lots or ones with dubious title."

"While we are on that subject, Mr. Chapman, Mick Myers informs me that Mr. Abrams and Mr. Reed have begun to accumulate piling logs on the riverbank in front of his house. He was informed that would be the site of the new steam sawmill, on land given to them by you and Mr. Coffin."

"As that is all correct, I fail to see the reason for you mentioning it."

"I mention it, Mr. Chapman, because the original townsite grid was for sixteen blocks from Front Street to Second and from Washington to Jefferson streets. The eight riverfront 'blocks' are for moorage and wharfage and are all part of the Pettygrove property purchased by Portland Provisions Company."

"Mrs. Llwellen," he said impatiently, "you must be mistaken. There are commerial ventures already built on the river side of Front Street."

Beth didn't bat an eye. "Naturally, the ones that we felt appropriate to the shipping line."

"You said you didn't bite, but you strike like a snake in the grass."

Beth laughed, but without humor in the sound. "I am willing to negotiate. You may have Block 8 for the mill, if we can have three more schoolrooms and two more teachers."

"The owners can't afford more teachers!"

"Then you shouldn't be owners," Elizabeth Caruthers snapped.

"I would think," Beth went on, before Chapman could retort to Elizabeth, "that if you can find a press, editor, and a building to house the . . . ah, what was the name you insisted it be called, Mr. Chapman . . . oh, yes, *The Oregonian,* then you could—"

"How did you find that out, woman?" Chapman growled.

"Thomas Jefferson Dryer is as sharp as a steel trap and will be a very astute editor. He checked with Francis Pettygrove to learn if you and Coffin were indeed owners here. But while he will bring along an old hard press and some rather battered type, I think you'd best prepare yourself for a shock. Sometimes it is difficult to keep secrets in the shipping business. Empire State Shipping has a manifest order for a new press to be delivered from New York to *The Western Star Printing Company,* Lot Whitcomb, Esq. Now, about those new teachers."

"No new teachers!" Chapman hissed, appalled at the news that Milwaukie was getting a newspaper. "You can cut down on students by stopping this inane practice of teaching those Indian brats."

"My, did we say something to ruffle his feathers?" Finice asked, after Chapman had quickly departed.

"I certainly hope so," his mother laughed. "Well, what do we do, Beth?"

"The same as we decided before he got here. If a carpenter wants his child to go to school, he will give a day's labor.

Pack will donate the trees for the acres he is clearing and
Katoro will mill them. Now, we need to raise eighteen hundred dollars to pay two teachers for nine months."

"I'm really not a part of the committee," Rhoda said, "but
I recall how they would celebrate the Fourth of July in
Boston. They surely made some money on the iced milk and
cake."

"How could you make ice milk in July?" Finice pondered.

"Kenwa's people surprised us one year by bringing ice
from Mount Hood in the summer." After she said it, Beth
wondered if salmon, packed in such ice, would last on a trip
to San Francisco.

"And we would need speeches," Rhoda encouraged.
"Maybe we could get Francis to come back."

Elizabeth had been silent. "Let's think a little bigger, so
we don't need the pockets of the owners. Back home I
always gave a horse for our celebration. They made enough
to pay me what feed and keep I had in the colt and make a
hefty profit."

"There were more people back home, mother, buying
those dollar chances."

"Nonsense! Town was no bigger than this. It was the
county folk who came in that made it a success. Old Granny
Hutchins would sell out of her gooseberry jelly by noon and
then would sell corn liquor out of the same booth."

"Booths!" Rhoda enthused. "That's what we need, but we
don't have a park."

"Sure do," Beth said. "We've got a four-acre park called
The Clearing."

Finice frowned. "Beth, I think you better know that Chapman has had a surveyor marking it out for lots for sale."

"Over my dead body!"

The quick, desperate charge of Daniel Lownsdale to the
Chapman house was born of frustration and despair at what
was happening to his town.

He and Coffin were always in agreement, only to find that
they were not in agreement with Chapman. The man thought

he was a puppet master, but some people wouldn't dance at the end of his string.

Before Daniel could get a word in, Chapman was demanding the firing of the "school board," the payment of the Front Street blocks he was cheated out of, and an immediate contract with the Milwaukie Line as Portland's authorized agent.

"Chapman," Daniel said slowly, "it takes more than a couple of planks and a few nails to make a town. It takes people. You can't fire volunteers, and that's what keeps the school going. Nor have you been cheated on anything. My hides come from Pack, my workers from Kenwa, my supplies from Mick, and I ship with Ian. That settles, in my mind, the Milwaukie Line statement. Now, I'm going to tell you, just as I told Steve Coffin, keep your damn hands off of The Clearing and forget about trying to sell it!"

Chapman was not about to listen to Lownsdale. By naming his loyalties, Daniel had given him cause to see that he and Coffin had to get rid of the man. Within the hour he had bags packed and took a scow to Milwaukie. Before boarding the *Ocean Bird* for San Francisco, he put in a manifest order with Lot Whitcomb for the bark *Keoka* to ship Dryer's press the first week in October. Being four months away Lot took it to mean that Portland was getting a new press and it would be in operation before his newspaper. That didn't set well. He didn't think it unusual for Chapman to give the order to the Milwaukie Line, because it was becoming common knowledge on the river that he did not like Beth Llwellen and her high-handed ways.

Twelve days later Dryer was given an advance on his salary and told to delay his departure until fall, because his building would not be completed until then. That was pure hookum on Chapman's part, because he had already determined to give him the log structure, which had been John Morrison's first house, because Chapman didn't want to waste money on a building.

Then, even though Steve Coffin was also in San Francisco, Chapman went to the offices of the Pacific Mail Steamship

Company and sold them his share in the steamer *Columbia* being built in New York for delivery in the fall. In exchange for buying his small share, he gave them exclusive "steamer" rights for Portland mooring.

Then he began looking up old friends from his gold mining days. Because the gold strike had created millionaires who were liars, and liars who pretended to have millions, Chapman had to play the role of being a major owner of a town, who had two minor owners who were curtailing its growth because they lacked the capital. He spent more on lavish dinners on potential purchasers for Lownsdale's interest than it would have cost for the salary of the two teachers.

The customers at the *Oyster House* were so insistent that the woman had no choice but to sing for them.

"Clancey," Chapman whispered, with open admiration, "who is that woman?"

Clancey O'Bannon preened with pride. "Willie, me boy, that's the 'Irish Thrush,' a darlin' woman of wealth."

As Chapman grew more impressed, he expressed a desire to meet the woman. As Kitty Flynn approached the table, the other women stared with frank envy. At twenty-three she had become showwoman enough to know that even a dinner gown was important to her image. She wore a wig to give her height, accented by white ostrich tips and aigrettes. The low-cut gowns brought men's attention to her well-molded endowment, while the women gawked at the hard blaze of her massive diamond necklace and matching earrings. Fashion was finally catching up with her hour-glass figure, and dressmakers in San Francisco were fighting to create her gowns.

"Kitty, may I present Mr. William Chapman of Portland, Oregon. William, Mrs. Flynn."

"My pleasure," Chapman said, reverting to his monotone. Her marital status reversed his desire to seek her out as a potential buyer.

"Portland," Kitty mused. "What a coincidence. I depart soon for an engagement in your town."

"Portland?" Chapman said thoughtfully. "We have no establishment like this for you to perform in."

"John McGraw is building it now," Kitty said—nothing on earth could bring her to call him "Pack."

"Then he'll go broke," Chapman chuckled, but glad for the bit of news. Because the foundation was so large, he thought Pack was just building another warehouse. "We don't have liquor in Portland, Mrs. Flynn, and our people are prone to eat dinner at home. Best you get your money from Mr. McGraw before you sing a note."

"Thank you, I'll take it under advisement. And how goes it with you, Clancey?"

"Same, same," he shrugged. "I'll be going back to me claim any day. About ready to talk William into a partnership and grub-stake."

Chapman turned pale. He had struck out again. Kitty saw the look and quickly excused herself. She knew the look of two men conning each other. She did not go in for philanthropy or dole out grub-stakes. Frankly, she couldn't do it if she wanted to. The lure of gold had brought seventy thousand to Sacramento and San Francisco, but only about one percent had become really wealthy. She had mined the miners and poured her profits into the ornate *Oyster House* and the less ornate *Flynn's Public House* on the Embarcadero. Both were financial failures, the first of her life. She was happy to grab at the "grub-stake" John McGraw had offered.

Joseph Lane had come quietly to Oregon in December 1849, with the official papers making Oregon a territory and confirming his appointment as Territorial Governor by President Zachary Taylor. He had been a general under "Old Rough and Ready" during the Mexican War, and knew little about his new territory upon arrival. He spent six months quietly learning that he was governor in name only and that George Abernethy still pulled the political strings. He was therefore quite pleased to be invited to participate in Portland's Fourth of July celebration. He had received an important dispatch from Thomas Ewing, Secretary of the Interior, which he felt would be an excellent topic for his speech, and he had a few personal things to announce. He had not been a successful general by letting the enemy dictate the course of the battle.

"I must say, ladies, I am most impressed. A street named for the President, already."

"Long before he became that," Beth laughed. "My cousin named it because of General Taylor's efforts in the War of 1812. You will meet him shortly at the speaker's platform."

"Which raises a rather delicate point."

Beth, Elizabeth, and Rhoda stopped dead in the street and let their silence demand him to raise his point. They had done everything possible to make the day a success, even to whitewashing the stumps, so no one would trip over them.

"I'm from North Carolina," Lane said timidly, almost apologetically, "and am therefore well versed in Caruthers Kentucky horses. I'm most eager to take some chances on today's prize, but am reluctant to do so and also do the drawing, as you have kindly asked."

"How many chances, General Lane?" Elizabeth asked, on a sigh of relief.

"Am I greedy to take fifty?"

"Most generous," Rhoda, who was in charge of raffle sales, gasped, "and I am sure we can find someone else to do the drawing."

"Hardly generous," he chuckled. "If I win that colt for fifty dollars, I will be most pleased. If I don't, I will talk to you, Mrs. Caruthers, about a purchase. I've always dreamed of owning one of your horses."

Rhoda made sure that the ladies in the raffle booth knew of the Governor's purchase.

"Must be an election coming, if he's buying votes."

"He don't have to buy votes, he was appointed."

For the day all rivalries were forgotten. By noon over two thousand were wandering about the booths, which had as much variety as a county fair. The Clearing was so packed that families had to take their picnic baskets into the shade of the fir trees, as far back as Tanner's Creek.

"Too bad Chapman can't see this," Daniel chuckled.

"Is he still trying to find someone to buy you out?" Stephen Coffin asked.

"That's the rumor I keep hearing. But, like most things Chapman does, he failed to take one thing into consideration. He never asked if I had a desire to sell. For your information, I do not. Where do you stand?"

"Daniel, I came here not as a wealthy man, like Chapman. I don't have to pretend to you that my advancement is due to the help from others. I won't sell out and let Chapman have a chance of hurting those who have helped me."

"Like Pack?" Lownsdale kept casting pious glances skyward. "What's Chapman going to say when he sees that new building and learns its business?"

"I can hardly wait!" Coffin rumbled in his Olympian bass. "Pack gave me a preview last night. I have never seen a bar that long in my life! The stage has a velvet curtain! We will just have to see if he gets any business on his opening tonight."

"I have no doubt that he will, Steve. Don't forget, we never went to the gold fields, like nearly every other man in this territory. They will come to see if it is like their gold-rush days. When the newness wears off, then he will learn if it is a long-range business. Let's move closer, they've just introduced the Governor."

Coffin studied Joseph Lane closely. It was the first time anyone, outside of a few in Oregon City and Salem, had seen the man. He was magnificently built, with a carefully trimmed Van Dyke beard and neatly combed hair. He looked like a military hero—and had the voice to match his appearance.

"My dear friends," he boomed, and people coming forward from their picnic area sat back down, because they could hear him, "today we are seventy-four years young as a nation. Today our states and territories stretch from the Atlantic to the Pacific, and from the 49th Parallel to the Rio Grande. To toast this day, the organizing ladies have made two excellent choices. In 1632, the first members of the Pettygrove family stepped ashore in Maine. That same pioneering spirit brought Francis Pettygrove to this very spot, called The Clearing, to establish this town. Mr. Pettygrove, your toast, sir."

Francis was nervous. He had never had to speak in public before and it was an emotional moment. To his left, Portland had expanded as far as Fifth Street. Front Street had wooden sidewalks from Washington to Taylor. Behind him there were four blocks of new wharves and warehouses. To his right was a foundry, a hand laundry, a second hotel, a barber shop, and Pack's new two-story building, which covered the entire two hundred square feet of a block. He looked down at Sophia and smiled. They could be proud of what they had started.

His eyes brimming with tears, he cleared his throat. "My friends, to our revolutionary struggle. It won a home for freedom in the world, and the echoes of its warfare still rumble about the rotten monarchies of Europe."

It received only polite applause, because the phrases were a little over the heads of most of the people.

"The other gentleman to toast was born in Canada as a British subject. He, too, is of fine pioneering stock, and because of his many years of creating a trading giant out of this one-time wilderness he can truly be called 'the father of Oregon.' I give you Dr. John McLoughlin."

"Thank you very much, General Lane," McLoughlin said, when the applause died down. "I probably am old enough to be the father to most of you, but my spirit is still young. Standing down here is Robert Benjamin Pettygrove. Robert and I share something in common. He was the first baby born in this town, and it was the first baby I had brought into the world since the birth of my youngest son. Since that time, I have brought my grandson into this world, to make sure there is a McLoughlin around for at least another sixty-odd years. My son and daughter-in-law have become citizens, and Dave made me promise that I would tell you today that Mrs. McLoughlin and I have made our intentions known to General Lane that we will become United States citizens." Again he had to wait for sincere applause. "Now, my friends, a toast to Oregon. From the fertility of its soil, the salubrity and mildness of its climate, the finest place in North America for the residence of civilized man."

Dr. McLoughlin was given a standing ovation. Governor Laner hoped that his words would be received that well.

"This is my first chance to address you as the Territorial Governor and I welcome the opportunity for so many to hear me firsthand. I have spent my few months here trying to learn the territory, so to speak, and the issues. Even though our main population base is right here in the Willamette and Tualatin Valley areas, we stretch clear back to the Rocky Mountains. For two years this has been a territory, but without certain rights that are to be expected by every citizen. So that the government can operate in an orderly manner, it is my pleasure today to announce the appointment of Asa L. Lovejoy as Territorial Judge, and of Timothy Steadholm as Territorial Marshal, to announce the relocation of the seat of government to Salem, the new Territorial Capital."

There was an audible gasp and then some from Oregon City began to boo him.

"I'll be damned!" Lownsdale gasped. "He just cut himself free from the Abernethy crew without a 'by your leave'!"

"But kept his options open by tucking Asa in his hip pocket."

"I didn't come here," Lane barked over the ruckus, "to run in a popularity contest. I came here to govern, wisely and fairly." From his breast pocket he took out a document.

"As your governor, I am happy to convey the regards of your government for your act in breaking this territory open for settlement. The Congress of the United States has passed the Donation Land Claim Law of 1850 and put it in the jurisdiction of the Department of Interior. Any male citizen over the age of eighteen who settled in Oregon prior to this coming December will receive three hundred twenty acres, providing he cultivates it for four years. His wife can also receive three hundred twenty acres. Those settling after December and until December of 1855 will receive only one hundred sixty acres. This land law does not apply to emigrants who are black or Hawaiian, although it does not exclude part-Indian settlers. The Department of Interior is even now working on treaties with the various Indian tribes to establish reservation lands for them, so that we can all live in peace and harmony. I thank you."

Instead of applause he was met with silence and groups murmuring among themselves.

"General Lane," Asa said, stepping up to the base of the platform. "I'm aware of the intent of this law, but I fear your announcement is leaving more doubt than joy. Do you mind?"

"Not at all, Asa. That's why you are the judge, to handle our laws."

"My friends, I can hear your doubts before they are raised. The Donation Land Claim Law does not affect your land under the Linn Act."

"Mr. Speaker," Peter Burnett interrupted. "I certainly hope that you are correct, but I strongly question it."

Francis leaned toward McLoughlin. "Probably disgruntled because he didn't get the judgeship."

"Sorry, Peter," Asa said, "but that is how I see it and how it should be. It wouldn't be fair, otherwise. Jason, you are a good example. For you new people, this is Jason Lee, who has been farming his land for ten years. That's his son David, who farms the six hundred forty acres next to his dad. Does this mean that Mr. and Mrs. Lee can keep their six hundred forty acres, but that David, being single, would have to give half of his back? Hell no, I say."

"Many of us," Lot Whitcomb said, on a worried frown, "started a townsite out of our claim. How do you cultivate a townsite?"

"Exactly, Lot!" Asa answered. "Because we are trying to confuse a homestead act, with no restrictions, as against a free land law, with a four-year restriction. Under the Linn Act we were able to sell our property, developed or not. Under this law you would have to cultivate for four years."

"Sounds like it was written by a Senator from a farm

state," Jason snickered. "What about the lumbermen and dairy and cattlemen?"

"You are thinking too narrow on the word," Finice said. "To cultivate means to civilize, refine, or make use of for a productive purpose."

"Guess I'll go home and cultivate my wife," one of the young men laughed, for which he got his ears boxed by a red-faced wife.

Joseph Lane had lost control, but wanted to win it back.

"My friends, let's don't crack the egg until the hen has laid it! I have studied the Title Deed Books very carefully and find them in excellent order. I have never known the Congress of the United States to give out a bushel and then ask for it back for half a bushel. The Title Book will stand, as is, and claims for the three hundred twenty acres will be taken and filed until December thirty-first. After that, it will be just the one hundred sixty acres. If we find that we have erred, it can be rectified by our own legislature, because they have that power. Now, I believe we are to have a drawing for the Caruthers horse."

"If the bastard wins it," Elizabeth whispered to Beth, "I'll kill the beast."

"What are you saying?"

"Not what I'm saying, it's what he didn't say. The way he smiled when he said the law didn't apply to blacks or Hawaiians was a pure Southern pro-slave smile. Mark my words, if he tries to move us toward statehood, it will be as a slave state."

She didn't have to worry, or kill the horse. It was won by Aaron Sellers, the young husband who had gotten his ears boxed.

"You got a place to raise him up?" Elizabeth asked.

"Golly, yes, ma'am," he beamed from ear to ear. "I'm working at the McGraw-Bellam Ranch."

"Good! Then you know about horses."

"Reckon I do, Mrs. Caruthers. Ran horses for General Sam Houston and was at the Battle of San Jacinto. Know more about horses, cattle, and battles than I do about gold, and that's for sure. Ulalie and I were down to our last bean when we got here a month ago. Told Ulalie this place would bring us luck and it sure has."

"He only bought one chance," Rhoda said.

"That's all it takes. Does my heart good. That's the kind of man who will cherish that horse, for both of their lives."

Pack McGraw did not want to offend any of the women. He donated the prizes for the children's games, brought in a puppet theater troupe from San Francisco, and coordinated with Beth so that his "grand opening" would be over by 9 P.M., leaving enough summer daylight for families to get safely home.

Many of the men had been in saloons before, but never one of such size and opulence. Everything was done in bright colors, from the Chinese red chairs, to the "titty" pink velvet stage curtain, to the candy-striped shirts of the six bartenders behind the one hundred-foot-long bar and buffet counter. Liza Boddick had stolen from the rainbow to create the costumes for the dance-hall waitress girls. Pack had nearly rebelled when he saw the suit, vest, and shirt she had made for him. The last time he had seen such an outfit it had been on a riverboat gambler in Independence. But when all two hundred seats were filled and men were standing three deep at the bar, he forgot what he was wearing.

He had been amazed when Francis and Asa came in, as though they had never fought, and joined Ian and Mick, at the table next to the two McLoughlins, Steve Coffin, and Daniel Lownsdale. Had George Abernethy still been governor, he would have had his full legislature present, but he had been conspicuous by his absence all day long.

Pack let them eat, drink, and anticipate for an hour, then signaled the girls to lower the ropes on John Terwilliger's proud invention.

High above the twelve-candle chandeliers they looked like lamp hoods on a wagon-wheel frame. As the six wheels, with twelve hoods each, came in contact with the candle flame, it snuffed them out and dropped the room to immediate darkness, except for the piano lamps, footlight lamps, and wall lamps on the back of the mirrored bar.

"My, my, my," Liza purred, as she slipped in next to Pack to see how her creations looked under lights. "It's the gents' night out."

Pack did not respond, for he was feasting his eyes on the effort of the curtain rising in folds, as Alfred made the piano music echo through the silent room. Then, as the music built higher and higher, the overhead stage lamps were lighted, revealing a formal garden scene backdrop, and the stage-hands started lowering Kitty from the second-floor catwalk, sitting on a swing.

It was the second standing ovation of the day.

Pack had seen Kitty Flynn in many guises, from the gaudy gowned madam in Independence, to the rowdy, boisterous belt-em-out singer in a saloon tent, to a nûde, playful kitten. Still, he was not prepared for this elegant woman in a picture hat and garden party gown, looking like a girl of sixteen.

Kitty kept her song's light and lively, with a few ballads thrown in so that her sky-blue eyes could suggest a secret sexual glint.

Pack felt instant arousal, because he felt the looks were for him alone. Only once had she invited him to her tent in California and that had ended up being only for a social drink. He had hoped that bringing her to Portland might rekindle the Independence flame, and had hinted at it earlier.

Kitty had laughed gaily, determined not to mention how penniless she really was. "As always, John, I can read you like an open book. Suddenly, I became your song-bird prop-erty. John, I still pick my men, they don't pick me."

"I've done everything you've wanted here!" he had growled.

She had leaned forward toward him and her voice had become curiously intense. "Because I am loyal to my people. My chef, Alfred, stagehands, bartenders, and the girls are family. My girls are not whores, John. The clients don't need to know that they are the wives of the bartenders. That's why I wanted rooms, here, for my staff. I don't want them to become a part of the community. No excess baggage when we move on."

"That will be some time, Kitty. The *Portland Public House* is yours."

Applause brought him out of his reverie. The "Irish Thrush" had captivated them. They hooted and howled for more, but Kitty only returned to take sweeping bows.

The girls opened the heavy drapes over the windows and front doors. Everyone was amazed to see that it was still daylight. They had been transported for an hour and a half into a nighttime dream. They stayed, mingling, chatting, drinking until a bartender rang the closing bell.

Once they were gone, Pack turned his attention back to Kitty. Congratulation drinks for the staff were poured, but Pack and Kitty eyed each other in silence and Alfred Smithson sensed there was more between them than he knew about. He had been with Kitty since her final days in Independence. He didn't like other men trying to crowd in on her.

"I know you keep a room here," Kitty finally said, smiling and adding, "which will be neutral ground for us to talk."

Pack nodded and took Kitty by the arm.

Inside the room, Pack poured two short drinks of Irish whiskey and handed one of them to Kitty. They drank.

"Mick Myers remembered what you used to like."

"He has hardly changed."

"Nor have you."

Kitty smiled. "That's a lie." She turned. "I'm even better looking, and Alfred has done wonders with my singing voice."

Pack walked over, took her gently by the shoulders, and turned her around. He leaned down and kissed her, firmly but gently. He pulled away, because she did not respond.

"Remember the last time we were really together? I was the one anxious to get away."

"I remember."

"I'm not anxious anymore," he said. He began unbuttoning the bodice of the garden dress. She didn't resist.

Kitty's flesh broke out in goose bumps at Pack's touch. She had taught him to undress her and she shivered as his hands moved from the soft, rounded shoulders and down to her breasts. His fingers found her nipples and spent some moments fondling and squeezing them. Pack's arousal returned. He had enforced a period of celibacy from the Kanaka girls when he knew she was returning, and he would now make up for lost time.

Kitty stepped back and pulled loose his string tie. It was invitation enough for him to move them to the bed to hasten the process of undressing each other. Minutes later they were side by side and touching each other as would a young couple who were together for the first time. They were exploring vaguely familiar territory, dusting off cobwebs of time which shrouded pleasant memories.

Kitty suddenly surrendered. She wanted to forget the faceless men of her youth, having to be nice to clients who smelled of sweat and whiskey. Only two men had ever treated her like a lady, not a whore. Pack she had once helped send away, and Alfred refused to go away—although she now refused him her bed, too.

Kitty blinked rapidly when she realized Pack could hold back no longer. Perhaps, she thought, it was better this way. Emotions would not get in the way of pleasure.

At the very peak of their passion, Kitty raised up and a euphoric Pack thrust all the way inside her. The combined effort was totally rewarding and they climaxed together in an all-too-short moment of total pleasure.

As though by mutual consent he rolled away and they were silent. The youthful moment had been recaptured, but neither wanted to address the present or future.

The door came flying open and Mick Myers gasped and turned.

"Goddammit, Mick!" Pack barked, pulling the bedspread over them. "Do you get your thrills barging in on Kitty and me?"

"Piano player said you were alone."

"That would be just like Alfred," Kitty said sourly.

"Well, Mick?"

"Trouble with the Kanakas, Pack. Beth says you better come quick."

"All right. I'll be along as soon as I dress."

Mick silently closed the door. He resented the piano player telling him that Pack was dead drunk and would have to be awakened. He hoped the man enjoyed his little joke.

"Do you always jump when she calls?" Kitty asked.

"Wasn't aware that I did," Pack said, swinging his legs to the floor.

"I've only been here a week and I've noticed it. She *is* quite beautiful."

He got up and began to dress. "And married."

"That doesn't seem to matter anymore." She got up and began gathering her clothes. "Do you belong to her?"

He smiled. It was, for Pack, a wistful smile. "I don't belong to anyone."

"Not even me?"

Pack said nothing. He finished dressing, except for the tie, and pulled on his coat. Kitty walked over to him and turned him around so that she could look into his eyes. She'd had a week to think things over and learn from Liza Boddick. He had said that the *Portland Public House* was hers, but men had made her grand offers before. She didn't want to play the patsy and be bounced on her ear. For the first time ever, she did not want to be independent. If ever there was a proper man to marry, it was John Packwood McGraw.

"I need to know where we stand, Pack."

It was the first time she had called him anything but John. He winced and then smiled, weakly.

"You knocked them dead tonight, Kitty. The take will cover the crew's salary for a month. Tomorrow you can start taking care of the real customers, the sailors."

She knew he had avoided her question on purpose. "Will you be back, later?"

"No, so you can go bed down with Alfred now."

Kitty slapped Pack's face . . . hard. Few women had mustered the courage to do that and, thought Pack, she didn't have any justification. He had eyes and ears and feelings. He had seen the way Alfred looked at her and treated her. He could hear what the bartenders and girls said about them. He had felt her surrender the moment that he had entered her and he knew the surrender was for some other gain. The playful kitten had turned into the mother tiger protecting her cubs. He had not felt cheated when Molly pulled her con game, he felt cheated now. No, he wouldn't be back that night, or any night soon. He had been a damn fool, trying to be a part of the town, when he belonged back on the ranch.

In a single sentence Joseph Lane had crushed the dream of over two hundred people. Without the right to own land or gain citizenship, there was no future for the Kanakas in Oregon. With the wages they had saved, they would be better off back home in the Sandwich Islands.

Pack quickly lost his labor force and foremen from the sawmill. But the Portland Provisions Company retained Katoro.

"We are sending Dexter and Karen to New York to open an agent's office," Ian told him. "We want you to take over the office and warehouses in Honolulu. It will really rock the *haloes* to have a Kanaka in such a position."

Pack lost something he thought he would never lose.

"The dairy girls want to go home," Joe Bellam told him. "Ain't setting too well with my wife, Pack. She won't have any of her folk to talk to, here or at the fort. She's been telling me about their big island. Sounds like good cattle country. Suppose you could buy me out without any hard feelings?"

"What will I do?"

"Pack, you ain't been around here much, so you don't know that Mick Myers's four sisters already do twice as much work as the Kanakas. Let young Sellers take on my foreman duties. Damn kid knows more about cattle than I've forgotten."

In one area Pack did not lose.

"Don't need land or citizenship," Matoa declared. "Nuua and I no wish to go home, bossman. We have good jobs, nice house, happy children. I stay if you say so."

"I say so."

* * *

In a crowd of a couple thousand, a stranger could go unnoticed, even if the stranger carried the height and girth of Forrest Wilkerson, who had an olfactory organ that couldn't simply be called a nose. Its bulb spread from the center of one fat cheek to the center of the other. It was so large that people seldom ever looked at his piglike eyes or his tiny mouth.

"It's also good for sniffing things out, Grover," he declared, with an admirable lack of modesty, "when I sense someone skating on the thin ice of skullduggery."

Grover Adams poured his guest another drink. Adams, a small and wily man, had arrived in March and rented the Nathaniel Crosby house. He did nothing to hide the fact that he had amassed considerable wealth in California and was looking for the proper business opportunity.

When the mail steamer, *Carolina,* arrived at Portland on May 31, Adams was only one of the crowd who marveled that it was only six days out of San Francisco. When the *Carolina* returned again, on June 25, it brought his houseguest, Wilkerson, who left the next day for Oregon City.

"Thank you, Grover. Now we can start to put some meat on your shrewd and sly skeleton report. Pacific Mail Steamship Company should be grateful to Mr. Chapman for selling his stock and opening our eyes. This has been a most interesting trip. I agree with you that Oregon City should not be considered."

"And Milwaukie? Do you agree with what they are building over there?"

Wilkerson chuckled, tapping himself on his round and sturdy chest. "It is as obvious as this. The keel structure gives it away—it's clear there'll be the addition of a sidewheel. But my real clue came in learning that the work is supervised by Captain John Ainsworth. Remember, Grover, when he tried to interest us in steamboats for a Sacramento run? He will captain this craft, I am sure, and it will be large enough for ocean going."

"But we have the mail contract. Now that the 'unofficial'

visits are successful, shall I open the agent office before she returns for you on the 15th?"

"Grover, I have not attained this very satisfactory status in life by undue speed. Even now in San Francisco our directors are discussing with Mr. Coffin the purchase of his shares in the *Columbia*. That leaves us open to make Astoria our only stop, and we will let these river towns worry about their own mail."

"Surely you don't want to leave it with the Portland Provisions Company."

"I want to leave them with nothing," he said with blameless innocence, "but will deny any plots."

Grover Adams was the plotter. "I understand. This town is really split by two cliques, with intertwining webs. They seem to hunger for their newspaper, which Chapman has fouled up. I think we can slyly help confuse that issue at the time. If we give the mail contract to the *Keoka* we would be able to hold her for a few days in Astoria."

"That's small potatoes, Grover. What of the stranglehold Llwellen has over Portland shipping? *That's* the plum we wish to pluck off the tree."

Grover grinned. He loved it when the plotting became nefarious, designed to bring confusion and ruin to others. "I came up on the *Yam-il II* so I could observe the man. His only interest is in his ships. Pettygrove was the master of merchandising and he is gone. I say they are overstocked and a couple of 'disasters' would leave them vulnerable."

"How vulnerable?" Wilkerson asked slyly.

"Very, with a bit of nastiness."

Knowing that Adams was extraordinarily intelligent, Wilkerson would leave it in his hands to bring down the house of the Portland Provisions Company. This area did not have enough population to make passenger travel alone profitable. Pacific Mail Steamship Company also needed the lucrative lumber and wheat trade.

CHAPTER

☆ 17 ☆

As fall turned to winter, Ian was conscious of a general undercurrent of uneasiness in the world of shipping. Profits from California sales had fallen off alarmingly. No one seemed to be heeding the overextended business market. On the lower Willamette, the towns and sawmills at St. Helens and Milton were expanding. The Pacific Mail Steamship Company was building a landing wharf at St. Helens, and Captain Nathaniel Crosby, Jr., was so pleased with the growth of his Milton townsite that he put his house and Portland property up for sale.

Another matter took people's mind off declining business. While Governor Lane had been speaking in Portland, President Zachary Taylor was speaking in the Capitol and grew ill. Four days later he was dead of cholera. Vice-President Millard Fillmore moved quickly to establish his own Presidency, moving out the Taylor appointees and naming his own. By mid-September, John B. Gaines had arrived to replace Joseph Lane as Territorial Governor. He did not agree with Asa Lovejoy on the question of the Linn Act and the Donation Land Claim Law. He determined the first to be invalid because of nonpassage and only the second valid. Because Peter Burnett sided with him, he replaced Asa as Territorial Judge. "Ain't gonna take my land without a fight" became the battle cry of the Tualatin and Willamette farmers and ranchers.

William W. Chapman, unable to find capital to buy out Lownsdale, came home on the July 15 trip of the *Carolina* to attempt to do it piecemeal. Ironically, on the same vessel was Lot Whitcomb, who had just purchased a fifteen-thousand-dollar engine for *The Lot Whitcomb of Oregon,* planned to be launched on Christmas Day of 1850. Abrams and Reed also announced that their steam-powered sawmill would be ready for operation in December.

Grover Adams rubbed his hands together, not because of the chill fall weather. From where he sat it appeared that the Portland Provisions Company was in a program of expansion and not curtailment. Because of his spurious business activities and ill-gained knowledge of some of the "minor" members of the company, Grover was of the opinion that there was infighting over authority and money. Mentally, he set the end of December as his target for the total collapse of Ian Llwellen. Because of his blandness no one in Portland paid much heed to his questions or the information he was trying to gain.

They hardly had time. The fir forest between Jefferson Street and the Caruthers's property was being cleared for the sawmill. A house and business building a day were being completed. The new house for Captain John Couch had an inside bathtub and a water tower on the roof. The bumper harvest hardly suggested a coming depression.

Secretly, in early October, the Portland Provisions Company altered their programs. No one, not even Grover Adams, questioned that Beth Llwellen's Sunday dinners were anything other than that. Grover's main weakness was probably that he never believed people other than himself could be intelligent—especially women.

"It may have been a stroke of luck, Pack," Ian said as the group took seats at the diningroom table after dinner, "that you lost the Kanakas and the sawmill. Lumber has fallen to two hundred dollars a thousand and we are paying one hundred dollars. We are already committed to the *Merchantman* getting a load at Milwaukie in December. I say we curtail lumber shipments until we see how the Portland mill does."

Beth, Pack, and Mick nodded their agreement.

Ian looked at the others around the table. "We may be the

owners, but we are nothing without you. Speak up when you disagree."

Dave McLoughlin was there because he knew every last item that was in their warehouses or stores in Portland, Oregon City, and Salem. Nicolas Zarundy was there not only for his sugar industry but also as representative of the Russian families who had started hog farms. Joe Bellam had been right about Aaron Sellers, also present—he did know more about the cattle business than Joe and Pack had forgotten. David Lee, fearing he might lose his farm, had sold it to his father and become an agent for a majority of the wheat farmers. He'd used his profit to lease the sawmill from Pack and was converting it into a grist mill. Seated next to him was John Kenwa, whose river service was still vital to all of them. Matoa had hired a German from Pittsburg, via California, as the new butcher, which gave him time to run the new slaughterhouse and packing plant on Tanner Creek, just below the tannery. He was seated by Asa Lovejoy, who was present as company attorney—because they were all wary of what rash decisions might come out of the "Salem Clique."

"Well, you've all heard my report on how the California market is overstocked and money is becoming exceedingly scarce. McLoughlin, what reaction did you get from Francis?"

Dave McLoughlin smiled. "Very favorable. His advance party has already laid claim to a peninsula in the Straits of Juan de Fuqua and laid out the townsite of Port Townsend. We can become his chief supplier, at once."

"How will we keep it secret?" Beth asked.

"Beth," Mick answered, "most of the things Francis requires—tools, broad and felling axes, nails and housewares—we have in ample supply, still uncrated. We will number the crates, but not label them as to content. Once the ship is over the Columbia bar, not even Astoria can see that it turns toward the Puget Sound."

"And," Dave interjected, "because he needs flour and foodstuffs, it will look like any other exporting shipment."

"Good thing he doesn't need lumber or good liquor," Pack said sourly.

Everyone ignored the double barb of the comment. Throughout the summer none had dared ask why he had left the full running of the *Portland Public House* to Kitty Flynn. The local clientele had dwindled away to those few who did not want to go all the way to Milwaukie or Oregon City for a drink, but the sailor clientele increased due to a handbill distributed to Portland-bound ships in San Francisco.

Grover Adams had made sure that the printer suggested that Portland could offer everything they might find on the Barbary Coast. Because they could not, it caused nightly fights and street brawls in and around the pub. Egged on by W. W. Chapman, the churches began demanding its closing.

The U.S. Navy Steamship *Massachusetts* had visited Portland on July 8, when the pub was only four days old and still respectable enough to keep the American sailors a little in awe. She returned in mid-September, after surveying the Pacific Coast ports to establish lighthouses. An "agent" for the Pacific Mail Steamship Company offered the 152 officers and crew a "free evening of food, grog, and female companionship" for their gallant efforts. They arrived en masse. No "agent" had contacted Kitty Flynn, so there was no food prepared, she had not replenished the liquor supply since the opening, and the bartenders were not about to let their wives become "female companions."

The riot left the bar in a shambles. By the time Pack arrived the next day, Kitty Flynn and crew had departed on the *Ocean Bird*, with every cent the public house had made since opening. With no Pacific Mail Steamship Company agent in Portland, and the U.S. Navy refusing to take responsibility, Pack was out of luck.

Without making any major repairs, he brought up three tough bartenders from the Barbary Coast, turned it into a saloon without a stage show, and became his own best drunken customer for two weeks.

"Ian," David Lee said, to break the silence, "now that Mick and Dave have brought up the need of wheat for Mr. Pettygrove, might I further address that issue?"

"To be sure."

"You have stockpiled five thousand barrels of wheat. I

have consignments from the farmers for an additional twelve thousand barrels, once it is threshed and culled. The farmers are willing to put it up for credit on trade."

"But where would we store it?" Beth asked.

"Not where it is stored now," Kenwa said. "My people are getting tired of being accused of breaking the barrels to steal the wheat. David, shall I go on with what we discussed?" David Lee nodded.

Kenwa took out a map he had drawn and spread it on the table. "These farmers take their grain to Abernethy in Oregon City. From here and here, they are prone to cart it to Whitcomb's ferry for the Milwaukie mill. Even if they only have their wheat milled, they have to hire me to get it here for the ships. People pay no attention to my scows being loaded with barrels. Pack, you've got thirty houses sitting vacant right next to the sawmill. David thinks they would be excellent for storing the twelve thousand barrels and would be right at hand when he needs them to mill."

"I like it," Beth mused. "No one will be able to see we have that much in storage and be able to cause a panic and force the prices up."

"I have done the same," Nicolas said, almost apologetically. "I have let all my crops go to seed, because my family has ten thousand pounds sacked in the barn lofts, and the unprocessed beets in the silos are in no hurry to meet the knife. I now have more money than the Czar, but not the poor corn farmers and you. Again, the corn crop has been a failure. You have a mountain of unsold ears that not even Kenwa's people wish to eat. Hogs do not count the missing kernels in each row or care that the ears are small. Mick, you paid a dollar per thousand ears—the hog farmers have authorized me to offer ten cents a thousand, and they will haul the mountain away."

"But they are already withering and drying. They are a total loss."

"Not to the hogs," Asa laughed. "They eat them dry all winter long. Better the ten cents than nothing."

"And building good will," Beth advised, "with the corn and hog farmers."

"The corn farmers were already paid," Mick said miserably, still kicking himself for the purchase.

"I see what Mrs. Llwellen means," Aaron Sellers said. "We bought several acres of the corn to let dry for chicken feed. The farmers are embarrassed that they can't come up with the right corn seeds for this climate and are afraid to come in and use their credit for what they did sell you, Mick."

"I usually only address shipping matters," Ian said, "but we can't have a feeling like that out there. The last thing we want is for them to give that impression to Crosby & Smith, Beck & Ogden, or even Couch's store. We can't let the sense of depression spread here, as it is in California. We've got to watch our expenditures, but not look like we're pulling in our neck like a turtle."

"How then shall I handle the slaughter of the cattle and hogs?" Matoa asked.

"That doesn't change," Pack said, "because we still have nine hundred people buying at this butcher shop retail, and Oregon City, Milwaukie, and St. Helens buying wholesale. How do you want to handle Honolulu, Ian?"

"No different than before and perhaps an increase. Putting that coating of salt on the carcass has greatly reduced the spoilage, and we are getting into cooler shipping weather."

Matoa grinned. "Mr. Lownsdale will be happy you say increase. He say Matoa not produce hides fast enough for him to tan into leather."

Beth had sat pondering the matter of the cattle. "For reasons of my own, I have not been able to view your . . . ah, plant, Matoa. However, I am curious as to how long the beef stays good after having been dressed out?"

"Longer, since Aaron's suggestion."

"Oh?"

Aaron blushed. He still felt uncomfortable being around Beth. She was so beautiful and intelligent. "Only something I learned from a Mexican in Texas. Down there, ma'am, we like our beef aged a spell. Once the quarters are hooked they hand them in an adobe building with a straw-thatched roof. The little *ninōs* would pour buckets of water over the straw, so the wind going through it would cool the room. It keeps the meat good for weeks."

Pack suddenly laughed. "Years from now they will never believe that the first brick building in Portland was a straw-roofed cooling chamber at the slaughterhouse. Good Lord, isn't there some way we could turn the mud of our streets into bricks, instead of importing the expensive little rascals from New England?"

"When we were primitive," Asa laughed, "we were smart enough to set up a glass-blowing foundry—it has since tripled in size."

"That's exactly the point I was getting at," Beth enthused. "We can't appear like we are being conservative. Chapman has always wanted us out of here, and every day he gets Stephen Coffin more and more into his corner and against Daniel. I know we can never prove who keeps breaking open the wheat barrels, or who pulled the peacocks so the *Alina* almost sank at the wharf, or all the other little mishaps of late—but we sure as hell have our suspicions. We've got to keep those two on edge, so why not announce we will soon construct a brickyard and drying ovens? And I think we should try Nate's house."

"Why?" Ian asked. "Isn't it rented?"

"It is, but that's not the point. Nate approached me first, so I know he has the whole block, all eight lots up for sale. Chapman will pee his pants if we steal it out from under his nose."

"If the company doesn't buy," Pack said, "I will."

Beth frowned. "I thought you wanted out of the urban sprawl."

"Do," he answered dully, "but I own the block on either side and Coffin wants 'em bad, for some reason. He's got a petition going around to close down the saloon as a public nuisance. Price goes up on the property each day, until the petition shit is stopped."

"Then you buy it," Beth laughed. "You've got cause."

"Speaking of buying," Kenwa said hesitantly, "I know that you do not like steamships, Ian, but without the Kanakas I'm having a hard time getting these new immigrants to work the scows for less than five dollars a day. I've been talking to James Frost in Astoria. An agent for the Pacific Mail Steamship Company has been giving him a hard time because he named his little river steamer *Columbia,* the same as their steamship. He's ready to sell out. I figure her seventy-five horsepower can tow four scows at a time. I will need only a tiller man on each, for which I have Cayuse already trained. I save the wages of twelve men there. Like Mr. Frost, I can be my own fireman, engineer, and captain."

"You're right," Ian scowled, "I'm not a lover of steam power, but I am impressed that it only takes that little tub twenty-four hours from Astoria to Portland, and that she can make it to Oregon City without difficulty. How much?"

"Twenty-five thousand dollars," he said, without changing expression.

"You're crazy!" Ian gasped.

"Yes, he's crazy," Asa chuckled. "Crazy like a fox. I've seen Kenwa's figures. He was paying his Kanaka boys three dollars a day. That's one thousand eighty dollars a month he will save in wages. That's half the cost of the steamer right there. But don't worry. Kenwa intends to pay cash and have me draw up a proper purchase title."

Beth suddenly remembered something that Old Wife had once said—a fleeting remark by a proud old woman: "Kenwa's grandfather once rich with horses, but died in the mountains with only one. Kenwa need no horses or *coup* feathers to be rich man. He has horses in his head."

Well, she mused, I wonder how that news will set with the Portland Trio?

Asa Lovejoy, because of his now frequent trips to Portland, had rented the former office and quarters of Dennis Landry. Walking back that Sunday afternoon, he paused to take a look at Nate Crosby's house for Pack McGraw. The one-story building with its dormer windows reminded him of early Boston homes that had been absorbed into the expanding business district. That, he could see, would be the fate of this structure.

Two blocks farther along he stopped. Eliza Boddick's

frame building stood between a shoe shop and a harness shop. Like little children they had been avoiding each other. Crossing the street very slowly, he saw that Liza was in her shop, which was also her sitting room. Her back was to the window, as she inspected the garments other women made for her by the piece.

Asa felt a strong urge to talk with her. The people he had just left were trying to look at the big picture, and Liza would have a grasp on the reality of the Portland scene. Then he realized that was only an alibi for his ego. He was lonely for the sound of her voice and her cheery laugh. He stepped inside the door and cleared his throat. She turned, her eyes widening in wonderment. For once, Eliza Boddick was caught without a word on the tip of her tongue. She walked forward, her legs feeling awkward and rubbery, and when she was close she put out her hand.

"Hello, you old fool!" she said.

Asa did not answer her. He stood there, staring down at her hand. Then he took it, holding it lightly, before he covered it with his other hand.

"Old fool!" he mimicked her. "Just because you haven't yet seen thirty, don't make me feel ancient because I've gone past forty. Hell, Liza, by pioneer standards I'm still a young pup."

"Hello, young fool, then," she whispered.

"Liza . . ."

"Yes, Asa?"

"Can we put our petty differences behind us?"

She took her hand away. "They didn't seem petty to me, or else I would have married you."

"Thunderation! At that time—"

"Which is not this time," Liza said slowly, patiently, as though she were talking to a child. "Our little world changes almost daily, Asa. New people. New ideas. I don't think Mr. Boddick would have been happy being a navigator on one of these new steam vessels. Still, as I see it, we need to put aside little quarrels."

"I didn't come here to be lectured, but to apologize."

"Accepted," she said. Then, leaning forward, she kissed his mouth, slowly, forgivingly, with so much tenderness that Asa shuddered. "That's to say you're forgiven. I've a kettle on, if you'd like a spot of tea."

After an hour, Asa sat back, grinning. Liza Boddick was better than a newspaper. Women talked while being fitted and he now had a good measure of business in every Portland store. For some their gold dust was drying up and they wanted to revert to a trade basis. In a piqued mood over the money her husband had spent in San Francisco, Mrs. W. W. Chapman had ordered six frocks in late June. Now, she claimed that four were not of the fabric or design she selected and would only pay for two. Asa put that down as Chapman being in a bit of a financial pickle.

"I have one cash customer who is quite generous," she said. "This Mr. Adams, who is renting the Crosby house, ordered four maid outfits. A morning, afternoon, and two evening serving ensembles. He hired that Sean Cassidy's daughter, Patricia. She's a nice little thing, but as dense as her father. I sometimes wonder how Hugh O'Bryant can afford to keep the drunken bum on. Lucky they have Patricia's salary, but I question that number of dresses when the man has had only two houseguests for dinner since he moved here in March. Patricia says he's interested in the shipping business, but I don't see the man doing a lick of work."

"When did she say that?"

"Just yesterday. He's having her fitted for a couple of dresses of her own. Apparently, he's quite intrigued that Kenwa might be buying that Astoria river steamer."

"I see," Asa said heavily. That was news that he and Kenwa had carefully guarded until that afternoon at Beth's. He made a mental note to find out how a stranger had learned it beforehand. Then he smiled. "I am now in Portland a couple of times a week. Might we have dinner?"

"Might, but I best make myself clear, Asa Lovejoy. If the talk turns to marriage again, I've no intentions of living in Oregon City. Portland's me home."

"I see," Asa mumbled. "Guess I can't blame you for that. Shall we say Wednesday evening? The food at the Union Hotel is quite good."

"Wednesday it is."

Then she kissed him lightly on the cheek and let him out the door. Asa was reminded once more of how much of life he was missing without a wife. He would let their relationship renew itself and then consider if it was profitable to make a move to Portland. His term as mayor was over in four months and he was not seeking reelection. He was trying to get John McLoughlin to run, because Morris Attwood had already announced his candidacy. Morris, in the opinion of Asa and George Abernethy, was too much a part of the "Salem Clique."

Grover Adams's information had come via Forrest Wilkerson, who did not want the river steamer operated by James Frost *or* John Kenwa. The Indian was to be discouraged, or bought out, because he was too closely associated with Ian Llwellen. Both erroneously thought it was Portland Provisions Company money behind the buy, because neither thought an Indian could afford such a purchase.

Adams did not want to approach Kenwa directly, so the first thing he did was to pump Patricia for all the information she could supply about the man. When she was finished with her glowing, enthusiastic report, he smiled. He would have no trouble getting Patricia to help in his gambit.

Patricia approached Kenwa the next evening as he was leaving the pub, where he had been meeting with Pack about putting the wheat in the fort houses, and handed him a note.

Puzzled, Kenwa opened it and then decided to play dumb. He knew that the thin and rather homely girl worked for the man living in the Crosby house. He also knew, from James Frost, that the man was somehow connected with another man, named Wilkerson, who was giving Frost a hard time over the *Columbia*.

"Don't read," he lied, handing it back.

"I can tell you what it says," she giggled. "My bossman,

Mr. Adams, would like you to visit him this evening at ten P.M."

"Why so late?"

"He's a strange man," she shrugged. "Sleeps most of the day and works at night."

"Tell him maybe, but no promise."

Without warning she put her arms about his neck and kissed him.

Kenwa pulled back and looked at her darkly.

"I'm a married man!"

"Don't matter," she sing-songed. "Had my eye on you since you brought Paw and me upriver on your scow. You still got a bed in that little cabin on the back of the scow?"

"Doesn't matter if I do," he growled. "I told you I am married!"

"Are you different?" she snorted. "Hear tell that Indians have more than one wife, because they've always got their pecker up."

"When they do," he hissed, "they are all legal wives and not sluts who want to find out if we do it differently!"

She reeled back, as though slapped, as he spun and re-entered the saloon.

Sean Cassidy had been taking a shortcut across the clearing from O'Bryant's house on Morrison Street. He had been turned down for an advance against his salary and was wondering who he could cadge for a couple of drinks when he saw the kiss. He stopped dead still, his Irish starting to boil at his daughter for taking up with the likes of a savage. Then, when he saw her reel back, he was torn between going for the Indian for a fisticuffs demand or boxing his daughter's ears until he learned how long this had been going on.

Being a man without luck, he decided on the latter, because if his daughter was a piece of damaged goods, the Indian might be willing to pay a little something to keep the news from his wife.

Once he had Patricia by the ear, he marched her on her tiptoes, screaming all the way home. Most paid no attention, because the father regularly beat the girl's salary out of her.

Sean had a savage style of questioning his daughter. When she was nearly unconscious he gained what he had been seeking. And he saw a potential for more money.

Kenwa arrived at the appointed time, because Pack was curious to learn of Grover Adams's game.

Adams opened the door and Kenwa entered. Instantly, each of Kenwa's arms was twisted behind his back and strapped together by a belt. He had not anticipated an attack, and now he tried to twist out of the two men's grasp, bellowing like an enraged bull. He was boxed on the side of his ear and pushed down onto the floor. Then Sean kicked him viciously in the stomach and groin. He grunted at the pain and everything went black for a second. He rolled into a ball to ease the pain. When his eyes began to clear, all that would come into focus were feet. A pair of women's feet in muddy slippers. He looked up. It was the girl, sitting in a chair. Her face was distorted with bruises and a black eye that was swollen completely shut. The other eye was wide with fright.

"Take a good look!" someone roared in his ear. "That's the way you left her!"

"Didn't—" he mumbled, and swung his torso so he could sit up. Far, far off he could see a cowering Grover Adams still standing at the open door. Closer was the burly Irishman, Sean Cassidy. Then, jutted into his view, was the grotesque, twisted face of William Chapman.

"Oh how I have been waiting for this moment," Chapman scathed. "I'm glad Mr. Adams had the good sense to send the father for me, instead of those weak-sisters Coffin and Lownsdale. Now, you friggin' savage, I've got you and will run all your people off my land."

"For what?"

"For *what?*" Chapman shrieked. "The bloody bastard rapes a girl, nearly beats her to death, and asks 'for what?' Scared the hell out of you when she escaped your scow, didn't it? After you followed her here, what were you going to do? Kill her? Kill him?"

Kenwa shook his head. Nothing was making sense. "He invited me here."

"That's a lie!" Adams protested.

"Note!" Kenwa got out. "He sent me a note by the girl."

Chapman grinned wickedly. "Then where is the note?"

"Back . . . she took it back before . . ."

"Before what?" Chapman asked, rubbing his hands together.

"Before she kissed him," came the deadly quiet answer from the doorway.

Pack McGraw filled the whole frame.

"McGraw!" Chapman barked. "Get the hell out of here! This does not concern you!"

"I'm making it my concern."

"You can't get your Indian friend out of this, McGraw," Chapman said, spitting out each word. "A great many of our citizens are not comfortable with Indians living this close. How do you think they will feel when they find out that he raped and beat this little girl?"

"Listen to the facts," Pack said fervently. "Ain't no way he could have raped her, because he was with me from the time she brought the note to the saloon, to when he knocked on this door."

"You lie," Adams gasped. "The girl . . . the father . . ."

"Yeah," Pack growled, "that's where I got confused, too, listening outside. If the girl came to you, escaping from Kenwa, where did the father magically appear from, for you to send for Chapman?"

"Quit trying to twist things in his favor," Adams said indignantly.

"Which he can't do." Sean Cassidy felt he better take charge, before the money slipped through his fingers. He was disgusted with Grover Adams for being so mealymouthed. He had seen no good reason to bring Chapman in on it. Nor had he expected Pack McGraw. But none of that mattered. He would handle everything in his way. "You ain't got all the facts straight, Pack. Hate to admit it, but I'm the one who sent her to the saloon to say her good-byes. I don't hold with a married man getting it on the side. Indian or no. When she didn't come back to the house, I came to see if she was here. About then she came stumbling in and told us what her 'lover' had done to her before he went back to the bar. Ain't got no law in this town. Owner seemed the next best thing."

Kenwa started to laugh. It started in his belly and rumbled upward. Each time he would almost stop, it would start up again. Throughout, he kept his eyes on Patricia. The eyes were not laughing, they were piercing. She could close her good eye to the sight, but not her ears. The laugh was haunting, accusing, shattering to her nerves.

"Stop it!" she screamed. "Everyone stop lying!"

The room fell into a sudden silence. All eyes were riveted on her, each with their own emotion.

"I kissed him," she said flatly. "He wouldn't kiss back . . . because he's married. I kept the note from Mr. Adams, who wanted to see him on business. My Paw caught me in The Clearing and hauled me home for a beating. Worse than ever. To stop it, I lied. He pulled me over here by my hair and got Mr. Chapman here so he would look good in one of the owner's eyes."

"Now look who is lying," Sean bellowed. "She told me this little pipsqueak was her lover and Adams cooked up the story to blame the beating on Kenwa."

"I beg your pardon!" Adams said fretfully. "The girl has not uttered a word since she stumbled through the door. I only had the father's report to go on. Patricia, did you say such a dastardly thing against me?"

"No, sir."

Cassidy started for her with a clenched fist and Kenwa thrust out his legs to trip him. Pack was there immediately to take away the belt strap and stand over Cassidy.

"My, this is a poser," Chapman said. "I'm still not sure what it was all about."

"As if you really cared, Chapman."

Chapman sniffed, his face filled with astonishment.

Clearly he wasn't used to being rebuffed. He took his hat from a chair and marched out.

Pack lifted Kenwa up and looked at Patricia. "Would you like for me to find you someplace else to stay?"

She looked beseechingly at Grover Adams and then fearfully down at her father.

Pack understood without words. "Get your ass up, Cassidy. That's my building that O'Bryant is working on, so you ain't got a job tomorrow. You ain't got a job anywhere in town. Your daughter is of age and gainfully employed. Your daughter won't say it, so I'll say it for her. Get your ass out of town."

He rose, cursing under his breath, and shuffled out the door. Pack helped Kenwa out. At the door, Grover Adams crisply nodded his head at their departure and closed the door.

Then he began to smile. Patricia had pulled the coals from a near fire of defeat. She had played her part well, not knowing that Grover had anticipated the beating. They each had gained what they sought out of this venture. She would be rid of her father, because Grover had paid him off on the blackmail lie. How foolish the man would feel if he knew that Grover Adams was impotent.

The payoff had been because Patricia had lured Kenwa and Chapman for Adams to have a close look. Chapman he now saw as a hothead who would not serve Adams well, not at all.

Kenwa, he now saw, as not easily bluffed or frightened. But the fascinating thing, which Adams had not been aware of, was the close camaraderie between Kenwa and Pack McGraw. Adams had been remiss. He had considered McGraw to be little more than a cattle rancher who also ran a saloon.

The expense of Patricia's new dress just went up. He was curious as to what the dressmaker knew about the man.

"You all right?" Pack asked his young friend.

"I've been better. First time I've been accused of rape.

What game was he playing, Pack? He hedged and lied more than anyone."

"So I noticed. I've a feeling it goes a lot deeper than just your river steamer, Kenwa. Curious how he got Chapman over there. I wonder if they are tied together in some way."

Kenwa laughed. "You might have let them kick me around a few more times and you might have learned."

"No, thanks, we can learn in other ways. For one thing, that's quite a fancy dress for a servant girl to be wearing. I'll take it up with Liza in the morning, to see if it's one of hers."

Kenwa stopped in front of his house. A lamp was still aglow in the kitchen, which meant Tama was home from the village. Old Wife was dying and would only let *Saki,* Little Flower Petal, care for her.

"Pack," Kenwa said grimly, "Chapman did speak one word of truth. The townspeople are uncomfortable with our village so close and we are uncomfortable with the townspeople so close. When we were small, we could all be friends. No more! Old Wife is dying and longs for the old village. What are your plans with all the fort land you bought? I know you bought more than just the houses and mill."

Pack stared at him incredulously. "I wasn't aware anyone knew, but the answer is simple. It has amazed me that everyone fights over their town sites on the Willamette when the fort has been there all the time on the Columbia. I'm going to sit on it until there's more settlement north of the Columbia."

"We could settle part of it right now."

Pack pursed his lips. "It would discourage squatters. What would the Indian commissioner say?"

Kenwa grinned. "What can he say to owned land? I'll trade you the village here for equal space to make a village there. My people will be happier. Salmon are always better on the Columbia. The old garden plots will be better because of this rest."

"What of your new river steamer?"

"And what is wrong with the old wharf at the fort? Nothing! Business can be done from there, as well as here."

"True! Well, we can't just tell people to get ahold of Kenwa at the fort. What shall we call it?"

Kenwa shrugged. "Why change? It's been known for years. Just drop the fort and call it Vancouver."

Pack frowned. "You've been thinking about this for some time, haven't you?"

"Almost since we got here. The older people, like Old Wife, long to rejoin our people, wherever they are scattered. The young wives resent Tama having a white man's house. When Old Wife is gone, they may have such, if they wish. I only want workers, not shirkers."

"Shades of Francis Pettygrove. Speaking of workers, Lownsdale will scream."

"No he won't," he smiled. "He and Ancho found a huge hemlock grove on a creek a couple of miles above the fort. Lownsdale didn't bother looking there originally because it was all under HBC control."

"Well," Pack said sadly, "if Daniel knows your desires, so must the other two."

"On that you are fortunate. They are not speaking to each other right now, because Coffin invested in the new sawmill without telling them."

"We'll see how long my fortune lasts. When would you like to do this?"

"Tomorrow!"

Pack whistled. "What's the hurry?"

"My grandfather was called 'cunning warrior.' He would put on a sham battle, let the enemy feel they had won that day, move the village that night, and let the enemy come screaming after him the next dawn. He always left traps where the old village stood. That would be the real battle. He would win and move the village back. If you are a cunning warrior, Chapman will think he won this sham battle."

They stood looking at each other. Only five miles would separate them, but it would never be the same again.

Portland had to grow, they knew, but with growth would be

a loss forever of those magical days when you would hear the music of English, Kanaka, and Cayuse voices blending in a pioneer chorus.

Even now, there were newcomers who would not build their houses until the carpenters had cleared the stumps from the streets of "Little Stumptown."

CHAPTER

☆ 18 ☆

Chapman was ecstatic, without knowing it would be a pyrrhic victory.

Liza was a wealth of information about John Packwood McGraw, all of it fiction.

Patricia was a chatterbox about Grover Adams, with no real information to be gleaned from her chatter.

Grover Adams did learn one thing about Pack McGraw. When Thomas Jefferson Dryer arrived on November 1, the *Ocean Bird* also brought the mail from Astoria. Wilkerson thought the time was ripe for Adams to purchase a suitable site for a PMSC agent's office. He had seen the Crosby property advertised for sale and paid a visit to Crosby & Smith General Merchandise. He came out utterly shaken after learning the name of his new landlord. His substantial ego was further deflated by learning that all the riverfront property was owned by Portland Provisions Company. His intelligence would have gone into a tailspin had he known that Forrest Wilkerson did not always wait for Grover Adams to act.

"It's from Ian," Beth told Asa, visiting his office. "Rather ironic that we use their mail service to get our fastest news. Even more ironic that the directors of PMSC hold a document from Chapman giving them exclusive steamer landing rights."

"Interesting." Asa whistled. "Our bland little sheep, Grover Adams, has shed part of his coat and has been digging around for a location for an agent's office. If he is tied up with Chapman, as Pack thinks, why isn't he going to him direct?"

"I'm judging by what Ian writes that the directors of that company are not bound to keep their field agents informed on majority policy. He paints a rather florid picture of his conversation with a Mr. Wilkerson."

"What is Ian proposing?"

"That we build a new wharf and building at the foot of Yamhill Street. He feels Kenwa would agree that a wharf would better serve his river steamer than just pulling the scows up onto the riverbank. With a new wharf and shipping building PMSC will agree to a lease with Portland as a terminus for mail and passengers."

"Again, I say, interesting. Do we contact this Adams fellow?"

"Why not," Beth said, with a sly grin. "Time we let him know the proper people to deal with in regards to shipping. I would appreciate your doing it, Asa, as I am back to afternoon naps again."

"When is this child due?"

"Early summer. I'm looking forward to another girl. That will give me two of each and I think that will be my limit."

Asa nodded. He would be happy with a single offspring. "Have you met our new editor, as yet?"

"No, only what I read about him in the *Spectator*. They make it sound like a race for who publishes first, Lot's *Western Star* or Dryer's *Oregonian*. Do either have their presses yet?"

"No. Dryer says the *Keoka* is in the river and Lot claims that he is impatiently waiting. I'm afraid I greatly question that, because two months ago he was boasting that the equipment would be on the *Desdemona,* and she has already arrived and left."

"I wasn't aware."

"I'm sure. She went directly to Milwaukie, because all the cargo was for Abernethy and Company. I fear George doesn't smell the depression, as we do."

* * *

T. J. Dryer, while awaiting his press, made a visit to Oregon City to meet his rival at the *Spectator*. Wishing to also meet the new editors of the *Western Star,* he visited Milwaukie on his way back downriver, but never got to the newspaper office.

"Mr. Whitcomb," he said, with pungent ardor, "I was assured by your agent that no detention could happen in river navigation, as the *Keoka* would be towed by a steamer from the mouth of the Columbia to Milwaukie. You can imagine my astonishment, sir, to see that said steamboat is still in construction and not employed to bring my freight to me."

Lot Whitcomb had taken a dislike to Dryer before he'd even met him. He wanted his new newspaper to have a progressive democratic feel, and Dryer, to him, smelled of pure conservative whig dogma.

"That's partially true," Lot said, indifferently, "but the advertisment did not say *when* we would use steam. *Keoka* sits in Astoria, sir, waiting more important cargo and mail. You can take delivery there, if you've a mind!"

Lot Whitcomb had more important duties that day than wasting time with an editor from Portland. First, it was the twentieth of November and the first "surprise" edition of the *Western Star* would be published the next day. Second, he was busy that day with his duties as Commissary-General for the Territorial Government.

Major John Grace, Lot had decided at once, was going to be a difficult customer.

"Army script? Major, we still ain't been paid for supplying the army when they came in to help on the Cayuse War. Why is this script any different?"

"We will be a permanent regiment," Grace said pompously, "with payroll and commissary payments coming out of the headquarters at The Presidio in San Francisco. I'm just the advance officer."

"Where shall you be headquartered, Major Grace?"

"It is General Wende's plan to supplant Hudson Bay's old fort. This way we shall not have to build."

"Are you aware," Lot murmured, sorry he had to inform him, "that the fort property was sold and is private property?"

Grace didn't bat an eyelash. "The owner will soon learn that we have first priority for the fort. General Wende received such assurance from Governor Gaines. I will have the man's name, sir. The Mounted Rifles are a spit and polish outfit, Mr. Whitcomb, and we must have the fort in top fettle for the general's arrival, in mid-December. You may wish to attend the 'taking of command' ceremony. It is most impressive when a general officer reviews the mounted lines, with the brass band playing and the squadron banners waving in the breeze."

"Band?" Lot mused. "Here just for the ceremony, I assume?"

"Hardly," Grace said, indignantly. "It is our own, comprised of musicians out of the Mounted Rifles. General Wende's idea, and an excellent one. For good public relations they did many concerts in San Francisco."

"You don't say." Lot grinned. "We are having a small public occasion here on Christmas Day, Major. A banquet, a ball, a christening of a new ship. It might be an excellent opportunity for the band to participate and let people know that we have the U.S. Army here to protect us."

John Grace was very aware that he was being conned, but thought he'd do a bit of conning himself. Merchants in Sacramento and San Francisco were still waiting for Congress to pay them for the "script" they held for supplying the Army throughout the gold rush days. Wende was moving the regiment out of the bay area, because California was now a state and would not support his troops.

Grace grinned. "Excellent suggestion. And as I am the officer in charge of the band, I can approve of their appearance right here and now. Shall we get on with the list of supplies we shall need and the name of the man I am to contact to take over the fort?"

Pack agreed to meet Major John Grace at Vancouver, and not because Grace had made it sound like an imperial order from Governor Gaines. With Dexter Farman in New York City, the Portland Provisions Company received news of events in Washington faster than Gaines. Pack was quite aware of the act moving through Congress to make a separate Washington Territory with the Columbia River as the southern boundary. The army could be of help.

Grace had only seen the fort from a distance, before his ship had turned to head up the Willamette. His eyes now wandered about it, seeing its ancient form and grim neglect as HBC had dwindled away. His heart told him that it would cost more to bring it back than it would have to build new. But, as a West Point graduate, he was more prone to follow orders than create new ones.

"It might work," he said. "With some changes. Before I'm through, I can see the single clerks' quarters as barracks. Their warehouse, inside the fort, can be converted to horse stalls. As we shall purchase hay and oats locally, that old wheat field can be used for drilling. Those houses are near poverty, but can be tidied up for officers' quarters. The Indians will have to move their village, of course."

"Afraid not, Major. It's their village property. Likewise, those houses, the grist mill, and the wharf are leased out to others. I'm willing to rent the fort and any property needed to the west, and that's it."

"You are dealing with the United States government," Grace said narrowly. "We shall take for our use what we deem is necessary and shall fix a rent figure that we feel is fair."

"Is that right," Pack said with a wry smile, taking a piece of paper out of his pocket. "We do have lawyers here in the territory, Major. Handy things to have around when you don't know all the answers. If you say it's for the government, then they have to abide by their own rules. This here's from a thing called the Bill of Rights. Their rules. Says you can't quarter soldiers without my consent as the owner. Now, I'm not an unreasonable man. I've told you what I would consent to, and the rent will be only a dollar a year for a two-year period. But the minute I hear of you giving the Cayuse any trouble, out you go!"

There was something the man was not saying, Grace thought. Something was not right for the man to have a dollar figure already in his mind. But he pigeonholed the thought for later consideration because he was quite elated at the price. He would leave the Indian situation for General Wende. The man was an expert in solving Indian problems, one way or the other.

General Nelson Wende, Pack thought grimly. Welcome to my turf! I can hardly wait to see your face when you learn of your new landlord!

Nelson Wende was undaunted by the news. He needed first to learn more about this version of John Packwood McGraw.

"Governor," he said with a laugh, "you did not mention in your dispatch that the fort was under private ownership." He put all his geniality, all his bluff into the laugh.

Gaines was furious. All of Hudson Bay's land and property sales had gone through John McLoughlin, who had recorded them with Asa Lovejoy. Judge Peter Burnett declared them valid, under the terms of the Boundary Settlement.

"I question the legality of the sales, General Wende, especially back to Indians. I am asking for a clarification from Washington. Until then, is everything else to your liking?"

"Seems to be. If not, we shall see each other again in five days' time in Milwaukie."

There was a gruff sound from Major John Grace's desk. Grace was contemptuous of the fact that he had planned a beautiful ceremony for that day and only Governor Gaines and a few curious Indians attended.

"Oh, yes," Wende corrected himself, "there is a matter that Major Grace has brought to my attention. To fix up the fort he hired carpenters from wherever he could find them. Because of the building boom he didn't get any from up the Willamette. One chap came down from Astoria, with a most curious tale. Cassidy, by name. Sean Cassidy. Claims he was beat up and kicked out of Portland. His daughter is still there, but as they have no law officer, he is afraid to go back to fetch her. Is it true that you have only one marshal for the entire territory?"

"No need for more," Gaines answered. He had not heard of any such incident in Portland. "Each town is powerful enough to handle its local problems."

"What if the problems become ours?" Grace snapped. "We need some authority to maintain law and order."

Gaines was unsure if he had the power to grant such authority. Gaines never made a decision without prior consultation with the "Salem Clique."

"I will look into it," he said weakly.

John Grace was embittered. He wanted the authority of law and order so he could become the police force over the Indian village. He found their young leader, John Kenwa, uncooperative and arrogant. He had refused to move the supplies from Oregon City and Milwaukie without pay. Grace, who had been born in Atlanta and had come from the East Coast to California by ship, had never really seen an Indian before this time. He discerned that they were little different than Southern black slaves and had no legal right to own property or a business. But what really embittered him was the tone in John Kenwa's voice. Such a man needed a good thrashing for addressing a white man in such a haughty manner.

Nelson Wende was more interested in the attitude of the governor. He saw that the man was a fool, and powerless, so he had refrained from even delving into his knowledge about Pack McGraw. He was certain he would have no useful knowledge.

He also knew, after one meeting, that John Kenwa was no ordinary Indian or man. He seemed thoroughly likeable, despite his ridiculous British accent. Still, Kenwa filled him with a certain panic. He was used to having power over his officers and men—the extraordinary power to mold them to his liking and thinking, as he had so successfully done with John Grace. But Kenwa had already been molded and some of Wende's panic came with the realization that Pack had been part of that process.

* * *

Folks from Portland had not attended the Fort Vancouver ceremony for three obvious reasons.

First, because Portland got the premier issue of their newspaper on December 4, and Major John Grace had failed to give the *Oregonian* or the *Spectator* news of the event for that issue or later issues. Their local pride slighted, the people of Portland and Oregon City ignored the event. Even though it was greatly heralded in the *Western Star,* everyone in Milwaukie was busy getting ready for their extravagant Christmas Day celebration.

Second, Portland had a minor celebration of their own on December 20. Abrams & Reed were to fire up the engine for the saw mill. "It drew a respectable crowd to the foot of Jefferson Street," T. J. Dryer reported.

Beth laughed. "I wonder if he is speaking of the size of the crowd or of those in attendance? Daniel and Chapman were quite obvious by their absence."

"I'm sure he wasn't speaking of my people." Kenwa snickered. "They heard all the chugging and huffing and came out of the trees to see if it was me ready to take them down home on the river steamer. I've never had reason to use the whistle on my boat, so they weren't prepared when Coffin let off a blast with that steam engine whistle. Damn, did you see them run! Took me most of the afternoon to get them out of the woods. Going downriver I showed them the whistle on the boat. Sounded puny in comparison."

"What were they doing at the old village?" Asa asked.

"When Francis and Daniel first let Old Wife move our family there, she made them a promise. Even though I had bought it from them, her deathbed wish was for the promise to be kept. So, this morning, we came back to return the area to the way that we found it. I can tell you why Chapman wasn't at the sawmill ceremony. He was too busy peeking at us and telling Henry Travis how he wants it laid out in three-hundred-square-foot blocks with hundred-foot-wide streets. An area for 'substantial' homes."

"I wasn't aware Pack had sold it to him," Beth said, on a puzzled note.

"Hasn't," Asa chuckled. "Chapman is being his typical self and has assumed that if the village has departed, the land reverts back to the trio. Pack is going to let him get his neck full into the noose before he tightens it."

The third thing to keep the people of Portland from attending Wende's ceremony was the Annual Llwellen Christmas Party.

Elizabeth Llwellen was the only woman with the audacious courage to bring the feuding Portland Trio together in the same house, plus mixing in the entire Portland Provisions Company gang, her normally large list of people from all corners of the valley and river, plus an invitation to Grover Adams, Esq., and guest.

Liza Boddick was quite sure the "guest" would be in attendance, because she had been paid a handsome sum to fashion a gown out of a bolt of moiré blue silk that Captain Crosby had brought back from China. It was common gossip scandal that Patricia Cassidy was living with Grover Adams, but Liza steered clear of that talk, for she knew some women who kept count of the nights that Asa Lovejoy never made it back from her house to his lawyer quarters or Oregon City.

"One nice thing about this party," Liza said, "it brings us girls together in Beth's kitchen. D'Arcy, I'll kill you if you don't leave your eggnog recipe to me in your will."

Nuua giggled. "You no like my roast pig?"

"I love it, but not the sight of Matoa bringing the poor little thing up out of the pit with its head still on."

"Gore!" D'Arcy said. "The Twelve Days of Christmas pig always had 'is head on when they marched him in on a platter."

"That was different, luvy. He still had a jolly pink face and an apple stuck in his mouth."

Tama was quiet as she put colorful pieces of hard candy in a bowl. She was missing Old Wife, who had become like a mother. She was also missing Katoro and Pelani. This would be the first Christmas without them in seven years.

"Oh my! Oh my!" Rhoda came fluttering into the kitchen like a little bird too heavy to take flight. Despite her girth, which had been steadily increasing, she had picked out a dress pattern that made Liza gasp. She was just too large a woman to wear "bo-peep" hip bustles and a fitted bodice. "I never thought I'd get dressed before—"

"And you look lovely," Liza broke in, glaring her to silence. "I do declare, everyone talks about money getting tight, but you wouldn't know it by my business. Those coming here, and to the ball in Milwaukie at Christmas, all ordered a dress for each occasion. Even the McLoughlins' daughter, visiting from England. My fingers are near raw from sewing. Tama, the candy bowl is lovely. Why don't you put it in the parlor. Oh, and be a luv and check on Beth. I didn't want to give her gown a maternity cut, but she pooches out more and more each day."

"Oh my! Oh my!" Rhoda repeated, as she left.

"I'll 'oh my' you, Rhoda Farman," Liza said when she'd closed the door behind her. "It has been hard enough keeping the fact from her that Katoro, Pelani, and the children arrived on the *Island Maiden*. Near fainted dead in my tracks when she came bounding in this morning. I'll kill the woman who forgot to sew button holes into that bodice. But when the young'un began to cry in the back room, I had to lie like a beefeater and tell Tama that my cleaning lady had to bring her child along today. Gore! What a morning. But, that's the present Kenwa wanted her to have for Christmas. And wait until you see the presents that Pelani has brought packed in wet leaves. A lei for each of us."

"Best you watch your language, Elizabeth Boddick!"

"D'Arcy Broome McLoughlin! Get your dirty little mind out of the London gutter! Nuua knows exactly what I meant."

Nuua giggled. "Gonna be most happy Christmas ever!"

For most it was also the happiest Christmas party ever.

Grover Adams was stunned that there was so much camaraderie between people who were supposed to detest one another.

Some of it, as with Mesdames Lownsdale, Coffin, and Chapman, was merely a case of keeping a stiff upper lip.

Beth as usual, was an expert in circulating people and discussions.

Mary Charlotte Foster had become an expert with children and delighted in turning Ian's study into a game and playroom. When one of the Spanish captains who had stayed to become a citizen brought a surprise from San Diego the year before, Mary Charlotte had paid him to bring several of the large, brightly decorated objects for this year. The squeals of the blindfolded children echoed through the house as they swung the wooden bat to break the swinging piñatas and be rained upon with candy and little wrapped presents.

The tradition of John Morrison and Hugh O'Bryant playing their pipes for dancing continued, with John McLoughlin as the caller.

Every year since the arrival of Mary Charlotte there had been a surprise guest each year. Laura McLoughlin Pierce and daughter didn't count. They had arrived in October. Tama bubbled with glee when Katoro, Pelani, and the children came down the stairs.

The flower leis were amazingly fresh, and filled the rooms with the aroma of a spring garden.

"You just wait," Mrs. Lownsdale winked at Rhoda. "When Henderson Luelling put in my orchard this spring, we added something extra—one hundred and fifty little rosebushes. The cuttings I brought with me from Kentucky have done so well in this climate that every yard in this town will have a rosebush before I am finished. Oh, don't these smell just grand?"

When Katoro put a lei over Patricia's neck, her mouth fell farther open in awe.

When she had arrived on the arm of Grover Adams, she had acted with what she felt was genteel aloofness. Mr. Adams, in her opinion, was the agent of a most rich and powerful company, and if they weren't treated with due respect, then she was prepared to tell these snobs which end to blow their gas out of.

The look on her face made Adams regret certain things he had in the works that he was now unable to stop.

"Finice, I am going to hit you!" Elizabeth Caruthers boomed with laughter. "How dare you say I will run right over to feed these lovely flowers to the horses? Get on over there and dance with one of those pretty belles."

He chuckled. He twined his arm affectionately in the arm of Elizabeth. "I always save the first dance for you."

Beth twined her arm in Ian's, although he did not dance.

"I think another tradition is holding true," she whispered. "This is the third dance David Lee has had with Mary Charlotte's oldest girl."

How quickly time did pass, Ian thought. It seemed like yesterday when they'd had a special Christmas Day celebration for the survivors of the massacre. The girl had whimpered the whole day and had seemed too small and withdrawn for sixteen. Only Mary Charlotte had been able to comfort her, and that had sparked her inspiration to adopt all six of the orphans. Now, he hardly recognized the happy, laughing, excitingly beautiful girl of eighteen. He could also tell that Philip Foster had no objection to his Alice being with David. Foster beamed each time the couple would sashay by him.

Ian suddenly realized that Beth had slipped away again. He stood and took everything in, as though wishing to burn it into his memory. Six-year-old Peter Kenwa almost up to his father's waist. The daughter and son of Katoro and Pelani as handsome as the parents. Matoa and Nuua's brood as short and wide as they were. Dave and D'Arcy's children looking like they had come out of an English mold factory. Mick and Anita's son with the best qualities of each.

For a man who hated being a child, he now loved children and especially his own: Dana, who was at home with every person at the party; Donnie, who only spoke when spoken to and eyed every person as though he were a doctor having him under examination for a hidden malady. And his lucky Penny, already showing signs of the heartbreaking beauty she would become.

A strange noise from the kitchen brought him out of his reverie. It came again, as though Nuua had dropped an entire tray of glasses. Without saying a word, he crossed through the dining room and entered the kitchen.

Nuua and Tama stood cowering at the sink. A burly man stood at the end of the preparation table and breathed in drunken gasps. In his hand was a length of firewood and on the table the broken glassware he had smashed.

"Who in the 'ell are you?" he slurred.

"I might ask you the same," Ian said evenly. "I am Ian Llwellen, the owner of this house. What are you doing here?"

Sean Cassidy squinted. He was not used to the effect of the good whiskey Grover Adams had left in the Union Hotel room for him. It had been so smooth that he had kept drinking and had lost track of time and now had to concentrate on why he was there.

"Llwellen," he repeated, stumbling over the name. "Aye, the Welshman." He burped. "Come fur me daughter."

Ian had handled his share of drunken sailors. What they said was not always what they thought they had said. You had to be calm to get to the root of their problem.

"That's fine. But how do I know your daughter is here, if I don't know your name."

"Know she's here." He shrugged. "Also know she's been sleeping with that saloon owner. First a friggin' Indian and now him. Want that Pack McGraw out here, too!"

Ian smiled at him softly. He had been able to take a step forward, stop, and then another step forward. "I'm surprised you didn't find Pack at the saloon. He never attends my wife's Christmas parties. A little too high-brow for him, he says. Are you sure your daughter isn't with him at the saloon?"

"Goddamit, I know she's here, you lying son-of-a-bitch. You want my name, huh! Sean Cassidy, if it means anything to you."

It meant nothing to Ian. When he had been introduced to Grover Adams, the young lady on his arm had been introduced simply as "Patricia." He could recall no person by the name of Cassidy at the party.

"All right, Mr. Cassidy," he said, within an arm's length of the man. "Give me the name of your daughter and I'll have Nuua and Tama go in and find her."

Tama gave out a muffled cry and Nuua held her closer. Tama had recognized the man the moment he had barged into the kitchen. The fear that he had come to beat up on Kenwa again had frozen the scream of warning in her throat. Her muffled cry now was having seen Kenwa out the window, on his way to the outhouse.

"They don't move," Cassidy flared, raising the piece of firewood. "Don't want them warning McGraw, so he can sneak up behind me again."

Ian moved, but not fast enough. The man moved to his side and swung forward with the log. It caught Ian on the side of the head, opening a gash. He reeled back, blood oozing down over his chin.

Now the screams did pour forth from Nuua and Tama.

Cassidy looked from Ian to them, as though stunned. He was only supposed to have caused enough trouble to ruin the party.

"No one was to get hurt," he said gruffly. He turned and fled out the door. Once in the street, his drunken mind became totally confused. He lost all sense of direction.

Even though the always late Zarundy family were coming down the street at a slow pace in their wagon, to the eyes of Sean Cassidy it looked as if the wagon were barreling down on him. A man was running toward him from the outhouse. Coming up the street were the two men he had seen checking into the hotel when he had come stumbling down the stairs. All his mind could rationalize was that they were coming for him, because he had cursed them out when one had called him "a drunken bum."

His luck worsened when he got near the front of the house. The front porch had filled with people, and some of the men were coming off the steps and starting to walk toward him. But all he could see was Patricia. Lord-a-mercy, he thought. She sure do look fine. But something was wrong. His little girl was crying and beating on Grover Adams's chest. Now his hatred centered on Adams. Why did the man bring him back from Astoria and pay him to ruin the party? Patricia looked so pretty, so it must be a party for her. Why would the little weasel pay him to ruin Patricia's party?

"Drop the log, Cassidy," Kenwa said, who was now right behind him.

Cassidy swung around, but didn't see Kenwa. All he could see was the face of Grover Adams.

He charged, swinging the log back and forth with all his burly might. Kenwa dodged the first blow, then caught the second blow on his shoulder and jumped back. He dove for Cassidy's middle and they crashed into the street. Kenwa struck with a devastating fist, catching Cassidy on the forearm. With a yelp of pain he dropped the log.

Captain James Coburn, an Abernethy barge man, began to urge Cassidy to get up and fight.

"He's the one who attacked the Indian," Governor John Gaines hissed at him indignantly.

"Lookee 'ere, guv," Coburn spat. "I barged yah from Oregon City to the fort and back up tah here. Ain't happy you decided to stay the night for this shindig. I'll root fer who I please."

"But that's the drunk who cursed us!"

"And that's the In'jun who steals river business away from white men like me. Here, man, cut the in'jun up some!" He tossed Cassidy his belt knife.

"You damn idiot!" Gaines growled, then looked around. "Someone stop this!"

It was too late for anyone to move in quickly. Cassidy grabbed the knife in mid-air, scrambled to his feet, and lunged. Kenwa could not raise the arm of his injured shoulder fast enough. The knife ate into that shoulder, was pulled out, and caught his right arm in the muscle as he swung. Kenwa staggered back. He was now powerless to fight with either arm.

Cassidy began to laugh maniacally. He crouched, ready to spring for the death lunge.

No one had a weapon. Everyone was stunned by the

swiftness with which it had turned into a knife battle. Those who might have gained their common sense back a little faster were all in the kitchen trying to stem the flow of blood out of the head of the unconscious Ian Llwellen.

Kenwa started to slowly step backward. His only hope of survival was to gain enough distance so that when Cassidy lunged he could leap into the air and kick out with his feet.

And just as Cassidy did spring, Kenwa heard the whistle of a bull whip over his head and its crack like a rifle. It was too late to wonder at it. He was high in the air, arching his back and locking his knees so his legs were solid weapons.

Nicolas Zarundy's aim was perfect. The Russian whip had a tiny metal tip. Nicolas used it to kill rattlesnakes in the beet fields. The thin leather brushed against Cassidy's hand as the metal tip fell and started twirling the leather whip around his wrist. At that instant Kenwa's feet hit Cassidy's kneecaps, shattering them. The man screamed out as his legs began to buckle. Nicolas jerked on the whip. It brought the raised knife arm down with a fierce force and the blade went deep into Cassidy's belly.

Cassidy, wide-eyed, began to laugh again; Kenwa lay on his back in front of him, and for a moment he felt he was responsible for it.

The laughter ceased abruptly. Cassidy threw back his head and a trickle of blood came out of the corner of his mouth. Nicolas let off the tension of the whip and flickered it to untwirl the end from the wrist. Then, as though the thrust of his head had been too much weight in that direction, Cassidy slowly fell over on his back.

Captain James Coburn silently turned away without retrieving his knife. He had heard the discussion between the Governor and General over law and order. By the time he reached his barge he had convinced himself that Kenwa was responsible for Cassidy's death. If the General didn't believe him, he was sure that smart-assed Major would. He took the moor lines off his barge and let it float out into the downriver current.

*   *   *

If this was a portent of things to come, no one thought about it.

W. W. Chapman bustled out importantly to usher the Governor into the house and assure him that this was the first "accident" of this nature ever to take place in Portland.

A visibly shaken Grover Adams took Patricia away and made arrangements for the undertaker to come for the tarpaulin-covered body.

Beth assured everyone that Ian was all right, and that Dr. McLoughlin was seeing to Kenwa.

Normally, such an event tended to break up a party. But in this instance they all seemed to want to stay together and not speak of their individual guilt feelings about not having stepped in and stopped it.

The news reached the saloon via the undertaker. Pack excused himself from the captain and crew of the *Island Maiden* and walked slowly across town. In a way he felt responsible. He had seen Patricia that morning buying an expensive bottle of liquor from one of the bartenders. Having learned that Grover Adams was a teetotaler, he had laughingly asked the bartender for whom she had bought the bottle. He thought she had been lying when she told the bartender that it was for her father. The thought didn't cross his mind again until the captain of the *Island Maiden* was telling him about being flagged down at Astoria for mail, and that the mail had included a burly passenger who'd complained about the forty-five-dollar fare, bellowing that he could go the same distance on a PMSC ship for twenty-five dollars. Pack had put two and two together and determined that Sean Cassidy was back in town. But he had done nothing about it, because he had not anticipated anything like this.

Passing the Crosby house—for even though he owned it, it would always be called that—he saw Patricia sitting by the front window, with Grover Adams serving her a cup of tea. He had the odd feeling that neither of them was feeling any remorse.

He himself had felt remorse the moment his father was

shot and the arrow pierced his mother's throat. The confident egoism of youth had given him the knowledge that he was of that rarified mountainman breed who could live within their own emotions and not share them. Few had been able to scratch below the surface of Pack McGraw. Kenwa was one who had, because they could communicate without speaking. They had both walked the same path, asking, "Where will I find friends, among these strangers?" "Where will I find soil appropriate to my roots?" And "Can there be a place in this new world for me?" Yes, Pack would feel remorse if he were to lose Kenwa, and with it would come a sense of guilt in overlooking the fact that Cassidy meant trouble when he got a bellyful of liquor. Damn Grover Adams for being the hypocrite without remorse!

He was amazed to hear fiddle playing as he cut up Madison Street to First. When he got close enough to see through the parlor windows, he saw that some people were dancing, while a group gathered around the dining room table had started in on the oyster stew. He almost turned back, but then he saw Liza sitting alone in the kitchen.

She didn't turn her head when he entered. She was staring off into space. He helped himself to a cup of coffee, refilled her cup, and sat down.

"How are they?"

She didn't move her eyes from the blank wall.

"Ian's head has been bandaged up and Nuua's feeding him some oyster stew. John McLoughlin is still up with Kenwa and Tama. One shoulder is broken and the knife severed some muscles in his other arm."

She was silent for a long time. "Poor thing," she sighed.

"Who?"

She looked down at the coffee cup. "Patricia. God, she was bloody pitiful. 'No tears,' she said. 'I can't cry tears over something I never had. He were only a man who used and abused me, but no father. No tears.' Oh, Pack, this was probably the only happy day of her life and look how it ended!"

Pack's bushy brows rose sharply.

"She may have brought it on herself. She's the one who bought the bastard the bottle. Damn expensive stuff for a maid to be buying. And where does a bum like that get forty-five bucks for fare from Astoria?"

Liza sat there staring at him, her wides widening and darkening in her long face.

"What are you saying, Pack?"

"I don't really know," he said. "I just don't like the smell of it, after what happened before. That man Adams makes my skin crawl."

"Don't mention this to Beth," she warned. "She's trying to remain the perfect hostess, but I know her mind is frantic over Ian and Kenwa. Take your coffee in, Pack. We talked her into sitting down with this group for a bowl of the stew. It will mean so much to her to have you here."

He hated the thought, but he would walk on live coals barefooted for Beth Llwellen. He had known a lot of women in his twenty-five years, but he only knew three real ladies: his mother, Sophia Pettygrove, and Beth Llwellen. Beth was the only one that sometimes troubled his dreams.

She was sitting at the end of the table, facing the door, when he entered. She looked up and her hand flew to her breast.

Instant teardrops brimmed her eyes, spilling over her lashes and making slow streaks down her cheeks.

"I am so grateful," she whispered and then brushed the tears from her cheeks and smiled. "Look who is here, everybody. Our dear, sweet Pack. Governor, I don't believe you've met Pack McGraw. Pack, Governor John Gaines. Pull a seat up, right next to me. You will love the tenor of the conversation."

Pack shook the Governor's hand, pulled up a chair, and sat. Beth took his hand and squeezed it, to further show her gratitude.

"The tenor is balderdash!" Chapman declared. "As an owner of this town I am totally against it."

"Then I shall probably be totally for it," Pack said candidly.

John Gaines laughed. "Then I like you already, young man. You should know that your name has been bandied about quite a bit at this table."

"If that is the case, I think I'd best be told the topic of discussion."

"It's very simple," Beth said. "Governor Gaines has suggested that if we were incorporated as a town, we wouldn't have to rely upon the Territorial Marshal. We could appoint our own sheriff."

"And," Asa interjected, "stories started flying about as to how you handled certain situations on the wagon trains."

"Whoa!" Pack laughed. "My mother didn't raise me to be a lawman!"

"Come on," Hugh O'Bryant urged. "They have jokingly talked me into running for mayor. And I'm sure Joe Terwilliger would be disappointed not to have a chance to pound you up a tin star."

"I was not joking, Hugh," Daniel Lownsdale said with deadly seriousness. "Chapman and Coffin are against it, because I am for it. We are a little over nine hundred. That seven hundred dollars we raised to buy supplies for that stranded immigrant train at The Dalles is going to reap benefits. Father Bernardo tells me that they number two hundred families, with a great many skills that we can use."

"But they are poor and destitute or else they would not have needed our charity," Chapman said acidly.

"Damn you to hell, Chapman!" Asa flared. "There is hardly a person in this house who did not come here poor and with only the ringing words of 'manifest destiny' as their hope. Charity? The first night that Pack and I pulled into Oregon City, it was that wounded boy upstairs who stood on a rock ledge and snatched a salmon out of the Willamette for our supper. Charity? How many lots did Francis Pettygrove give away free so families would settle in this town? We are growing too fast to be left only in the hands of a couple of money-grubbers."

"And who are you to talk of money-grubbing!" Coffin snarled. "When you had your chance, you sold out to make a quick profit."

"That is quite enough, gentlemen," Lownsdale barked. "Even though Asa may have used an ill-advised expression, Stephen, I must come to his defense. Last week you sold a lot at Fifth and Yamhill for us. What was the price?"

"I don't see that it's material," Coffin glared, "but it was four hundred dollars."

"Oh, I find it very material, when you consider that Asa sold his one-half interest in the entire townsite for three hundred ninety dollars. Oh, I know that each of us paid considerably more for our interest, but we would be liars not to admit that our investment has long since paid for itself."

"Well," Gaines said, rising. "This has been most enjoyable, Mrs. Llwellen. The barge is taking me to Oregon City early in the morning, so I must get back to the hotel. Please tell Mr. Llwellen that I shall look forward to meeting him on my next visit. Good night, everyone."

"Oh, let me fetch my wife," Chapman shot up quickly, "and we will walk you along."

"We shall join you," Coffin chimed in.

Beth sat, a slow grin creeping across her lips as they departed. "How nice of them to remember to say good night."

"Do you realize," Lownsdale said, as though to change the subject and yet not change it, "that I arrived in time for your very first Christmas party. But, I am not going to say those were the good old days, because our good days are yet ahead. I'm not a betting man, but from what I know about 'Hesitation Johnny,' those two will have Gaines claiming tomorrow morning that he doesn't even know what incorporation means. Asa, what does it mean and how do we bring it about?"

"Well, it's no different for a town than it is for a company. You are just uniting and forming into a legal body. As a town it would require a petition of the eligible voters to ask for a vote on incorporation. If it passes, then they elect a committee to determine the type of town government they desire. They then vote on that, and then elect a mayor."

"By that time we will be in our graves."

"Excuse me," Finice said, who had sat quietly through

everything. "I have two questions. First, what about property owners outside of the townsite, such as John Couch, myself, Joe Terwilliger, and even you, Daniel? Portland is bound to expand. Are we incorporated now, or at some future expansion date?"

"Good question, Finice," Asa said. "Yes, you can ask to be incorporated at this time, or you can wait."

"Then my second question, which is really more of a statement. I think we can have a Kentucky shortcut. Have a town meeting of property owners and let those in favor of the petition stand. If it passes, go right ahead and elect a mayor and let him get the committee together to iron out the government structure."

Daniel smiled. "I like it. What about you, Beth?"

"I can't vote, remember? But I like it. Pack?"

"Count me in. Better be right after the first of the year or the 'Salem Clique' will tell us how to do it. Dryer will love it. He's only put out two issues and is already fed up with Chapman telling him what to write. Where is he tonight, by the way?"

"He had to excuse himself, it being press night."

"And my eyes are pressing on me to say good night," Asa said.

With that, the party did start to break up. Beth was thankful. Nuua had her children in bed. Tama had made a bed for herself and Peter in Kenwa's room. Now Beth yearned for peace and quiet, and the traditional moments of sitting in front of the fireplace with Ian.

"Are we better?"

He put out his arms to her and she came to him gladly.

"Still a mite fuzzy," he sighed. "I'm glad it is not tomorrow we have to be in Milwaukie."

"Why?"

"A show of Portland's support," he said gruffly. "Coffin, knowing we have the *Merchantman* there loading lumber, asked for its use as part of the ceremony. Bunting and flags, you know. The Milwaukie Committee on Arrangements have even got the loan of a cannon. They want it on the *Merchantman* for us to give a salute at the time of launch."

"Well, only if you feel up to it."

"I shall, Beth. Now kiss me, quickly. I've got to tell you about your Christmas present."

Beth kissed him softly, then hung back against the circle of his arms, looking at him.

"I've been giving more thought to this steam business. I never want to skipper one of the things, but I think we should stay in line with progress and competition. Do you recall the visit of the *Gold Hunter*?"

"Yes. That was the private steamer out of San Francisco, right?"

"That's what Coffin wanted everyone to believe it was. When he sold his shares in the PMSC's *Columbia* he put the money into the *Gold Hunter*. As yet, Chapman and Lownsdale are not aware. Coffin is quietly asking our help. I thought you might like a few shares as your Christmas present."

Beth was silent for a moment. After the discussion in the dining room she was not sure if she wanted anything to do with Stephen Coffin at the moment. But she decided this was not the time to trouble Ian's head with that. "What changed your mind?"

"Coal. Lot wasn't very clever in hiding the fact that some miners, looking for gold up here, found coal on the Cowlitz River. Every time I passed the mouth of the river I noticed a heavy deposit of something on the bank. This last trip I stopped, on the excuse that the wind was not right to bring us farther up the Columbia. My dear, as a Welshman, I should know a heap of coal when I see it."

She smiled at him softly. Now she was sure she would not mention her disenchantment with Coffin.

CHAPTER
☆ 19 ☆

By noon the next day a smoky haze hung over Portland. As it had been a very wet fall, there was no fear that it could be a forest fire.

When Crosby's bark *Louisiana* came downstream from Milwaukie, a longboat put a passenger ashore.

The normally dapper Grover Adams was disheveled, sooty, and reeked of smoke.

"Where was the fire?" Mick Myers asked, coming out of the store.

"Milwaukie," Adams said wearily. "Lot Whitcomb's sawmill has been totally destroyed. Too far along by the time it was spotted. Took every man available to put it out and keep it from spreading to the shipyard."

William Chapman had come out of the store and stood listening with interest. "And what were you doing in Milwaukie, Adams?"

They eyed each other warily. Neither had any love for the other anymore.

"Fulfilling my duty," Adams said simply. "The *Louisiana* brought up a cannon for use at the festivities."

"No one has left this wharf all morning," Chapman said suspiciously.

Adams looked at him with glaring hatred. "I am not about to pay a five-dollar fee to Milwaukie, when a healthy body can walk up to the ferry and pay ten cents to cross. And put your next question back in your head, Mr. Chapman. As a goodwill gesture the cannon was loaned by the Pacific Mail Steamship Company and I was charged with the duty of

314

seeing to its arrival. Now, if you will excuse me, I have need of a bath!"

Chapman was full of further questions as to this "cozy" new relationship between Milwaukie and PMSC, but another arrival took his immediate interest away.

At the far north wharf, Captain James Coburn was tying up his barge, the *Skookum Chuck*. Stepping ashore were two officers and an armed guard of four. They headed directly toward Pack's public house. Feeling that he was the "dignitary" they should be addressing, Chapman waddled quickly down the wharf. He was too late to stop them and had to follow them inside.

The saloon was not yet open. Pack sat at a window table figuring out a liquor order.

Wende was only halfway into the long room when he ordered the guards to stand at the ready.

"So," he sneered, "when murder is in the air, we can always find John Packwood McGraw lurking about."

"Vastly different this time, Wende," Pack said casually. "I wasn't at the scene when the man stabbed himself. Right, Chapman?"

"General," Chapman oozed, "I am William W. Chapman, one of the owners of Portland."

"And not doing a very good job of it, it would seem. Well, was McGraw there?"

"I don't really know," Chapman said, miffed at the tone the General had taken with him.

"It doesn't matter for the moment," Major John Grace said gruffly. "It is the Indian, Kenwa, we are after. Captain Coburn, here, came down to the fort on orders from the Governor for us to investigate a brawl that ended in the murder of one Sean Cassidy. According to Coburn's eyewitness account, the Indian attacked Cassidy, who picked up a fire log to defend himself. The Indian disarmed him and stabbed him. We have already done a turnout search of his village and will now search this place! Men!"

Pack sighed, taking the pistol from his lap and putting it on the table. "I think they'd best stand pat, General. You know I can drop all four of them before they get their bolts pulled back."

"Have them remain at ready, Major."

"Good! As usual, Wende, you jump an issue to suit your own facts. Seems odd to me that Governor Gaines was pretty damn furious this morning when he had to pay seventy-five cents to rent a horse to get him to Oregon City. Seems his chartered barge had deserted him. Odd he didn't mention sending for the military when he had breakfast with Daniel Lownsdale and me at the Union Hotel this morning."

"Why was Daniel meeting with him, without Coffin and me?" Chapman demanded.

"Wait your turn, Chapman. I've got questions for Coburn, first."

"What right do you have asking him questions?" Grace flared.

Pack studied the Major, his brow furrowed in a frown.

"And what right do *you* have turning the Cayuse out of their homes and searching for Kenwa either there or here?"

"They are savages and have no rights!" Wende declared.

"And you're a fool to think that way! I'm afraid it has always colored your outlook, but I am no longer a little boy you can intimidate. You're on my turf, so don't get any funny ideas."

"How dare you talk to the General that way!" Grace sputtered.

"He knows damn well how I dare!" Pack said coldly. "All right, Coburn, why all the lies?"

"I am not lying!" he snarled. "Chapman, you'd better come clean and back up my story, because you saw it that way. Right?"

Chapman hesitated. Pack had not been there, that he knew. Coburn's story had convinced the military. No one was going to back up the Indian, unless it was some of the Portland Provisions people. With an ego as great as that of Grover Adams, he felt his word would carry more weight than anyone elses.

"Well, yes, it happened much as Coburn said. He should know. He was standing right there in the street with Governor Gaines."

"Curious," Pack said, turning the barrel of the gun around and around on the table with his index finger. "A man is murdered, in the terms of Coburn, and yet you, Mr. Chapman, sit down to a bowl of oyster stew and never once discussed apprehending Kenwa, who lay wounded right above you."

"I—I—"

"And now you can't think of a new lie fast enough to cover up your lie of siding with Coburn."

"Now see here—" Grace started.

"No, you start seeing a few things, Major. See that gold five-dollar piece? That's from Governor Gaines. Lownsdale asked him to send up the marshal from Salem. Gaines thought differently. He made me a Deputy Marshal to handle this case. He was my first eyewitness. I've spent the morning talking with others, including the first man attacked by Cassidy."

"I beg your pardon?" Wende glared at Coburn.

Pack sat back and put his feet up on the table. "It's a long story. Gaines is sending Judge Burnett up the day after Christmas. Everyone will have their say at that time, including you, Coburn."

"I've said my piece!"

"You seem to be missing your knife out of its sheath."

Coburn felt of it, and it was as though he had suddenly gone naked. "I'm always losing the damn thing."

Pack unfolded a piece of cloth on the table. "This is the weapon that was removed by the undertaker from Cassidy's hand. You can see that carved into the handle are the letters *J. C.* Yours Coburn?"

"I told you," he stammered, "I'm always losing the damn thing!"

Pack slowly recovered the knife. "I've got five witnesses, including the Governor, who will testify as to how you lost it last night, Coburn. I also have a written record of exactly what you said to the Governor before you threw your knife to Cassidy."

Coburn began to sweat. "I'm no more responsible than

the Russian with his damn bullwhip. He's the one who caught Cassidy by the wrist and jerked his arm so that the knife came down into his stomach—" He stopped, suddenly realizing what he had said.

"Oh, my God!" Grace said miserably. "No murder, but self-defense on the part of the Indian."

"Yes," Wende said honestly.

Chapman opened his mouth and closed it. Nothing he could say would remedy the impression he had given General Nelson Wende. He didn't even consider Pack, whom he seldom considered, anyway. Then, as though it didn't matter, he turned and marched out of the saloon.

"Not so fast, Captain," Wende barked, as Coburn started to follow Chapman out. "You brought us here, and you will take us back. Major, take the men to the barge so he doesn't try to leave."

When Pack and the General were alone, the silence stretched between them, rearing up ghosts from the past.

"I gather," Wende said, at last, "that there is much more to this story than you have reported?"

"Right," Pack said drily. "This part I could prove and only needed Coburn to break down. In case you didn't smell it, he was egging Cassidy on, because he feels Kenwa is stealing his business. Hell, Wende, Oregon City and Portland wouldn't be here for ocean traffic if Kenwa and his Cayuse paddlers weren't here for river service. He's a businessman now. Paid twenty-five thousand dollars cash for that river steamer. The land in Portland, which he traded me for the village land at the fort, is worth another twenty-five thousand dollars. That's one hundred twenty-five months' wages at your salary. The real savages are those who want to take it away from them without working for it."

Wende studied him with his eyes.

"For someone who lost his family to Indians, this seems quite unusual. Why did you rent us the fort for just a dollar a year?"

Pack's answering gaze was cool and frank.

"I was going to make you sweat, like I made Coburn sweat. Seeing you, it was a shock to discover that I no longer cared about wasting my time in hating you. I've got more important things to do with my life now."

"From what I understand, you are doing quite well."

"Maybe I owe that in part to you. When that soldier threw the knife that killed Moshe Shamir, I had to become Moshe Shamir. Judge, jury, and sheriff of a wagon train."

"I've often wondered if that were not the case, not hearing about you after that."

That answered one question. Molly had lied about killing the soldier.

"But that doesn't make us friends," Pack said ominously. "The Indian Agent for that northern region is Chester Harbinger. He's been with the agency since it was founded in 1824. He remembers your Washington days well. I pumped him enough to piece together how you survived what should have been a disgrace. Funny, I laughed when I figured it out. I always felt you were yellow to run from the massacre the way you did. Harbinger sees it differently. He credits you with creating a sense of urgency and training that was responsible for saving lives rather than losing them against an enemy too cunning for the military mind of that time to grasp. You'll still get your chance, though. Harbinger sees the worst Indian wars ahead—when we try to put them on reservations."

"I would have to agree with him, but I fear we face an even greater battle. In light of that coming struggle, this territory is wise to prohibit slavery. Well, I must get back, McGraw. Thank you for sharing what you learned of my Washington days. I stood in fear of you for a decade because of your knowledge of that massacre day. I now stand in fear of you because of the manner of man you have become."

Pack frowned. "Exactly what do you mean?"

"You were all primed and ready for Coburn and me. You had the gun in your lap, because you knew I would bring guards. Playing with it to let the soldiers know that you wouldn't draw unless drawn upon. You had your facts, but you let the knife undo Coburn's lies. But the fearful thing is the manner in which you didn't handle Chapman. You branded Coburn a liar and left Chapman dangling like a cat playing with a mouse. If he has never been your enemy before, he is now."

"I hope so," Pack said, without a trace of emotion.

Nelson Wende shuddered as he turned to leave. He would make the Cayuse village off limits and cancel the harrassment plans Major Grace had drawn up. He no longer wanted to cross swords with John Packwood McGraw. He knew he could only lose.

Thomas Jefferson Dryer refrained from printing an account of the incident, other than a brief item to say Ian Llwellen would be well enough to represent the Portland Provisions Company at the Milwaukie celebration, and that John Kenwa had been moved to his home in Vancouver to recover from his accident.

He did not say that Kenwa's left arm was strapped to his chest to help the broken shoulder heal, and that he had only regained partial use of the thumb and forefinger of his right hand.

Wedding plans were announced by Mr. and Mrs. Philip Foster, of Foster Farms, for their daughter Alice to marry David Lee of Salem.

Mrs. W. W. Chapman informed the editor that her husband had taken to his bed with the sniffles.

Mr. Grover Adams announced that Patricia Cassidy had been elevated to the position of housekeeper at the Crosby House.

The Lone Fir Cemetery received its first internment.

The one-line "filler" statement did not mention that it was accomplished without a service, mourners, or a grave marker.

Lot Whitcomb could not have asked for a more perfect day. The sun rose in a cloudless blue sky and it was near summer-warm by noon.

"It's like going back in time," Mrs. J. D. Schnelby told Mrs. William Kilborn. "We came early, because as the editor of the *Spectator* my husband had not met his counterparts at the *Western Star*. The boy at the dock didn't even know they had a newspaper. Well, my dear, am I glad I brought my ball gown separately. Look at my shoes and hem. Why they would put their office on a muddy path, at the top of a hill, is beyond me. Are you and Mayor Kilborn staying the night?"

"Hardly, Bessie. The Milwaukie Hotel only has sixteen rooms and if you look at its construction you'll understand that I wouldn't sleep a wink, fearful it would burn over my head like the sawmill."

Bessie drew close. "That's our very reason for wanting to talk with Editor Waterman. *We* think it is quite curious for it to burn just as 'Little Stumptown' starts up a mill. Even more curious when you consider that the *Merchantman* had just finished loading all the available lumber. I wouldn't put anything past those pushy, pushy Portlanders!"

"I would hardly know," Mrs. Kilborn sniffed. "I've never visited the hamlet and never intend to. Everything we do in Oregon City they copy. Why visit a copy?"

"Pushy, pushy, pushy! Just look at us sitting here and them on the ship. Oh, I know this poor committee has tried to be cosmopolitan, but we, the dignitaries, are sitting on plank benches and look at them!"

Beth had felt near the same thing. The *Merchantman* had been moved to the center of Johnson Creek during the fire and then left there at anchor. The Oregon City barges, Whitcomb's ferry boats, and even the Cayuse boys with the scows had to move around it. With the badly draped bunting on its prow it stuck out like a sore thumb.

She also noticed the wooden platform, small strip of bunting, and wooden planks to accommodate the governor, legislative members, and guests. As though segregated on purpose, all the Portland people in attendance were being told to climb the ladder to the deck of the Portland Provisions Company ship.

Frederick Morse had been accommodating, because most of his owners would be on board. All of the proper chairs on board were brought to the main deck and set in comfortable rows. Benches from the crew's dining room had been put along the railing for the children.

Even though the ceremony was not scheduled until 3 P.M.,

the Portland people had been informed that the ship's company would serve a buffet luncheon from noon on. The ship's cook had outdone himself with a well-decorated table of food on the main deck. From the main deck of the *Lot Whitcomb of Oregon,* the guests of Lot Whitcomb and the members and family of the Committee on Arrangements could look down on the feasting. No food or drink had been provided on the ship to be launched, and Whitcomb took offense at Portland showing such a lack of courtesy.

No one was quite sure why everyone was placed on the reviewing stand at noon. The women chatted until there was nothing left to chat about. The men gazed longingly at the three taverns, which were doing a booming business. The only acceptable excuse to get off the platform was a need to go to the outhouse, and it quickly became a regular excuse.

Henderson Luelling, who was not a committee member, finally approached Major John Grace and asked if the Vancouver Brass Band couldn't play a few tunes to entertain the people who were waiting.

"Might get boring," Grace said. "They only know 'The Star-Spangled Banner,' 'Hail Columbia,' and 'Yankee Doodle.'"

"What will they play for the ball tonight?"

"Music to dance by! But we can't play that now."

Henderson headed for the tavern, shaking his head in disgust.

"Captain Llwellen," Morse saluted. "Might I show you, sir, our placement of the cannon on the bridge."

"Of course, Fred. Excuse me, everyone."

Climbing the stairs to the bridge, Ian stumbled. Morse was behind him and caught him by the elbow.

"Are you all right, sir?"

"Fine. Just a second of dizziness. Sun is mighty bright today. Not used to staying in bed and being pampered."

Ian went to the stern of the bridge and began to laugh.

"Did they bring that relic up from a sunken galleon?"

"I'm told that PMSC got it from the old Mexican fort at the Presidio. It's a twenty-four-pounder."

"Well, Mister Morse, I feel it needs to be lashed down

better. It probably has a kick that would send it over the side."

He inspected the brazier, heating the firing-rod to white hot. Then, moving around the cannon, he determined that the fuse was of adequate length and then peered down the barrel.

"Doesn't the wadding seem a little extreme?"

"She's not carrying a cannon ball, sir. They wish quite a reverberating roar, so it has an extra charge of powder and cotton padding."

Ian tapped the side of the cannon to hear the returning echo. "It seems like more than just an extra charge. To be on the safe side aim the damn thing down the creek toward the Willamette. It should produce quite a tongue of flame, and if left in this position I'm afraid it would singe Governor Gaines's beard."

"I'm sure glad you are going to touch her off, Captain Llwellen. Never have trusted the blasted things."

"What is our timing to be?"

"If they are on schedule, the band will play a number or two before the Governor does the christening. Mayor Kilborn will present her new colors and as they are raised Mr. Whitcomb will say a few words in accepting them. As they loosen her fastenings you are to fire the cannon, then the band strikes up again."

"Humph!" Ian frowned. "I will have my back to all of that. You will have to stand with me, Mister Morse, and give me a verbal order at the proper time."

Frederick Morse nodded, but it was not to his liking. He had served in the U.S. Navy during the Mexican War and had seen too many cannon accidents. He was tempted to give the assignment to one of the junior officers, but he owed a deep debt to Ian Llwellen.

At the close of the war the naval appropriation had been cut in half. Despite the California gold rush, eastern seaboard shipping was falling into a depression. Everyone wanted steam-powered vessels because of their speed and the ability to keep moving when their auxiliary sails were dead in a calm. Dexter Farman had found him "on the beach" in New York and had sent him to Ian in San Francisco. He would have been content with a junior officer position, but was stunned to be placed immediately as the master of the *Merchantman*. He would do anything that Ian Llwellen desired.

Several times Beth was tempted to call for a scow and take Ian back to Portland. He picked at his food, paid little attention to what people were saying to him, and complained at the loudness of the band.

"The brass seems to throb in my head."

"What throbs in my head," W. W. Chapman snorted, "is the deliberate insult to Portland. Look at that reviewing stand! That's where I belong."

He was totally ignored. Once Daniel Lownsdale had heard of his actions in the saloon, it was all over town.

Stephen Coffin leaned close to Ian's ear. "Enough of the California shareholders of the *Gold Hunter* are willing to sell to give us control here in Portland. You said you might be interested."

"I am, but you said the majority interest was sixty thousand dollars. That's steep with money so tight."

"We only have to raise twenty-one thousand dollars in cash. They will take a note for the remaining thirty-nine thousand dollars."

"Captain," Morse said, "time for us to get back on the bridge."

"Thank you. Stephen, that is encouraging news. Let's talk tomorrow. Beth's Christmas present will be a good quarter of what you will need."

Mrs. W. W. Chapman, sitting right behind them, had made sure that she had heard every word of the whispered conversation. Not a single word about the steamship had been mentioned to her husband, or she would have known about it. She feared that Coffin was cutting her husband out again, as he had done on the sawmill. When, she wondered bitterly, would they learn that her husband was the enterprising genius behind everything that was important for Portland? She determined to make sure that the Portland Provisions Company would have no part of a new steamship.

For a reason that Frederick Morse could not determine, the band began to play "Hail Columbia" for a second time.

"Finally," he said, more to himself than to Ian. "The Governor is beginning to speak."

He turned to see if Ian was in place. Ian was supporting himself, by one hand, against the bulkhead of the wheelhouse. He was shaking as though he had the ague.

"Captain!" Morse gulped with alarm. "You are not well, sir! Let me get you below."

"No," Ian said weakly, "let's give them their blast first."

He turned, took a step, and then leaned back against the bulkhead.

"Mr. Morse," he said quietly, "on second thought, I'm afraid I am not going to be of much use to you. It would seem that I am suddenly blind."

Morse was stunned. He waved a hand in front of Ian's face and saw no eye movement. He started to call for help, but the air was suddenly filled with applause coming from the reviewing stand, the deck of the ship to be launched, his vessel, and the Milwaukie riverbank. He took a quick look. The fastenings had been loosened and the three hundred-ton vessel was sliding rapidly down the stocks. The band did not wait for the cannon report, but immediately began playing "The Star-Spangled Banner." Morse didn't need to see more. He turned back and took the heated rod of iron from the brazier and touched it to the fuse. It did not take and he had to touch it again. The fuse was old and brittle. It had not been primed by a dip in whale oil, because Grover Adams did not know that navy trick.

Morse had to lean down over the cannon and gently blow on the fuse to keep it ignited. When it was down to an inch in length it suddenly flared from the power residue that had leaked from the fuse hole when the cannon had been upright for the powder loading and tamping.

There was no time for Morse to pull his head back. The powder was exploding inside of the iron chamber and could not escape.

The cannon had been prepared four days before, in the back of the sawmill. After the overcharge of powder had been poured down the muzzle, Adams began packing the chamber with cotton wadding that had been dipped in Johnson Creek water and mud. When it was a good four inches thick, he began to add dry wadding and packed it firm with the long wooden tamper rod.

After the lumbermen had wheeled the cannon down to hoist up to the *Merchantman* bridge, Adams shook the residue out of the black powder barrels onto a sawdust mound, touched a sulphur match to the base of the mound, and went to see that the cannon was safely on board. In four days' time, he determined, the wadding next to the powder would dry to rock hardness.

The explosion fragmented the thick iron into hundreds of pieces of flying shrapnel. Being that close to the exploding chamber, the head and torso of Frederick Morse virtually vanished. There had been no time for him to utter a sound.

Four feet away, the explosion was of such intense volume that Ian was instantly deafened. If he screamed, he did not hear it.

The jagged, red-hot metal ripped into both of his legs and right arm. The pain was so excruciating that he was unconscious before he collapsed to the deck.

The explosion rocked the *Merchantman* so violently that the food trays slid off the table. Sensing that the roar was too close, and not out over the water, Mick and Dave McLoughlin raced up onto the bridge.

They gagged at the side of what little remained of Captain Morse, then began moving carefully toward Ian. The bridge was strewn with hot metal fragments seering into the wood deck. They turned pale when they saw that Ian's legs and one arm were nearly severed in several places.

Instantly, Mick's composure became like tempered steel. He went to the railing and cupped his hands to his mouth. "Scow boys to the port side," he roared. Then he leaned over the railing. "All officers to the bridge."

Dave," he said, his voice even and steady, "take the first scow that touches and go get your father off the reviewing stand."

Dave moved, as though in a trance. He had always liked

Mick Myers, but had never considered him to be a full man. What he was doing now was something David knew he himself would not be capable of doing.

Mick didn't even give the officers time to think. "Get something to cover your Captain. Prepare the hoist with a stretcher. Tear up some cloth for tourniquets to stem the flow of blood. Have the sailors bucket up water to douse this deck so it doesn't smolder into fire. I'm going to speak with Mrs. Llwellen and get her into a scow. Under no circumstances do I want her to see this."

"Couldn't we get him to Portland faster by weighing anchor?"

"I hardly see how!" Mick said firmly. "There is no breeze, whatsoever! Who was Morse's second in command?"

"Me, sir! First Officer Philip Goerner."

"Please take immediate command, Captain Goerner. As soon as we have the patient and his wife away, you can weigh anchor and get to Portland with the current flow. I will leave the rest of our party in your care, because I want to triple up on the paddle boys on the scow."

"Have you considered taking him ashore here in Milwaukie?"

"I have," he said gruffly. "It will be quicker getting him to Portland than through that throng and up their steep banks to the hotel. Here's Dr. McLoughlin. He can make the final determination."

John McLoughlin didn't even greet them, but went directly to squat down and examine Ian. He tested each tourniquet that a junior officer was applying and releasing. He nodded and then nodded again, as a stretcher was brought and roped to a hoist hook.

"Shock," he muttered to Mick. "He's lost a great deal of blood, but the tourniquets are holding it stable."

"Shall we keep him here or on board?"

"No. I'm glad to see you've made quick arrangement to move him. I'm afraid I shall have to amputate one, and possibly both, of his legs. He can't be moved after that for some time. I'll see to things here. Go help my son. He's white as a ghost, fearing he will have to tell Beth."

Mick was immediately aware that Dave had just done his duty. Beth swayed toward D'Arcy, as though ready to faint, but only lowered her head and gulped. Then she straightened up with firm resolve, and when she spoke, her voice did not quaver.

"There has been an accident. Mick has made arrangements for me to take Ian back to Portland. Mick?"

"Dave, help Beth down into the scow. Nuua, please see to the children. Ladies and gentlemen, this ship will see you back to Portland, as we shall have need of the scow boys. Those wishing to stay for the festivities can be rowed ashore now. The scows will come back for you after the ball. Please don't rush to the rail, as we don't want to cause a commotion."

Beth sat on the scow with great dignity. John McLoughlin had covered the stretcher so that only Ian's pale face was visible. He sat beside Beth and held her hand, patting it with his huge bear's paw.

"Everyone seems to be going back to Portland," Mrs. Chapman whispered.

"Then they are fools," Chapman said firmly. "I have already paid for our night's lodging at the Milwaukie Hotel and see no reason to lose my money."

"How bad?" Daniel Lownsdale asked Mick.

"Very bad! McLoughlin may have to amputate both of his legs."

"I feared it was bad when the sailors wouldn't let anyone go up to the bridge. John will need help, my boy."

"He has the Cayuse paddlers."

"I'm not talking about carrying the stretcher to the house, Mick. They had to take off my father's leg. Even though he was unconscious, it took all six of us boys to hold Paw down as the doctor did the surgery."

"Damn! I've sent all the best paddlers on that scow."

"In a pinch like this I'm sure some of us men can handle our own paddle. You, Dave, and me are three. Who else?"

Chapman had talked the Coffins into staying and they had departed. David Lee, Philip Foster, Finice Caruthers, and Matoa were quick to volunteer. T. J. Dryer, feeling he had ample notes on the festivities, also offered his services.

Elizabeth Caruthers and Mary Charlotte Foster were concerned about Beth. They, along with D'Arcy and Nuua, demanded to be taken along, leaving the children in the care of the other women.

"I am really most useless in an emergency," Grover Adams said pitifully. "Perhaps we should go ashore."

Patricia Cassidy nodded in agreement. She had come mainly for the ball and was not about to let some minor little accident ruin it for her.

Asa Lovejoy, Eliza Boddick, and Rhoda Farman had been on the deck of the launched ship, as the guests of Captain John Ainsworth. It had not pleased Lot Whitcomb, but Ainsworth was not exactly pleased with Whitcomb. He had been promised a salary of three hundred fifty dollars a month, had not been paid a cent, and a week before the launch had been offered a two-thousand-dollar share in the ship. He respected Asa Lovejoy as a lawyer and had him draw up the agreement. His new bride, a former Oregon City schoolteacher, was greatly concerned over Asa, announcing he would be escorting Liza. To soften the blow of gossip, Mrs. Ainsworth had insisted that Miss Rhoda Farman be included in the party.

"Asa, I think you'd best take a look," Ainsworth said, handing over his spyglass.

Asa looked at the battered cannon and then at the departing scow with a feeling of dread.

"Ian was to set off the cannon," he said, his voice quavering.

"I'll let down a boat and have our sailors row you to Portland."

John Ainsworth had lead a riverboat life from his youth on the Mississippi, and he was greatly superstitious of the portents at a ship's launching. The accident was like an albatross landing on his wheelhouse.

Matoa had run for Pack McGraw the moment they landed.

It was like walking into a house with no one in command. The women paced, while Beth sat rigid on the edge of a parlor chair. The men stood silent, waiting, unable to find a topic for conversation.

McLoughlin was on his knees, next to where they had put down the stretcher, cutting away the trouser cloth with a pair of kitchen shears. The moment Matoa came in, the doctor sent him right back to the butcher shop. Being a butcher, the instruments he was told to bring back gave him the horrible realization of what must be done.

"All right, all right," McLoughlin said testily, "the dining room table will need all its leaves. Nuua, I will need a lot of sheets. Ladies—" He faltered. He was too old and too close to the man not to feel emotion.

"See to the patient, John," Pack said quietly to McLoughlin. "I think I know most of what you need."

Mick was glad to no longer be in charge. He was mentally drained. And as though Pack were the wagonmaster again, everyone quietly listened and obeyed.

The kitchen fires were started and water put to boil. Mary Charlotte took a brandy bottle and glass into the parlor and closed the door. The table was covered with sheets and all the lamps lit, even though it was daylight. The men lifted Ian from the blood-drenched stretcher and onto the table.

Then they waited again. Elizabeth Caruthers came from the kitchen, her hair covered with a towel, with a steaming basin and wash cloth. She had been around enough injured animals to know the blood would have to be washed away before the doctor could see what he was doing. The other women busied themselves in the kitchen. Matoa brought in a boiling kettle of tools. With tongs, McLoughlin lifted them out and put them on a towel on the sideboard.

"Close the dining room door," he said. "Elizabeth, tell the ladies not to enter from the kitchen."

"I'm going to stay to assist you, Doctor."

"I won't have time to attend you if you faint."

"I never faint. Finice, instruct the ladies."

When the Lovejoy party arrived, Nuua showed them into the parlor, informing them that if they wished anything from the kitchen they would have to go outside and enter through the back door.

Elizabeth did not faint, but some of the men grew queasy and had to look away as the sharp knives cut into the mangled flesh. When McLoughlin's strength began to wane, Matoa had to assist with the saw.

They were a quiet, well-functioning team. Because Ian was so deep in shock, it took only three of them to keep the torso rigid from the nerve spasms. This left David Lee and Daniel free to help Pack with his assigned chore.

Ian had become fascinated with the irons that the California ranchers had used to brand their cattle. Every chance he got he had purchased one and used them as decorations in his study. They were now stuck in the coals of the kitchen stove and run back and forth to Pack when they were ready.

As soon as the doctor would cut and pull the flesh away, Pack would touch the stump with the hot metal. To forget what he was really doing, he mentally told himself that he was branding calf after calf.

Elizabeth continually wiped the sweating brows of John, Pack, and Matoa. Without a qualm she took a sheet, covered the first amputated limb, and removed it so that McLoughlin could dress the stump.

The body jerked violently and went still. McLoughlin reached quickly for the good wrist and the heart area. No one breathed.

John McLoughlin closed his eyes so they would not see his tears. "I am sorry, my friends. We tried very hard, but he had just lost too much blood."

No one moved, but wanted to run away to be alone with their thoughts and sorrow.

"She can't see him this way. I'll get water to wash him."

Half of Portland was shocked that Beth did not cry. The other half called it Puritan dignity.

Then came the grief. A grief she would not, could not share.

Friends were turned away politely by Nuua. The Sunday dinner business meeting ceased. If any individual portion of the Portland Provisions Company required Beth's attention, she would give them a short appointment during the afternoon, but only one at a time. In most cases they went away perplexed, having been told to make the decision on their own.

John Morrison came to build a new hallway, eliminating the study and pantry.

"She's closed the door to the dining room and won't enter it," Morrison said later. "Now that she can get to the kitchen, she eats there. Told her I was moving to the San Juan Islands, but I don't think she heard me."

Hugh O'Bryant came to tell her that he had been elected mayor. She congratulated him and walked him back to the door.

The children had been delighted that they were going to be able to spend the rest of the holidays with "Auntie" Mary Charlotte on the farm. Because their father had always been gone so much of the time, they had not understood the funeral, and felt he was just off on another of his trips.

As January turned into February, Beth would weekly postpone the return of the children.

The parlor lamps would burn throughout the night. When the town was quietly asleep, a cloaked figure would walk to the Lone Fir Cemetery. The sailors of the *Yam-il II* had pulled up its anchor, attached a new one, and embedded Ian's anchor at his gravesite.

Beth would touch the massive anchor lovingly, and leave with a sense of having touched Ian.

She never knew that Pack McGraw shadowed her nightly. He shared her grief, but cried more for her than for Ian. He was the only member of the company who had not run to her with a problem, real or imaginary. He could not figure out what he was going to say to her when they were alone.

"Again? Nuua, you are in here almost every other day for a bottle of brandy."

"Never see her drinking it, though, Mr. Pack. Just find the empty bottle and money on the kitchen counter. I'm so worried."

"Tell her I will be there tomorrow."

Pack had watched a situation develop that had disturbed him. When he had approached Stephen Coffin on the subject, he had been given the cold shoulder. Because Ian had approached him on the subject, Pack thought it only fair to raise it with Daniel Lownsdale. Daniel was shocked and then embarrassed over the manner in which Coffin and Chapman had handled the matter. For Beth's sake, Lownsdale pleaded that she never be told.

Pack now felt she had to be told to break her out of the grip of grief.

"To tell the truth," Beth told him over coffee, "Ian did mention something about a share in a steamship as a Christmas present, but I don't recall the name."

"Gold Hunter," he reminded her. "Ian had asked me if I thought he could afford five thousand dollars and I assured him that he could. Went out of my mind until I heard the rumor that Coffin was looking for investors. He was inferring that Ian had put in a substantial amount before his death, but it shouldn't be mentioned to you because of your state of grief. That's how he suckered Daniel in, even though they were barely speaking. When they had their twenty-one thousand dollars, without Ian's money, Chapman quickly organized a joint stock company, using Daniel's promise to invest as part of their personal note against the remaining thirty-nine thousand dollars. Without Daniel really knowing it, the Portland Trio control the only steamship to Portland."

"Of all the low, contemptible tricks . . . just a minute! Oh, damn, my mind is such a jumble. Was Marsha here for the funeral or after the funeral?"

"After. She didn't even know about Ian until her arrival and was amazed to find Sophia here."

Beth rose and took the coffee cup to the desk. She opened its cupboard door, poured the cup from a brandy bottle, and put it back.

"Drinking quite a bit of that, aren't you?"

She froze, and when she turned her cheeks were flushed with wrath.

"I'll fire Nuua for telling on me!"

"She doesn't drink," he said firmly. "When she continued to come to the saloon for brandy, I knew it had to be for you."

Looking at his face she saw concern and compassion, not condemnation. She stilled the other hot words on the tip of her tongue.

"It helps," she whispered. "Mainly at night, to help me sleep."

"You were saying something about Marsha Tolcott?"

"Yes." She sat and sniffed the aroma of the coffee-laced brandy. "But, it's no longer Tolcott. Bern—Burn—Barn—Barnley. Mrs. Horace Barnley." She took a sip. "That was the joke she and Sophia were giggling over. She had gone to California as a gold hunter and her husband named his ship the same."

"So?"

"It has to be the same ship, Pack. If it is, we just sit back and wait."

He looked at her as though she might have been nipping on the brandy bottle before his arrival. "Wait for what?"

"Simple. Marsha told Sophia that the ship was so expensive to run that it lost money on every trip. They were looking for a buyer, but would have to hide a pile of old debts unless they got a full cash payment."

Finally Pack began to grin. "They may already be in trouble at this end. Chapman has named himself as agent, without knowing the first thing about manifests."

"What has this done to PMSC?"

"I could say it's forced them into Crosby's hip pocket, but I don't believe it. I don't think they planned on coming any farther than St. Helens."

"What does that do for your tenant?"

"Adams? He's still in the Crosby House and has moved into the office in the building we built at the new wharf. I don't know what he does, but he goes to the office each day."

She sat for a long moment, taking tiny sips. "I want to go away for a while."

Pack sat stunned. He didn't think he could live with her gone. He could hardly live with her there.

"I said—" Beth began again.

"I heard!" he snapped. "Where? How long?"

She did not hear the demand in his voice. The thought had

not crossed her mind before that moment and that was all she was hearing.

"The children have never seen their grandparents. I would like to go home to the other Portland. Last year Ian got a letter from his mother, when his father died. I will go to Wales. I don't know how long. I can't be that close without seeing Harold Tucker in London."

"Another man in your life?" he spat.

Beth laughed. It was the first time she had laughed since the funeral. "He would be more prone to take an interest in you than in me." Then she frowned. "Speaking of men, Pack, who are we going to get to run the ships?"

"I won't lie to you, Beth. We have still been meeting each Sunday. It's been a concern to us, just as you have been a concern. Our recommendation, if you agree, is to bring Katoro back from Honolulu."

She sat up straight. "Yes! Let's send for them. I'll need time to show him how Ian ran things. They can stay here while I am gone."

"When would you like to leave?"

"Not until it is spring in New England."

Pack stood up, looking down at her.

"I shall miss you," he said quietly. "I shall miss you very much."

It was very still after he had gone. His words had not been of love, but they were filled with such a feeling of passion that it had made her heart thump. She rose and took the cup back to the desk. But this time when she extracted the brandy bottle, she picked up the cup again and started for the back of the house.

When she started to turn left, into the new hall, she stopped. Slowly she turned and stood facing the closed dining room doors. She shuddered and then opened the sliding pocket doors.

It was only a room with a table, chairs, a sideboard, and a china closet. It held no ghosts, but a great many marvelous memories. She had been selfish living only for the ghost of Ian. She had her children to live for, and a company to run.

"You're thirty years old, Elizabeth Llwellen," she said

aloud. "You don't look good in black, so don't even think about widow's weeds."

During the next two months Beth concentrated on two things: her planned trip and a new project.

"Finished?" Beth growled. "Are you quite finished, Stephen Coffin!"

"Yes, Beth, I'm finished."

"You've had your say. Now I'm going to have mine. I am not running away from a ghost, as you thinly imply. I need a new house for my children. The bedroom space here is already inadequate and I've another child coming in June. Where I build is no concern of yours or Mr. Chapman. My purchase of land from Pack McGraw is quite legal. You two are deeply mistaken if you feel you are going to get back the ten acres of the old Indian village. Try it and I might start screaming fraud over you using the name of a dead man to sell your steamboat scheme. Get out of my house! You have become completely contemptible in my eyes."

Coffin was stunned. He had wanted to handle this conversation quite differently, but had taken the advice of Chapman. William Chapman saw Beth Llwellen as a woman still in grief, with little business sense, and therefore easily swayed. Because she had been so much in the background, Coffin had forgotten how dynamic a woman she could be at times. But now it was too late to throw himself on her mercy. Dejected, he left.

He was not gone two minutes before there was another knock at the door and Nuua ushered in Daniel Lownsdale.

His face was so ashen that Beth took immediate fright that something dreadful had happened.

"Daniel? What is it?"

"I am not a sneak," he said, with great agitation, taking a seat without invitation, "but when I saw that Coffin was here, I had to see you. Might I inquire as to his mission?"

"For me to pay him for the two acres I intend to buy from Pack."

"Without the courtesy to explain his reasons, I'm sure. We

are all hard-pressed for money, but particularly Coffin and Chapman."

"Oh?"

"We have been swindled in the steamer stock," he told her with grim satisfaction.

"My understanding was that you three had the majority of the shares," she answered calmly, playing dumb.

"That's how Chapman recorded it, with small interests held by Captain Hall, the purser Dennison, and others in town. Chapman told us that if any shareholders sold, they could only sell to us. Hall and Dennison sold out to the minority stockholders in California, giving them the majority. Beth, they've sold the *Gold Hunter* to cover her bad debts. We've lost our entire investment in the venture!"

"I'm sorry for you," she said genuinely, "but not for them."

"Don't feel sorry for me. I was not man enough to come and tell of the double deal they pulled using Ian's name."

"I've known, Daniel. Pack told me about it, just after you learned the full truth. You were trying to save my feelings and I appreciate it."

"Then you'd best know the worst. It wasn't all our money or notes. Several, thinking that Ian Llwellen was interested in steam, invested. When Coffin had accumulated their five thousand dollars, he stopped using Ian's name. I'm all right to cover my notes, but not pay them back. I'm insisting that they be paid, but those two want to cover their own hides first. I'm sorry, Beth, but it looks like I will have to side with them and sell The Clearing."

She wanted to scream out her disapproval, but something he said and what Coffin had said mixed together to stop her.

"He wasn't here to discuss my purchase from Pack," she mused. "He was here to feel me out on the sale of The Clearing. What if they can't sell it, Daniel?"

He sighed. "Then they will be obliged to sell a majority of their lots at bargain prices to meet their losses."

"Doesn't that affect you?"

He shook his head. "When we started falling out, we

divided up the unsold into equal sections. Each man responsible for selling his own. On this day I am protected because the note I signed was against the money I tucked away when Kenwa bought from Francis and me."

"So," she mused again, "the only unprotected property is The Clearing. Can it be sold in such a way that it would go to those small stockholders you want to protect?"

"Of course it can, but even lot prices have fallen by thirty percent since January. It would have to go by the acre and there are only four acres. It would never fully cover their loss."

Beth rose and went to her desk. "When Morrison took out Ian's study, to make the new hallway, I had all of his things put in the back storeroom. When I decided to put away his ghost, I had to search through his papers to find his mother's address in Wales. I came across his Christmas present, Daniel. All wrapped and ready to give to me when we came back from Milwaukie. Five thousand dollars for shares in the steamer. I think he would want it to go for The Clearing. I will have Asa put it in the children's name so that it can't be touched until they are of age."

That afternoon she walked with Pack to pick the location of her new home. It was a brisk March day and the old Indian path was becoming overgrown. She had to hold on to his arm to keep from falling.

Pack was acutely conscious of the thin arm resting on his great one, her warmth seeping right through the thick wool dress and cape.

She can't go away, he told himself. I want her too much to let her go! It's not just wanting, he corrected himself, it's this horrible animal I thought I would never face. Damn it, I love her! Any woman could satisfy his basic needs, but she had become every portion of his dreams.

"Why are you frowning? Don't you want me to build up here?"

"I just don't want you to leave," he got out honestly. "I know it's too early for you to think of anyone else but Ian. But it scares the hell out of me that you're going to come back married to someone else."

"I have no thoughts of marriage," she said suddenly, fiercely, "and would not want to marry a man I would have to break into our way of life. If I marry, it will be to someone like you!"

"Do you mean that?"

"I always mean what I say, Pack McGraw!"

Pack bent down and sought her mouth, but she turned her head so that his lips only brushed her cheek.

"Pack, no," she said gently.

"Will you ever say yes?"

"When I do say yes, I shall be naked in your arms!"

She turned and fled before her resolve melted.

Beth's intention had been to be gone a year.

It might have been shorter if all her experiences were like those in Portland, Maine. Her mother looked on her and her children as strangers. George Pettygrove did not even invite her to Residency House or inquire after Francis or Mary Charlotte. Nelson Cleeve was now with the Tucker Line offices in London.

Ian Llwellen, Jr., was born in Wales.

Although the welcome from the elder Widow Llwellen was more friendly, the poverty of the coal mining village was depressing. The woman had lost a husband and two sons in the mines, and a son to the seas. After fruitless attempts to convince the woman that Ian had not been lost at sea, Beth came to the realization that the woman wanted to live in the past and could not be changed.

Little Ian had been her most difficult birth yet. For some reason her breasts would not produce milk for him. A goat was bought and although the child would drink the milk, the aroma nauseated Beth. Daily she lost strength, instead of gaining it.

When Ian was three months old, she made her excuses and took the train for London.

Exhausted, depressed, and feverish, she arrived at Waterloo Station. She breathed a sigh of relief upon spotting the familiar faces of Nelson Cleeve and Harold Tucker. Then she fainted.

"Cholera!" the doctor said, and shook his head hopelessly.

That she was alive six months later amazed the hospital staff. She was skin and bones, had lost all her hair, and was barely able to speak above a whisper.

"There is nothing more that we can do, Mr. Cleeve. Home care is all I can now recommend."

Harold Tucker had a garden cottage in Kensington. The governess who had been hired for the children remained, and a cook-housekeeper was found in the village. They moved Beth into the cottage a year to the day that she had left Portland.

It was almost a year before her hair and fingernails began to grow back in, and another year before she could walk without the aid of two canes.

Nelson Cleeve kept Mary Charlotte informed of her progress, and Mary Charlotte kept Beth informed on Portland.

Mary Charlotte wrote Beth explaining that when Milwaukie had finally gotten around to asking how they could pay for the ruined cannon, the PMSC claimed no knowledge. Because it had been responsible for dual deaths, its origin was traced back to the Presidio and a surplus sale, where it had been purchased by a Mr. G. Adams.

According to Mary Charlotte, this greatly troubled Forrest Wilkerson, who made a hasty trip to Portland to discharge Grover Adams. He gave Adams until that evening to tidy up his books. When he returned later that night to the Crosby House, he found Adams and Patricia Cassidy dead from the poison they had eaten in their lunch. Wilkerson hastily removed the remaining uneaten oysters he had brought them from Astoria. Portland could only speculate on their deaths, called a double suicide.

The *Lot Whitcomb* had proven to be too expensive for Whitcomb to sustain and was forced to put her up for sale. John Kenwa and Abernethy & Co. fought each other for the controlling stock, but George Abernethy won for Oregon City.

Another blow for Milwaukie, Mary Charlotte revealed in

her letter, was the removal of the *Western Star* to Portland, with a new name, the *Oregon Weekly Times*.

Portland now had a population of 1,500; Milwaukie, 210.

But there was not one mention of Pack McGraw in the letter.

In the next year Beth's hair was fully grown, she was back to 103 pounds, and she and the three older children spent the summer touring France and Spain.

The Portland Provisions Company now possessed a propeller-driven steamer for the New York–San Francisco run, and a smaller sidewheel steamer for the San Francisco–Portland run, leaving the five sailing vessels for the Honolulu, China, and new Japanese runs.

The company sold its retail operation to Henry Failing, who put up an imposing fireproof building on Front Street, between Stark and Oak. The company was now exclusively an import/export wholesale dealer. Because they needed a better form of exchange with New York, the Portland Provisions Bank was established, David McLoughlin, Cashier.

Mr. and Mrs. William W. Chapman departed Portland in 1853 to settle in southern Oregon.

Mrs. Eliza Boddick married Asa Lovejoy of Oregon City, but retained her Portland business.

"They seem to be doing very well without me," Beth commented after receiving a letter in London from Mary Charlotte. She wondered privately why there was no news of Pack.

One month later, the floor plan of her completed house arrived. Hugh O'Bryant had suddenly left Portland, and Mick had hired an architect and several carpenters to complete the project, because Hugh had left with the original plans.

"Then it's time for me to start thinking about going home," Beth reflected. For the next six months, she went from room to room selecting furniture and having it shipped. Then, whether Liza liked it or not, she had a whole new wardrobe designed and made. Her breasts and hips had come back full, but her waist remained as small as when she was sixteen. She was thirty-five years old, but her strawberry-blond hair had come back in still naturally thick and curly, and her complexion was creamy smooth. But the fever of the cholera and the years of reflecting on how close death is at all times had created in her a quiet dignity and respect for life.

She was not fully aware of the change in herself until a week before their departure. As a farewell gift, Harold Tucker had taken the entire family to sit in his private box at the opera.

The nearly nine-year-old twins had been delighted that they would be able to wear long-trousered evening attire. Penny, who had become enthralled with music in England, was a little princess. Ian, a throwback to his father, refused to go at the last moment and stayed with the governess.

By the intermission, Dana was bored to the point of becoming a distraction with his fidgeting. Penny just wanted to sit and absorb the first act. Harold took his mother, Lady Tucker, from the box and Beth followed.

At the head of the promenade stairs, leading down to the champagne tables, Beth was suddenly aware of someone standing beside her.

Very formally, Donnie put out his arm. "May I escort you down, Mother?"

Beth was stunned, because only that morning they had had been in a pitched battle over his not wanting to return to America.

"It will be my honor, Donald. But I thought you didn't like me."

"Oh, I like you, Mother. You just didn't hear me correctly. I said I don't love you. I don't think I shall be capable of ever loving anyone."

Beth did not understand, but quietly accepted it. Then, out of character with his last statement, he giggled. "Oh, how exciting! Every eye is on us. That's why I wanted to escort you. You are the most dignified, beautiful woman in the whole opera house. I just know that they think we are European nobility!"

At that, Beth had to giggle, then gleefully laugh.

Below, Lady Agatha Tucker had been watching them descend. "Harold, I used to think that baggage was a disgrace to the Pettygrove family. Lord, what a man she married in that Captain Ian Llwellen. Sorry we had to lose him. He not only turned her into something regal and beautiful, but she is so intelligent. We had tea yesterday. Her Oregon area is apparently becoming quite a producer of wheat, Harold."

"I didn't know that."

"I didn't think you would," she said, sarcastically. "Tucker Lines never took advantage of the Corn Law after it was repealed and we could import grains. England has not been able to get wheat out of Russia since the start of the Crimean War. I think we need an agreement with Mrs. Llwellen for the Tucker Line to import Oregon wheat."

Beth departed England in March of 1856, with one concession to Donnie: Miss Beatrice Chumley, the governess, would go with them.

In New York they were met by Dexter Farman, for transfer to the *Ajax*.

Dexter had lost his first wife in childbirth and had remarried. Beth almost commented that for a man who was over forty before his first marriage, his brides seemed to get younger and younger, but bit her tongue.

"I hope you don't mind, Beth, but we have changed our schedule. The railroad from Colon to Panama City has now been completed. The *Pacific Star* will meet the train."

"I really hate another change in San Francisco."

"No change." He grinned. "The *Star* goes direct to Portland. The *Pacific Sun* is the San Francisco ship."

"Two more propeller-driven ships?"

"The competition with the Pacific Mail Steamship Company has become fierce. Most of the lumber now comes out of Port Townsend and Seattle."

Beth tucked all of that information away. The Tucker Line still relied heavily on its clipper ships. She would pay attention to this railroad to see if it would be faster to ship the wheat to Panama City and railroad it to Colon.

Beth had forgotten how humid the Caribbean could be. She soon learned that it, at least, had the sea breeze. The tropical jungle of the Isthmus convinced her that the wheat could mold, even if it was only less than a fifty-mile run. Even that short a trip left them drained of energy, and uncomfortable from their clothes sticking to them.

Boarding the *Pacific Star* was like entering heaven. The staterooms were attractively furnished, with a wash closet instead of a mere chamber pot.

Dana, the inquisitive one, stood gazing into a 3' by 3' steel-lined chamber.

"What is that?" he asked the steward, as he brought the twins' luggage into their stateroom.

The steward looked at him as though he were an immigrant. "A shower bath, son. You stand in here, pull on the cord, and you get a bath."

A bath to Dana meant a porcelain tub. His sense of humor was thin-skinned when it came to adults who thought him naive. He stepped into the stall, pulled the wooden knob on the cord, and was instantly drenched.

Donnie and the steward broke into peals of laughter.

Dana glared, but mainly at his brother. He had always been his father's favorite, he knew. But his father was dead and of late it seemed like Donnie was becoming his mother's favorite. He hated Donnie and would get even with him for laughing at him.

Beth, too, laughed at the shower story and then delighted in trying hers out.

To retain the body coolness the shower had created, she selected a chiffon gown of light pink for dinner. It seemed to bring out the sparkle in her emerald eyes.

The ship had a complement of fifty-five passengers. The dining salon was elaborate in its use of rosewood panels and plush chairs. The service was crystal and china.

The table steward looked at the arriving Llwellen party with dreadful misgivings. He did not enjoy waiting on children. He began to relax when he noticed the firm discipline of the governess.

"Excuse me, Captain. I see an old friend I must greet!"

Pack McGraw rose from Captain Ohlson's table and started across the crowded dining salon.

When Beth saw him coming, she didn't say a word to the children. Instead, she sat quite still and looked at him strangely.

It was hardly the same Pack McGraw. This was the first time she had ever seen him in a tailored suit and cravat tie. The moustache was trimmed to just his upper lip and his hair at earlobe length. At thirty-one, his face had attained a firm maturity. The lantern jaw no longer appeared as though it were held by gritted teeth and the chin lean enough to make the cleft more pronounced. Although there was a twinkle to his eyes, they still held the quality of hard flint.

Then, slowly, she rose, her lips not smiling. She watched him come, holding her breath hard in her throat. She was unsure how best to handle five years of silence.

"Hello, Beth! Children! How good to see you all again. This must be Baby Ian. My God! He's hardly a baby!"

His voice was warm, rich, friendly. There was in it the pure joy of seeing them again.

"Children, you recall Mr. McGraw. Ian, this was a very good friend of your father. This is their governess, Beatrice."

She couldn't bring herself to utter his name, even if the reminder and introduction had stretched out to the boundaries of forever.

"It's been a long time, Beth."

"Yes, it has. What puts you on this ship?"

"Cattle. I've been down in Argentina. They raise quite a hardy breed of cattle there. I've got ten bulls in the hold, for cross-breeding on my ranch east of the Cascades."

"I was not aware that you had moved." She was beginning to feel uncomfortable standing, while the tables around them were starting on their soup course. Still, she could not help but to get in a reproach. "We never heard from you."

Pack laughed. "And the only information I received about you was secondhand from Rhoda Farman. Mary Charlotte, I'm afraid, has never approved of my being in the saloon business. Might we have after-dinner coffee together?"

Beth hesitated, but saw it as an opportunity to be rid of him for the moment. "If you wish," she said, with a faint smile.

"You have most charming old friends," Captain Jon Ohlson said, as Pack retook his seat.

"You are not aware of who that is?"

Ohlson shook his head. He rarely invited family groups to sit at his table, and had paid no attention to the name when he had crossed it off his list.

"That is Mrs. Ian Llwellen," Pack said, adding with sardonic heaviness, "The majority stockholder of this line."

Ohlson smiled broadly. "I will have to include her at my next sitting."

"I don't think that will be necessary. She is not one to flaunt her position."

The blaze of having two owners on board vanished from Ohlson's moon face, and was replaced by a look of bewilderment. The young woman was obviously of high breeding and riches. Having just left the employment of Commodore Vanderbilt, he knew that women of her station demanded, and got, attention. Commoners did not travel with an English governess. He did not understand and looked at Pack for translation.

"This is your first run to Oregon, Captain. People like Mrs. Llwellen brought the best of the old world and New England with them, but are not prone to forget they were pioneers. I'm having coffee with her later, and will ask if she'd desire a change in table arrangements."

Coffee was served in the card and writing salon. Beth was seated at a small table near the open doors to the promenade deck, and waited for Pack to excuse himself from the Captain and a most striking woman in her mid-twenties.

Still unsure of what to say, she thought it safe to pick up near where they had left off.

"You mentioned a new ranch, I believe."

"Yes. Do you recall young George Curry? He was once editor of the *Spectator*."

"Yes, I recall him. Got fired because he was too much of a Democrat for Abernethy's Whig thinking."

"His being a Democrat paid off. When Pierce was elected President, the 'Salem Clique' tried to convince him that the territorial governor should be one of our own—namely George Abernethy. Pierce shocked them by naming George Law Curry. He began pushing for more settlement in eastern Oregon. I took a look, liked what I saw, and bought ten thousand acres from the Umatilla tribe. I've got Aaron and Ulalie Sellers on the property. We run five thousand head of cattle."

"What of the Tualatin ranch?" she asked, to be polite.

"Use it mainly to graze before slaughter. Got a Minnesota family, the DeHaans, running the dairy operation since all of Mick's sisters got married off. Testing a herd of Angus on the western claims. They're used to being around sheep, which had taken over most of the western valley to the mountains. Bought the Angus back from Scotland about three years ago."

Beth had been listening to be polite, but that last sentence touched a raw nerve.

"Scotland?" she said, with an icy edge. "You were in Scotland and did not come to see us in London?"

He had been regarding Beth benevolently, with warm kindliness in his hazel eyes. Now those eyes were like agate marbles.

"I came to London. I dined with Nelson Cleeve. He determined that you would be devastated if I tried to see you in the condition you were in. He refused to even give me your address. I knew then why Rhoda had not given me the full story of how ill you had been."

"Nelson the protector," she sighed. "He never told me, Pack."

Suddenly, she realized she had been able to say the name automatically. That he had tried to see her was like a cloud lifting after a storm.

"His reason was obvious," he said, with good humor. "The man is in love with you, which I can't fault him for."

"Nels?" she laughed, the old natural sound returning. "He has been in love with me since we were children, when I would get him and Francis into all manner of mischief. Like Mary Charlotte, they were just being too protective of me."

"Now, I am glad that they did. You look marvelous. As a friend, I am most thankful that you will be back home in Portland."

The young woman came up behind Pack and affectionately put her hands on his shoulders.

"Pack, dear, you promised to join us for whist. Please excuse yourself, now."

"Oh, Katie, you haven't met Beth Llwellen. Beth left for England before your parents arrived. Beth, this is Katrine DeHaan."

Beth nodded, her heart sinking. She had to admit that the woman was beautiful. Tall, blonde, with Nordic high cheekbones and cornflower blue eyes. Eyes that looked at John Packwood McGraw with a smoldering love.

Beth should have realized that things were different when Pack only referred to her as a "friend." Had she been listening more carefully, she would have also realized that he was now under the guidance of someone who was dressing him properly and had taken a rasp to the rough edges of his speech. But the woman calling him "dear" was final evidence enough.

"How do you do, Mrs. Llwellen. Please excuse us."

"Perhaps Beth would like to join us?"

"The table is already full, Pack. Let's not keep them waiting."

Pack rose. "I will see you tomorrow, Beth."

Beth nodded and felt a moment of pity. Pack was not even aware that he had a ring in his nose. She almost laughed. Pack had been worried that she would find another man in England. She had never once considered that he might find another woman in Oregon.

Beth looked in on the children. Penny was asleep in the upper bunk and Ian in his trundle bed. Beatrice Chumley sat reading. At last, Beth thought, someone to make use of Finice Caruthers's library.

In the twins' compartment Dana was snoring in the lower

bunk and Donnie stood in the wash closet, a wet wash cloth held to a bleeding nose.

"You two fighting again?"

He turned, a twinkle in his eye. "This time I hit him back. He was so shocked, he went right to bed. The snoring only started when he heard the click of your heels in the passageway."

"Is that right, Dana?" she asked.

"He's such a know-it-all," Dana carped, without opening his eyes. "The bloodied nose will teach him to laugh at me."

"I laughed about it, too. Are you going to bloody my nose?"

"Your nose needs to be bloodied, if you are thinking of marrying that Pack McGraw. Nobody is going to take the place of my father!"

That caught Beth off guard, but only for a second. "That will be quite enough of your insolence, young man. You will take all of your meals in this cabin tomorrow and not be allowed on deck."

He buried his head in the pillow and made a rude sound.

"Make that two days. And I suppose you have something to say on the matter, Donald?"

He shrugged. "I haven't even considered it could be a possibility."

"Well, it isn't! Good night!"

She undressed, realizing the possibility was no more. She blew out the cabin lamps, and in the darkness crawled into her bunk. She turned her head into the pillow, and it became wet with the most terrible tears she had ever shed.

As if to punish herself, she stayed in the cabin for breakfast and lunch.

When the room steward came to take away the luncheon tray, he had a note from Captain Ohlson.

"I'm to wait for your answer, Mrs. Llwellen."

Beth hesitated. "Will it be the same group as last night, dining with Captain Ohlson?"

"He has a different group each evening. But with your family—"

"Oh, no," Beth cut him short. "That is hardly necessary. Miss Chumley will dine with the children, separately."

"Thank you. I shall inform the Captain."

Before she could correct him, he was gone.

Then she decided she was being foolish. Not only for this voyage, but for the rest of her life, she would have to work with Pack as a director of the Portland Provisions Company. He had extended the hand of friendship and she would have to accept it. Still, she spent the rest of the afternoon agonizing over the proper gown for dinner.

Beth stood in the doorway of the dining salon and almost headed for her family table. To her disgust, Pack and Katrine were already at the Captain's table. The table had been set for five, and a sixth chair and place setting were being quickly added.

"I'm sorry, Mrs. Llwellen," the table steward said. "It will only be a moment. The Captain had only planned on you, Mr. McGraw, and Mr. and Mrs. Sherlock. But Miss DeHaan got to the table first and refuses to move, unless Mr. McGraw moves also."

"I wonder if the ring hurts."

"I beg your pardon?"

Beth blushed. "Sorry, I was just thinking out loud."

"I can seat you now."

Beth had selected a gown the same emerald shade as her eyes. The bodice was tightly fitted, but the semi-hoop let her float, rather than walk to the table.

The only vacant seat was opposite the Captain at the round table. To his left were Katrine and Pack. To his right were Irma and Stanley Sherlock.

Captain Ohlson and Pack looked slightly embarrassed, but Katrine slyly smiled in triumph, until she saw that it would still put Pack next to Beth. Then Beth was given the most glaring and malevolent of glances, before the woman turned to dominate the conversation with Captain Ohlson in Swedish.

Beth turned to the Sherlocks. "Did I hear right, Mr. Sherlock? You now live in Portland."

"Please, it is Stanley and Irma. We've been in Portland since '53. Bought the last piece of property that Mr. Chapman had for sale on Front Street."

"Rhoda wrote he had left," Beth said, turning to Pack. "What finally got rid of him?"

Before he could answer, Katrine broke off with the Swedish and turned to whisper and giggle in Pack's ear.

"And your business, Stanley?"

"Saddles, harness, bridles, and the like. Been in New York to get hardware and bits. And some special things for Elizabeth Caruthers."

"How grand to hear a name from home. How is she and her horses?"

Irma Sherlock leaned around her husband. "Her horses are fit as a fiddle, but she's been poorly."

"Oh? Pack, what seems to be the problem with Elizabeth?"

Again Katrine went into her little act. It was growing rude and insulting. Pack tried to turn back to Beth, but Katrine pulled him back roughly by the arm.

"I was not finished talking with you, Pack!" she hissed.

"Nor have you been with me," Ohlson said curtly. "As long as we are in America, Miss DeHaan, let's keep our conversation in English, so everyone can join in."

It phased Katrine DeHaan only to the degree that she stopped speaking to him at all and concentrated mainly on Pack. Beth's disgust with Pack grew as he refused to admonish or correct her throughout the entire meal. She could have scratched his eyes out, because he just sat there and grinned.

When the children started to depart, Beth used it as an excuse to see them to bed.

Instead, once on the deck, she headed toward the prow and let the ocean breeze play through her hair. She didn't need to be told who was approaching her. She could almost see the feline walk of the woman without turning.

Katrine put her back against the railing and shook out her hair.

"I want you to stay away from Pack," she said crisply.

"No decent woman goes running after . . ."

"I think," Katrine said cruelly, "that you are hardly in a position to call yourself decent."

"Precisely what is that supposed to mean?"

"It means I've heard all I need to hear from Mrs. Stacey and D'Arcy. Give D'Arcy a slug of gin and she will tell you anything. You've already chased after two men and gotten them killed. Don't chase after this one. He's mine."

Beth's head reeled, her face white and still.

"I don't even know a Mrs. Stacey," she murmured.

"One of Pack's old girlfriends, whom he took pity on and is letting run the taverns. I find it rather charming of him, in a crude sort of way, doing things like that. He sent me back home to Sweden for two years of school. My mother had forgotten how liberal Sweden was. She called me a viper and kicked me off the dairy farm. It didn't matter to me. I found out Pack was in Argentina, so I just came down to Panama City and waited for him."

Beth had been wrong about one thing. This could not be the woman who had polished Pack. Stacey? The name rang a bell, but she couldn't place it. Still, Pack was a fool! Knowing Pack she could see where he would want Katrine, but could he really be in love with her?

"I thought I might find you two together," Pack said gruffly, approaching them. "Beth, I apologize for Katie's horrible table manners. It would have done no good to scold her, as she's a 'liberated woman.' I never should have sent her to Sweden. Katie, go to your cabin, I wish to talk with Beth."

"Don't mind me, but I'm not going anywhere!"

"We are now in shark-infested waters," he said stoutly. "Mind, or you are going for a swim you will not come back from."

Katrine, surprisingly demure all of a sudden, turned and left the deck.

"I don't know what she told you," he said, "nor do I really care." Then he added, truthfully: "Yes, I have slept with her, before Sweden and after Sweden."

"That's hardly my affair."

Pack glanced at her uneasily. "I'm no angel, you know that. Her folks are the ones who are running the dairy farm. Hardworking, and determined for their children to get an education. Katie is the oldest. Sent her to Sweden to learn animal medicine. I think she learned more about Swedish boys."

"I said it doesn't matter," Beth said quietly. "What does matter to me is what lies she has heard about me from a Mrs. Stacey and D'Arcy."

"Damn!" This was going to be annoying, he thought. "Molly Spragge is now Molly Stacey, Beth. She married the bastard captain and stayed on board with him, until he ran out of money in Hong Kong and sold her to a white slaver. When she finally wound up on my doorstep again, I took pity and gave her a job in the saloon."

"After what she did to you before?"

"No man could have turned her away, no matter what she had done to them before. The sailors on Crosby's ship used her to pay for her passage back from Hong Kong."

Beth looked at him with a new respect dawning in her eyes.

"But it wouldn't be from D'Arcy that she learned anything. That's part of the problem. When she got back from Sweden she started this marriage talk. I put her in her place and went over to the Cascade ranch. I was gone for three months. When I got back I noticed D'Arcy sitting with Molly a few times, but paid it no mind. Then, one night she was so drunk I had to take her home. Dave McLoughlin wasn't there and Nuua had the children. In a crying stupor I learned from D'Arcy that Dave had been secretly seeing Katrine."

"Oh, what a fool!"

"And a damn liar," Pack said dryly. "Saw him at the bank the next day. He admitted it was only a sexual attraction and that he would break it off at once. I left for Argentina that week and have been gone for six months."

Beth frowned. "Six months? She said her mother kicked her out and she came down to wait for you. Was she in Panama City that long?"

Now it was Pack who frowned. "No. I paid her hotel bill. It was for a week. Let's walk the deck, Beth. We get to the rough part, now. She's pregnant. Started claiming it was mine the moment she saw me. That's why I was quick to say I had been with her before and after Sweden. You've seen her. She couldn't be more than a couple of months along. She is frightened and unstable as hell. That's why I put up with her tantrums and let her believe I've accepted her story. Last thing I wanted was her blaring out she was carrying my bastard child. Our clientele on this trip is a little different than the gold rush boys."

"Dave again?"

"The only reason I can think of Marti DeHaan kicking her out. No one in Portland knows, so she claims. I'm not quite sure how we will handle it when we get back."

"Why me?" Beth mused. "And why would Molly say anything about me or my husbands?"

"I would strongly question if Molly said anything. Katie is a cunning animal. I would venture that she pumped Dave McLoughlin in more ways than one. Beth, you are not one of Dave's favorite people, you know."

"No, I didn't know. Why?"

"Goes back to when we started the Sunday dinner meetings. Ian thought that some, like Dave, Kenwa, and Nicolas should be given a token share in the company and a vote. You came down on the idea pretty hard, and he grumbled that you had always cheated D'Arcy and were now cheating him."

"What a bunch of crap! He was on a damn good salary. We were taking the risk." She paused. "Still doesn't answer, 'Why me?'"

He blushed deeply. It was something she was not aware he was capable of.

"My fault, there. I must have been murmuring your name in my sleep one night. She shook me awake and demanded to know who you were. I was honest. She said there was no way I could love you, after having been with her. She painted you as a namby-pamby New Englander with ice-water for sexual desire. It must have been maddening for her to see you in the flesh. You scared the hell out of her and she is fighting her cunning game."

Beth laughed throatily. "What would she have done if you had mentioned Rhoda Farman's name in your sleep?"

"I don't dream about her."

"You haven't been acting like you dream about me, either."

At once Pack was abject.

"I'm no longer a wild-eyed mountain boy, Beth. None of us realized what we were losing when we lost Ian and then you. Our head and our heart were gone. Mick is great, but when we clashed horns there was no one there to break our deadlock vote. In a fit of rage he accused me of wanting to marry you just so it would be a two-to-one vote. I took a poke at him!"

"What were you fighting over?"

"Your damn house! Got so furious I built one on the hill behind it. The way I thought it should be."

Beth hid her smile. "I can hardly wait to see both of them."

He stopped in his tracks. "How petty that sounded and not what I started to say, Beth. The days of Francis, Lot, Asa, and Daniel are drawing to a close. Bigger men than Chapman and Coffin are moving in. John Couch is back with his whole family, and they've brought their New England money to invest here. I wasn't ready for this new phase in Portland's life, nor ready for you. These businessmen, like Sherlock, are not where they are by some lucky gold strike. They'll split hairs over a tenth-of-a-cent profit. I had to know how to cope with that and deal with them. Finice and Elizabeth have been helping me. Damn hard job learning to read and write. When the time is right, we can talk about us."

"Very well. In the meantime, there is nothing keeping you from kissing me."

Pack looked at her and the agate marble shattered in his eyes.

When he broke away from the embrace he was shaking.

"I'll not do that again," he gasped, "until we are married.

It's too dangerous. I want you to be Mrs. John Packwood McGraw, not just one of the women who came in and out of his life. Here's your cabin. Good night, Beth. I'll see you tomorrow?"

"Pleasant dreams," Beth said. I'll worry about Dana later, she thought as she slipped into her room.

Captain Jon Ohlson was waiting for Pack in his cabin.

"I'm afraid we have a problem on our hands, sir. I thought it best to discuss it here, in your cabin."

Pack sat down and waited for him to go on.

"Miss DeHaan came on the bridge and first claimed that you threatened to throw her overboard and, in almost the same sentence, demanded I bring you to her cabin and perform a marriage ceremony. After her little stunt at dinner, I am most baffled and concerned."

"No more than I am, Captain. Mrs. Llwellen also came under her sharp tongue. I certainly wish to maintain the dignity of your ship."

There was a frantic knocking on the door.

"Come in!" Pack barked, expecting it to be Katrine.

A wide-eyed and frightened Donald Llwellen opened the door. "My mom . . ." he stammered, "says come quick, Mr. McGraw. Some lady has taken Ian!"

So much for dignity, Captain Ohlson thought, as he raced after Pack.

The stateroom was a bedlam of noise. Penny was crying hysterically on her bunk. Dana stood whimpering in a corner, the front of his pajamas wet. A wailing Miss Chumley sat in the middle of the floor, with Beth beside her, trying to pump a rational sentence out of her.

"Captain," Pack said quickly, "get the room steward to close off this passageway. You go and stand outside Miss DeHaan's cabin. It's A-3, just four doors down. If she pops out and asks for me, tell her I'll be right there."

He went over and picked up Penny and let her cling to him. "You're getting to be a big girl, for seven."

"Al-al-most e-e-eight," she said, through her sobs.

"Good. I'll remember that. Now, Beatrice is still frightened, so maybe you can help me. Were you awake or asleep?"

"Pack, don't badger the children! Beatrice, stop wailing and talk sense!"

"We were all awake," came the quiet, logical voice of Donnie. "We were in here and Miss Chumley was reading us a story."

Beth sat down flat on the floor. "You didn't tell me that."

"You sent me immediately for Mr. McGraw."

"All right," Pack said, "now we seem to be calming down." He put Penny down on the lower bunk. "Beth, come and sit with Penny. Dana, stand in the doorway and let me know if Captain Ohlson signals for me."

"But—I . . ." He looked down at his soiled pajamas.

Pack leaned over him, so no one could hear. "I didn't notice until you mentioned it. Don't mention it." Then he turned to Donnie. "Where were you sitting or standing?"

"Sitting on the top bunk with Penny."

Pack lifted Donnie up to the bunk and whispered, "I'm keeping Dana busy so he doesn't start blubbering again. Now for the other cry-baby."

"Really, Miss Chumley," he said, with real sarcasm, "you look most ridiculous in that position. Let me help you up to your chair. This is not London, so the culprit can't get very far." He didn't wait for her to respond. He picked her up by the armpits and plunked her into her chair. She gasped and nearly fainted. A real man had actually touched her. If nothing more, it had stilled her with the shock.

"Now, everybody, Captain Ohlson and I have a very good idea that Miss DeHaan is in her cabin. We're almost certain because a short while ago she went up on the bridge and told the Captain to bring me to her cabin to marry us."

He looked at Beth, but she just looked back blankly. All she could think about was little Ian.

"What we don't know is why she would come here and take Ian. Who answered the door?"

"No one," Miss Chumley said weakly. "Thinking that it was Mrs. Llwellen, I just called for her to come in. She entered and seemed confused, as though she had gotten the wrong cabin. I rose and asked if I could help her. She answered something, but already her hand was coming from behind her back. She struck me with that candlestick."

"Miss Chumley fell," Donnie went on calmly, "but I recall what she had said. 'He'll marry me if I've got his . . .' She never finished. Just dropped the candlestick, grabbed up Ian, and ran out."

"I heard Penny crying as I came down the stairs," Beth said. "There was no one in the passageway when I turned into it. The rest you know."

Dana had left his post when Pack had lifted up Miss Chumley and was now back. Back also was his I-was-the-first-born strut. "Captain says he can hear her muttering in her cabin, but no sound from Ian. Wants to know what you want to do."

"Who are you addressing?" Pack said shortly.

"You."

"When you address me it is 'Mr. McGraw.'"

"Yes, sir," he said, his lip quivering. "What shall I tell him, Mr. McGraw?"

"That he had best get ready to perform a marriage ceremony."

"Oh, no, Pack!" Beth said as Dana left.

"Beth, that is what she is expecting and that is the only way that Ohlson and I are going to get into that room. Donnie, you come with me. I'm going to leave you and Dana on either side of her door. We'll try to leave it open. If the Captain can distract her, I'll try to get Ian out to one or the other of you. Let's go, my young man."

"Yes, sir, Mr. McGraw."

Ohlson had sent Dana to have the room steward go for his Book of Services. When he returned, Pack thought it would be wise if he went for the ship's doctor and his bag. Then he knocked and opened the door.

"Hello, darling," Katie said, running to kiss his cheek. Then she smiled at the Captain. "I see you are ready. The baby is asleep, but we can tell him about it later."

"Ian's asleep?" Pack said gently. "Let me see him."

"It's not Ian." She giggled. "It's Karl. I named him Karl, before the State took him away from me. You wouldn't marry me, and the Swedish government said it was more important for you to get your education than be a father. But you can see your son." She lifted back the spread on the upper bunk. Ian was curled in a ball, sucking his thumb. Pack sighed with relief. He was peacefully asleep. Probably had hardly waken up from the transfer from his trundle bed to the bunk. But the bunk would make it nearly impossible to lift him down without Katie seeing.

"He's a fine-looking boy."

Katie looked at him with grim amusement.

"I knew it was the only way to get you here to marry me. It wasn't nice for you to laugh and say the child might be that of any man. My mother knows that it is your child, but she kicked me out. She'll have to take me back, once we are married. That will solve everything."

Pack took a gamble. "Even if I am married?"

Katie smiled, sly and cunning. "You are so stupid. You once said you could get it from any London girl for a dollar. Isn't that what your wife is, a low London girl? Give her a dollar and she will go away and leave us alone."

"You're smart, Katie. I always said you were a smart girl. But what about the plan of blaming it on Pack?"

She laughed throatily. "He's been with so many girls and no bastard children come calling his name. I'm a good example that he is not able."

"There's always the possibility of the first time."

Katie came and put her hand on his chin. "It doesn't matter, my darling. I cried all the way to Panama City, when you sent me away. Now, it doesn't matter. You are here and I don't have to marry him."

Pack put a rough edge on his voice. "But, Katie," he protested, "I am not about to marry you in that dress. Why must you always look like a street market peddler? You disgrace me everywhere we go! Change, at once!"

Ohlson looked at Pack in startled confusion. The entire

conversation had baffled him, but to be curt with her, given her strange mind, he thought was highly dangerous.

Pack held his breath. He had often heard the fussy Dave McLoughlin get at D'Arcy in that manner. He prayed that it would work with Katrine.

"Oh!" Katie grasped. "I—I—er—" But it was impossible for her to focus in on the reality of the moment. Her mind was terribly confused. She knew how badly she wanted Dave—and she knew that he did not love her. Nor was he any longer in love with D'Arcy. The London domestic had saved herself so long for the right man and husband that once gained she was incapable of knowing how to keep him. And Katie's sensual beauty had been Dave's antidote.

Now that Dave was here, now that he wanted to marry her, it was possible for her to forget his ugly act of betrayal and vengeance in going to her mother and denying that he was the father. In a cruel manner he exposed the fact of her having born a child while in school. A fact that she had shared in secret with Dave, because she loved him so. She pushed the pain from her heart that he had caused. How wonderful that he was there to marry her.

She nodded demurely, took a dress from the clothes press, and went into the wash closet and closed the curtain.

Pack signaled Ohlson for quiet. He took the pillow from the lower bunk and turned back the spread on the upper bunk. The moment he had Ian in his arms, Ohlson sensed his chore.

Pack handed Ian out to the boys. There was a moment of silent altercation as each reached for Ian and tugged him back and forth. Dana won and strutted down the passageway. He wanted the honor, in his mother's eyes, of returning his baby brother.

To Donnie it didn't matter. He was far too fascinated in what had been transpiring to leave. The words and the meaning behind them did not make sense to him, but the manner in which the drama was being enacted was better than the opera. It was as though Dana were the woman and he were Pack. Dana had spent his nine years surviving on his "pretty, handsome boy" looks, cunning little "white" lies, threats, and tantrums. Donnie had been the quiet observer of life.

For one so young he could now see that this would be the mold of their lives. Dana would skim the waves; he would plow through them. In business, he wanted to be like Pack McGraw at this moment. Quiet, unflappable, probing, and giving no quarter until victory was achieved.

"Doctor," Pack said quietly, "Ian Llwellen once told me that they also kept something in the medicine chest in case a sailor got too far into his rum ration and became belligerent. This woman seems to be living in three different periods of time, at the same time. I need something to relax her and quickly put her to sleep."

The doctor grinned. What Pack sought had been around longer than both of them. The British had used it to drug tavern drinks and impress men into the navy. Now that trade with China was so frequent, they had an even better drug for such a purpose. He quietly gave instructions to the room steward.

Pack was pleased when he stepped back into the cabin. The crumpled pillow, under the spread, looked just like Ian. Nor was he surprised when Katie came out of the wash closet wearing the same dress as when she entered.

"You look charming, my dear."

Katrine laughed—a cool, amused sound.

"Probably not the first service where the honeymoon came first."

The room steward came in with a bottle of wine, four glasses, and the doctor.

"What are they doing here?" Katie growled.

"We cannot have a service without a toast or a witness. How will you prove that we are married unless we have this ship's officer here as a witness? Steward, pour the wine so that we can have our toast."

Ohlson looked at Pack with amazed relief. He had gotten around the impious girl each time.

Katie was smiling now. She took the offered glass of sparkling wine, without questioning where the toast came in the service. While they sipped, she downed the glass in three quick swallows and came to put her arm through Pack's.

"I'm ready," she said dreamily.

Ohlson gulped. He had not imagined it would reach this point. He leaned forward to whisper in Pack's left ear.

"She could later claim it was official!"

Pack took his Book of Services, opened it at random, and handed it back.

"What did he want?"

"To know if I had the ring. The steward has it."

Even as Ohlson began reading from "Service for the Dead" she was resting her cheek on Pack's arm. With each droning sentence she became weaker until she wilted like a cut flower out of water. She was not aware when the steward laid her out on the bunk.

The doctor waved them out and his nurse-wife in and closed the door. They would know how to care for her.

Beth was standing in the passageway with Dana and Donnie.

"Thank you," Beth whispered. "Thank you very much."

"This whole thing has made me stop and think about what I said earlier, Beth. No more waiting. The time to marry me is now!"

Beth didn't hesitate in reaching for his hand. She, too, saw the need, and her love was ready.

Neither was aware of Donnie's broad grin, or that Dana's face was suddenly bleak. Bleak and fierce. He would never accept another man taking his father's place.

Two nights later Beth giggled over the narrowness of the bunk and the thought that all three of her "real" wedding nights had been on board a ship. But this night was a memory she could hold on to forever.

John Johns had been a man to every other woman but his wife. Ian Llwellen had a wife and a mistress—the sea was his wife and Beth his mistress.

Pack McGraw, to her amazement, was a gentle lover for being such a big man. His other women had wanted to conquer his rugged manliness, to give back steel for the steel that he gave. The more they had wanted him to be rough, the rougher he was, because it was only a sensual moment that was out of his mind the next day.

Beth was his mind, every fiber and throb. He absorbed every square inch of her body as he had panned for gold. Slowly, methodically, his heart thumping with each nugget found. A treasure to be cherished and handled with care.

Not since his early days with Kitty Flynn had he taken a woman two nights in a row. He now savored the heady thought that the exciting and sensual body of his wife was his and his alone. And each night he found something new to love about Beth. She filled his cup so that he had to keep expanding it. He had waited thirty-one years to find out what real love and manhood was all about. He would have waited another thirty-one years, if it had meant waiting for Beth.

CHAPTER

☆ 21 ☆

In later years, Beth McGraw would curse the years that had been wasted in England, and in the same breath curse the years since her return.

It had been heartbreaking to see the destruction of the Indian village at the fort. General Nelson Wende had come to the viewpoint that "people show their best traits when well treated." With Washington as a separate territory, there were those who coveted the former HBC lands. They were able to get Wende removed and all HBC sales north of the Columbia declared null and void. Pack and Kenwa fought them from 1853 to 1855, when the army was ordered to raid the village and move the people to the Umatilla Reservation.

Leaderless, they didn't fight back. Kenwa, Tama, and eleven-year-old Peter escaped with nothing more than the river steamer. His scows and wharf were burned. By a "small error" the marauder directed that troops also burn the grist mill and wheat-storage houses.

Pack and Kenwa could not get compensation. They were not alone. Lot Whitcomb and George Abernethy were going broke because Congress would not pay them for supplying the troops and militia.

The Washington territorial government put the land up for claim, except for the old fort. Because the quartermaster could show they had paid a dollar-a-year charge, since 1849, it was deeded to the army and renamed Vancouver Barracks.

Portland and Pack McGraw did get a bit of revenge. When

developers tried to form a townsite and port, the Portland
Provisions Company boycotted any ship or wholesaler doing
business with them.

That didn't help Kenwa. A new prejudice against the Indians had cropped up. The only business he could muster
was from Portland Provisions.

When John McLoughlin opened the HBC trading post at
The Falls, in 1829, there were three thousand Cayuse in the
Willamette Valley. Seventy-eight Cayuse were removed from
the village in 1855. John Kenwa was the last Cayuse in the
area.

For Beth, 1857 was a year of sorrow after sorrow.

In September, 1856, Katrine DeHaan gave birth to a girl,
but was hardly aware of it. Katie's mind had regressed to a
point where she was again twelve and would speak only
Swedish. On January 3 she had left the dairy farm early in
the morning to deliver the milk and take the baby to the
doctor. Midmorning, Nicolas Zarundy couldn't get by a
wagon that was half-on and half-off the Plank Road. It wasn't
until he and his son had the abandoned wagon back on to the
road that they discovered the baby. The length of the Plank
Road, Portland, and the upper third of Tualatin Valley were
searched. There was no trace of Katrine DeHaan.

D'Arcy McLoughlin grew hysterical when Dave came
home that evening with scratches on his cheek. He claimed
that a branch had snapped back at him while inspecting a
piece of property with a client, because he was not about to
admit that he now spent an afternoon a week with Molly
Stacey, or one of her girls. D'Arcy had packed and unpacked
a hundred times in the last few years, but this time she would
go home to London for a long visit.

A week later, Rhoda Farman never woke up from a peaceful sleep.

It seemed they had hardly left Lone Fir Cemetery and
Rhoda when they were right back for Elizabeth Caruthers.
While nearly every school child in Portland seemed to know
Rhoda, it was sad, now that they were a population of two

thousand, how few really knew Elizabeth—other than that she owned a 640-acre horse farm.

Finice was devastated. He would speak to no one but Beth and Pack. Others had to take over the library, because he refused to leave the farm.

Along the planked sidewalks of Milwaukie's muddy streets, a thousand mourners marched behind the Douglas fir coffin of Lot Whitcomb. It was eerie, because none of the closed businesses were closed for the funeral, they were just closed. Milwaukie was dying right along with Lot. Even his steamship no longer graced the river. It had been sold and was on the San Francisco–Sacramento run, where John Ainsworth had wanted to be in the first place.

Oddly, when the "Father of Oregon" passed away it was like a private family service. Dr. John McLoughlin, "the white eagle," had lived alone the last few years in McLoughlin House. The man and the house were so legendary that many thought he had died years before. The listing of his accomplishments in the *Spectator* brought a quite common response—"I didn't know that!"

Asa Lovejoy gave the main eulogy, followed by George Abernethy and Governor George Curry. There was a buzz when the minister called upon Mrs. John Packwood McGraw.

"Why her?"

"She was a Pettygrove, you know. Cousin to Francis Pettygrove. She built one of the first homes in Portland."

"How could that be. She looks little more than a girl right now."

Beth thought that Dave had asked her to soften the blow that D'Arcy was going to leave him for good. She was doing it for a man she loved and respected.

"We have heard of the history, accomplishments, and awards of this man. We have not heard of the man. The husband, the father, the grandfather, the doctor, the gentle soul. We will no longer hear his magical voice calling a lively reel, or see his nimble feet do the 'Flora MacDonald.' But a hundred years from now, nay two hundred years, you will not be able to walk this land that he called 'the residence of civilized man' without still seeing the giant footprints that he left behind. May we trod in them with humility and reverence."

The Portland–Oregon City road had been improved to the point where it was now a comfortable carriage journey. That afternoon it would be an enjoyable trip back, because during the service it had been renamed the "McLoughlin Road."

"Thank you," Dave said, "but in the next breath I have to disappoint you. I find that Father was near penniless and his affairs are in a shambles. I'm afraid that I must resign from the bank and come back to Oregon City. They didn't steal all of his land, but I shall have to move quickly to salvage it."

"I'm sorry," Beth said, but she was not.

"I think ten thousand dollars would be a fair price," he said, without preamble.

"For what?" Pack demanded.

"Mick said that if I would move out of wholesale and open the bank I would get shares equal to the years I put in building it up. I've put in five years."

"Well, Mick," Pack said gruffly, "what's this all about?"

Mick Myers was brick red. "Beth was in England, and you were going to look over the Cascade property. You said get the bank started and Dave said he wasn't going to be cheated again. I thought it was fair and I think his price now is fair."

"Let's agree," Beth said helplessly, "everyone is listening."

"I'll have the books audited in the morning. If everything is in order you will be paid at once!"

It was silent in the carriage for a long time and then Mick cleared his throat.

"Anita and I have been talking much the same. I have an opportunity to buy a wholesale firm in San Francisco. I'm sorry, but San Francisco seems to be expanding by the block and we are still at the house-to-house stage."

"And what do you think you are worth?" Beth asked coolly.

"We figure it roughly at two hundred thousand dollars."

Pack whistled. "Quite a showing for an investment of twelve hundred dollars."

"And the work!" Anita snapped. "Don't forget the work and the burden you put on Mick's shoulders while you were off traipsing here and there."

Beth started to remind her that her illness was no "traipsing" matter, but something stilled her tongue. She had been home for nearly a year and a half. Anita and Mick had been more like strangers than old friends. Anita, more than Mick, had taken great offense when Beth had decided that Pack's house would be her house and not the one that Mick and Pack had fought over. Nor did she think this was something new that had recently cropped up. Mick had made a half-dozen business trips to San Francisco since her return, but she couldn't recall him discussing if it was Portland Provisions Company business. From the beginning she had felt Mick had been the weakest link. It was time to forge a new chain.

"Beth?"

"Sorry, darling, I was mulling it over in my mind. I will do what you say."

Pack shrugged. "Get your books in order tomorrow, too."

"Well," Mick stammered, "I was not expecting it to be—"

"Sooner the better, now."

Pack sat back glowering. A corner of his mouth came up in a sly quirk after they were let out at the Myers's house. The lips were in a full grin by the time the carriage climbed the hill and pulled into the circular drive before "Pack's Monstrosity."

No one dared call it that to his face. But for a man who had never seen the eastern part of the United States until he was ready to turn thirty, it was exactly that. It was haphazard in design—a bit of this house he had admired, a wing from that house, a certain window design, the size of certain rooms, a feel, a texture, a book of verses without a theme—but overall its feel was towering gothic.

Beth had gasped, but accepted the fact that at least the

interior would be hers, although all the furniture that she had purchased and shipped covered only a tenth of its needs.

The children, except for Dana, had fallen instantly in love. They each had their own bedroom, playroom, and private bath with running water. Beatrice Chumley's quarters also had a little kitchenette for her to make her own meals and tea. Her quarters were quite separate from the first-floor-rear rooms for the cook and maid. Behind the house was a livery and carriage house, with quarters for the driver and groom. Thunder had been put out to pasture on the Cascade ranch. Pack now rode a Caruthers horse.

Amazingly, it was Dana Llwellen who accidentally named the house that he hated. From any of the second-floor bedroom windows, and from Beth and Pack's sweep of the entire third floor, you did get a "far view" of Portland: the Willamette, and the rows upon rows upon rows of the Luelling fruit orchards.

The size of *Farview* was excellent for entertaining, but except for a few small dinner parties, Beth and Pack were trying to build a family relationship first.

Both would join the children for their dinner hour, with their private dinner two hours later. No business, unless Pack was away, was allowed to intrude upon their weekends. Cook, maid, Miss Chumley, and the stable boys were scattered to the winds. The only outside person they saw for two whole days was the Sunday morning ritual of seeing Finice at the Caruthers farm. Dana delighted in getting to ride the horses and Donnie sat enthralled with Finice. Pack was beyond what Finice could teach him, but Donnie was like a never-filling sponge. Penny and Ian were never too thrilled with the Sunday visit, but were polite. Ian, even at six, liked Saturday, when his "father" would take him down to the wharf to see whatever ships were in. Penny liked Saturday afternoons, because she could visit "Aunt Liza," who was up from Oregon City each Saturday to check on her seamstresses and her new sewing machines.

Beth enjoyed it all. She was happy, content, and pleased over the rapport between Pack and the children, except for Dana. Because she did not want to force Ian out of their memory, each child had taken easily to calling him Pack, except he was still Mr. McGraw to Dana. Because it would all be theirs someday, business was discussed openly at their dinner table. But that evening Pack avoided the subject and was animated in telling every antidote he had heard about John McLoughlin. The one they liked best was the one about their second cousin Francis getting the best of the man over the fur deal.

But when Beth and Pack sat down to their own dinner, he did begin to laugh.

"Well, my darling," he said, "if those two put such little stock in themselves, I wonder how much they have lost us on other deals."

"I am still angry at Mick offering him shares without our approval."

"Just be thankful that Dave McLoughlin was so pumped up with his own importance that he didn't hold us up for what a share might really be worth."

"Oh? What do you anticipate the audit to show as assets?"

He stood up to carve the roast, grinning. "I had Henry Blake prepare the books yesterday, while Dave was making arrangements for the funeral. Not counting cargo on the way from Hong Kong, our poor little bank holds $24 million in Portland Provisions Company assets."

"Twenty-four!" Beth shrieked in delight. "I guess I keep thinking of things in piecemeal."

"And that, sweetheart, is the way Dave and Mick have been thinking. Dave only saw the million in gold and cash in the vault and thought 'Ah! I am worth one percent of that.' Knew what he was up to the minute he mentioned the figure."

"Pack!" she snorted. "You knew about that share deal all along!"

"Damn right! The lying bastard hit me with it when I first confronted him about Katie. Told me he would give her up for an increase to a share and a half. Told him to give her up or I'd fire his ass and there would be no share. I would love to send the whole amount to D'Arcy."

"Don't worry about her," Beth laughed. "I got a marvelous letter from Harold Tucker. He's made D'Arcy his housekeeper, which for Harold will mean his official hostess. He's retained a governess for the children." She frowned and played with her wine glass. "The strange part is that she feels that Dave will end up being the one who suffers the most."

Pack reared back his head and roared with laughter. "Of course! We are forgetting that was the first Catholic marriage in Portland. He can't get a divorce and remarry."

"I'd forgotten. D'Arcy's right. Well, who do we replace him with?"

Pack mashed at his potato with his fork. "Blake is an excellent bookkeeper and teller, but not strong enough a personality to deal with the sharks in these waters. We'll be a state by next year, Beth. That will mean state-chartered banks and not private ones like ours and the one John Couch is putting together. We'll have to be damn competitive. We are our own best customer right now. I had considered mentioning Mick to you, until he and Anita pulled what they did in the carriage. He's not strong enough either. Hell, Beth, we do two hundred thousand dollars a month in importing and exporting. I don't understand his figure, but I won't fight him on it. Still, who's the sharpest businessman we know in Portland? Want more roast?"

"No more, thank you. Please pass the peas, though. I can think of several who are sharp, but wouldn't want to give up their business."

"I can think of one," Pack grinned. "What would you say to elevating Henry Blake to Cashier and naming John Kenwa as President?"

"I love it! But you would be causing a revolution."

"That what I want. Let's see some of them try to buck him!"

Beth frowned. "It just dawned on me. It's just you and me. We are the company."

Pack pushed his plate away. "That's why we can have this quiet little directors' meeting tonight and be ready to roll some heads in the morning. I would like to offer Katoro and Kenwa the option of buying voting shares now or on a long-term basis."

"I agree."

"Nicolas Zarundy is our largest depositor, Beth. His oldest son, Nick, has been Mick's assistant for the last two years, because that Russian doesn't want all of his sons to be farmers. Nicolas has been good for us. Let the old man buy his son into the import division and we'll let David Lee buy in for the export division."

"How many shares?" Beth said thoughtfully.

Pack winked. "Ten percent each for Katoro, Kenwa, Nick, and David. That leaves us with sixty percent. Not that I don't trust them, but I see us heading for a slump. We will have to be very conservative in our negotiations."

"There is one thing I would like to negotiate right now."

"Oh?"

"A trip to the bedroom."

Pack grinned and came to kiss her. He was finding that love was something that deepened day by day, night by night.

☆ 22 ☆

Pack had foreseen what other men had failed to consider. The major depression they had escaped in 1851 had been minor, which helped to build a sense of false security. Like a pump losing its prime, the California business became a trickle.

Those suffering the most were the one-industry sawmill towns of St. Helens and Milton. Oregon City lost its barrel factory to Portland.

With the end of the Crimean War, Beth had feared that the English wheat orders would dry up, too.

"Actually," Katoro told them, "we can lower our shipping charges to them and still hold our price stable to the farmers and the coopers for the barrels."

"Why lower it for them?"

"Mainly to keep our ships from dead-heading back from Panama City. Now that the British government has taken over India and Hong Kong from the East India Company, those ports are open to the Tucker Line. We ship their wheat to Hong Kong. Granted, it is more distance for the Tucker ships back, but they will also have the markets in India and South Africa for the wheat, as well as England. Also, if we make the wheat shipping charge lower, and David and Nick agree with me on this, it will double their demand for our sugar."

"How do you three figure that?" Pack asked.

Katoro grinned, having just returned from Hong Kong. "The British keep up with our politics more than we do. We have an election coming up in less than two years. Slavery is already the question. Britain has been in enough wars to think far ahead, and they predict a civil war. The wheat they import from our northern states would go for the war effort, and sugar and cotton from New Orleans would be hard to come by. They are even giving government grants for immigrants to start cotton plantations in India and Egypt."

"Well," Beth sighed, "at least their orders are keeping us afloat right now."

"Which brings up the matter of the Fuller loan," Kenwa said. "He and his brother want to buy the grist mill equipment from Milwaukie."

"What is your recommendation?"

"Well, now," Kenwa said, in a sarcastic tone, "they don't believe this Indian when he tells them they are not thinking big enough. Tanner Creek has nowhere near the waterpower drop as Johnson Creek. Ten barrels a day does not justify the loan. I haven't told them, but Nate Crosby has a one hundred-horsepower steam engine sitting on his wharf at St. Helens. Nate's hurting, as we know by his loan. Let's call his loan and accept the engine as payment. I'll approve the Fuller brothers loan, if they can then turn out two hundred barrels of flour a day."

Wheat, flour, and sugar gave the Portland Provisions Company a steady market through the first months of 1860. The narrow margin of profit was poured back into company improvements.

The original Pettygrove warehouse was rebuilt with Portland bricks. From the river, its four-story facade looked like an imposing office structure. Giant doors opened right onto the wharf and a rope-pulley elevator serviced each floor. A portion of the wharf was elevated, extended thirty feet out in the river with wide, sturdy ramps at each end. It was the home berth for the new freighter *Wheat Queen*. Its three holds had been steel-lined in Oakland. For the whole kernel wheat the farmers could drive their wagons right up onto the high wharf and shovel the wheat onto chutes that dropped the wheat into the hold. The coolie labor in Hong Kong, to off-load it by baskets, was eighty percent cheaper than the cost of barrels. The savings would pay for the holds in a year's time.

The directors were not quite sure why John C. Ainsworth had asked Asa Lovejoy to set up a meeting between them and some of his friends. He had been "on the beach" since the *Lot Whitcomb* had been sold a third time, because of the stagnation of business in California, as well.

It had been a very hot July in 1860. As they waited for Ainsworth, the only thing to talk about was politics.

"Hard to believe," Asa said, "this Lincoln is the same age as me, fifty-two. It's going to be a different race, with four men in the field."

"Just hope," Beth laughed, "that our Democrat friends in the valley don't vote Southern Democrat. I can't stand the thought of Joseph Lane becoming Vice-President."

"Hardly matters," Pack said sourly. "Georgia and South Carolina have already said they'll leave the Union if Lincoln, Douglas, or Bell is elected."

Asa pursed his lips. "I really feel that is just a scare tactic to get people to vote for Breckenridge. Ah! Here's John."

Ainsworth was a warm, rosy man who wore a well-cut black broadcloth, with a plain white linen shirt and a black stock cravat. His face was cleanshaven except for a white beard that he wore on the lower part of his chin, which looked like a white rabbit-fur neck warmer.

"Thank you, gentlemen, and Mrs. McGraw. Although you probably all know one another, I've brought with me Jacob Kamm, former engineer on the *Lot Whitcomb;* Robert Thompson, who has the brick yard; and William Ladd and Simeon Reed. I believe you do most of their importing of wines and liquors for Ladd and Tilton."

"Shall we get down to business?" Pack said, trying to smile pleasantly, but miffed at the manner in which the meeting was requested.

"It is a banking matter," Ainsworth murmured.

"Then it is a matter that should have been brought before John Kenwa first."

Ainsworth fumbled in the tails of his coat and brought out a thick group of papers. He smiled with thin embarrassment, and actually blushed.

"We are most aware that he is the head of your bank. We mean no offense. The nature of our business is such that we did not want speculation rising—which no doubt would be the case if we were seen sitting around his desk in the bank lobby."

Pack threw himself back in his chair. In his opinion, that was a lame excuse. He gazed at Ainsworth with a look that had never failed to intimidate wrongdoers on the wagon train. The man seemed not in the least intimidated.

"As a matter of fact," Ainsworth said, "John Kenwa's expertise will be essential to make this project successful."

Kenwa coughed roughly. "You have us at a disadvantage, Mr. Ainsworth," he said, ironically. "Are you here to hire me or seek a bank loan?"

"I wish the first was possible," Ainsworth said, with gentle regret. "You will be able to evaluate if we are reasonable men or foolish dreamers. May I give the background and outline our proposal?"

Pack sat silent. The question had been directed at Kenwa, which was proper. When Kenwa waved his half-paralyzed hand for him to continue, Pack smiled to himself. They wanted something big and were showing Kenwa respect to get it.

"As you know, there have been some gold strikes in eastern Oregon, the Idaho section of this territory, and the Montana section of the Washington Territory. Steamboats are making it up the Missouri to Great Falls and then the miners are going over the Rockies to the diggings. Hence, St. Louis is getting the profits out of those supplies. California wasn't ready for her gold strike and had to rely upon Portland for the majority of her imports. I am just back from San Francisco and they are thumbing their noses at us. The wagon trains are going back up the California and Oregon trails, Mr. McGraw. This time they are taking supplies out of California for the overland trip to the mine sites. Their business was as bad as it's been here in Portland. Now they are booming again."

He seemed very wrought up, and leaned across the table toward Kenwa. "Mr. Kenwa, you have traveled all of the Columbia and Snake rivers. Can river steamboats, like yours and larger, get up and down those rivers?"

"Without a doubt!"

For the first time the other four began to smile. Ainsworth thumped his fist resoundingly on the table. "And you don't have to finish your thought, John Kenwa, because I can read it in your face. 'But there has never been a need before.' Damn right! But here is an opportunity to create an *Inland Empire*."

"Where would be your headquarters?"

Ainsworth smiled genially. "I believe the Portland Provisions Company has convinced many that Portland is the import-export hub of this market area."

"What shall you require?"

Ainsworth smiled delightedly at the papers in his hands. "We anticipate starting with ten river steamers, of which there is a surplus in San Francisco. Jacob Kamm has inspected them from an engineering point of view and has his eye on nine. Mr. Kenwa, we would like to discuss the purchase of your vessel for shares in this new company."

"That will have to be taken under advisement by this board, as it is now company property."

"Then we'll talk with all of you," Kamm said, in his clipped accent. "She's the finest one I've ever seen built."

"Yes, yes," Ainsworth said, wanting to get on. "We will want to get a monopoly of the key portages at The Dalles and the Cascades. The trading posts and warehouses at those locations, plus the trading posts at the mine sites, will fall under the direction of Mr. Ladd and Mr. Reed. We will look to the Portland Provisions Company for importing and exporting. In our meetings we have determined what ready capital we have as individuals and what additional loan money we shall need to capitalize at one hundred seventy-two thousand dollars."

"Which is?" Kenwa asked, as dry as any banker ever sounded.

"We have twenty-two thousand dollars in cash and require one hundred fifty thousand dollars in loan, with all of our combined property as collateral."

There was no sound in the room except the dry rustling of the papers that Ainsworth nervously fingered.

"One hundred fifty thousand dollars," Kenwa repeated slowly. "Surely that doesn't include the twenty-five thousand dollars it will take to buy our river steamer?"

"Oh, yes it does!" Kamm shot out.

Kenwa shook his head, smiling unpleasantly. "Then I think you gentlemen are greatly underfinancing this venture. Your vessels alone will eat up that amount. You will need ten crews and should figure in three months' wages before you turn a profit. You will have building costs and labor wages at your trading posts. Do you expect this company to extend credit on the shipped supplies until the goods are sold? And major expenses I have not heard addressed—are you figuring in the expense of the boats having to dead-head back without a paying cargo?"

"We said we needed your expertise," Ainsworth said, in a meditative voice. "You have opened many doors, which we have only peeked behind. We had anticipated making only a downpayment on the vessels and the supplies, leaving the rest for the majority of the other matters you astutely raised."

Before he could stop himself, Kenwa said brutally, "Which puts you in a losing position from the start. Double interest. Interest on the boats and interest on the loan. That is not very smart business!"

William Ladd cleared his throat. "I could not agree with you more. I have been arguing that point for days. But, things being what they are, we know that to ask for one hundred fifty thousand dollars is steep. We here, in Portland, can see what you people do. Every bit of your profit you pour right back into your company and the growth of the town. No fat laying around to go to waste. Funny thing is that none of us has ever had to borrow before. We'll take any recommendations you have for us."

Kenwa didn't change his expression. "Would you gentlemen excuse us for a moment. At the end of the hall you will find a room with coffee available. Shall we say ten minutes?"

They left as though they had failed already.

"Well?" Pack asked.

Kenwa grinned broadly. "It's the most exciting thing I have heard in years."

"Then they are not underfinanced?" Beth asked.

"They are, but there are ways to get around that, if you all agree. Let them have the river steamer, but for shares. Let them have the one hundred fifty thousand dollars, but we will put up the extra money to buy the vessels outright. We might as well get the interest as nine different boat owners in San Francisco. As long as we hold the monopoly on what supplies they are shipping, we can afford to give them a six-month line of credit. Pack, I would recommend that David Lee get some people into that 'Inland Empire' to determine what could be shipped back. Last, I think we are within our rights to ask for representation on the board that they form."

Pack laughed. "That took two minutes. We have eight left to put it to a vote."

"Sure puts all my ships back in business!" Katoro chortled.

"And just in time for all the valley produce to start coming to market," Nick added.

"I think it is time we started talking to Henderson Luellìng about shipping his fruit," Beth enthused.

"Wool," Asa said, then laughed. "I'm thinking of those sheepherders who thought the Tualatin Valley was too crowded and settled east of the Cascades. That woolen mill in Salem handles the local stuff, but if enough wool comes down river, I know a perfect spot in Oregon City for a mill."

"Traitor!" Beth kidded him.

"That brings a point to mind," Pack said. "I don't think we

need to be greedy over this. Everyone has been hurting and this will help all of Portland. If it is something we have here, let's buy local and ship it on."

This last point pleased the quartet and Ainsworth the most, although they were overwhelmed at the speed of the decision and the generous terms on all the conditions.

Immediately, Asa Lovejoy was asked to draw up the papers for the *Oregon Steam Navigation Company,* with John C. Ainsworth as president, with boardmembers Reed, Thompson, Ladd, Kamm, and Kenwa. They determined the board should be seven members.

"For the seventh member, Mr. McGraw, I trust your feelings would not be hurt if I suggested Mrs. McGraw," Ainsworth said.

"Hurt?" Pack boomed with laughter. "I couldn't be prouder—as long as there are no night meetings. We're newlyweds, you know."

"Pack McGraw!" Beth scolded. "We've been married for four years."

Pack smiled at her with his eyes, but his heart was sad. He had hoped by this time they would have a child. Perhaps Katrine DeHaan had been right. Perhaps he spent his last seed sometime in his youth.

By the fall of 1860, the Oregon Steam Navigation Company was forced to buy four more vessels with larger passenger space. They had not considered that they would become a major terminal for those wishing an easy route to the gold diggings. The numerous strikes in the region were not as lucrative and legendary as the Sutter's Mill strike, but for the people of Portland it was longer lasting and did not produce large cities and farms. The small mining towns continued to rely upon the Oregon Steam Navigation Company for its food and supplies.

"It makes my head swim," Henry Blake told Kenwa. "I've just got to have a couple more people for the OSNC account. Captain Ainsworth is in here daily with deposit bags. I just don't have enough hands to count all the money."

"You can have the extra help, but keep their books current, daily. We're plowing the profits back into improvements faster than the ink can dry on the deposit ledger."

"Sure is one hell of a millionaire-making machine."

Kenwa had to agree. And now that Mr. Lincoln was President-elect, it could only expand in importance and profits.

"Oh, Beth! Has Amos from the Caruthers Farm caught up with you?"

"No."

"He was in the bank about a half-hour ago. Said Finice was ill and was asking for you."

"I'll go right out. Tell Pack where I am when he comes for me."

Beth's worry increased when she saw Dr. Ditmar's buggy at the house. His face turned her worry to alarm.

"It's his heart again, Beth. You'd best say good-bye quickly."

Finice was propped up in bed by a half-dozen pillows so he could breathe. He smiled weakly when he saw her and waved her close.

He was so drawn and gray. My God, Beth thought, he is only a year older than I am, but he looks sixty. She knelt by the bed and took his hand.

"Mother and I are old fools," he got out. "She didn't worry about a will, because I was all she had left." He had to wait to let a coughing fit pass. "On the desk is a letter I wrote yesterday. It's not really a will—things I want you to do for me."

"Anything, Finice. Don't tire yourself talking."

He gave off a dry laugh. "If not now, no time left." He paused, as though seeing the list in his mind. "Plenty of money in the bank to care for Mother's horses and pay Amos Tuttle's wages. Let Amos and Alma move in here. Closer to the horses. They still miss Mother, but are most fond of Dana. The four new colts are his."

"Oh, no, Finice!"

"Hush your pretty face. My things and I'll do what I want. Books go to Portland for a real library."

He was silent for so long she thought he had finished. His lips had a wry little smile, as though recalling a fond memory.

"Never had a wife or son. My mistake. I thought my proudest moment was seeing Pack grow in wisdom. Mighty proud of him. But my fondest is with Donnie. First person I ever saw, man or boy, who was so frank or honest. I put it down. Donnie is to get the land."

"He's too young, Finice. He's only thirteen."

He didn't answer, just smiled. When he didn't speak again, she knew it was over. He had made his wishes known and had gone to sleep.

After they returned from Lone Fir Cemetery she handed the note to Asa.

"Pack and I have discussed it," she said, "but don't know quite what to do. We've said nothing to the boys about it."

Asa started frowning as he read. "Certainly not any form of a will. It's an unsigned list of things he wished done, but he doesn't even name you by name, Beth."

"What do we do?" Pack asked.

"For the time being just carry out his wishes. He never consulted me, so I can't shed any light on what he might have wished, other than this. Even then it is vague. Amos to take care of the horses, with the colts to Dana. What about the other horses? You say he told you that the land went to Donnie. The way this reads could have a whole different meaning: 'Books to Portland, all else to Donnie.' Does that mean the house and lot that the books are in? It's not very clear. Good thing there are no relatives to come crawling out of the woodwork. Well, just follow his instructions for the time being. We'll have to wait and see on the rest."

They had nearly put the matter out of their minds, except for paying Amos and approving his purchases of feed and hay. Dana was old enough to go out and see the horses on his own, but Donnie steered clear of the farm. His reason for going there was gone, as was the reason for that being a family outing place.

There was another matter more pressing. After the March inauguration everyone waited tensely to see whether Lincoln would oppose secession by force or let those states depart the Union in peace.

Ironically, Portland was able to get their news faster than San Francisco. St. Louis had a steamboat arriving in Great Falls every third day, with the *St. Louis Dispatch* newspaper a regular delivery. Thomas Jefferson Dryer panted for every word out of Washington, so he paid two men to be alternating dispatch riders, meeting every steamboat upon its arrival, getting the newspaper over the Rockies and onto an Oregon Steam Navigation Company ship. In many cases he was printing news out of Washington no later than three or four days after the happening.

Friday morning had become the traditional time for the OSNC Board to meet in their new block-long building on Front Street, which fortunately hid from view Portland's growing tavern and slum area. Every tavern seemed to bring with it a certain number of little shacks for those who worked in the tavern, or worked the sailors, or menial laborers who liked the cheap rent.

The building only hid the view from the river, but not when you made your exit from the building, as Beth did that day, just before noon.

She debated whether to wait for Pack or walk on down Front Street and meet him at Orlando's Seafood House for lunch. She was about to turn, when two burly men stepped into her path; they didn't even bother to doff their bowler hats.

"Mrs. McGraw, I'm Joseph Dolph and this is one of my associates, John Mitchell. We need to talk with you about the Caruthers-Thomas property."

"The what?"

"The Elizabeth Caruthers-Thomas property."

After all of these years Beth had forgotten that Elizabeth had another married name.

"What about it?"

"The law firm of Dolph-Mitchell is representing Mr. Amos Tuttle. He claims he was given the land by Mr. Caruthers, for his long and faithful service, but you seem to think it was given to one of your sons."

Beth stared at him, incredulous. Then she let out a short and caustic laugh.

"A single year can hardly be long and faithful, Mr. Dolph. I should know, because my husband brought him and his wife here from his ranch."

He smiled faintly. "He said that you would deny it."

"What is it, darling?" Pack asked, coming up. "Oh, hello, Joe, John. Didn't think you got out of bed this early in the day, John."

Mitchell's flabby face colored. "In practice with Joe, now. Gotta get out early to beat a buck out of the bushes."

"And the buck they are trying to beat," Beth said angrily, "is Elizabeth and Finice's property. Amos is trying to claim that Finice gave it to him for 'long and faithful service.'"

"Amos?" Pack laughed. "Joe, I've known you since you came to town. You know I'm a little softhearted when it comes to firing people. Amos was a waste of my money, east of the Cascades. When Finice started feeling poorly, I brought Amos and his wife here. Don't take much upstairs to care for a couple dozen horses that are fenced in."

"Be that as it may, Amos says Finice promised him the property, and that your wife pressured him to change his plans on his death bed."

Beth regarded him, white with anger. "Tuttle was not even in the room, as Dr. Ditmar can tell you. And I have Finice's note of last instructions. If Tuttle was to get the property, why am I charged with the responsibility of paying his wages and the bills?"

"Seems to me," Mitchell said slowly, "that with he and his wife living in that grand house, it says something about their getting the land that goes under it."

"That is also in the note. They were to be allowed to live in the house, so they would be closer to the horses. Prior to that they were living in one of those damn shacks."

"Well, this isn't getting us anywhere. Can we come along and take a look at that note?"

"I think not," Pack said. "I don't think we care to discuss this matter further until our attorney, Asa Lovejoy, is present."

Joseph Dolph rolled his eyes. He could hear Tuttle's low and toneless voice telling him how easy it would be. He had been shocked in hearing about the note, but had kept his lawyer composure. He doubted his real client wanted Lovejoy involved, but the fat was in the fire.

"All right," Dolph said. "It's Friday, April twelfth. Rumor is you don't work on the weekends and I've got a trial in Salem on Monday. Lovejoy's here on Tuesdays, so let's meet then in his office over the library."

As the two lawyers departed, Beth flung back her head angrily, closing her eyes. "Is it just my impression, or are they always that rude?"

"They are," Pack said, taking her arm, "and crude. Joe is feeling his oats because he's the head of the Republican Party. Quite a feather in the hat of that young party to deliver Oregon's three electoral votes for Lincoln."

"He's not as bad as the other one."

"Molly's husband?"

"You've got to be kidding."

"I wish I were. Here we are. I'll tell you about it over lunch."

Because it had become a very popular luncheon spot, they had to say hello to several people and were into their meal of oysters and steamed clams before he could go on.

"The afternoon that Molly and I were wrapping up the deal for her to buy my three taverns, back in mid-January, that fellow was hanging around the bar. I thought he was just another of her pick-up boyfriends. When I came back with the draft papers, Molly said she wanted Mitchell to look them over. Butter wouldn't melt in his mouth, but he did make some sound suggestions in Molly's favor. Later, when I came back with the final papers for her to sign, came the shocker."

"That they were married?"

"Hell no! Molly told me how he'd deserted his wife in Pennsylvania and brought his three-year-old daughter and mistress to California for the gold strike. Changed his name from Hipple to Mitchell. And he'd done it again, leaving the kid and his mistress in California for Molly."

"How can Molly marry him if he is not divorced?"

"Actually, she hasn't. She's just using the name Mitchell so she can be Molly Mitchell, owner, and not Molly Stacey, bar girl–madam. I've a hunch it's his money backing her. For the taverns it was full cash and not payments, as I thought it would be."

"How did she get so much background dirt on him?"

"Molly has a way of getting things out of men when she has them in bed."

"Do you know that from being in bed with her yourself?"

"No," he laughed. "It was only a stand-up job when I was fourteen. Let's get out of here. I want to nail Amos to the stable wall!"

Amos didn't like the look on Pack's face. He realized he had made a dangerous mistake.

"Weren't really me," Amos cackled. "Finice told me that Coffin man had been after him to sell the land ever since his Maw died. I didn't hear nothing. Coffin told me he heard that from Doc Ditmar and it made Coffin fume. Coffin's the one said it wasn't fair, because Finice told him that he was aiming to give me and Alma the ranch so his Maw's horses would always have a home and care."

Alma turned an amazed face toward her husband.

"That ain't the story you told them lawyer men, Amos. You told them Mrs. McGraw talked Finice out of that idea."

"Told them what Mr. Coffin told me to tell them, so shut up!"

"Don't you tell me to shut up, Amos Tuttle. This is the first decent home I've lived in since I married you. Don't lie us out of a good home and job."

"Woman, shut up!"

"Sorry, Amos," she said quietly. "I'd like to oblige you, but I can't. Mr. McGraw, might be something even more important that he told them lawyer men. Mr. Finice got quite lonely, except for your Sunday family visits. We'd take our supper with him quite often. Better than a meal back in that shack."

"Woman, you are going to ruin us!"

She ignored him. "Over supper he'd get to talking about his Maw and their life in Kentucky. He told about his Maw getting married to this Joe Thomas and the pranks he'd pull to get rid of the drunken bum. His Maw came west thinking she had been deserted and Joe was dead. Finice knew it a little differently. Oh, his stepdaddy did desert them, but with a pocket full of cash from the horse sale. When his high living ran through it, he contacted Finice for more money, knowing Finice hated him enough to pay him to stay away. Finice got a metal money box, filled it with horse manure, and told the man that's all he'd get from the horse farm. Last Finice heard about him was he'd become a wrestler in a circus."

Beth and Pack were silent. Was the stepfather alive, or was this another of Finice's stories? He had been known to tell a few tall tales in his time.

"Now you done it, woman. They'll never pay me for information again."

"And I should break your neck for taking it in the first place," Pack barked. "I don't know what to do with you, Amos. But don't count on staying here after we get this mess straightened out."

But his real disgust was with Stephen Coffin. After he sent Beth home, he walked back to the sawmill. He was greeted cordially, as one of their best customers. But Pack did not waste time or mince words.

"You've done some dirty deeds before, Stephen, but this cuts it. Asa will be here Tuesday and we're going to resolve the Caruthers land question. I would advise you to have a better set of lawyers than Dolph and Mitchell, because I'm going to cream those bastards for paying Amos to lie. And when you see Doc Ditmar, you'd best tell him that I'm going to ruin him in this town."

Coffin blinked at him. He was not to have been involved. It was only supposed to have come down to a simple case of Amos's word against Beth's. That would throw it into court, and he could handle any judge in the state. Something had gone wrong, that was for certain. The last thing he wanted was to lock horns with Pack McGraw. He had tried that before and lost.

Pack gave him no chance to reply, but stormed out.

A gleam stole into Coffin's eye.

"I'll be gone the rest of the day," he called to Abrams.

The news that the Confederates had fired on Fort Sumter that Friday, April 12, was in the *Oregonian* the morning of the meeting.

Joseph Dolph was a little shamefaced. "We learned, on our return from Salem last evening, that Mr. Amos Tuttle has departed the region."

Beth and Pack were not amazed. Alma Tuttle had come to them in tears on Sunday evening. Amos had blamed her for all his misfortunes in life and ruining his one chance to get rich. Even though she had seen him packing a great deal of money, he had refused to take her with him. He had taken one of the finest Caruthers horses and headed east.

"And," Dolph continued, "after reading this note of instructions, I see where Mr. Tuttle was under a bit of misconception as to staying in the house. I believe you have asked Mrs. Tuttle to stay on for the time being?"

"Someone has to look out after the horses," Beth said.

"Even though her husband is a horse thief?" Mitchell sneered.

"As you say, counselor," Asa said, "the man is a horse thief—not his wife."

As yet, the name of Stephen Coffin had not been brought into the picture. Without Amos, they couldn't openly accuse him of anything.

"The man is gone," Dolph said, "so let's don't pick over those bones again. In Salem I looked over the Donation Land Claim books. The claim was filed under the name of Elizabeth Thomas. We have understood that she was a widow, but on the advice of the Attorney General we shall write her former home in Kentucky to be certain. Is that agreeable?"

Asa nodded, having heard the Joe Thomas story.

"Then we will honor the intent of the note, at least for the time being."

Joseph Dolph was happy to leave it at that. He had purposely refrained from telling John Mitchell that he had seen Coffin that morning. He thought Coffin a damn fool for paying Tuttle to go in search of Joe Thomas. He considered the best plan to be the one laid out by the State Attorney General: wait seven years, and the land would revert to the state.

CHAPTER

☆ 23 ☆

War was not the only tragedy of the spring of 1861.

The Columbia rose and rose with the spring run-off. It backwatered into the Willamette, also receiving an unusual run-off, forming a great lake.

The villages of Milton and St. Helens had four inches of mud and water on the streets. Portland's Front Street riverbank was leveed up with sandbags to the height of the "wheat pier." On Tanner Creek it was easier getting to the grist mill and tannery by rowboat than by horse and buggy. Driving the marshy areas of the Plank Road was like taking a ship through choppy waves.

Upstream, the Clackamas Rapids were under ten feet of rolling water and The Falls were one giant cascade. Asa's original wharf was under four inches of water, and the Methodist Church had water lapping at the door.

Then the rains came, hard and heavy, continuing day after day.

Again, man had taken from nature and not put back. The denuded forests could not hold back and absorb so much moisture. Trickles became rivulets that cut new streams that merged to become flash-flood rivers.

Hollow booming shook the hills and pulled the people of Oregon City from their beds. Then, moments later, the wall of water ate through the waterfront section of the town. It tore buildings from their foundations inch by inch, and the sound of their crashing together in the river echoed back and forth between the encircling hills. Then the wreckage started crashing down the river.

The gathering roar pulled the people of Portland to their waterfront to gaze in horror as familiar portions of Oregon City floated by: the Pettygrove building, the roof of Abernethy & Company, after the brick walls had collapsed, a steeple with a clanging bell, a wall from the Main Street House Hotel, and boats and barges with their bottom sides up.

Katoro and Joe Kamm had been fearing something like this. Every day that the rain had increased, they had kept their ships and boats away from Portland. That left a clear river channel for the debris to rush through.

Milton and St. Helens were not so fortunate. The lower branch of the Willamette had flooded over Sauvie Island to become part of the main river. This new flood rise swept away every building in Milton and washed away the sawmill and the Pacific Mail Steamship Company wharf at St. Helens.

The biggest loser of the night was George Abernethy. He lost his buildings, his home, his merchandise, all his boats, and the safe from the Abernethy Oregon City Bank.

He and his wife started walking down McLoughlin Road to Portland. He couldn't look back. His heart and too many years of work were left behind.

For years they had been calling the principals of the OSNC millionaires. By April 9, 1865, they were quite correct.

They were not the only ones. The war for Oregon had been like far-off thunder. Somewhere out there was a storm whose destruction never touched them or their men.

Many did put on uniforms, like Colonel Stephen Coffin, but their four years were spent in eastern Oregon making sure that the Indians didn't rise up to do battle. Nor did the war stop those, who wished, to stop searching and finding gold.

Along the Columbia and Willamette the war was a case of supply and demand.

The demands coming from the Federal government and Great Britain.

The Union troops were wearing out three million pairs of boots and one-and-a-half million uniforms a year. Their food demands were staggering.

As quickly as Pack could slaughter and ship the salted beef, Daniel Lownsdale was turning the hides into boot leather.

Asa's Oregon City Woolen Mill, hard pressed for labor, brought in five trained weavers from San Francisco. At first no one questioned that they were Chinese. They would be like the Kanaka labor—there for awhile and then back home. As the demand for wool for uniforms grew, so did the need for additional imported weavers, until they numbered more than one hundred.

The idea of cheap labor was not lost on others. Hundreds of men had gone off to fight. A great many had joined the Oregon Militia. There were many Southerners in Oregon, and the Willamette and Tualatin Valley farms lost over a thousand hot-headed young rebels, gone off to join the Confederacy in those first glorious summer days of 1861, when the "gentlemen" of the South set out to whip the "damn Yankees" in a matter of weeks.

For the harvest that fall, only a few Chinese field laborers were brought in. Daniel kept them on afterward to work in the tannery, helping them to build temporary homes on the west bank of Tanner's Creek. That necessitated a new import for the following year's harvest—three times as many, in fact. They didn't leave, either, and by the end of the war "Little Chinatown" numbered over three hundred.

There were as many conflicts on the homefront that final year as on the eastern battlefields.

"Mr. Mitchell, I do not have the authority to sell any portion of the Caruthers land. And, even though my son is about to turn eighteen, as you point out, he is at school in England."

Beth's hatred of Mitchell had grown with the years. After living with Molly for a year, he had suddenly married another woman, still without benefit of divorce, and was now seen daily with his sister-in-law in his carriage. Because only men could vote, his lifestyle did not stop him from being elected to the Legislature. The year before, Dolph-Mitchell had tried to get the Caruthers land deemed public domain, on the very anniversary of Elizabeth's death. But the judge, refusing to be pushed by Coffin, denied it until the anniversary of Finice's death arrived.

"My son is in love," Kenwa said. He sounded so sad about it, Beth thought, although Tama sat glowing with radiant pride.

Beth looked at Peter Kenwa. Was it possible, she thought, that this was the same chubby little boy who had been taken off the burning scow? He was so tall and muscular, with a face that was a noble blend of Cayuse and Kanaka. But in the deep, dark eyes was a peace and contentment she had never seen before. It was an all-consuming love.

"Father makes it sound so sinful," he laughed. "I have come for your blessing Aunt Beth, Uncle Pack. Father Bernardo received the letter from Rome this morning. I have been accepted to study at the American Seminary in Rome. I will only be gone seven years."

Beth almost wished that there was some way to get rid of Dana for seven years. He did not wish school. He did not want to know anything of the family business. When Alma Tuttle died, he'd moved to the Caruthers house on the excuse that someone had to look after the horses. When rumors reached Beth that some of Molly's tavern girls were visiting the house, she had confronted him.

"Deny it all you want, young man. But don't be surprised if I send your father to check up on you."

"He is *not* my father!" Dana hissed with hatred. "He has no authority over me!"

"But I do, and your allowance has just ended! Let's see how you manage without it!"

He only smiled cunningly. He had already figured out how he could sell small portions of the farm without her ever knowing.

"At fourteen," Pack grinned, "I'm quite pleased that Ian

marched in on his own, looked old Joe Kamm in the eye, and
applied for a job as cabin boy for the summer."

"He certainly is his father's son," she sighed.

"Shall we take Penny to London this summer to be with
Donnie and D'Arcy?"

Beth gave it some thought. Penny was beautiful, head-
strong, and wise beyond her years. She made Beth think
back to when she herself had been sixteen.

"No," she said finally. "I'm perfectly content with letting
Penny stay with Mr. and Mrs. Ainsworth. I think just the two
of us should get away. I would really like to see China and
Japan."

"What about your board meetings?"

"Pack," she said softly, "I'm forty-four, and it seems like
I've been working since the day I arrived in Oregon. I need a
change. Oh, we don't really have to go away, but I'd at least
like to start working on something different. John Ainsworth
and I were talking the other day about the fact that we've got
quite a city, with all the mansions being built and the new
businesses coming in—but what we don't have is culture.
You'll probably laugh, but I'd like to start planning for an
opera, a symphony, an art museum—and a library that's
more than just one room."

"You're the one who could do it, Beth," Pack said. He
kissed her. "Look, right now I've got to go see Nick Zarundy
and some agricultural nut who's been pestering him. I'll see
you later this evening."

Pack was not quite sure why he was to meet the young
couple in Katoro's office. All he knew was that they had
arrived from Louisiana three months before with little more
than a wicker suitcase apiece.

He took Lucien Breaux to be a man nearing thirty and his
wife, Anne, to be a woman just entering her twenties. They
both seemed highly nervous. Pack studied them as he had
people on the wagon train.

Breaux was a small, slight man with thick black hair and a
moustache that for the moment seemed unkempt. The dark
eyes were introspective, but glinted with love each time he

would look at or speak of his wife. Pack, who had no knowledge of the Cajuns of Louisiana, thought from the name that the man must be French.

But Anne Mailhot Breaux was the epitome of what he expected of a Southern belle: petite, pale, with luxuriant black hair. Here, in front of strangers, she seemed unassertive and shy, but the way she moved bespoke a genteel upbringing.

"After the Battle of Baton Rouge," Lucien continued, after giving a brief summary of his early life, "the man on the cot next to me, in the field hospital, was a young Union sailor."

"You were wounded in the battle?"

"I'm afraid not," he laughed. It was a rich, full sound. "My wound came from being the second in an unfortunate duel just prior to the battle."

"Unusual," Pack mused. "Oh, not the duel. We call them shootouts here in the West. I mean, wounded from both sides in the same hospital."

"War is itself unusual, Mr. McGraw," Anne said softly, the Southern Creole notes of her voice like a mellow harp. "That was a situation with two armies and two navies stepping on each other's toes. When they fell, or a riverboat was shelled, the wounded ceased to be enemies. We were close, so we got as many Northern boys as our own."

"We?"

"From the day the war broke out, Mr. McGraw, my wife dedicated herself to nursing the wounded."

"Very admirable work indeed, Mrs. Breaux."

Anne rewarded Pack with a gracious smile. "Your words are pleasing, sir, for I shocked the Creole aristocracy by doing what was considered improper work for their young women. But I am interrupting the flow of my husband's purpose. Lucien . . ."

"Oh, yes, I was about to tell Mr. McGraw about Cyrus. He served on one of the Portland Provisions Company ships before the war. When I met him, all he could talk about was this part of the country. While the other sailors would be doing . . . well, what most sailors do in port, he was out walking in the valley from farm to farm. He certainly loved it here."

"Has he returned to our service?"

"He died in battle, sir."

There was a long silence, which Katoro broke.

"He is speaking of Cyrus Wheatley, Pack."

"Pack," Nick Zarundy interjected. "I've had Anne and Lucien out staying with my folks. Lucien has done a lot of experimenting with sugar cane and corn, and I thought he would be interesting in studying sugar beets. Apparently what has caught his fancy is our failure to produce corn as a major crop."

"Not your failure," Lucien laughed, "but the failure of Mother Nature to cooperate. This area lacks sufficient hot days and humid nights for the plants to flourish to fully productive earing. And yet, in talking to some farmers who have been here for over twenty years, they talk of the beautiful maize grown by the Indians. Sir, I have spent hours cultivating and cross-breeding different strains of corn. My wife claims that my suitcase contains more seed samples than clothing."

"In short," Pack said, "you're saying you want to tackle our corn problem."

"He would like to," Nick jumped in, so the man would not be embarrassed, "but the question is where? There's no good farmland left in the Tualatin or Willamette. You know what the war and the droughts in Europe have done to wheat prices the last three years. No one is going to give up acreage to corn while wheat prices stay high."

"You know," Pack said, "when I was bringing cattle up from Spanish California, the Mexican women used to squeeze the fresh corn and cook in its oil."

"Its uses are many, Mr. McGraw."

"Please, call me Pack." He thought for a moment. "I don't know if this will work, but I've got an idea. Nick, ever since we started doing most of the slaughtering at the Cascade ranch, we don't use but a third of our Tualatin grazing land. That's all it is, Lucien—grazing land that has never been plowed or cultivated. Would it work?"

"Work?" Lucien gasped. "Nothing could be better for experimenting than land with only natural growth before."

"Well, that's great, then." Pack grinned. "About a mile from the DeHaan Dairy you'll find a log house that Aaron Sellers built when he was foreman on the range. Furniture is still there, too. Nick, get David Lee to set him up a bulk credit account like the other employees, and also an account at Failings."

"Excuse me, sir . . . Pack. I don't quite understand."

"Lucien, these boys can tell you that I don't waste time. Mrs. McGraw and I are going away on a trip and won't be back until late fall. Let's take a look at your results then. If it works, we'll talk about the next step then. Katoro, you and I need to talk about ships to the Orient."

That night, lying in bed, Pack began to chuckle.

"Forgot to tell you one thing about my meeting today, darling. When Breaux started talking about people who had been here twenty years or more, I realized that I fit into that category. Damn, did it make me feel like an old coot!"

She snuggled close. "You'll never be old, you old coot!"

"Beth," he said softly, sadly, "are you sorry we've never had a child of our own?"

"Yes, now that mine are all flying from the coop. But I don't think I'd want to start again, at my age."

"Besides, we'd never get Beatrice back from Mrs. Pittock."

"Speaking of babies," she laughed, "with the war over for a week, I bet every baby boy born since has been named Abraham."

Reading the headline of the *Oregonian* the next morning she gasped and then cried. Stunned and bewildered, the people of Portland mourned the death of Lincoln. Though they had never seen the man, the grief they felt was real.

Beth and Pack were gone only six months, but they could sense the change the moment they stepped ashore. The mood sweeping America had already reached Portland.

Immigration, checked somewhat during the war, had rapidly increased. Portland was in a new building boom.

Fighting an emotional letdown after the war, Yankee restraint had been quickly replaced by a mad race for personal gain. Everyone seemed in pursuit of their own profit.

Unable to afford farmland near Portland, the new immigrants began to develop the lands north of the Columbia and east of the Cascades. The woolen companies, continuing to feel an increase in demand, brought over shiploads of Basque shepherds and sheep.

The OSNC were up to twenty-nine river steamers and had five on order from an Oakland shipyard.

The farmers felt that they were being robbed by OSNC and Portland Provisions. They demanded higher prices, threatening not to deliver that fall, but both companies turned a deaf ear. The boycott collapsed when the stores in Portland started offering imported California produce.

Pack felt as though he'd returned from his vacation to a frantic hell.

"What will a new shingle job on the livery cost?"

"What are you worth, Mr. McGraw?"

It took him back that the carpenter was asking for his material worth to use as a yardstick for his labor charge.

"What are we worth?" he asked at the next board meeting.

"Seventy-two million," Kenwa said.

"That's enough to understand why stones might be thrown at us," Pack laughed. "This time the farmers picked up a stone, but didn't throw. They might the next time. I had an enlightening experience in China—after my meeting with an importer, I went to see an exporter only to discover it was the same man. Later, when I went to meet with a shipper, there he sat again! Each time a different business, but always the same owner. When I asked him how and why, he said that the Chinese do not resent the entrepreneurial spirit, and will tolerate the grossest waste and corruption on the part of the small businessman. But let it become an octopus, and a hatred born of envy makes even the coolie want to throw stones at it. Am I making sense out of what he was saying?"

They could see the sense immediately. On the books it was a matter of mirrors. For public perception it looked like the octopus had shed its tentacles. It took Asa a month of paperwork before the new signs went up:

LLWELLEN SHIPPING COMPANY, T. Katoro, president
PORTLAND IMPORTING COMPANY, N. Zarundy,
    President
OREGON EXPORTING COMPANY, D. Lee, President
PORTLAND MARITIME BANK, J. Kenwa, President
CASCADE CATTLE COMPANY, J. P. McGraw, President
PORTLAND MEAT PRODUCE COMPANY, A. Matoa,
    President
COLUMBIA CATTLE COMPANY, A. Sellers, President
DEHAAN DAIRY PRODUCTS COMPANY, H. DeHaan,
    President
ZARUNDY SUGAR MANUFACTURING COMPANY,
    N. Zarundy, Sr., President
TUALATIN VALLEY EXPERIMENTAL FARMS, L. Breaux,
President
FARVIEW REAL ESTATE AND DEVELOPMENT,
    E. Pettygrove-McGraw, President

And not one hint of a connection with Oregon Steam Navigation Company.

"But what is this Farview thing?" Harold Tucker asked, sipping his sherry, "and why the Pettygrove-McGraw handle, dear boy?"

Pack sat back with his whiskey and water and laughed. After all the stories he had heard about the infamous Harold Tucker, he thought he would loathe the man. But from the moment he'd "popped up" on the doorstep and announced " 'ere for the 'olidays, me luvs. I've read the posts each year on Elizabeth's fabulous Christmas soirees and determined this year I would partake," he was welcome. As masculine and effeminate as each were, an instant camaraderie was born.

"When Beth started listing all the lots and rental houses

she and I had in Portland, Asa thought we'd better put them into a company and hire someone to handle them. Because she was a Pettygrove and Francis Pettygrove founded the town, there is a certain snob appeal for some to know that they are buying from an original settler family. Also, there is the problem we are having over the Caruthers claim and her son."

"Dear boy, Donald is no problem. Peach of a lad, real peach!"

"It's not Donnie, it's Dana. He sold over twelve thousand dollars' worth of the land while we were in the Orient. Forged his mother's and brothers' names to the sales documents. We couldn't kick the people out who had already started building, so the real estate company was also formed as a blind. We had to put twelve thousand dollars into a Caruthers-Thomas account, so that if the land is ever settled the proper party can get the money. Beth doesn't know this, but the little bastard now has a dancehall girl pregnant."

"Oh, buggery! I'd tan his little bottom!"

"It isn't so little anymore—in fact, he's becoming a fat pig. He drinks too much. If you are fortunate, he won't show up for the Christmas party." Pack leaned close. "Has she started talking to you yet?"

Harold giggled. "Things are becoming more civilized. Frankly, I think it's a marvelous opportunity for Penelope, or I would not have used my influence to open so many doors for her."

"Then you really believe she has the talent?"

"The voice instructors at the London Opera, who turn down hundreds each year, called her the most natural soprano they've had their hands on in years. In five years, by the time she is twenty-one, I predict she will be the rage of Europe. Oh, I can hardly wait! At last, a soprano who is not built like the rear end of a horse!"

"And Donnie?"

Harold sat back, looking at Pack with real admiration in his eyes.

"He will make a remarkable businessman. Gives his credit for intellectual understanding to this Finice Caruthers. But, you, dear boy, are his guidepost for accomplishment. You did a remarkable job in the years he was under your guidance. Everything is 'Would Pack do it this way?' or 'I wish Pack could see this.' Pack, Pack, Pack! I was weary of hearing your name. Dear boy, I believe you're weeping!"

"Sorry, Harold. Those are the things a father likes to hear, even if he isn't a blood father. Beth and I have been married nine years. I've always resented the fact that we never had a child of our own, until this moment. It's going to be the happiest . . ." He stopped.

"Something the matter?"

"Superstition, I guess. Nuua uttered that phrase before the Christmas party fifteen years ago. That was the Christmas Ian was killed."

"Then we shall just break the superstition and say it's going to be a jolly time."

☆ 24 ☆

What Pack had once loved, he now hated. The "tavern section" of town was a boiling pot of sailors and working men. Narrow, crowded streets with loud voices and loud noises. He felt like an outsider.

He turned into the door of the old public house. It was hot and close in there, even though the June night was cool. Except for the long bar, he hardly recognized the place. It was filthy, the walls aged by smoke. Hanging heavy over the room was the sweet yet sourish smell of beer, ale, and whiskey. The place was packed, but Molly was easy to spot.

After she'd used Mitchell for her purposes, she had gone back to being Molly Spragge. At forty-three she had grown fat; she wore bright-red garments to match her henna-dyed hair, garish lipstick, and cheekbone rouge. Wealthy in her own way, she was shrewd, good-natured to her customers, and obscene with everyone. She saw Pack and waddled over to him.

"It's a wonder he ain't dead, Pack," she said to him in her hoarse, thick, whiskey voice.

"What was it this time?" Pack sighed.

"Not the usual drunken brawl. This time he decided to pick on two limey sailors who carried big knives. Sliced him up like he was a cured ham."

"Can he be moved?"

"Give it a few days, Pack. He ain't a bad one when he's sober."

"Sober?" Pack scoffed. "I can hardly remember the last

403

time I saw him sober. We'll pay for his keep, as always. Has he set a date to marry her yet?"

Molly raised her penciled eyebrows. "That's what the fight was all about. He tried to set her up with the sailors, thinking that if she was working again he wouldn't have to marry her. They took offense to his offering a woman who had just popped a kid, and somehow it got started before I knew what was happening."

"Damn him to hell!"

Molly was silent for a moment. Then she said contemptuously, "Should have let me get rid of the kid before it was born. He resents being forced into a marriage he doesn't want at nineteen."

"Age has nothing to do with it, Molly. He thinks he can make his own rules in life."

Molly grew stern. "You always leave out Lily, Pack. It wasn't love that got her in bed with Dana, it was money. Pursuing the world's oldest profession. I'm tired of being your go-between. Come on! It's time you asked her what she wants."

Pack didn't want to go upstairs, much less meet the girl. There'd be time enough for that, he had thought, once they were married and settled into a house. He was tired of hearing the snide remarks about "the Llwellen bastard born in a whorehouse."

He cringed. The second floor was little better than the first, and her room was dark and dingy.

On the narrow bed was a blanket-wrapped bundle, but Pack focused on Lily.

She was pretty, in a coarse and common way. She had the kind of figure that would serve her well in her trade. I've seen her, he thought, in every brothel from Independence to California. The same bold and defiant air, and the head held high. No pathetic coquetry here. And to think that for all these past months he had thought of her as a poor young creature cruelly used by Dana!

"Lily, I'm Pack McGraw. Molly tells me that Dana is bucking at marriage again."

She flung up her head, and her pale face flushed.

"Again? He's never wanted it from the start!" she bellowed, her voice high-pitched and squeaky.

"Then why did you let it go on for so long?"

She laughed, harshly. "You were paying for me to carry the baby. He kept paying me, because I couldn't be with any other man. Thought the kid would change his mind. She's twelve weeks old and he ain't taken a peek at her yet."

"And so, Lily, what do you think is the best thing to do?"

He had expected her to hesitate, but she spoke right out. "Do? If I had a choice in the matter I'd get rid of the kid and him. I'm losing money on this deal."

"You want to go back to work?"

"Look, buster, there's still lots of gold and silver out there. I was going to go upriver, but Molly talked me into staying here. Said the sailors were good to the girls. Hah! They're a bunch of cheap brutes! At least a miner who ain't had it for a long time is a generous man who treats a girl with respect."

Pack eyed Lily severely and spoke with cold authority.

"I take it you want to get away from here, without the child. What would that cost?"

She was taken aback, more by his tone than his words.

"I figure you've already paid for the kid, and Molly's been takin' care of me room and board. I could sure use some new clothes, and enough traveling money to get me to the Colorado Territory."

Pack didn't even take time to think about it. He pulled out a roll of greenbacks and peeled off ten fifties.

She came to him, her eyes hypnotized by the money. It was two months' wages, if she was lucky enough to work every night.

"There's a river steamer leaving for Lewiston, Idaho, within the hour. They have a stage line east from there."

She could not believe her ears. She gazed at him, stupefied.

"I'll be on it!"

"No good-byes! Not to Dana or Molly!"

"Yes, sir. Ain't got but this dress, a cape, and a few personal things. Gone in a jiff, if you'd like."

"I would like," Pack said.

She had already taken a small suitcase out from under the bureau and was scooping the contents of the drawers into it. "The baby ain't got a name yet. Been waiting to see what Dana had to say about it. What are you going to do with her?"

Pack hated her for asking. He really didn't know. He handed her the money and went toward the bed.

He turned back the baby blanket and was met by two huge blue disks. To his amazement, the rosebud mouth opened to a smile. The baby gurgled contentedly.

He was touched, and a little pleased. The baby would not make a fuss when he took her away. He heard Lily depart without a word. He reached for the baby and took her up in his strong arms. The child studied his face and smiled again.

"One thing I do know, little one, is that you are going to carry the name McGraw. I was always partial to my mother's name. Think you'd like being a Fiora McGraw?"

He became aware that someone was standing in the open doorway. He turned.

Molly stood there, tears making heavy tracks through her heavily made-up face.

"Figured you might do something like this, John Packwood McGraw. Right decent thing to do, too. You once said you owed me . . . well, the slate's clean. Now get out of here before I say something foolish."

They were able to get Beatrice Chumley back. A single baby, after the six Pittock children, was a blessing as far as she was concerned.

At first, Beth seemed merely resigned to a new child. Then Fiora stole into her heart, too.

CHAPTER

☆ 25 ☆

Beth thought that 1872 would be the best year ever.

Josiah Failing had done wonders as the president of the Portland Art Museum and Public Library Association. Although he had been in Portland for nineteen years, he was accepted as a "newcomer" by the progressive thinkers who had arrived in the last decade and wanted to change everything so that it was like St. Louis, San Francisco, or Chicago.

"If they liked it so well where they came from," Pack fumed, "why in the hell did they leave!"

"Oh hush! At least Josiah's getting money out of them to build a civic building."

"While they stick up their noses and forget where the land came from."

"Naturally." She laughed. "We're the dinosaurs who are supposed to be long dead."

Josiah had been delighted with Beth's suggestion that they build in The Clearing. The children, with the exception of Dana, had agreed to give up their claim. Beth bought Dana out for what it had cost her in the first place. Stephen Coffin, feeling the land was back in the grasp of the town again, tried to get the city council to table the "cultural" concept and build a town hall and police station on the property. Henry Failing, Josiah's son, had been one of the small investors in the *Gold Hunter*. He was quite aware of how Beth Llwellen had acquired the property. As Mayor, he pointed out that the land had been donated by Mr. and Mrs. John Packwood

McGraw with a specific intent in mind. Only a civic art center could be built on the property, which would house a library, an art museum, and a one-thousand-seat performing arts theater.

Beth had arranged for the grand-opening performers, but she let Josiah announce it to the Civic Center Committee.

"I'm happy to announce that for our July Fourth opening we have been able to secure the services of the London Symphony Orchestra, Sir Charles Bern-Hume, conducting. The featured concert soloist will be Miss Penelope Llwellen, who was born and raised right here in Portland."

"Of the shipping Llwellens?" Amanda Peabody asked, on a raised eyebrow.

Beth held her silence. After sixteen years of marriage she was only known by this group as Mrs. McGraw.

"Yes," Josiah answered.

"Well," Amanda sniffed, "I'm thrilled with the news of the London Symphony Orchestra, but is this local girl worthy of performing with them?"

Josiah smiled wryly. "Amanda, she is the reason they will be here. They have been on a world tour—London, Paris, Rome, New York, Buenos Aires, and San Francisco. At their expense, Llwellen Shipping is bringing the group from San Francisco."

"So let's don't look a gift horse in the mouth," T. J. Dryer said.

Beth was going to have her children home.

The only cloud that she anticipated was a settlement on the Caruthers property. It seemed fantastic, but they had now been in litigation over the land for twelve years. It had been a complex and costly legal brawl. Beth was fighting to keep it for Donald, Dana was fighting to keep it for himself, those who had bought parcels from Dana were fighting to get additional parcels, Dolph and Mitchell were fighting for Joe Thomas, who they had now promised to produce for the court, and Coffin—with new lawyers—was just fighting. No one anticipated that the trial would be so lengthy, vindictive, or petty.

"I object, Your Honor. It is only hearsay on the part of Mr. Coffin that Finice Caruthers promised him the land."

"I object, Your Honor. Counsel is treading on thin ice with the word *fraud*. We have already proven that the twelve thousand dollars for those land sales is in trust."

"I object, Your Honor. That question implies that Mr. Coffin paid to get Mr. Tuttle out of town. He has addressed that question time and time again. He hired Mr. Tuttle to go in search of Joe Thomas."

"If it please the court, we are again in the realm of hearsay evidence. Mrs. Alma Tuttle has been dead these many years, and I question Mrs. McGraw's motives."

"Your Honor, we have sat through four solid days of testimony from a man who does not even show this court the courtesy of appearing sober. The evidence is clear that Dana Llwellen has received compensation for his duties, both in salary and free lodging. On behalf of the other claimants, we move that his claim be set aside as frivolous and unjustified."

The court agreed, but the crowd was disappointed. It had been four days of high drama. Even though the majority of the questions were stopped by objections, from one counsel or the other, the tenor of the questions announced the enormous rift between Dana Llwellen and his family.

When Donald Llwellen was called to the stand it was quite a contrast. Where twenty-four-year-old Dana was fat and uncooperative, his twin was a near reincarnation of Ian Llwellen—tall, muscular, and extremely handsome. He wore his tailored clothes with a casual flair and moved with the grace of a man quite content with himself and life. The older people recalled him as a shy, introverted boy. He was hardly that now.

"Frankly, sir, I am not here seeking anything!"

"Mr. Mitchell, I have been gone for ten years. I can hardly comment on things that transpired during my absence."

"Mr. Dolph, that would be conjecture on my part."

"No sir, it is not up to me to say what is fair. I trust in the good judgment of this court and jury, or else I would not have come all the way back from England at this time."

Several young ladies came to the courtroom daily to measure this eligible bachelor.

Then, one day, the courtroom buzzed with even greater interest.

The eighty-two-year-old man hardly looked the wrestler, although he gave as one of his names "Wrestling Joe" Thomas. He was small and wiry, and his beady little eyes looked with as much suspicion on Dolph and Mitchell as they did everyone else. He was crisp and clean with his answers, as though they'd been well rehearsed. No amount of cross-examination swayed him from his story. He played on the harp strings of sympathy until Finice Caruthers became the culprit for keeping Joe Thomas from his lawful wife.

Eventually, the jury found in favor of Joe Thomas as the *bona fide* husband and heir to the Caruthers-Thomas property.

The counsel for Stephen Coffin and the counsel for the other property owners immediately announced they would file an appeal.

"To protect ourselves," Asa said, "we must file, too."

"I'm tired of it," Beth sighed. "Let the little man have it. Donald doesn't need it."

"It's not a question of need," Asa said, leaning to her confidentially, "but of possible perjury. I've got ten days to file the appeal."

"What are you fishing for, Asa?"

"The hides of Joseph Dolph and John Mitchell."

That would be very pleasing to Beth. They had been brutal with her on the stand.

She also sensed Asa's reason for wanting their hides. At one time people snickered about the "Salem Clique" and now they feared to even question the running of the Republican Party. The two men now ran the party and were more powerful than the governor in the awarding of political "plums." No one accused them of graft, but they had been responsible for the election of the state's Senators and Representative, and their man had just defeated Henry Failing in his bid for another term as Mayor. If this case stood, they would surely throw even more weight around.

Asa was delighted that the information he had been seeking from Macon, Georgia, arrived within the week. But he did not use it for his appeal; it was bait for a different hook.

On the final day for filing, Judge Peter Burnett announced he would have a judgment on each within twenty days.

The first tree to fall was Stephen Coffin. Burnett made an enemy for life, but found the Coffin claim to be as frivolous and unjustified as that of Dana Llwellen.

Asa and Donald then moved quickly and secretly, not even letting Beth know their plans.

"Mr. Bollen," Donald began. "A study of the plat books has been most interesting to me, having been gone for a decade. A two-wheel rut connects Second Street with the development you have going on the Terwilliger claim."

"And the Caruthers land I bought," he snapped.

"My very point, sir. Difficult for you to do anything more with your land until all of the streets are properly cut through. How long will that be? Oh, I don't fear the length of the appeals, but how long will it take to acquire the land from Mr. Thomas?"

"When he names a price," Darren Bollen growled, "I'm ready to buy what portions I need."

Asa opened a thick file, with pages already earmarked. He had paid seven hundred fifty dollars to have every word uttered during the trial transcribed for him. It wasn't that he mistrusted the Court Recorder, just that he had wanted his copy at the end of each day.

"Mr. Bollen," he said, "you won't be dealing with Joe Thomas, nor will he be setting the price. This wasn't germane to the trial, but it's damn important now. Thomas testified that he was found by the lawyers Dolph and Mitchell in St. Louis. It went right over our heads at the time, but he said they had purchased an option on any land that he might inherit."

"I'll be damned! So that's why they're strutting like peacocks. That about cuts it, doesn't it?"

Asa smiled knowingly and outlined what was really on his mind.

In the next three days, trying to make them appear like mere neighborly chats, Bollen talked with Keith Henderson, who in turn talked with Marcus Whipple. Whipple was able to talk that night with his brother-in-law, Frederick Thompson.

On the fourth morning they wandered in, one by one, to Asa's office.

"We agree, Asa, it's a sensible and workable plan."

"Don't credit me." Asa grinned. "It all came out of Donald Llwellen's head. You five are the last remaining claimants. Donald, here, felt it was far more logical for you to join forces."

They immediately drew up papers forming the South Portland Real Estate Association and called for a meeting with Dolph and Mitchell and their client.

"Settle out of court?" John Mitchell said slyly. "What are you gentlemen willing to settle for?"

"We are willing to pay Mr. Thomas fifteen thousand dollars for his claim to the estate."

"What kind of an idiot do you take me for?" Thomas screamed.

"A well-trained idiot," Asa said quietly.

The old man blinked at him. Asa gave him no chance to reply."

"I have your birth records here from Macon, Georgia. Would you care to reply?"

"Damn right, you whippersnapper. I was born in Perryville, as I've stated."

"Yes, there was a Joe Thomas born in Perryville in 1790, but it wasn't you, sir."

John Mitchell came to stand by the frail old man, as though to protect him. "You are wrong, Asa. I went to Perryville to check the records, to make sure we did not have an imposter. I talked to the people who used to know Elizabeth, Finice, and this Joe Thomas. So don't try to pull any funny tricks."

"It is not the same Joe Thomas," Asa said stiffly. "The Joe Thomas born in Perryville was a black slave."

"How can you prove that?" Dolph demanded.

"I don't have to," Asa grinned. "You did it for me. I borrowed this newspaper clipping back from the Court Recorder. You gentlemen put it into evidence, I believe. The announcement of the Caruthers-Thomas nuptials. Of course you only presented it as evidence of the marriage, but I read it with a little deeper interest, recalling how Finice had once kidded Pack McGraw and said, 'My mother robbed the cradle once before, you know.' According to this, Joe Thomas, of Macon, Georgia, was no relation to the Thomas family of Harmony Horse Farms, where the other Joe Thomas was a slave. Joe Thomas of Macon, Georgia, was born June 4, 1815."

Mitchell and Dolph looked at each other. They had been pulled into a tight trap. They had no choice but to surrender and save what they could.

"If the court agrees, we'll accept the settlement."

Joe Thomas was piqued. "Like hell, you say. You ain't going to use me and just dump me."

"We are not dumping you," Bollen said softly. "We will still settle for the fifteen thousand dollars and you can quietly leave Portland."

"Fat chance! These thieves have an option and will get most of that. Knew it was just too damn good a con game. Yeah, that's all it was. I ain't the Joe Thomas who was the erstwhile spouse of Elizabeth Caruthers. Pay me something and I'll be gone."

For a small sum, "Wrestling Joe" Thomas departed Portland, refusing to give his real name.

Joseph Dolph and John Mitchell didn't get mad, they just planned to get even.

"How in hellfire do we get back at the bastards?"

"Spill a little blood," Dolph said. "We've had the White Laborers Association formed for three years, John. We've had them screaming a lot of anti-Chinese labor talk, but no action. Seems to me that Asa Lovejoy and his people bring in more and more Chinks to work the woolen mill and that Kanaka is using them to load and unload ships. That's taking a lot of jobs away from white men. This is an election year. If we don't get them jobs, they don't vote the way we tell them. If Grant isn't reelected, our gravy train out of Washington is going to get mighty lumpy."

"How do we get them jobs?"

"Seems to me we have to scare away a few Chinese—maybe a strike could get out of hand."

"Some of ours could get killed, too."

Joseph Dolph shrugged. "Cheapest commodity we have around here, John, are laborers, white or Chinese."

"When?"

"I think July first would be an excellent day to start the strike. We'll let it rumble on for several days."

"They're planning a big to-do for the Fourth."

Dolph elegantly wrinkled his nose. "I didn't want to leave Beth McGraw out of the fireworks."

☆ 26 ☆

"**U**nbelievable," Donnie cheered. "Turn around and let me get a good look at my baby brother!"

Ian stuck out his tongue, which made six-year-old Fiora giggle, but proudly turned around to show off his uniform.

"Hardly the baby," he laughed. "Purser Ian Llwellen of the *China Wind*. I will have you know, big brother, that at twenty years old I am addressed as 'sir,' and other impressive names."

"Then you really love the sea—as much as Father did?"

He frowned. "Maybe even more, Donnie. They can talk railroads all they want around here, but try building a railroad to China. As long as there is a ship that goes to sea, there will be a Portland."

"And a girl in every port for you?"

"Hey, little doll, why don't you check with Maggie and see if there is time for us to have a drink before dinner?"

"I am not a little doll, Uncle Ian," Fiora declared, stamping her foot.

"Are too! You're a little Dresden doll that we wind up so she can walk and talk."

She ran out on a fit of giggles.

"Dana won't even discuss her," Donnie said sadly.

"Then you've seen him?"

"I've tried. He ignored me at the trial. I went out to the house to let him know I had made arrangements for him to keep it and enough land to keep his four horses on. He wouldn't let me in and said it was 'his due.' I tried to say something about Fiora and he cut me cold. He doesn't look well, Ian."

"He's not! Did you take a good look at him? He may be fat, but he's not healthy. It's the opium."

"How do you know?"

Ian laughed roughly. "We import it for the Chinese, Donnie. Mai-Li met the boat today to pick up her father's supply. Some people run taverns, he runs an opium parlor in China Town. Oh, sorry, you don't know about Mai-Li. Your twin brother's play thing. I'm amazed you caught him at home—he's normally with her and his opium pipe."

"Isn't there anything we can do for him?"

"Damn little," Ian said. "We have seventy-five taverns in town and he has been kicked out of every one and told never to come back. People run when they see him coming. He's a leech, Donnie."

"Let's change the subject. This one is getting depressing."

"All right," Ian said indulgently, "I need you to be my best man."

"Holy cow! Who is it and when?"

Ian sighed with pride. "You know her, but not all grown up. It's Katoro and Pelani's youngest daughter, Sarah. Scared the hell out of me getting up enough nerve to ask Uncle Katoro. He is my boss, you know. We plan to be married in the fall, after my next trip."

"Congratulations! I'm very happy for you. Now we do need a drink."

"Can an old man join you?"

"Come along, Pack," Donnie said gaily. "It's not every day I get to have a drink with my new boss."

Pack, too, was excited at having them home. In three years he would be fifty, and it would be time to let Donnie take over. It was happening all around him. Matoa, Katoro, and Aaron Sellers all had sons in the business. Kenwa had a son in a more important business. Father Peter Kenwa was the priest at the Umatilla Reservation.

They were a city of twelve thousand. It was time for the next generation to show their mettle.

*   *   *

Liza covered her ears with her hands.

"Won't they ever stop?" she cried. "They've been going on like this for over thirty hours."

"We can't give in," Asa said grimly. "I was willing to listen when they started the protest strike, but not now. That was senseless violence, attacking those Chinese workers. You don't strike to put someone out of a job so you can have that job. Let the bastards starve for a week or two."

"Their poor families."

"The Chinese have families too!" Asa said angrily. "They are now too afraid to come to work."

"Ready for the next, Mr. Lovejoy," Harvey Quiggley said, his face also white with fear.

"Those two cases are the last, Harvey. Mrs. Lovejoy will be right down."

Liza stood up, looking sad.

"You should come to Portland, too, Asa."

"It's all right, my dear. All of the other owners of the mill are hiding like frightened rabbits. I'll come as soon as this settles down."

"You know it won't," she murmured, "or else you would not be sending all of your valuables and money away with me. Do you really think they will try to burn you out?"

"Best to be on the safe side, my love." He kissed her and helped her out to the carriage.

Near sundown, the protesters broke up long enough to go to their homes for some supper. Then they came back and marched between his house and the mill until eleven. By midnight it was quiet. Too quiet, Asa thought. Keeping to the shadows he returned to the mill. He wasn't challenged by the guard, which worried him even more. Moving across the dark yard he stumbled and nearly fell. Putting out his hand to stop his fall he had touched warm fur. He struck a sulphur match and cursed.

The watchman's dog lay in the agony of death, its mouth foaming from poison. Then, as though touched off by a thousand torches, the mill exploded in a ball of fire.

"Oh, my God!" Asa cried, running for the corner of the building and the fire alarm bell.

He grabbed at the rope and pulled. The rope was falling down around him. From deep within the inferno he heard the watchman screaming.

Then all he could hear was screaming. The protesters came out of the night as though they had been a part of its shadows. But what they were screaming turned him sick. The Chinese were being blamed for the fire.

Asa Lovejoy's worst fear was becoming a reality: it was turning into a race riot. He knew it would not be safe to return to his house, so he raced around the burning building to the mill dock. Earlier, he had hidden a rowboat under the wharf, just in case it was needed. Now he let it drift quietly out into the current, so as not to draw attention to himself.

Then when he did begin to row, he was thankful he had not decided to take McLoughlin Road. It had filled with running, panicky Chinese. Then two horses slashed their way right through the throngs and rode rull gallop for Portland.

By the time Asa got to Portland, fingers of flame were already licking the dark sky to the west of Tanner's Creek. Now he knew the mission of the two riders. The hatred was spreading like wildfire.

Workmen had been fighting the calendar to complete the structure before the Fourth. Herman Leonard had been forced to increase production at his gas plant to supply lighting for the auditorium. His White Laborers Association workers had just finished running all the necessary lines that morning. In the cavernous building, still to be furnished, the smell of the oil-based paint was so heavy that the smell of gas went undetected.

Whether a flying shingle from China Town or a well-placed torch, no one ever knew.

The men of the volunteer fire department were just getting their equipment out for the run to China Town when the ground rumbled beneath their feet. Then a tongue of flame, five hundred feet high, shot from the roof of the stage portion of the auditorium. The entire building was a ball of fire in seconds.

China Town would have to burn. Burning shingles, like

falling stars, were dropping onto the roofs of the riverfront buildings. Men raced to ring every alarm bell in town.

The bells woke everyone at Farview. Pack fumbled to light the gas lamp by the bed. Even after twelve years he still marveled at what Herman Leonard had brought about to make life so much easier. But the blue-green flame did not whoosh up like normal. It sputtered and then gave out only a weak flame.

"What is it, Pack?" Beth yawned.

"Not sure," he growled, rising and putting on a robe. He shuffled to the window and gasped.

"The new building's afire! I'll go down and wake the boys!"

He found Donnie in the second-floor hall, but looking out the back balcony windows.

Pack looked at the spreading fires in China Town, speechless.

"How many live in that labyrinth?" Donnie asked.

"I don't know," Pack answered, his voice dry. "Has to be over two thousand."

Ian stumbled sleepily from his room.

"Big fire downtown. What are you two looking . . . Jesus! Dana!"

"What has that to do with Dana?" Pack demanded.

"Pack and Mom don't know about Mai-Li, Donnie. She came down to the ship this afternoon to see me and get me to talk with Dana. That's why I was late for dinner. Dana has been taking the side of the Chinese. He's been getting some ugly threats, but he said he was safer in the opium house than the farmhouse."

"Dress!" Donnie said hoarsely. "We've got to get him out of there!"

Pack looked at them, his face filled with the hurt Dana had caused them all.

"He is still our brother," Donnie said firmly.

"I'll dress and go help downtown."

Even though Ian had been there just a few hours before, it was like entering a different world.

They had to fight against the wave of frightened Chinese, filling the narrow streets to flee the advancing flames. Some, thinking they were more of the white men come to do them harm, spat and cursed at them.

"This way," Ian called, yanking Donnie into an alley. "Mai-Li took me this way!"

The roar of the fire pounded upon their eardrums like the waves of a stormy sea. It was racing now from rooftop to rooftop. Each street and alley swirled with thick smoke that burned their eyes and caused them to cough wildly.

On they went, twisting and turning. Fear crawled agonizingly along Donnie's nerves. They would never, ever be able to find their way back out.

Then, at long last, they came to the opium house. The fire had played a game of hit-and-miss.

The front of the first floor had been eaten away, leaving the second floor hanging precariously. They went to the back outside stairs. The smell of burned opium was thick.

"Ian," Donnie croaked. "Don't you think he would have already left?"

"I've got to find out," Ian said clearly, surprised at the strength of his own voice. "That's the room she took me to. There's still a lamp lighted in the window."

A step at a time he tested the rickety stairs. Donnie followed.

The hallway looked as though it had been destroyed by a tornado, littered with broken furniture from some of the rooms. Here and there on the walls were crimson streaks that Ian and Donnie knew were not paint.

Ian pushed in the partially open door of the room he had visited and sighed with relief. Dana and Mai-Li sat against the headboard of the bed, half-covered by a silk sheet, staring at him. He moved in to take a closer look.

"God!" he cried. "God!"

He backed out and turned to block Donnie from entering.

"Let's get the hell out of here!" he rasped. "Their throats have been slit!"

Numb, they stumbled back into the street and determined

that their quickest escape would be through the burned-out section and east to the Plank Road.

The fire, hungry for fuel, reversed itself, coming back to find buildings it had not touched, among them the opium house.

In downtown Portland the fire became a building-by-building battle.

Even before he got to them, Pack knew that the warehouses and import-export building were not worth saving. Ironically, the fire had already started eating in the other direction, consuming the public house and starting to devour the shacks that many of the White Laborers Association members lived in. Pack's next concern was the bank.

The new mayor was frantic, giving an order, countermanding it, then giving it again.

Katoro, too, knew that there had been little hope for the buildings. He had raised the port alarms, directing the sailors to save the most valuable stored goods, then moving the ships away from the wharf. Now they were using their bilge pumps to send streams of water back onto the Front Street buildings.

Pack found Kenwa and Father Peter, who was down for the concert, chopping at the bank floor with axes. Working with them, with mighty blows, was George Abernethy.

"This building is going to go at any time!" Pack called.

"Mud only buried my safe," Abernethy panted. "A fire will char everything black and melt the gold inside this metal monster."

"Henry Blake and Tama have already moved the greenbacks and stocks to the house," Kenwa said. "We've crammed the safe full of the most important records. Peter recalled having to mop the floor when the spring rises. The ground should still be good and muddy and the safe should sink a quarter of the way into it."

Without a further word Pack began to help chop away the floor around the safe.

By dawn the fire had consumed six blocks of Front Street on each side. Carpenters began to tear down the next two blocks as a fire break. Knowing that the fire could continue that way, Katoro sent word for the *New Englander* not to come upriver.

The sleek, 728-foot passenger liner had been steaming casually up the Columbia since summer daybreak at 4:00 A.M. Now all four of the *New Englander*'s engines were stopped, and the massive anchor was dropped.

Penelope Llwellen stretched her long, lithe body and reached out to touch the shoulder of the man who lay in bed beside her. Then she pulled back her hand.

Penny had found her original fierce resolution to blot John McLoughlin II from her life a difficult one to keep. The first few months of the concert tour it had not been so hard. Everywhere she had been the toast of the critics and the center of attention at reception after reception. Many men had tried to woo her. Still, there was the recurring memory of John's arms about her, his lips crushing hers with mad, unasked-for kisses.

No, she had not wanted to fall in love with John, or any man. Her music was her life. In the six years they had lived in the same house—with D'Arcy as the surrogate mother and John and Sarah almost like brother and sister to her—she had never even been given a clue that John was romantically interested in her. The only man in her life for concerts and dinners had been her own brother Donnie, when he was down from Oxford.

Then one night, when the two of them were alone in the house, it had happened.

The strongest memory was of the terror she had felt in his arms—the sudden fear of the brute quivering in his muscles and passionate kisses. She had thought John to be a gentleman, but in that flash of passion he was a caveman beast. It had unsettled her whole attitude toward life. For the first time she began to fear the darker side of passion. If this were love, she told herself, she would have none of it.

In Paris, in Vienna, in Rome she resolved to banish the last thought of him. In Madrid the concert manager grew ill. Sir Charles immediately thought of John, who had become the assistant manager of Albert Hall. He cabled John to meet them in New York.

John had been chivalrous and charming. They were forced into almost daily contact, and Penny found herself drawn to him, but always found an excuse for the rehearsal pianist to be present. She loathed herself for such deceit. Why did he attract her so? Why—why—why? The very question kept her away.

Then, departing San Francisco, they began to talk of home at the Captain's table. Sir Charles had been looking forward to seeing primitive America. Their tales suggested he still might get that chance. Only Penny noted that John only talked about his grandfather. In a flash she realized that he feared his lusty moments with her, because his amorous appetite for women was making him just like his lecherous father. She also knew that she loved him. She had accepted the fact at last in a burst of bitter tears.

The next morning they found themselves alone together at breakfast. It was easier to talk of home on a more personal note.

"I'm a frank man, Penny. I cannot hide the fact that I am unhappy in returning home. Ours was not a happy growing up. I matured too quickly with the conversations that passed between my mother and father. Mother made us almost hate the man. I can't. But I don't know how to handle the situation."

Penny had laughed. It was as flutelike as her singing voice. "Handle him as you do Sir Charles. The rough, stern schedule-master."

"I'm satisfied I can do that. I'm not satisfied that I can answer him truthfully should he ask us about us."

"What about us?"

"I've been a bloody fool, Penny! I don't blame you for hating me for taking advantage of you. I was being the insufferable male, thinking I could make you love me by being the dominate male. The tour has taught me that your music will always be your great love. There is no room for me."

"I'm only a woman," she had said, softly. "After this

concert I shall have to get a business manager and booking agent. It might keep the wolves away from the stage door if he were also my husband."

Now, she did touch John's shoulder. He rolled over and, blinking the sleep from his eyes, smiled up at her.

"Good morning, my darling new husband. We've come to a stop, and they've dropped the anchor. Don't you think we'd best dress and find out why?"

By the time the *New Englander* was allowed to continue on to Portland, the fire was out.

Penny stood at the railing and cried bitter tears. Her childhood memories were all ashes or charred black skeletons. Gone was Portland Provisions, the *Oregonian* log house, Finice's library, Aunt Liza's dress shop, the home in which she was born. Gone!

Every building along the riverfront, from the public house to the sawmill, lay in smoldering ruin. Front Street had been leveled by the fire . . . the firebreak hadn't worked.

Penny recalled how once, on a dare from the twins, she had gone to peek into the Portland Public House, to see what made it so evil. Now she couldn't remember where it stood in the black swath that stretched from The Clearing to John Couch's store and wharf.

Beyond First Street the fire had played gleeful hop-scotch, taking only a building here and a building there. Only the tops of the alder trees were singed in front of the Crosby House.

The Mayor resigned over the disaster of his firebreak order. John Mitchell was conveniently in Salem, and Joseph Dolph held his silence. He had never dreamed it would go this far. He had never imagined the mob they'd unleashed could get so ugly, and the brutality of it terrified him. He had worked to put out the fires until his hands were soot-grimed and his head swam dizzily, his nerves raw and quivering. A major apprehension was that a rampaging laborer would approach him and ask if they had "done good." His conscience was heavy.

The men and women of the London Symphony Orchestra

retained their cabins on the *New Englander*. That evening, they gave a solemn concert from the deck of the ship. People sat in their homes and listened to it through their open windows. It was too soon to meet in a crowd. They all needed some time to consider their personal losses. Tomorrow would be soon enough to dig through the rubble and make plans to rebuild.

Penelope Llwellen-McLoughlin sang only one song in Portland: Shubert's "Ave Maria"—at the memorial service for Dana Randolph Llwellen.

CHAPTER

☆ 27 ☆

"**V**ictorian!" Beth muttered, coming into the parlor. "We are surrounded by a forest of Victorian mansions."

Pack didn't look up. He was in the company of Lucien and Anne Breaux's five stairstep daughters, who stood fascinated as he turned the electric lamp off and then on again. The water-powered electricity lines had not yet extended out to the Tualatin Valley.

"Yes, a shame," sixteen-year-old Fiora McGraw laughed, sailing into the room. "Daddy's house is just a poor little shack next to all these magnificent structures."

It didn't get a rise out of him. Hardly a day now passed that he didn't grumble about their high-brow neighbors and the growth of Portland by "annexation." The city was twenty-two thousand strong, with a metropolitan area comprising all of the Couch, Lownsdale, Caruthers, and Terwilliger claims. Across the Willamette was the middle-class town of East Portland and the working man's town of Albina, which sprang up after the fire of 1872, and grew even larger in 1873 when a second great fire destroyed the hastily rebuilt shacks and taverns. But the type of people now living on his own hillsides irked Pack the most.

"Pack," Beth said gaily, "I never would have believed you'd be such a fool over an electric light bulb."

"I'm only demonstrating for these sweet little things, dear." He grinned. "I must say Lucien and Anne have raised a crop of girls as fine as their corn."

"Why, thank you kindly, sir," Anne said merrily, making

her entrance. "I'll share those words with my husband when he returns from the Grange meeting with Donald."

Pack's face clouded. Beth and Fiora cringed. Anne had said the wrong thing. "Damn farmers," he grumbled, "don't have any reason to fight us with their damned Grange. Oh, excuse me, young ladies. Your Uncle Pack's been told that, now his hair is as white as snow, he can't cuss anymore. At least not in front of you. But if the farmers have robbed me of a profit, there's no way in hell I'll be able to keep my tongue."

"Pack McGraw!" Beth snapped. "It no longer concerns you! You are retired, remember?"

"Humph!" He turned to the Breaux girls. "Do you know what *retired* means, my fair lovelies? It means I've got not much better to do than walk around town, subjected to the sight of the hideous homes people are building in Portland these days. If Mrs. So-and-So has fifteen rooms, Mrs. Uppity-duppity has to have twenty. Lord save me from those . . . Lord have mercy! Elizabeth McGraw! What have you done to yourself?"

The women broke into peals of laughter and the Breaux girls joined in.

Having finally caught his attention, Beth paraded about the room like one of Liza's fashion models. "It was Anne and Fiora's idea. A special hairdo for this special day. It's called a 'pompadour.' Do you like it?"

"Very much," he said quietly, eyeing the masses of curls piled up from her ears to the top of her head. "I've always said I married the most beautiful woman in town."

"And raised the prettiest daughter?" Fiora kidded.

"The sassiest at least," he chuckled. "Mrs. Fuller filled my ears over what you said to her daughter the other day."

"Oh, Daddy, Imogene Fuller is always bragging over the fact that her father's store is the tallest in town and has electric elevators."

"And how did you quote me to Imogene?"

"I repeated exactly what you said at the dinner table. That you'd seen better-looking log cabins built by mountainmen half-blind on Blue Ruin!"

"Oh, Fiora!" Beth said in mock wrath. "We never repeat Pack's words to the social elite. Now, march upstairs and get changed. I want to get to the station in time to find a good seat."

Anne looked at her in surprise.

"Lucien told me last week that you and Pack would be on the reviewing stand."

"Turned 'em down," Pack said uneasily. "After all Portland Maritime Bank did to help get this railroad here, our beloved and honorable Senator Joseph N. Dolph did not feel it was fitting for Useless S. Grant to be greeted by an Indian."

Beth laughed and turned to Anne. "My husband remembers Lieutenant Grant from when he was assigned to Fort Vancouver, back in 1852. When he came back to Portland four years ago, Pack told him that though he'd been useless to the army during his year here, he'd made many friends at the Portland Public House. I don't think General Grant appreciated Mrs. Grant hearing the comments."

Pack smiled, remembering. "Neither did our illustrious mayor or the town council. They were trying so hard to impress the General, what with putting him up in the mayor's new Clarendon Hotel and all. Worst thing that ever happened to this town was that damned fire. Everything had to be fireproof after that. Brick and quarried stone. Now, wood has warmth—but just look at those Victorian monsters as a good example. Cold stone for colder-hearted people to live in."

"This is where I came in," Beth said, shaking her head. "I'm going to put on my hat and get my wrap. Anne, I hear Donnie's surrey on the drive, so get the girls ready. Pack, go brush off your boots. They look like you've been walking in manure."

Portland had wondered if it would ever see this day. Many had dreamed railroad. Of course, there were short lines—but while people had been able to get from coast to coast for years, Portland was only now being connected to the transcontinental rail lines.

Many manipulators had come to Portland after the Civil War, but none more flamboyant than the controversial Ben Holladay. Having organized the largest stagecoach business in the country, he'd sold Wells Fargo for one point five million dollars in 1866.

When he'd reached Portland, in August of 1868, he was quick with his schemes—and shrewd enough not to let anyone see inside of his wallet.

"Well, sir, I need a small loan to bring the Iron Horse to this country. The same kind of Iron Horse your kin chased across the plains."

Kenwa hadn't cracked a smile. "How much of a loan and what have you for collateral?"

"I'm aiming to capitalize the railroad for six million dollars and have bought a piece of land across the river that's damn good collateral."

Still Kenwa did not smile. "We are a small private bank, Mr. Holladay. At the present land prices over there, you would need six hundred thousand acres to secure such a loan."

"Look here, Chief, when I get finished building a town over there for a railroad to come into, that will be the business center and there will be grass growing on Front Street."

Then Kenwa smiled. "A funny thing about the banking business, Mr. Holladay. The same men who come in to borrow during their meteoric rise are back in to borrow when they have a comparable fall."

And the fall had come, but without Portland Maritime money at stake.

Many Portlanders and other Portland banks did lose. Holladay had raised over two million dollars in Oregon and six million dollars from banks in Germany.

Henry Villard, an eastern railroad owner and builder, was eventually asked by the German bankers to go to Oregon and determine why the interest payments on the loans were in such serious default.

Holladay played hide-and-seek, as though the thirty-nine-

year-old man were a petty bill collector. Villard's early training had been as a newspaper reporter. He knew how to sniff
out the real facts.

Kenwa had immediately recognized him as a gentleman,
with a worried concern for his German associates. Kenwa
was brutally frank.

"Mr. Villard, the man is overextended on his and the
resources of others. Your banking friends have waited four
years without an interest payment. If they are wise bankers,
they will wait two more years. By then, because of his
diversified ventures and extravagances, he will be bankrupt.
A railroad man, such as yourself, could then acquire his
right-of-way holdings in Oregon and Washington, and his
combined holdings with the Great Northern in Idaho and
Montana. Your clients would then be protected after their
long wait."

Villard had looked at him in surprise.

"You know of my railroad background?"

"When a man seeks an appointment with me, sir, I try to
learn something about him in advance."

Villard had smiled, for he'd played the same game. When a
bank was worth over eighty million dollars, and had not dealt
with Ben Holladay, then that was the banker he wanted to
talk with.

Kenwa's prediction was good almost to the day. The day
Holladay did go bankrupt, Kenwa quietly started buying up
Holladay's bad paper at a great discount as Villard's agent.
By the time Villard arrived back in Oregon, Portland Mar-
itime Bank had acquired all of Holladay's holdings for him.
That had been September 11, 1876. On September 11, 1879,
Kenwa put together a package for Villard to purchase the
Oregon Steam Navigation Company and create the Oregon
Railway and Navigation Company. The date had become
such a goodluck charm in the mind of Henry Villard that he
picked September 11, 1883 for his first train to arrive in
Portland.

It wasn't the first steam engine Portlanders had seen pull
into the depot, north of the John Couch land. The Willamette

Valley line of Holladay's uncompleted Oregon and California Railroad had been shipping wheat to Portland for six years. But this was different. Oregon wheat and lumber could now go by rail all the way to New York City. Portland was in a festive mood.

John H. Mitchell, who made no bones over the fact that he used his political machine to serve the interests of the railroad, smiled wickedly. "Well, Mr. Katoro, not a very good day for the steam shipping business, I would say."

"Perhaps it's not altogether bad," Katoro said. "As of next week Llwellen Shipping will become a part of the Oregon Railway and Navigation Company. You don't look well, sir. Crow for breakfast?"

Like Pack McGraw, Timothy Katoro was ready to spend some time with his grandchildren.

Two years earlier, Francis Pettygrove had returned for the thirty-fifth anniversary of the founding of Portland. He and Katoro had walked for hours, recalling the early days.

"It fills my heart with joy," Francis told Katoro, "to see this great city where I once saw dense woods."

Now, walking away from Mitchell, Katoro smiled. The few hundred people in the reviewing stand bleachers would be comparable to the Portland population when Francis sold in 1848.

"Here you are at last," Asa enthused, rushing out of the depot to greet the McGraw carriage. "Liza is saving spots for you on the depot platform."

"Are Indians and mountainmen accepted?" Pack growled, with concealed amusement.

"Half of the depot building is owned by the Oregon Telegraphic Company. I'll invite who I want to stand on my property." Then Asa's face broke into a broad grin. "You know, Pack, my telegraph operators have kept me informed on the progress of the train since the 'last spike' ceremony in Montana. If only T. J. Dryer were alive to see that we can now get news almost as soon as it happens. What a day!"

On the surface, Asa Lovejoy was a happy man. Under the surface, he was hiding a troublesome worry. Unknown to

Liza, the doctor had forbidden him to attend the ceremonies. But at seventy-four, Asa wanted to live every last minute of his life to its fullest.

It was easy to pick Eliza Lovejoy out of the crowd. Over the years her infamous hats had become bigger and more flamboyant. Where most people seemed to shrink with age, at sixty-one Liza seemed taller and more buxom. In the decade since her permanent return to Portland, her booming voice had taken up the cause of women's suffrage.

"Hello, me luvs! Better viewing here than up with the 'silk top hats.' Where is Lucien? Oh, there you are, luv. Come with me! There is a man in the telegraph office who has come all the way from Illinois to meet you."

"Don't let him steal you away," Pack warned.

Lucien smiled. Nothing could take him away from his beloved farm. Once he had solved the problem of Oregon corn, he had begun work on a strain of wheat that could be grown in the more arid eastern portion of the state in the wintertime. For the Luelling family he was cross-pollinating several strains of pears and cherries. He had ample work, and wouldn't leave now no matter what the man had to offer.

"Frederick Weyerhaeuser, Mr. Breaux. A great pleasure to meet you."

At forty-eight, Weyerhaeuser was the central figure in the Midwest lumber industry. He was a latter-day Francis Pettygrove in that he never seemed to sit down.

"I have been on a three-month tour of the sawmills in Washington and Oregon. There is enough timber here for a century, but what of the century after that? In Illinois I have attempted to weed out seedlings and transplant them. Some live, but the majority do not. A hundred years is not long in the life of a tree, but very long in the life of a man. Before I decide to establish in this area, I want to know the feasibility of a tree farm with stock that can be transplanted and mature in a man's lifetime."

"A very noble venture, sir, but my line of research is in agriculture."

"I look at timber as an agricultural product, sir. Unfortunately, while we harvest, we do not sow back. And if we harvest too much, the floods will wash away your farms—no matter how hardy a seed you have developed. I would at least appreciate your consideration on the matter. My card."

"I shall give it some thought, thank you," Lucien said. "Now, I believe the scheduled arrival is near. Will you excuse me?"

"Do you actually expect the train to arrive on schedule, Mr. Breaux?"

Lucien laughed. "Even if Mr. Villard has to get out and push it. A contractor for the railroad bridge over the Columbia was five minutes late for a meeting. When he arrived, Mr. Villard was already walking away. The man ran to catch up and when he said he was only five minutes late, Mr. Villard said, 'That, sir, puts me five minutes early to meet the other man wishing to bid on the job.'" Lucien laughed. "The train will be on time!"

As Lucien walked away, he had to admit he was intrigued. He had been working on an apple tree with a degree of success, with a goal of having it produce fruit in half the normal time. Why couldn't that same knowledge be applied to the Douglas fir?

As though watching the seconds tick away on Villard's pocket watch, the engineer brought the train right up to the platform at 11:00 A.M.

"How very nice," Beth said, seeing the wreath of roses on the front of the engine. "I wish the Lownsdales were here to see that. Mrs. Lownsdale said she would make Portland the 'city of roses.' Lucien, someone has to develop a rose and call it the Lownsdale Rose. Oh, there's the General! Gracious, how old he is beginning to look."

To the chagrin of the Mayor and council, their lengthy pomp-and-circumstance ceremony was supplanted by Henry Villard's own agenda. He was not a man to be crossed. His comments were like the ticking of his second hand, each one precious and not to be wasted. He cut the Mayor out a second time by introducing General Grant personally.

"My humble thanks, Mr. Villard," Grant said. "I do appreciate an introduction that can be accomplished in a single sentence. The last time I visited your fair city, my good friend, Mayor David Thompson, went on at such length that it left me only time to say 'I thank you.'

"On that occasion I wasn't given time to recall my first visit to this area, although one local gentleman reminded me I was 'Useless' Grant in those days. It's my time to get even, John Packwood McGraw. General Nelson Wende, back thirty years ago, let me know why you were called Pack. Born in the mountains, everything you owned could be put into a pack. Back then, a man could live out of his pack and survive.

"Coming down the beautiful Columbia River Valley today, I couldn't help but think of that pack and the Oregon Trail. We would not be here today if wagon masters like McGraw had not seen the pioneers through, or if men like Asa Lovejoy and Francis Pettygrove had not dreamed of cities rising from the forest, or if men like John Kenwa had not been here to help them settle in peace.

"Now the wagon ruts are covered by iron rails, and the conestoga wagon has been replaced by a passenger coach. But men will still come, with packs on their backs which contain all their earthly goods. Let them grow and prosper as the first wave of pioneers has done.

"Oh, I said I was going to get even with Pack McGraw. I left here owing him a bar tab of seventy-two cents. Would you believe that thirty years ago you could still get a shot of good whiskey for two cents? You can imagine my chagrin at now having to pay five cents for a cigar. Pack, I've got your seventy-two cents—and I hope you don't mind that it's in Confederate money!

"I thank you."

During the laughter and applause, a telegraph operator touched Pack gently on the arm.

"Please come with me, Mr. McGraw. Mr. Lovejoy has collapsed."

Epilogue

"Noisy beasts!"

The Oldsmobile chugged around the highly polished Landau.

In the June air along the Willamette, the woman rode alone in the carriage. The silver hair still held a hint of strawberry. Behind the spectacles the eyes were still emerald bright. Eighty-four years of wrinkles could not hide what had once been raving beauty. With gnarled hands, Elizabeth McGraw pulled the fur boa closer around her neck. During the four years since Pack's death, it seemed to her that summer came later and later.

She still lived in his "monstrosity"; she would not dream of living anyplace else. It had been her home for over forty years. Once, she had closed a door—to keep Ian's ghost inside. Now she moved from room to room, and could feel Pack constantly with her.

Beth had not wanted to take this ride. She was a homebody. There was no one left to visit, anyway. She felt like that lone fir in the cemetery. The last survivor in what had once been a forest of dear and beloved friends.

Still erect in her declining years, she felt more comfortable at home. People could just come to see her.

Why, Robert Pettygrove had been there just the week before. He had smiled brightly and talked about the Lewis and Clark Exposition as if she were a doddering old fool who was not aware that his father had been a walking book of knowledge on the Lewis and Clark expedition.

And there were the children and grandchildren and great-grandchildren. The latter two thanks only to Ian and Sarah.

Penny's stellar musical career had given way to the teaching of others. Donald had never married, but remained a caring son and formidable guardian of the family interests.

Nor could she any longer be fretful with Fiora and Father Peter.

"People should not come back into other people's lives unannounced," she muttered.

Not having ever met Lily Dawson, she was not aware to whom she opened the door. Pack knew instantly, and denied the woman's request to see her daughter.

Age had made Lily cunning to gain whatever she desired. She had learned from a reluctant Molly Spragge that the girl was getting a good education at St. Mary's Academy. In 1882 the Sisters of the Holy Name had one hundred twenty pupils, none by the name of Llwellen, but one by the name of McGraw. Lily promptly introduced herself to a shocked Fiora.

Beth and Pack were then frank with the truth, but a gulf had opened between them. Too many of Fiora's school friends had overheard Lily. To satisfy her maternal desire, Lily had almost destroyed her daughter.

Fiora refused to graduate with her class and Father Peter counseled her to go into retreat with the Sisters. She came out of the retreat quiet and content with her decision to give her life to the church. It had taken Pack a long time to accept and forgive Father Peter Kenwa.

"Why are you turning here, Charles?"

"We are to pick up your son, Donald, Mrs. McGraw."

The street was new and quite different, she noted, with the warm smell of roses. The bushes were massive, almost brushing the side of her carriage. Nothing in this world, she determined, was as sweet as the scent of the spring rose.

The street made a wide turning and she gasped. From Farview she had been able to see the construction in the distance, but had never had a desire to see the Lewis and Clark Exposition up close. Now it stretched before her, with the thrusts of its mighty buildings against the clouds, the strength of their lines clean and proud. She was amazed at the throngs of people milling about. She had seen no one on

the street. Then she saw the reason: from all directions the
people were arriving by the new electric trolleys.

Her carriage pulled up in front of a most impressive building, where a large crowd had gathered. She spotted Donald
and waved. Standing next to him was a short, stocky man,
wearing a pince-nez and a toothy grin. The man waved at her.
Recognition was like a blow—she was not properly dressed
to meet the President of the United States!

"Bully meeting you!" Theodore Roosevelt boomed. "It is
my honor to name this 'Elizabeth McGraw' day at the 1905
Lewis and Clark Centennial Exposition. Before I escort you
into the Forestry Building, Mr. Lucien Breaux has a presentation to make."

"My dear friend, you once asked for a rose for someone
else, but nothing for yourself. I know you may hit me for this,
but today you are Portland's oldest living original resident. A
sixty-year resident. A year ago, the Portland Rose Association began to develop a new rose. Beth, we have here the
'McGraw Rose.' God love you!"

For once Beth was speechless. She let the President and
Donald take her by the arm into the reception that awaited.

Later, returning in the carriage with Donald, she took his
hand.

"Do you think I was born a generation too early, as President Roosevelt proclaimed?"

Donnie gave her a slow smile. "I think it would have been
very boring around here if you had not been born exactly
when you were. I would have been lost with any other
mother but you."

She patted his hand, lovingly. Turning in the seat, she
caught a glimpse of the huge anchor through the trees. For
the first time she was aware of the multitude of other crosses
and monuments. Lone Fir Cemetery was well populated, but
she did not belong there for a long, long time.

"So many marvelous advancements. Quite a marvel to
view. It is hard to believe that millions of people will come to
Portland to see all this. Education is a marvelous thing."

"You have now used 'marvelous' twice, and 'marvel' once
in the same thought. Mother, what are you up to?"

Beth laughed. It was still a full, rich sound. "Fiora gave me
. . . pardon, *Mother Superior Agnes* gave me a most interesting idea. Oh, Donnie, she will always be Fiora in my mind.
Still, I love her idea, because it will upset the neighborhood.
Are you aware that any young lady who wishes a college
education must be shipped all the way back East? Now, we
have several adjoining parcels . . ."

He sat back and smiled. Give her an idea to sink her teeth
into and she was good, no matter the generation.

Beth's schedule was firmly in her mind as they slowly rode
up their hill. Behind them, the facade of the Forestry Building still challenged the skies, with the Willamette shining
below and Portland awaiting whatever destiny the morrow
would bring.

KNIGHTSBRIDGE

Order Form

In order to receive books by mail, please check the appropriate title, remove that page from its binding, and send it along with this order form to:

Knightsbridge Publishing
208 East 51st St.
New York, NY 10017

Please send me the book(s) I have checked on the included page(s). I am enclosing a total of $_____._____ (Please add $1.00 for one book and 50¢ for each additional book for shipping and handling.*) My check or money order made out to Knightsbridge Publishing is enclosed. (No cash or C.O.D.s please.)

Name: _____

Address: _____

Apt.: _____

City: _____

State (Prov.): _____

Zip (P.C.): _____

DISCARD

*NY residents add 8.25% sales tax, CA residents add 6.75%.